Operator precedence and associativity

Operators at the top of the table have higher precedence than operators below. In expressions beginning with arguments in the innermost set of parentheses (if any), programs evaluate operators of higher precedence before evaluating operators of lower precedence.

Unary plus (+) and unary minus (–) are at level 2, and have precedence over arithmetic plus and minus at level 5. The & symbol at level 2 is the address-of operator; the & symbol at level 9 is the bitwise AND operator. The * symbol at level 2 is the pointer-dereference operator; the * symbol at level 4 is the multiplication operator. In the absence of clarifying parentheses, operators on the same level are evaluated according to their left-to-right or right-to-left
evaluation order.

Level	Operators	Evaluation Order
1 (high)	( ) . [ ] -> ::	left-to-right
2	* & ! ~ ++ -- + - sizeof new delete	right-to-left
3	.* -> *	left-to-right
4	* / %	left-to-right
5	+ -	left-to-right
6	<< >>	left-to-right
7	< <= > >=	left-to-right
8	== !=	left-to-right
9	&	left-to-right
10	^	left-to-right
11	|	left-to-right
12	&&	left-to-right
13	||	left-to-right
14	?:	right-to-left
15	= *= /= += -= %= <<= >>= &= ^= |=	right-to-left
16 (low)	,	left-to-right

C++ data types

Type	16 Bits	32 Bits	Range
unsigned short int	2 bytes	2 bytes	0 to 65,535
short int	2 bytes	2 bytes	−32,768 to 32,767
unsigned long int	4 bytes	4 bytes	0 to 4,294,967,295
long int	4 bytes	4 bytes	−2,147,483,648 to 2,147,483,647
int	2 bytes	4 bytes	(16):−32,768 to 32,767; (32):−2,147, 483,648 to 2,147,483,647
unsigned int	2 bytes	4 bytes	(16):0 to 65,535; (32):0 to 4,294, 967,295
char	1 byte	1 byte	256 character values
wchar_t	2 bytes	2 bytes	65,535 character values
bool	1 byte	1 byte	True or False
float	4 bytes	4 bytes	1.2e−38 to 3.4e38
double	8 bytes	8 bytes	2.2e−308 to 1.8e308
long double	10 bytes	10 bytes	3.4e−4932 to 1.1e+4932

C and C++ keywords

and (&&)[1]	and_eq (&=)[1]	asm	auto	bitand (&)[1]
bitor (|)[1]	bool[1]	break	case	catch[1]
char	class[1]	compl (~)[1]	const	continue
default	delete[1]	do	double	else
enum	explicit[1]	extern	false[1]	float
for	friend[1]	goto	if	inline[1]
int	long	mutable[1]	namespace	new[1]
not (!)[1]	not_eq (!=)[1]	operator[1]	or (||)[1]	or_eq (|=)[1]
private[1]	protected[1]	public[1]	register	return
short	signed	sizeof	static	struct
switch	template[1]	this[1]	throw[1]	true[1]
try[1]	typedef	typename	union	unsigned
virtual[1]	void	volatile[1]	while	xor (^)[1]
xor_eq (^=)[1]				

[1]C++ only
Reserved words followed by parentheses are synonyms for the operator in parentheses.

What's New

In the Third Edition

The third edition of this book has been revised and updated. This edition features:

- Updated information to comply with the new ANSI/ISO standard

- A CD-ROM containing the Dev-C++ compiler, a full-featured Windows-based C++ development environment that allows you to build C++ programs to distribute without commercial restrictions

- Easy-to-follow installation instructions for the Dev-C++ compiler

- The DJGPP C++ compiler, which will run on virtually any DOS or Windows-based PC

- Programs fully tested on the software that accompanies the book

- A glossary of important terms to serve as a reference throughout the 24 lessons and afterward

SAMS
Teach Yourself

C++

in 24 *Hours*

THIRD EDITION

Jesse Liberty

SAMS   *201 West 103rd St., Indianapolis, Indiana, 46290 USA*

Sams Teach Yourself C++ in 24 Hours, Third Edition

Copyright © 2002 by Sams Publishing

International Standard Book Number: 0672322242

Library of Congress Catalog Card Number: 2001089630

Printed in the United States of America

First Printing: August 24, 2001

04   03   02   8   7   6   5

Trademarks

Warning and Disclaimer

EXECUTIVE EDITOR
Michael Stephens

ACQUISITIONS EDITOR
Carol Ackerman

DEVELOPMENT EDITOR
Christy A. Franklin

MANAGING EDITOR
Matt Purcell

PROJECT EDITOR
George Nedeff

COPY EDITOR
Seth Kerney

INDEXER
Chris Barrick

PROOFREADER
Rowena Rappaport

TECHNICAL EDITOR
Paul Strickland

TEAM COORDINATOR
Lynne Williams

MEDIA DEVELOPER
Dan Scherf

INTERIOR DESIGNER
Gary Adair

COVER DESIGNER
Aren Howell

PRODUCTION
Ayanna Lacey

Contents at a Glance

Contents

About the Author

Jesse Liberty is the president of Liberty Associates, Inc.
(http://www.LibertyAssociates.com) where he provides training and custom programming. Jesse is the author of numerous books on C++, C#, Web development, and object-oriented analysis and design. He was a Distinguished Software Engineer for AT&T and Vice President of Citibank's Development Division.

Dedication

*This book is dedicated to Edythe, who provided life, Stacey who shares it,
and Robin and Rachel who give it purpose.*

Acknowledgments

With each book there is a chance to acknowledge and to thank those folks without whose support and help this book literally would have been impossible. First among them are Stacey, Robin, and Rachel Liberty.

I must also thank everyone associated with my books at Sams and Que for being professionals of the highest quality. The editors at Sams did a fantastic job, and I must especially acknowledge and thank Carol Ackerman, Christy Franklin, and Paul Strickland. A special thanks to Rich Halpert.

Finally, I'd like to thank Mrs. Kalish, who taught my sixth-grade class how to do binary arithmetic in 1965, when neither she nor we knew why.

Tell Us What You Think!

As the reader of this book, *you* are our most important critic and commentator. We value your opinion and want to know what we're doing right, what we could do better, what areas you'd like to see us publish in, and any other words of wisdom you're willing to pass our way.

As an Executive Editor for Sams Publishing, I welcome your comments. You can fax, e-mail, or write me directly to let me know what you did or didn't like about this book—as well as what we can do to make our books stronger.

Please note that I cannot help you with technical problems related to the topic of this book, and that due to the high volume of mail I receive, I might not be able to reply to every message.

When you write, please be sure to include this book's title and author as well as your name and phone or fax number. I will carefully review your comments and share them with the author and editors who worked on the book.

Fax: 317-581-4770

E-mail: feedback@samspublishing.com

Mail: Michael Stephens
           Executive Editor
           Sams Publishing
           201 West 103rd Street
           Indianapolis, IN 46290 USA

Introduction

This book is designed to help you teach yourself how to program with C++. In just 24 one hour lessons, you'll learn about such fundamentals as managing I/O, loops and arrays, object-oriented programming, templates, and creating C++ applications—all in well-structured and easy-to-follow lessons. Lessons provide sample listings—complete with sample output and an analysis of the code—to illustrate the topics of the day. Syntax examples are clearly marked for handy reference. To help you become more proficient, each lesson ends with a set of common questions and answers.

Who Should Read This Book

You don't need any previous experience in programming to learn C++ with this book. This book starts you from the beginning and teaches you both the language and the concepts involved with programming C++. You'll find the numerous examples of syntax and detailed analysis of code an excellent guide as you begin your journey into this rewarding environment. Whether you are just beginning or already have some experience programming, you will find that this book's clear organization makes learning C++ fast and easy.

Should I Learn C First?

The question inevitably arises: because C++ is a superset of C, should you learn C first? Stroustrup and most other C++ programmers agree: Not only is it unnecessary to learn C first, it is a bad idea. This book assumes you are not a C programmer. If you are a C programmer, however, no problem. Read the first few hours for review and then hang on tight. You're not in Kansas any more.

Conventions

Notes: These boxes highlight information that can make your C++ programming more efficient and effective.

Cautions: These focus your attention on problems or side effects that can occur in specific situations.

These boxes provide clear definitions of essential terms.

Do	**Don't**

DO use the "Do/Don't" boxes to find a quick summary of a fundamental principle in a lesson.

DON'T overlook the useful information offered in these boxes.

This book uses various typefaces to help you distinguish C++ code from regular English. Actual C++ code is typeset in a special monospace font. Placeholders—words or characters temporarily used to represent the real words or characters you would type in code—are typeset in *italic monospace*. New or important terms are typeset in *italic*.

In the listings in this book, each real code line is numbered. If you see an unnumbered line in a listing, you'll know that the unnumbered line is really a continuation of the preceding numbered code line (some code lines are too long for the width of the book). In this case, you should type the two lines as one; do not divide them.

PART I
Introducing C++

Hour

Hour 1

Getting Started

Welcome to *Teach Yourself C++ in 24 Hours*! In this very first hour you will learn:

- How to set up and use the features of your compiler
- The steps to develop a C++ program
- How to enter, compile, and link your first working C++ program

Preparing to Program

C++, perhaps more than other languages, demands that the programmer design the program before writing it. Trivial problems, such as the ones discussed in the first few chapters of this book, don't require much design. Complex problems, however, such as the ones professional programmers are challenged with every day, do require design. The more thorough the design, the more likely it is that the program will solve the problems it is designed to solve, on time and on budget. A good design also makes for a program that is relatively bug free and easy to maintain. It has been estimated that fully 90 percent of the cost of software is the combined cost of debugging and maintenance. To the extent that good design can reduce those costs, it can have a sig-nificant impact on the bottom-line cost of the project.

The first question you need to ask when preparing to design any program is, "What is the problem I'm trying to solve?" Every program should have a clear, well-articulated goal; and you'll find that even the simplest programs in this book have one.

The second question every good programmer asks is, "Can this be accomplished without resorting to writing custom software?" Reusing an old program, using pen and paper, or buying software off the shelf are often better solutions to a problem than writing some-thing new. The programmer who can offer these alternatives will never suffer from lack of work; finding less expensive solutions to today's problems will always generate new opportunities later.

Assuming you understand the problem and it requires writing a new program, you are ready to begin your design.

C++, ANSI C++, ISO C++, Windows, and Other Areas of Confusion

C++ is a language. DOS, Windows, UNIX, and MacOS are operating systems. When you learn C++, you'll want to learn it as a portable language without regard to which machine and operating system you'll run your programs on.

Teach Yourself C++ in 24 Hours makes no assumptions about your operating system. This book teaches *ANSI/ISO C++*. ANSI/ISO C++ is just another way of saying "standard" C++—the internationally agreed-upon version that is portable to *any* platform and *any* development environment.

The code presented throughout the book is standard ANSI/ISO and should run on almost any compiler. Therefore, you will see few references to windows, list boxes, graphics, and so forth. All that is operating system-dependent.

You'll see output accomplished through standard output. To make this work, you might need to tell your compiler to create a console application. This is the case with the Bloodshed Dev-C++ compiler. Some compilers, written to be used with Windows or the Mac or another windowing environment, call this a quick window, or a simple window, or perhaps a console window.

NEW TERM   A *compiler* is the software you will be using throughout this book. It translates a program from human-readable form into machine code, producing an object file that will later be linked and run. A *linker* is a program that builds an executable (runnable) file from the object code files produced by the compiler.

There are two compilers included on the CD-ROM with this book. The next section walks you through the set-up and installation process for the Dev-C++ Bloodshed compiler. It is designed to run in a windows-based operating environment and provides an integrated development environment (IDE) that permits you to edit, compile, debug, and more from a graphical interface. Eventually you might want to consider using another compiler that is not dependent on a Windows environment, but that is a matter of personal choice.

Installing and Setting Up the Compiler

To use the Dev-C++ Integrated Development Environment (IDE) supplied with this book, you need to use a Microsoft Windows operating system. If you are not going to be working in this environment, this section will not apply to you. You will need to find a compiler for your operating system.

If you are working in Windows, then proceed with the installation of the Bloodshed C++ compiler, which is the graphical interface you will use for the remainder of the book. You might also see this graphical interface referred to as the Bloodshed Compiler, Bloodshed Dev-C++, Dev-C++, or Dev-C++ IDE. They are all the same.

Insert the CD and it should run automatically. If not, you can start it manually by running start.exe from the CD. Click Compiler Center, then click Launch Dev-C++ Installer. You will use the default settings, so click Yes, then Next, then you must wait until you get the Setup Complete window. When you see the Setup Complete window, click Finish. This brings you back to the original screen. Click Exit. You have now installed the Dev-C++ IDE, but need to configure it in order to make it easier to use.

If you don't already have compression software installed on your computer, install the WinZip software from the CD-ROM. To start the installation process, you will follow similar steps to those outlined for the compiler installation.

Unzip the file from the CD, extracting it into the \Dev-C++ directory (or, if you did not use the default directory, the directory where you installed the compiler). Click Yes any time you get a Confirm File Overwrite window. This process will upgrade your Dev-C++ IDE from version 4.0 to version 4.01.

After you complete the installation of the compiler and the upgrade, install the debugger. It is also located on the CD-ROM and can easily be installed by following the prompts. It is the Cygnus Insight debugger, version 5. The Dev-C++ compiler comes with a standard command line debugger. The Cygnus Insight debugger is graphical and easier to use.

Now open the Dev-C++ IDE to do a bit more configuration. Menu items that you need to choose are listed in the order you will see them. From the Desktop click Start, Programs, Dev-C++, Dev-C++. You will see a Dev-C++ first time configuration window. Choose the defaults for the associations. At this point, choose the default icon set. If you want to change it later, you can. Click OK to continue.

FIGURE 1.1

The Dev-C++
Integrated
Development
Environment (IDE).

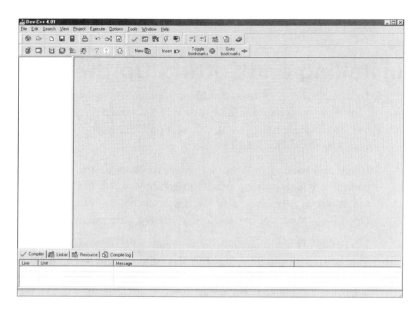

Notice in Figure 1.1 that there are two rows of icons below the menu bar. This is the toolbar. By moving your mouse over an icon, you will see a description of what the button does. On the first row, the first four icons from left to right are New project, Open project, New source file, and Save current file. The checkmark icon in the middle of the first row is Compile project. To its immediate right is Run project icon, and three icons to the right is Debug project. The first two icons on the second row are Compiler options and Environment options. Spend a minute comparing these icons to the Menu items from the menu bar.

You may notice that the word *project* is used in several of these icons. A project permits you to have several files bundled together. Dev-C++ project files have the extension .dev. Most of the projects in this book use single files. You will see how to use the IDE shortly, but first you must finish your configuration setup.

You will set up the Dev-C++ IDE to permit you to debug (find errors in) your programs. Click Compiler options from the toolbar, then in the Linker tab, check Generate debugging information. Finish by clicking OK. This option is not used until later in the book, but it is easiest to set it up now.

Now change the default settings to more closely match those used in this book. Choose Environment options, and click the Misc. tab. In the Default code when creating new source files: section, make the following changes: Remove the .h and capitalize iostream from the first line so it reads: #include <iostream>. Remove the 2nd line, #include <stdlib.h>, entirely. Remove the line that reads: system("PAUSE"); entirely. Click OK to save this as your default. You can always come back to this window and click Default to restore the original settings. After you read Hour 5 on functions, you might want to restore the defaults to see what system("PAUSE"); does. It will permit you to see the output of your programs without having to leave the IDE. In the meantime, you might find it helpful to run your programs from a command prompt in order to see your program's output to the screen. This will depend on what your program displays.

The Bloodshed IDE has a built-in editor. Click the New source file icon to bring it up. This is how you enter single file programs. To work with multiple files, click the New project icon and choose Console Application in the project tab. Click OK to continue. Save the project and all related files in a separate directory. The project file has the extension .dev, while the C++ source files have an extension .cpp. It is worthy to note that the editor appends the extension .cpp automatically for the source files when you save the file. To save the file you are working on, click the Save current file icon.

To compile and link a project or an individual source file, click the Compile project icon. Some compilers require two separate steps: first a compile, and then a link. Most integrated environments, including this one, however, do both whenever you tell it to compile. To run a program from the IDE, click the Run project icon. To debug a program, click the Debug project icon.

If you downloaded the visual debugger, after you click the Debug project icon you will see a Source window. The first executable line is highlighted. You will see a toolbar below the menu bar. By moving your mouse over the icons, you will see a description of what that icon does. The first icon, Run, starts your debugging program. At this point you might need to manually select the Source window to continue. This will give you a screen similar to the following figure.

FIGURE 1.2

*Source Window in the
Cygnus Insight Visual
Debugger.*

As you see it on your screen, the green highlight indicates which line is the next one to
be executed, and the red square is a *breakpoint*. A breakpoint temporally stops your program. When you first start debugging your program, a breakpoint is automatically set on
the first executable line. You can set your own breakpoint by clicking to the left of that
line. The Step icon executes one line, then stops on the next line. The Continue icon
keeps executing your program until it finishes or it gets to another breakpoint. The other
icons let you examine various aspects of your program. One word of warning: Do not
forget to compile before you try to run or debug.

If you click the About icon, you will see you are using Version 4.01 of Bloodshed Dev-
C++. If you click the Help on Bloodshed Dev-C++ icon, you will see the Standard C
Library Reference help file, as well as the help files that initially come with the Dev-C++
IDE. Let's look now at what the compiler does.

Your Compiler and Editor

A compiler often has its own built-in text editor. To write C++ source files, you can use
the built-in editor, or a commercial text editor or word processor that can produce text
files. As discussed previously, the Bloodshed compiler does come with a built-in editor.
Whatever editor you choose to use, be sure that it saves simple, plain-text files with no
word processing commands embedded in the text. Examples of safe editors include the
Windows Notepad, the DOS Edit command, Brief, Epsilon, EMACS, and vi. Many commercial word processors, such as WordPerfect, Word, and dozens of others, also offer a
method for saving simple text files.

The files you create with your editor are called source files, and for C++ they typically
are named with the extension `.cpp`, `.cp`, or `.c`. In this book, all the source code files are
named with the `.cpp` extension, as that is the default for the Bloodshed compiler.

Most C++ compilers don't care what extension you give your source code, but if you don't specify otherwise, many will use .cpp by default.

Do	Don't

DO use a simple text editor to create your source code, or use the built-in editor that comes with your compiler.

DO save your files with the .c, .cp, or .cpp extension. (The Bloodshed compiler defaults to .cpp.)

DO check your documentation for specifics about your compiler and linker to ensure that you know how to compile and link your programs.

DON'T use a word processor that saves special formatting characters. If you do use a word processor, save the file as ASCII Text.

Compiling and Linking the Source Code

Although the source code in your file is somewhat cryptic, and anyone who doesn't know C++ will struggle to understand what it is for, it is still in what we call human-readable form. Your source code file is not a program, and it can't be executed or run as a program can.

 To turn your source code into a program, a compiler is used. How you invoke your compiler and how you tell it where to find your source code will vary from compiler to compiler; check your documentation.

If you compile the source code from the operating system's command line, type the following:

For the Bloodshed compiler	`gcc <filename> -o <output executable name>`
For the Borland C++ compiler	`bc <filename>`
For the Borland C++ for Windows compiler	`bcc <filename>`
For the Borland Turbo C++ compiler	`tc <filename>`
For the Microsoft compilers	`cl <filename>`
For the DJGPP compiler	`gxx <filename> -o <output executable name>`

Compiling in an Integrated Development Environment

Most modern compilers provide an integrated development environment. In such an environment, you typically choose Build or Compile from a menu, or there can be a function key you press to build your application. For the Dev-C++ IDE, click the Compile project icon, or review the Dev-C++ installation section for further details.

Linking Your Program

After your source code is compiled, an object file is produced. This is still not an executable program, however. To turn this into an executable program, you must run your linker.

NEW TERM C++ programs are typically created by linking together one or more object files with one or more libraries. A *library* is a collection of linkable files that were supplied with your compiler, that you purchased separately, or that you created yourself. All C++ compilers come with a library of useful functions (or procedures) and classes that you can include in your program. A *function* is a block of code that performs a task, such as adding two numbers or printing to the screen. A *class* is the definition of a new type. A class is implemented as data and related functions. I'll be talking about classes a lot as they are explained in greater detail throughout the book.

The steps typically followed to create an executable file are:

1. Create a source code file, with a `.cpp` extension.
2. Compile the source code into an object file.
3. Link your object file with any needed libraries to produce an executable program.

The Development Cycle

If every program worked the first time you tried it, that would be the complete development cycle: write the program, compile the source code, link the program, and run it. Unfortunately, almost every program, no matter how trivial, can and will have errors, or *bugs*, in it. Some bugs will cause the compile to fail, some will cause the link to fail, and some will only show up when you run the program.

Whatever the type of bug you find, you must fix it, and that involves editing your source code, recompiling, relinking, and then rerunning the program. This cycle is represented in Figure 1.3, which diagrams the steps in the development cycle.

FIGURE 1.3
The steps in the development of a C++ program.

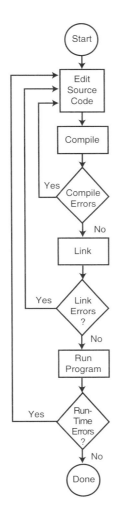

HELLO.CPP—Your First C++ Program

Traditional programming books begin by writing the words Hello World to the screen, or a variation on that statement. This time-honored tradition is carried on here.

For the Dev-C++ IDE, click New Source file to bring up the editor.

Type the first program directly into the editor, exactly as shown. After you are certain it is correct, save the file, naming it `Hello.cpp`, compile it, link it if your compiler does not do so automatically, and then run it. It will display the words `Hello World` on your screen. Don't worry too much about how it works; this is really just to get you comfortable with the development cycle and using your compiler. Every aspect of this program will be covered over the next couple of days.

> The following listing contains line numbers on the left. These numbers are for reference within the book. They should not be typed in to your editor. For example, in line 0 of Listing 1.1, you should enter:
>
> `#include <iostream>`

LISTING 1.1   HELLO.CPP, the `Hello World` Program

```
0:  #include <iostream>
1:
2:  int main()
3:  {
4:      std::cout << "Hello World!\n";
5:      return 0;
6:  }
```

Make certain you enter this exactly as shown. Pay careful attention to the punctuation. The << in line 4 is the redirection symbol, produced on most keyboards by holding the shift key and pressing the comma key. Line 4 ends with a semicolon; don't leave this out!

Also check to make sure you are following your compiler directions properly. Most compilers, including the Bloodshed compiler, will link automatically, but check your documentation if you are compiling with a different program. If you get errors, look over your code carefully and determine how it is different from Listing 1.1. If you see an error on line 0, such as `cannot find file iostream`, check your compiler documentation for directions on setting up your include path or environment variables. If you receive an error that there is no prototype for `main`, add the line `int main();` just before line 2. You will need to add this line to every program in this book before the beginning of the `main` function. Most compilers, Bloodshed included, don't require this, but a few do.

Your finished program will look like this:

```
0:  #include <iostream>
1:
2:  int main;
```

```
3:   int main()
4:   {
5:       std::cout << "Hello World!\n";
6:       return 0;
7:   }
```

Try running HELLO.EXE; it should display

```
Hello World!
```

on your screen. If so, congratulations! You've just entered, compiled, and run your first C++ program. It might not look like much, but almost every professional C++ programmer started out with this exact program.

Compile Errors

Compile-time errors can occur for any number of reasons. Usually they are a result of a typo or other inadvertent minor error. Some compilers will not only tell you what you did wrong, they'll point you to the exact place in your code where you made the mistake. And some will even suggest a remedy!

You can see how your compiler will react by intentionally putting an error into your program. If HELLO.CPP ran smoothly, edit it now and remove the closing brace on line 6. Your program will now look like Listing 1.2.

LISTING 1.2   Demonstration of Compiler Error

```
0:   #include <iostream>
1:
2:   int main()
3:   {
4:       std::cout << "Hello World!\n";
5:       return 0;
```

Recompile your program and you will see an error that looks similar to

```
Line    Unit         Message
7       Hello.cpp    parse error at end of input
```

This error tells you there is a source code error at the end of the code segment (although I admit it is somewhat cryptic). Note that this error message points you to line 7. In the Bloodshed compiler, line 7 would be the next numbered line. Sometimes the errors just get you to the general vicinity of the problem. If a compiler could perfectly identify every problem, it would fix the code itself.

Remember when looking at the code listings throughout the book, the line numbers are for reference only. The numbered listings in the book begin, as some compilers do, with 0. However, the Bloodshed compiler numbers lines beginning with 1.

Summary

In this first chapter, you've installed your compiler and learned a bit about its editor and tools. You have learned how to write, compile, link, and run your very first C++ program. You've learned what the normal development cycle is. You even took a brief look at compile errors and how the compiler reacts. Now let's move on to Chapter 2, "The Parts of a C++ Program."

Q&A

Q What is the difference between a text editor and a word processor?

A A text editor produces files with plain text in them. There are no formatting commands or other special symbols required by a particular word processor. Text files do not have automatic word wrap, bold print, italics, and so forth. Word processors usually can produce text files, but you must be careful to save your file as plain text.

Q My compiler has a built-in editor; is that the right thing to use?

A Almost all compilers will compile code produced by any text editor. The advantages of using the built-in text editor, however, might include the capability to quickly move back and forth between the edit and compile steps of the development cycle. Sophisticated compilers include a fully integrated development environment, enabling the programmer to access help files, edit, and compile the code in place, and to resolve compile and link errors without ever leaving the environment.

Q Can I ignore warning messages from my compiler?

A Absolutely not. Get into the habit of treating warning messages as errors. C++ uses the compiler to warn you when you are doing something you might not intend; heed those warnings and do what is required to make them go away.

Q What is compile-time?

A Compile-time refers to the actual time your compiler is running, as opposed to link-time (when the linker is running) or runtime (when the program is running).

Hour **2**

The Parts of a C++ Program

Before we dive into the details of C++, classes, variables, and so forth, let's take an hour to get a sense of how a program fits together. In this hour you learn:

- Why C++ is the right choice
- The parts of a C++ program
- How the parts work together
- What a function is and what it does

Why C++ Is the Right Choice

C++ is the development language of choice for the majority of professional programmers because it offers fast, small programs developed in a robust and portable environment. Today's C++ tools make creating complex and powerful commercial applications a pretty straightforward exercise, but to get the most out of C++ you need to learn quite a bit about this powerful language.

C++ is a relatively new language. Of course, programming itself is only about 40 years old. During that time, computer languages have undergone a dramatic evolution.

Early on, programmers worked with the most primitive computer instructions: *machine language*. These instructions were represented by long strings of ones and zeroes. Soon, *assemblers* were invented that could map machine instructions to human-readable and manageable mnemonics, such as ADD and MOV.

NEW TERM In time, higher-level languages evolved, such as BASIC and COBOL. These languages let people work with something approximating words and sentences, such as Let I = 100. These instructions were translated back into machine language by interpreters and compilers. An *interpreter*, like BASIC, translates a program as it reads it, turning the programmer's program instructions or code directly into actions.

NEW TERM Compilers translate the code into what is called object code. The first step in this transformation is called *compiling*. A *compiler* produces an object file. The second step is called *linking*. A *linker* transforms the object file into an executable program. An executable program is one that "runs" on your operating system.

Note: the term "object code" is not related to the concept of objects as used in object-oriented programming (described later in this book).

Because interpreters read the code as it is written and execute the code on the spot, they are easy for the programmer to work with. Compilers introduce the inconvenient extra steps of compiling and linking the code. On the other hand, compilers produce a program that executes faster than the same program executed by an interpreter.

For many years, the principal goal of computer programmers was to write short pieces of code that would execute quickly. The program needed to be small because memory was expensive, and it needed to be fast because processing power was also expensive. As computers have become smaller, cheaper, and faster, and as the cost of memory has fallen, these priorities have changed. Today the cost of a programmer's time far outweighs the cost of most of the computers in use by businesses. Well-written, easy-to-maintain code is at a premium. Easy-to-maintain means that as business requirements change, the program can be extended and enhanced without great expense.

Procedural, Structured, and Object-Oriented Programming

NEW TERM In *procedural programming*, programs are thought of as a series of actions performed on a set of data. *Structured programming* was invented to provide a systematic approach to organizing these procedures, and to managing large amounts of data.

The principle idea behind structured programming is as simple as the idea of divide and conquer. Any task that is too complex to be described is broken down into a set of smaller component tasks, until the tasks are small and self-contained enough that they are easily understood.

As an example, computing the average salary of every employee of a company is a rather complex task. You can, however, break it down into these subtasks:

1. Find out what each person earns.
2. Count how many people you have.
3. Total all the salaries.
4. Divide the total by the number of people you have.

Totaling the salaries can be broken down into:

1. Get each employee's record.
2. Access the salary.
3. Add the salary to the running total.
4. Get the next employee's record.

In turn, obtaining each employee's record can be broken down into:

1. Open the file of employees.
2. Go to the correct record.
3. Read the data from disk.

Structured programming remains an enormously successful approach for dealing with complex problems.

Yet, there are problems. The separation of data from the tasks that manipulate the data becomes harder and harder to comprehend and maintain as the amount of data grows. The more things you want to do with that data, the more confusing it becomes.

Procedural programmers find themselves constantly reinventing new solutions to old problems. This is often called "reinventing the wheel" and is the opposite of *reusability*. The idea behind reusability is to build components that have known properties, and then to be able to plug them into your program as you need them. This is modeled after the hardware world—when an engineer needs a new transistor, she doesn't usually invent one; she goes to the big bin of transistors and finds one that works for what she needs, or perhaps modifies it. Until object-oriented programming, there was no similar option for a software engineer.

NEW TERM The essence of *object-oriented programming* is to treat data and the procedures that act upon the data as a single "object"—a self-contained entity with an identity and certain characteristics of its own.

C++ and Object-Oriented Programming

C++ fully supports object-oriented programming, including the three pillars of object-oriented development: encapsulation, inheritance, and polymorphism.

Encapsulation

When an engineer is creating a new device, he wires together component pieces. He can wire in a resistor, a capacitor, and a transistor. The transistor has certain properties and can accomplish certain behaviors. He can use the transistor without understanding the details of how it *works*, as long as he knows what it *does*.

NEW TERM To achieve this, the transistor must be self-contained. It must do one well-defined thing, and it must do it completely. Doing one thing completely is called *encapsulation*.

All the properties of the transistor are encapsulated in the transistor object; they are not spread out through the circuitry. It is not necessary to understand how the transistor works in order to use it effectively.

C++ supports the properties of encapsulation through the creation of user-defined types, called classes. Once created, a well-defined class acts as a fully encapsulated entity; it is used as a whole unit. The actual inner workings of the class should be hidden; users of a well-defined class do not need to know how the class works, they just need to know how to use it. You'll see how to create classes in Hour 7, "Basic Classes."

Inheritance and Reuse

In the late 1980s, I worked for Citibank building a device for home banking. We didn't want to start from scratch; we wanted to get something out into the market quickly. Therefore, we started with the telephone and "enhanced" it. Our new enhanced telephone was a kind of telephone; it just had added features. Thus, I was able to reuse all the calling features of a plain old telephone, but add new capabilities to extend its utility.

NEW TERM C++ supports the idea of reuse through *inheritance*. A new type can be declared that is an extension of an existing type. This new subclass is said to derive from the existing type, and is sometimes called a derived type. The enhanced telephone is derived from a plain old telephone and thus inherits all its qualities, but additional features can be added to it as needed. Inheritance and its application in C++ are discussed in Hour 16, "Inheritance."

Polymorphism

The enhanced telephone (ET) behaves differently when receiving a call. Rather than ringing a bell, the screen lights up and a voice says, "You have a call." The phone company doesn't know this, however. They don't send special signals to each kind of phone. The company just pulses the wire and the regular telephone rings, an electronic telephone trills, and ET speaks. Each phone does "the right thing" based on its understanding of the message from the phone company.

NEW TERM C++ supports this idea that different objects do "the right thing," through what is called *function polymorphism* and *class polymorphism*. *Poly* means many, and *morph* means form. *Polymorphism* refers to the same name taking many forms, and is discussed during Hour 17, "Polymorphism and Derived Classes," and Hour 18, "Advanced Polymorphism."

The Parts of a Simple Program

The simple program from the first hour, HELLO.CPP, had many interesting parts. This section will review this program in more detail. Listing 2.1 reproduces the original version of HELLO.CPP for your convenience.

LISTING 2.1 HELLO.CPP Demonstrates the Parts of a C++ Program

```
0:  #include <iostream>
1:
2:  int main()
3:  {
4:      std::cout << "Hello World!\n";
5:      return 0;
6:  }
```

OUTPUT Hello World!

ANALYSIS On line 0 the file iostream is included in the file. As far as the compiler is concerned, it is as if you typed the entire contents of the file iostream right into the top of HELLO.CPP.

Examining the #include, Character by Character

When you run your compiler, it first calls another program—the preprocessor. You don't have to invoke the preprocessor directly; it is called automatically each time you run the compiler.

NEW TERM The first character is the # symbol, which is a signal to the *preprocessor*. The job of the preprocessor is to read through your source code looking for lines that begin with the pound symbol (#). Each time it finds a line beginning with the pound symbol, the preprocessor modifies the code. It is the modified code that is given to the compiler.

The term include is a preprocessor instruction that says, "What follows is a filename. Find that file and read it in right here." The angle brackets around the filename tell the preprocessor to "Look in all the usual places for this file." If your compiler is set up correctly, the angle brackets will cause the preprocessor to look for the file iostream in the directory that holds all the header files for your compiler. These files are called "h files" or "include files" because they are *included* in source code files and traditionally ended with the extension .h.

The new ANSI-standard include files often do not have any extension at all. In fact, your compiler probably comes with two versions for each of these files. For example, if you check your installation you might find that you have both the older traditional iostream and the new, ANSI-standard iostream. We'll use the new files in this book, as the old files are now obsolete.

The file iostream (Input-Output-STREAM) is used by cout, which assists with writing to the screen.

Notice that cout has the designation std:: in front of it; this tells the compiler to use the standard input/output library. The details of how this works and what is going on here will be explained in more detail in coming chapters. For now, you can treat std::cout as the name of the object that handles output, and std::cin as the name of the object that handles input.

The effect of line 0 is to include the file iostream into this program as if you had typed it in yourself. By the time the compiler sees this file, the included file is right there, and the compiler is none the wiser.

Line by Line Analysis

Line 2 begins the actual program with a function named main(). Every C++ program has a main() function. In general, a function is a block of code that performs one or more actions. Functions are invoked, (some programmers say they are *called*) by other functions, but main() is special. When your program starts, main() is called automatically.

The function `main()`, like all functions, must state what kind of value it will return. Once again, `main()` is special; it will always return `int`. The keyword int refers to an integer (a whole number) as explained in Hour 3, "Variables and Constants." Returning a value from a function will be discussed in detail in Hour 4, "Expressions and Statements."

All functions begin with an opening brace (`{`) and end with a closing brace (`}`). The braces for the `main()` function are on lines 3 and 6. Everything between the opening and closing braces is considered a part of the function.

The meat and potatoes of this program is on line 4. The object `cout` is used to print a message to the screen. We'll cover objects in general beginning in Hour 8, "More About Classes." The object `cout` and its related object `cin` are provided by your compiler vendor and enable the system to write to the screen (cout) and read in from the keyboard (cin).

Here's how `cout` is used: Write the word `cout` followed by the output redirection operator (`<<`). You create the output redirection operator by keyboarding shift-comma twice. Whatever follows the output redirection operator is written to the screen. If you want a string of characters to be written, be sure to enclose them in double quotes (`"`) as shown on line 4. Note that a text string is a series of printable characters.

The final two characters, `\n`, tell `cout` to put a new line after the words `Hello World!`

On line 5 we "return" the value `0` to the operating system. On some systems, this is used to signal to the operating system success or failure; the convention is to return `0` for success and any other number for failure. On modern windowing machines, this value is almost never used, and so all the programs in this book will return the value `0`.

The `main()` function ends on line 6 with the closing brace.

Comments

When you are writing a program, it often seems clear and self-evident what you are trying to do in the program. Funny thing, though—a month later, when you return to the program, it can be quite confusing and unclear. I'm not sure how that confusion creeps into your program, but it's always there.

To fight the onset of confusion and help others understand your code, you'll want to use comments. Comments are simply text that is ignored by the compiler, but that might inform the reader of what you are doing at any particular point in your program.

Types of Comments

NEW TERM A *comment* is text that does not affect the operation of the program, but is added to instruct or inform the programmer. There are two types of comments in C++. The double-slash (//) comment, which will be referred to as a C++-style comment, tells the compiler to ignore everything that follows the slashes until the end of the line.

The slash-star (/*) comment mark tells the compiler to ignore everything that follows until it finds a star-slash (*/) comment mark. These marks will be referred to as C-style comments because C++ inherited them from C. Remember, every /* must be matched with a closing */.

Many C++ programmers use the C++-style comment most of the time, and reserve C-style comments for blocking out large blocks of a program. You can include C++-style comments within a block "commented out" by C-style comments; everything, including the C++-style comments, is ignored between the C-style comment marks.

Comments are free; they don't cost anything in performance, and the compiler ignores them. Listing 2.2 illustrates this.

Listing 2.2   HELLO.CPP Demonstrates Comments

```
 0:  #include <iostream>
 1:
 2:  int main()
 3:  {
 4:      /* this is a c-style comment
 5:             and it extends until the closing
 6:             star-slash comment mark */
 7:      std::cout << "Hello World!\n";
 8:      // this c++-style comment ends at the end of the line
 9:      std::cout << "That comment ended!";
10:
11:      // double slash comments can be alone on a line
12:      /* as can slash-star comments */
13:      return 0;
14:  }
```

OUTPUT
```
Hello World!
That comment ended!
```

ANALYSIS The comments on lines 4 through 6 are completely ignored by the compiler, as are the comments on lines 8, 11, and 12. The comment on line 8 ends with the end of the line; however, the comments on 4 and 12 require a closing comment mark.

Using Comments

Writing comments well is a skill few programmers master.

It is best to assume your audience can read C++, but can't read your mind. Let the source code tell *what* you are doing, and use comments to explain *why* you are doing it.

Functions

Although `main()` is a function, it is an unusual one. Your operating system invokes `main()` to start your program. Other functions are called, or invoked, from `main()` or from one another during the course of your program.

The function `main()` always returns an `int`. As you'll see in the coming hours, other functions might return other types of values or might return nothing at all.

A program is executed line by line in the order it appears in your source code, until a function is called. Then the program branches off to execute the function. When the function finishes, it returns control to the line following where the program called the function.

Imagine that you are drawing a picture of yourself. You draw the head, the eyes, the nose, and suddenly your pencil breaks. You "branch off" to the "sharpen my pencil" function. That is, you stop drawing, get up, walk to the sharpener, sharpen the pencil, and then return to what you were doing, picking up where you left off. (I think you were adding a cleft to your chin.)

When a program needs a service performed, it calls a function to perform the service. When the function returns, the program resumes where it was just before the function was called.

Listing 2.3 demonstrates this idea.

Listing 2.3 Demonstrating a Call to a Function

```
0:  #include <iostream>
1:
2:  // function Demonstrating a Call to a Function
3:  // prints out a useful message
4:  void DemonstrationFunction()
5:  {
6:      std::cout << "In Demonstration Function\n";
7:  }
8:
9:  // function main - prints out a message, then
```

Listing 2.3   continued

```
10:  // calls DemonstrationFunction, then prints out
11:  // a second message.
12:  int main()
13:  {
14:      std::cout << "In main\n" ;
15:      DemonstrationFunction();
16:      std::cout << "Back in main\n";
17:      return 0;
18:  }
```

OUTPUT
```
In main
In Demonstration Function
Back in main
```

ANALYSIS The function DemonstrationFunction() is defined on lines 4–7. As a definition, it shows what to do, but does not do anything until called. When it is called in line 15, it prints a message to the screen and then returns.

Line 12 is the beginning of the actual program. On line 14, main() prints out a message saying it is in main(). After printing the message, line 15 calls DemonstrationFunction(). This call causes the commands in DemonstrationFunction() to execute. In this case, the entire function consists of the code on line 6, which prints another message. When DemonstrationFunction() completes (line 7), it returns to where it was called from. In this case, the program returns to line 16, where main() prints its final line.

Using Functions

Functions either return a value, or they return void, meaning they return nothing. A function that adds two integers might return the sum, and thus would be defined as returning an integer value. A function that just prints a message has nothing to return and would be declared to return void.

Functions consist of a header (line 4) and a body (lines 5-7). The header consists of the return type, the function name, and the list of parameters (if any) to that function. The parameters to a function allow values to be passed into the function. Thus, if the function were to add two numbers, the numbers would be the parameters to the function. Here's a typical function header:

```
int Sum(int a, int b)
```

A parameter is a declaration of what type of value will be passed in; the actual value passed in by the calling function is called the *argument*. Many programmers use these two terms, *parameters* and *arguments* as synonyms; others are careful about the technical distinction. This book will use the terms interchangeably.

NEW TERM The name of the function and its parameters (that is the header without the return value) is called the function's *signature*. The body of a function consists of an opening brace, zero or more statements, and a closing brace. The statements constitute the work of the function. A function might return a value using a `return` statement. This statement will also cause the function to exit. If you don't put a `return` statement into your function, it will automatically return void at the end of the function. The value returned must be of the type declared in the function header.

Listing 2.4 demonstrates a function that takes two integer parameters and returns an integer value.

Listing 2.4 `FUNC.CPP` Demonstrates a Simple Function

```
0:   #include <iostream>
1:
2:   int Add (int x, int y)
3:   {
4:       std::cout << "In Add(), received " << x << " and " << y << "\n";
5:       return (x+y);
6:   }
7:
8:   int main()
9:   {
10:      std::cout << "I'm in main()!\n";
11:      std::cout << "\nCalling Add()\n";
12:      std::cout << "The value returned is: " << Add(3,4);
13:      std::cout << "\nBack in main().\n";
14:      std::cout << "\nExiting...\n\n";
15:      return 0;
16:  }
```

OUTPUT
```
I'm in main()!

Calling Add()
In Add(), received 3 and 4
The value returned is: 7
Back in main().

Exiting...
```

ANALYSIS The function `Add()` is defined on line 2. It takes two integer parameters and returns an integer value. The program itself begins on line 10 where it prints a message.

On line 12 `main()` prints a message and then prints the value returned from calling `Add(3,4)`. This invokes the function and processing branches to line 2. The two values passed in to `Add()` are represented as the parameters x and y. These values are added together and the result is returned on line 5.

The return value is printed on line 12, and is shown in the output (7). `Main()` then prints a message on lines 13 and 14 and the program exits when `main()` returns (returning control to the operating system).

Summary

In this hour you examined a program in some detail. You learned how to include files using `#include`, and you learned how to use comments well. You also learned what a function is and how it is used in a program.

Q & A

Q What does `#include` do?

A This is a directive to the preprocessor, which runs when you call your compiler. This specific directive causes the file named after the word `include` to be read in as if it were typed in at that location in your source code.

Q What is the difference between `//` comments and `/*` style comments?

A The double-slash comments (`//`) "expire" at the end of the line. Slash-star (`/*`) comments are in effect until a closing comment (`*/`). Remember, not even the end of the function terminates a slash-star comment; you must put in the closing comment mark or you will get a compile-time error.

Q What differentiates a good comment from a bad comment?

A A good comment tells the reader why this particular code is doing whatever it is doing, or explains what a section of code is about to do. A bad comment restates what a particular line of code is doing. Lines of code should be written so that they speak for themselves: Reading the line of code should tell you what it is doing without needing a comment.

HOUR 3

Variables and Constants

Programs need a way to store the data they use. Variables and constants offer various ways to work with numbers and other values.

In this hour you learn:

- How to declare and define variables and constants
- How to assign values to variables and manipulate those values
- How to write the value of a variable to the screen

What Is a Variable?

NEW TERM From a programmer's point of view, a *variable* is a location in your computer's memory in which you can store a value and from which you can later retrieve that value.

To understand this, you must first understand a bit about how computer memory works. Your computer's memory can be thought of as a series of cubby holes, all lined up in a long row. Each cubby hole—or memory location—is numbered sequentially. These numbers are known as memory addresses.

Variables not only have addresses, they have names. For example, you might create a variable named myAge. Your variable is a label on one of these cubby holes so that you can find it easily, without knowing its actual memory address.

Figure 3.1 is a visual representation of this idea. As you can see from the figure, we've declared a variable named myVariable. myVariable starts at memory address 103.

FIGURE 3.1

A visual representation of memory.

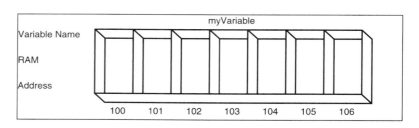

NEW TERM   *RAM* is Random Access Memory. It is the electronic memory your computer uses while executing programs. Any information in RAM is lost when your computer is turned off. When you run your program, it is loaded into RAM from the disk file (hard drive storage). All variables are created in RAM as well. When programmers talk of memory, it is usually RAM to which they are referring.

Setting Aside Memory

NEW TERM   When you define a variable in C++, you must tell the compiler not only what its name is, but also what kind of information it will hold: integer, character, and so forth. This is the variable's *type*. The type of the variable tells the compiler how much room to set aside in memory to hold the variable's *value*.

Each cubby is one byte large. If the type of variable you create is two bytes in size, it needs two bytes of memory, or two cubbies. The type of the variable (for example, int) tells the compiler how much memory (how many cubby holes) to set aside for the variable. Because computers use bits and bytes to represent values, and because memory is measured in bytes, it is important that you understand and are comfortable with these concepts.

Size of Integers

A char variable (used to hold characters) is most often one byte long. A short int is two bytes on most computers; a long int is usually four bytes, and an int (without the keyword short or long) can be two or four bytes. If you are running Windows 95,

Windows 98, or Windows NT, you can count on your int being four bytes as long as you use a modern compiler.

Listing 3.1 will help you determine the exact size of these types on your computer using your particular compiler.

LISTING 3.1   Determines the Size of Variable Types on Your Computer.

```
0:   #include <iostream>
1:
2:   int main()
3:   {
4:       std::cout << "The size of an int is:\t\t";
5:       std::cout << sizeof(int) << " bytes.\n";
6:       std::cout << "The size of a short int is:\t";
7:       std::cout << sizeof(short) << " bytes.\n";
8:       std::cout << "The size of a long int is:\t";
9:       std::cout << sizeof(long) << " bytes.\n";
10:      std::cout << "The size of a char is:\t\t";
11:      std::cout << sizeof(char) << " bytes.\n";
12:      std::cout << "The size of a float is:\t\t";
13:      std::cout << sizeof(float) << " bytes.\n";
14:      std::cout << "The size of a double is:\t";
15:      std::cout << sizeof(double) << " bytes.\n";
16:
17:      return 0;
18:   }
```

OUTPUT
```
The size of an int is        2 bytes.
The size of a short int is   2 bytes.
The size of a long int is    4 bytes.
The size of a char is        1 bytes.
The size of a bool is        1 bytes.

The size of a float is       4 bytes.
The size of a double is      8 bytes.
```

On your computer, the number of bytes presented might be different!

ANALYSIS   Most of Listing 3.1 will be familiar. The one new feature is the use of the sizeof() function in lines 5 through 15. sizeof() is provided by your compiler, and it tells you the size of the object you pass in as a parameter. For example, on line 5 the keyword int is passed into sizeof(). Using sizeof(), I was able to determine that on my computer, an int is equal to a short int, which is two bytes.

signed and unsigned

NEW TERM In addition, all these types come in two varieties: `signed` and `unsigned`. Sometimes you need negative numbers, and sometimes you don't. Integers (`short` and `long`) without the word "unsigned" are assumed to be `signed`. `signed` integers are either negative or positive. `unsigned` integers are always positive.

Because you have the same number of bytes for both `signed` and `unsigned` integers, the largest number you can store in an `unsigned` integer is twice as big as the largest positive number you can store in a `signed` integer. An `unsigned short` integer can handle numbers from 0 to 65,535. Half the numbers represented by a `signed short` are negative, thus a `signed short` can only represent numbers from –32,768 to 32,767.

Fundamental Variable Types

Several other variable types are built into C++. They can be conveniently divided into integer variables (the type discussed so far), floating-point variables, and character variables.

Floating-point variables have values that can be expressed as fractions—that is, they are real numbers. Character variables hold a single byte and are used for holding the 256 characters and symbols of the ASCII and extended ASCII character sets.

NEW TERM The *ASCII character set* is the set of characters standardized for use on computers. ASCII is an acronym for American Standard Code for Information Interchange. Nearly every computer operating system supports ASCII, though many support other international character sets as well.

The types of variables used in C++ programs are described in Table 3.1. This table shows the variable type, how much room this book assumes it takes in memory, and what kinds of values can be stored in these variables. The values that can be stored are determined by the size of the variable types, so check your output from Listing 3.1.

TABLE 3.1 Variable Types

Type	Size	Values
unsigned short int	2 bytes	0 to 65,535
short int	2 bytes	–32,768 to 32,767
unsigned long int	4 bytes	0 to 4,294,967,295
long int	4 bytes	–2,147,483,648 to 2,147,483,647
int	4 bytes	–2,147,483,648 to 2,147,483,647
unsigned int	4 bytes	0 to 4,294,967,295

TABLE 3.1 continued

Type	Size	Values
char	1 byte	256 character values
bool	1 byte	true or false
float	4 bytes	1.2e–38 to 3.4e38
double	8 bytes	2.2e–308 to 1.8e308

Defining a Variable

You create, or define, a variable by stating its type, followed by one or more spaces, followed by the variable name and a semicolon. The variable name can be virtually any combination of letters, but cannot contain spaces. Legal variable names include x, J23qrsnf, and myAge. Good variable names tell you what the variables are for; using good names makes it easier to understand the flow of your program. The following statement defines an integer variable called myAge:

```
int myAge;
```

Remember that C++ is case sensitive, so myAge is a different variable name from MyAge. As a general programming practice, try to use names that tell you what the variable is for. Names such as myAge or howMany are much easier to understand and remember than names like xJ4 or theInt. If you use good variable names, you'll need fewer comments to make sense of your code.

Try this experiment: Guess what these pieces of programs do, based on the first few lines of code:

Example 1

```
main()
{
    unsigned short x;
    unsigned short y;
    unsigned int z;
    z = x * y;
}
```

Example 2

```
main ()
{
    unsigned short Width;
    unsigned short Length;
```

```
    unsigned short Area;
    Area = Width * Length;
}
```

Case Sensitivity

NEW TERM   C++ is *case sensitive*. In other words, uppercase and lowercase letters are considered to be different. A variable named age is different from Age, which is different from AGE.

 Some compilers allow you to turn case sensitivity off. Don't be tempted to do this; your programs won't work with other compilers, and other C++ programmers will be very confused by your code.

Many programmers prefer to use all lowercase letters for their variable names. If the name requires two words (for example, my car), there are two popular conventions: my_car or myCar. The latter form is called camel notation, because the capitalization looks something like a hump.

Keywords

Some words are reserved by C++, and you may not use them as variable names. These are keywords used by the compiler to control your program. Keywords include if, while, for, and main. Generally though, any reasonable name for a variable is almost certainly not a keyword.

Do	DON'T
DO define a variable by writing the type, then the variable name.	
DO use meaningful variable names.	
DO remember that C++ is case sensitive.	
DO understand the number of bytes each variable type consumes in memory, and what values can be stored in variables of that type.	
DON'T use C++ keywords as variable names.	
DON'T use unsigned variables for negative numbers.	

Creating More Than One Variable at a Time

You can create more than one variable of the same type in one statement by writing the type and then the variable names, separated by commas. For example:

```
unsigned int myAge, myWeight;    // two unsigned int variables
long area, width, length;        // three longs
```

As you can see, myAge and myWeight are each declared as unsigned integer variables. The second line declares three individual long variables named area, width, and length. The type (long) is assigned to all the variables, so you cannot mix types in one definition statement.

Assigning Values to Your Variables

You assign a value to a variable by using the assignment operator (=). Thus, you would assign 5 to Width by writing

```
unsigned short Width;
Width = 5;
```

You can combine these steps and initialize Width when you define it by writing

```
unsigned short Width = 5;
```

Initialization looks very much like assignment, and with integer variables, the difference is minor. Later, when constants are covered, you will see that some values must be initialized because they cannot be assigned a value.

Listing 3.2 shows a complete program, ready to compile, that computes the area of a rectangle and writes the answer to the screen.

LISTING 3.2   Demonstrates the Use of Variables

```
 0:   // Demonstration of variables
 1:   #include <iostream>
 2:
 3:   int main()
 4:   {
 5:       unsigned short int Width = 5, Length;
 6:       Length = 10;
 7:
 8:       // create  an unsigned short and initialize with result
 9:       // of multiplying Width by Length
10:       unsigned short int Area = Width * Length;
11:
12:       std::cout << "Width: " << Width << "\n";
13:       std::cout << "Length: "  << Length << std::endl;
14:       std::cout << "Area: " << Area << std::endl;
15:       return 0;
16:   }
```

OUTPUT
```
Width: 5
Length: 10
Area: 50
```

 ANALYSIS Line 1 includes the required `include` statement for the `iostream`'s library so that `cout` will work. Line 3 begins the program.

On line 5, `Width` is defined as an unsigned short integer, and its value is initialized to `5`. Another unsigned short integer, `Length`, is also defined, but it's not initialized. On line 6 the value `10` is assigned to `Length`.

On line 10 an integer, `Area`, is defined, and it is initialized with the value obtained by multiplying `Width` times `Length`. On lines 12 through 14 the values of the variables are printed to the screen. Note that the special word `endl` creates a new line.

 `endl` stands for *end l*ine and is end-ell rather than end-one. It is commonly pronounced "end-ell."

typedef

NEW TERM It can become tedious, repetitious, and, most important, error-prone to keep writing `unsigned short int`. You can create a synonym for an existing type by using the keyword `typedef`, which stands for type definition.

It is important to distinguish this from creating a new type (which you will do in Hour 7, "Basic Classes"). `typedef` is used by writing the keyword `typedef` followed by the existing type and then the new name. For example,

```
typedef unsigned short int USHORT
```

creates the new name `USHORT` that you can use anywhere you might have written `unsigned short int`. Listing 3.3 is a replay of Listing 3.2 using the type definition `USHORT` rather than `unsigned short int`.

LISTING 3.3   Demonstrates `typedef`

```
0:  // ****************
1:  // Demonstrates typedef keyword
2:  #include <iostream>
3:
4:  typedef unsigned short int USHORT;        //typedef defined
5:
6:  int main()
7:  {
```

LISTING 3.3   continued

```
 8:     USHORT Width = 5;
 9:     USHORT Length;
10:     Length = 10;
11:     USHORT Area = Width * Length;
12:     std::cout << "Width: " << Width << "\n";
13:     std::cout << "Length: " << Length << std::endl;
14:     std::cout << "Area: " << Area << std::endl;
15:     return 0;
16:  }
```

OUTPUT
```
Width: 5
Length: 10
Area: 50
```

> On some compilers, this code will issue a warning that the "conversion may lose significant digits." This is because the product of the two USHORTS on line 11 might be larger than an unsigned short can hold, and assigning that product to Area can cause truncation. In this particular case, you can safely ignore this warning.

ANALYSIS   On line 4, USHORT is typedef'd as a synonym for unsigned short int. The program is otherwise identical to Listing 3.2, and the output is the same.

When to Use short and When to Use long

One source of confusion for new C++ programmers is when to declare a variable to be type long and when to declare it to be type short. The rule, when understood, is fairly straightforward: If there is any chance that the value you'll want to put into your variable will be too big for its type, use a larger type.

As seen in Table 3.1, unsigned short integers, assuming that they are two bytes, can hold a value only up to 65,535. Signed short integers can hold only half that. Although unsigned long integers can hold an extremely large number (4,294,967,295), that is still quite finite. If you need a larger number, you'll have to go to float or double, and then you lose some precision. Floats and doubles can hold extremely large numbers, but only the first 7 or 19 digits are significant on most computers. That means that the number is rounded off after that many digits.

Wrapping Around in `unsigned` Integers

The fact that `unsigned long` integers have a limit to the values they can hold is only rarely a problem, but what happens if you do run out of room?

When an `unsigned` integer reaches its maximum value, it wraps around and starts over, much as a car odometer might. Listing 3.4 shows what happens if you try to put too large a value into a `short` integer.

LISTING 3.4   Demonstrates Putting Too Large a Value in an `unsigned` Integer

```
0:   #include <iostream>
1:
2:   int main()
3:   {
4:       unsigned short int smallNumber;
5:       smallNumber = 65535;
6:       std::cout << "small number:" << smallNumber << std::endl;
7:       smallNumber++;
8:       std::cout << "small number:" << smallNumber << std::endl;
9:       smallNumber++;
10:      std::cout << "small number:" << smallNumber << std::endl;
11:      return 0;
12:  }
```

OUTPUT
```
small number: 65535
small number: 0
small number: 1
```

ANALYSIS   On line 4 `smallNumber` is declared to be an `unsigned short int`, which on my computer is a two-byte variable able to hold a value between 0 and 65,535. On line 5 the maximum value is assigned to `smallNumber`, and it is printed on line 6.

On line 7 `smallNumber` is incremented; that is, 1 is added to it. The symbol for incrementing is ++ (as in the name C++—an incremental increase from C). Thus, the value in `smallNumber` would be 65,536. But `unsigned short` integers can't hold a number larger than 65,535, so the value is wrapped around to 0, which is printed on line 8.

On line 9 `smallNumber` is incremented again, and its new value, 1, is printed.

Wrapping Around a `signed` Integer

A `signed` integer is different from an `unsigned` integer in that half of its values are negative. Instead of picturing a traditional car odometer, you might picture one that rotates up for positive numbers and down for negative numbers. One mile from zero is either 1 or

−1. When you run out of positive numbers, you run right into the largest negative numbers and then count back down to zero. Listing 3.5 shows what happens when you add 1 to the maximum positive number in an `unsigned short` integer.

LISTING 3.5   Demonstrates Adding Too Large a Number to a `signed` Integer

```
0:   #include <iostream>
1:
2:   int main()
3:   {
4:       short int smallNumber;
5:       smallNumber = 32767;
6:       std::cout << "small number:" << smallNumber << std::endl;
7:       smallNumber++;
8:       std::cout << "small number:" << smallNumber << std::endl;
9:       smallNumber++;
10:      std::cout << "small number:" << smallNumber << std::endl;
11:      return 0;
12:  }
```

OUTPUT
```
small number: 32767
small number: -32768
small number: -32767
```

ANALYSIS   On line 4, `smallNumber` is declared this time to be a `signed short` integer. (If you don't explicitly say that it is `unsigned`, it is assumed to be `signed`.) The program proceeds much as the preceding one, but the output is quite different. To fully understand this output, you must be comfortable with how `signed` numbers are represented as bits in a two-byte integer. For details, check Appendix B, "Glossary."

The bottom line, however, is that just like an `unsigned` integer, the `signed` integer wraps around from its highest positive value to its highest negative value.

Constants

NEW TERM   Like variables, *constants* are data storage locations. But variables can vary; constants, on the other hand and as you might have guessed, do not vary.

You must initialize a constant when you create it, and you cannot assign a new value later; after a constant is initialized, its value is, in a word, constant.

Literal Constants

NEW TERM   C++ has two types of constants: *literal* and *symbolic*.

A literal constant is a value typed directly into your program wherever it is needed. For example:

```
int myAge = 39;
```

myAge is a variable, of type int; 39 is a literal constant. You can't assign a value to 39, and its value can't be changed.

Symbolic Constants

A symbolic constant is a constant that is represented by a name, just as a variable is. Unlike a variable, however, after a constant is initialized, its value can't be changed. If your program has one integer variable named students and another named classes, you could compute how many students you have, given a known number of classes, if you knew there were 15 students per class:

```
students = classes * 15;
```

| * indicates multiplication. |

In this example, 15 is a literal constant. Your code would be easier to read and easier to maintain if you substituted a symbolic constant for this value:

```
students = classes * studentsPerClass
```

If you later decided to change the number of students in each class, you could do so where you define the constant studentsPerClass without having to make a change every place you used that value.

Defining Constants with #define

To define a constant the old-fashioned, evil, politically incorrect way, you would enter:

```
#define studentsPerClass 15
```

Note that studentsPerClass is of no particular type (int, char, and so on). #define does a simple text substitution. Every time the preprocessor sees the word studentsPerClass, it puts 15 in the text.

Because the preprocessor runs before the compiler, your compiler never sees your constant; it sees the number 15.

Defining Constants with const

Although #define works, there is a better, less fattening, and more tasteful way to define constants in C++:

```
const unsigned short int studentsPerClass = 15;
```

This example also declares a symbolic constant named `studentsPerClass`, but this time `studentsPerClass` is typed as an `unsigned short int`.

This takes longer to type, but offers several advantages. The biggest difference is that this constant has a type, and the compiler can enforce that it is used according to its type.

Enumerated Constants

NEW TERM *Enumerated constants* create a set of constants. For example, you can declare `COLOR` to be an enumeration; and you can define that there are five values for `COLOR`: `RED`, `BLUE`, `GREEN`, `WHITE`, and `BLACK`.

The syntax for enumerated constants is to write the keyword `enum`, followed by the type name, an open brace, each of the legal values separated by a comma, and finally a closing brace and a semicolon. Here's an example:

```
enum COLOR { RED, BLUE, GREEN, WHITE, BLACK };
```

This statement performs two tasks:

1. It makes `COLOR` the name of an enumeration, that is, a new type.
2. It makes `RED` a symbolic constant with the value `0`, `BLUE` a symbolic constant with the value `1`, `GREEN` a symbolic constant with the value `2`, and so forth.

Every enumerated constant has an integer value. If you don't specify otherwise, the first constant will have the value `0`, and the rest will count up from there. Any one of the constants can be initialized with a particular value, however, and those that are not initialized will count upward from the ones before them. Thus, if you write

```
enum Color { RED=100, BLUE, GREEN=500, WHITE, BLACK=700 };
```

then `RED` will have the value `100`; `BLUE`, the value `101`; `GREEN`, the value `500`; `WHITE`, the value `501`; and `BLACK`, the value `700`.

Summary

In this hour you learned about the built-in C++ types, such as `char`, `bool`, `int` and `float`. You also learned about numeric and character variables and constants.

You must declare a variable before it can be used, and then you must store the type of data that you've declared correct for that variable. If you put too large a number into an integral variable, it produces an incorrect result.

This chapter also reviewed literal and symbolic constants, as well as enumerated constants, and showed two ways to declare a symbolic constant: using #define and using the keyword const.

Q&A

Q **If a short int can run out of room, why not always use long integers?**

A Both short integers and long integers will run out of room, but a long integer will do so with a much larger number. However, on most machines a long integer takes up twice as much memory every time you declare one. Frankly, this is less of a problem than it used to be, because most personal computers now come with many thousands (if not millions) of bytes of memory.

Q **What happens if I assign a number with a decimal to an integer rather than a float? Consider the following line of code:**

```
int aNumber = 5.4;
```

A A good compiler will issue a warning, but the assignment is completely legal. The number you've assigned will be truncated into an integer. Thus, if you assign 5.4 to an integer variable, that variable will have the value 5. Information will be lost, however; and if you then try to assign the value in that integer variable to a float variable, the float variable will have only 5.

Q **Why not use literal constants; why go to the bother of using symbolic constants?**

A If you use the value in many places throughout your program, a symbolic constant enables all the values to change just by changing the one definition of the constant. Symbolic constants also speak for themselves. It might be hard to understand why a number is being multiplied by 360, but it's much easier to understand what's going on if the number is being multiplied by degreesInACircle.

Hour **4**

Expressions and Statements

A program is really nothing more than a set of commands executed in sequence. The magic emerges from the capability to branch from one set of commands to another depending on whether a particular statement is true or false. In this hour you learn

- What statements are
- What expressions are
- How to work with operators
- The meaning of Truth

Statements

NEW TERM   A *statement* controls the sequence of execution, evaluates an expression, or does nothing (the null statement). All C++ statements end with a semicolon.

A common simple statement is the assignment:

```
x = a + b;
```

Unlike in algebra, this statement does not mean that x equals a+b. This is read, "Assign the value of the sum of a and b to x," or "Assign to x, a+b." Even though this statement is doing two things, it is one statement and, therefore, has one semicolon. The assignment operator assigns whatever is on the right side to whatever is on the left side.

Whitespace

NEW TERM Spaces, along with tabs and new lines, are called *whitespace*. Extra whitespace is generally ignored by the compiler; any place you see a single space you can just as easily put a tab or a new line. Whitespace is added only to make a program more readable by humans; the compiler won't notice.

The assignment statement previously discussed could be written as

```
x=a+b;
```

or as

```
x                              =a
+              b               ;
```

Although this last variation is perfectly legal, it is also perfectly foolish. Whitespace can be used to make your programs more readable and easier to maintain, or it can be used to create indecipherable code. In this as in all things, C++ provides the power; you supply the judgment.

Compound Statements

NEW TERM Any place you can put a single statement, you can put a compound statement. A *compound statement* begins with an opening brace ({) and ends with a closing brace (}).

Although every statement in a compound statement must end with a semicolon, the compound statement itself does not end with a semicolon. For example, consider this piece of code:

```
{
    temp = a;
    a = b;
    b = temp;
}
```

This compound statement swaps the values in the variables a and b.

> **Do**
>
> **DO** use a closing brace any time you have an opening brace.
>
> **DO** end your statements with a semicolon.
>
> **DO** use whitespace judiciously to make your code clearer.

Expressions

NEW TERM   Any statement that returns a value is an *expression* in C++.

There it is, plain and simple. If it returns a value, it is an expression. All expressions are statements.

The myriad pieces of code that qualify as an expression might surprise you. Here are three examples:

```
3.2                     // returns the value 3.2
PI                      // float const that returns the value 3.14
SecondsPerMinute        // int const that returns 60
```

Assuming that `PI` is a `const` equal to `3.14` and `SecondsPerMinute` is a constant equal to `60`, all three of these statements are expressions.

The complicated expression

```
x = a + b;
```

not only adds a and b and assigns the result to x, but yields the value of that assignment (the value in x) as well. Thus, this statement is also an expression. Because it is an expression, it can be on the right side of an assignment operator:

```
y = x = a + b;
```

NEW TERM   The *assignment operator* (=) causes the operand on the left side of the assignment operator to have its value changed to the value on the right side of the assignment operator.

NEW TERM   *Operand* is a mathematical term referring to the part of an expression operated upon by an operator.

This line is evaluated in the following order:

Add a to b.

Assign the result of the expression a + b to x.

Assign the result of the assignment expression x = a + b to y.

If a, b, x, and y are all integers, and if a has the value 2 and b has the value 5, both x and y will be assigned the value 7. Listing 4.1 illustrates evaluating complex expressions.

LISTING 4.1   Evaluating Complex Expressions

```
0:  #include <iostream>
1:
2:  int main()
3:  {
4:      int a=0, b=0, x=0, y=35;
5:      std::cout << "a: " << a << " b: " << b;
6:      std::cout << " x: " << x << " y: " << y << std::endl;
7:      a = 9;
8:      b = 7;
9:      y = x = a+b;
10:     std::cout << "a: " << a << " b: " << b;
11:     std::cout << " x: " << x << " y: " << y << std::endl;
12:     return 0;
13: }
```

OUTPUT
```
a: 0 b: 0 x: 0 y: 35
a: 9 b: 7 x: 16 y: 16
```

ANALYSIS   On line 4, the four variables are declared and initialized. Their values are printed on lines 5 and 6. On line 7, a is assigned the value 9. On line 8, b is assigned the value 7. On line 9, the values of a and b are summed and the result is assigned to x. This expression (x = a+b) evaluates to a value (the sum of a + b), and that value is in turn assigned to y.

Operators

NEW TERM   An *operator* is a symbol that causes the compiler to take an action.

Assignment Operator

An operand that can legally be on the left side of an assignment operator is called an l-value. An operand that can be on the right side is called (you guessed it) an r-value.

Constants are r-values; they cannot be l-values. Thus, you can write

```
x = 35;        // ok
```

but you can't legally write

```
35 = x;         // error, not an l-value!
```

NEW TERM   An *l-value* is an operand that can be on the left side of an expression. An *r-value* is an operand that can be on the right side of an expression. Note that all l-values are r-values, but not all r-values are l-values. An example of an r-value that is not an l-value is a literal. Thus, you can write x = 5;, but you cannot write 5 = x;.

Mathematical Operators

There are five mathematical operators: addition (+), subtraction (-), multiplication (*), division (/), and modulus (%).

Addition, subtraction, and multiplication act pretty much as you might expect. Not so with division.

Integer division is somewhat different from everyday division. When you divide 21 by 4, the result is a real number (a number with a fraction). Integers don't have fractions, and so the "remainder" is lopped off. The value returned by 21 / 4 is 5.

The modulus operator (%) returns the remainder value of integer division. Thus 21 % 4 is 1, because 21 / 4 is 5 with a remainder of 1.

 You read 21 % 4 aloud as "twenty one modulo four." Modulo is the operation performed by the modulus operator. The result of the modulo operation is also called the modulus. Thus the remainder, 1, is the modulus.

Surprisingly, finding the modulus can be very useful. For example, you might want to print a statement on every 10th action.

It turns out that any number % 10 will return 0 if the number is a multiple of 10. Thus 20 % 10 is zero; 30 % 10 is zero, and so on.

Combining the Assignment and Mathematical Operators

It is not uncommon to want to add a value to a variable and then to assign the result back into the variable. If you have a variable myAge and you want to increase the value by two, you can write

```
int myAge = 5;
int temp;
temp = myAge + 2;   // add 5 + 2 and put it in temp
myAge = temp;                // put it back in myAge
```

This method, however, is terribly convoluted and wasteful. In C++ you can put the same variable on both sides of the assignment operator, and thus the preceding becomes

```
myAge = myAge + 2;
```

which is much better. In algebra this expression would be meaningless, but in C++ it is read as "add two to the value in myAge and assign the result to myAge."

Even simpler to write, but perhaps a bit harder to read is

```
myAge += 2;
```

The self-assigned addition operator (+=) adds the r-value to the l-value and then reassigns the result into the l-value. This operator is pronounced "plus-equals." The statement would be read "myAge plus-equals two." If myAge had the value 4 to start, it would have 6 after this statement.

There are self-assigned subtraction (-=), division (/=), multiplication (*=), and modulus (%=) operators as well.

Increment and Decrement

NEW TERM The most common value to add (or subtract) and then reassign into a variable is 1. In C++, increasing a value by 1 is called *incrementing*, and decreasing by 1 is called *decrementing*. There are special operators to perform these actions.

The increment operator (++) increases the value of the variable by 1, and the decrement operator (--) decreases it by 1. Thus, if you have a variable c, and you want to increment it, you would use this statement:

```
C++;                    // Start with C and increment it.
```

This statement is equivalent to the more verbose statement

```
C = C + 1;
```

which you learned is also equivalent to the moderately verbose statement

```
C += 1;
```

Prefix and Postfix

NEW TERM Both the increment operator (++) and the decrement operator (--) come in two flavors: *prefix* and *postfix*. The prefix variety is written before the variable name (++myAge); the postfix variety, after (myAge++).

In a simple statement, it doesn't much matter which you use, but in a complex statement, when you are incrementing (or decrementing) a variable and then assigning the result to another variable, it matters very much. The prefix operator is evaluated before the assignment; the postfix is evaluated after.

The semantics of prefix is this: Increment the value and then fetch it. The semantics of postfix is different: Fetch the value and then increment the original.

This can be confusing at first, but if x is an integer whose value is 5 and you write

```
int a = ++x;
```

you have told the compiler to increment x (making it 6) and then fetch that value and assign it to a. Thus a is now 6 and x is now 6.

If, after doing this, you write:

```
int b = x++;
```

you have now told the compiler to fetch the value in x (6) and assign it to b, and then go back and increment x. Thus, b is now 6 but x is now 7. Listing 4.2 shows the use and implications of both types.

LISTING 4.2   Demonstrates Prefix and Postfix Operators

```
0:   // Listing 4.2 - Demonstrates
1:   // prefix and postfix and increment and
2:   // decrement operators
3:   #include <iostream>
4:
5:   int main()
6:   {
7:       int myAge = 39;        // initialize two integers
8:       int yourAge = 39;
9:       std::cout << "I am:\t" << myAge << "\tyears old.\n";
10:      std::cout << "You are:\t" << yourAge << "\tyears old\n";
11:      myAge++;           // postfix increment
12:      ++yourAge;         // prefix increment
13:      std::cout << "One year passes...\n";
14:      std::cout << "I am:\t" << myAge << "\tyears old.\n";
15:      std::cout << "You are:\t" << yourAge << "\tyears old\n";
16:      std::cout << "Another year passes\n";
17:      std::cout << "I am:\t" << myAge++ << "\tyears old.\n";
18:      std::cout << "You are:\t" << ++yourAge << "\tyears old\n";
19:      std::cout << "Let's print it again.\n";
20:      std::cout << "I am:\t" << myAge << "\tyears old.\n";
21:      std::cout << "You are:\t" << yourAge << "\tyears old\n";
22:      return 0;
23:  }
```

OUTPUT

```
I am       39 years old
You are    39 years old
One year passes
I am       40 years old
You are    40 years old
Another year passes
I am       40 years old
```

```
You are   41 years old
Let's print it again
I am      41 years old
You are   41 years old
```

ANALYSIS On lines 7 and 8 two integer variables are declared, and each is initialized with the value 39. Their value is printed on lines 9 and 10.

On line 11 myAge is incremented using the postfix increment operator, and on line 12 yourAge is incremented using the prefix increment operator. The results are printed on lines 14 and 15, and they are identical (both 40).

On line 17, myAge is incremented as part of the printing statement, using the postfix increment operator. Because it is postfix, the increment happens after the print, and so the value 40 is printed again. In contrast, on line 18 yourAge is incremented using the prefix increment operator. Thus, it is incremented before being printed, and the value displays as 41.

Finally, on lines 20 and 21 the values are printed again. Because the increment statement has completed, the value in myAge is now 41, as is the value in yourAge.

Precedence

In the complex statement

```
x = 5 + 3 * 8;
```

which is performed first, the addition or the multiplication? If the addition is performed first, the answer is 8 * 8, or 64. If the multiplication is performed first, the answer is 5 + 24, or 29.

NEW TERM Every operator has a *precedence* value, and the complete list is conveniently located on the tear card at the front of the book. Multiplication has higher precedence than addition, and thus the value of the expression is 29.

When two mathematical operators have the same precedence, they are performed in left-to-right order. Thus

```
x = 5 + 3 + 8 * 9 + 6 * 4;
```

is evaluated multiplication first, left to right. Thus, 8*9 = 72, and 6*4 = 24. Now the expression is essentially

```
x = 5 + 3 + 72 + 24;
```

Now the addition, left to right, is 5 + 3 = 8; 8 + 72 = 80; 80 + 24 = 104.

Be careful with this. Some operators, such as assignment, are evaluated in right-to-left order! In any case, what if the precedence order doesn't meet your needs? Consider the expression

```
TotalSeconds = NumMinutesToThink + NumMinutesToType * 60
```

In this expression you do not want to multiply the `NumMinutesToType` variable by 60 and then add it to `NumMinutesToThink`. You want to add the two variables to get the total number of minutes, and then you want to multiply that number by 60 to get the total seconds.

In this case you use parentheses to change the precedence order. Items in parentheses are evaluated at a higher precedence than any of the mathematical operators. Thus

```
TotalSeconds = (NumMinutesToThink + NumMinutesToType) * 60
```

will accomplish what you want.

Nesting Parentheses

For complex expressions you might need to nest parentheses, setting one pair within another. For example, you might need to compute the total seconds and then compute the total number of people who are involved before multiplying seconds times people:

```
TotalPersonSeconds = ( ( (NumMinutesToThink + NumMinutesToType) * 60)
➥ * (PeopleInTheOffice + PeopleOnVacation) )
```

This complicated expression is read from the inside out. First, `NumMinutesToThink` is added to `NumMinutesToType`, because these are in the innermost parentheses. Then this sum is multiplied by 60. Next, `PeopleInTheOffice` is added to `PeopleOnVacation`. Finally, the total number of people found is multiplied by the total number of seconds.

This example raises an important issue. This expression is easy for a computer to understand, but very difficult for a human to read, understand, or modify. Here is the same expression rewritten, using some temporary integer variables:

```
TotalMinutes = NumMinutesToThink + NumMinutesToType;
TotalSeconds = TotalMinutes * 60;
TotalPeople = PeopleInTheOffice + PeopleOnVacation;
TotalPersonSeconds = TotalPeople * TotalSeconds;
```

This example takes longer to write and uses more temporary variables than the preceding example, but it is far easier to understand. Add a comment at the top to explain what this code does, and change the 60 to a symbolic constant. You then will have code that is easy to understand and maintain.

4

The Nature of Truth

In previous versions of C++ all truth and falsity were represented by integers, but the new ISO/ANSI standard has introduced a new type: bool. This new type has two possible values, false or true.

Every expression can be evaluated for its truth or falsity. Expressions that evaluate mathematically to zero will return false, all others will return true.

> Many compilers previously offered a bool type that was represented internally as a long int and thus had a size of 4 bytes. ANSI compliant compilers will now often provide a 1-byte bool.

Relational Operators

NEW TERM *Relational operators* are used to determine whether two numbers are equal, or if one is greater or less than the other. Every relational expression returns either 1 (true) or 0 (false). The relational operators are presented in Table 4.1.

If the integer variable myAge has the value 39, and the integer variable yourAge has the value 40, you can determine whether they are equal by using the relational "equals" operator:

```
myAge == yourAge;   // is the value in myAge the same as in yourAge?
```

This expression evaluates to 0, or false, because the variables are not equal. The expression

```
myAge > yourAge;   // is myAge greater than yourAge?
```

evaluates to 0 or false.

> Many novice C++ programmers confuse the assignment operator (=) with the equals operator (==). This can create a nasty bug in your program.

There are six relational operators: equals (==), less than (<), greater than (>), less than or equal to (<=), greater than or equal to (>=), and not equals (!=). Table 4.1 shows each relational operator, its use, and a sample code use.

TABLE 4.1 The Relational Operators

Name	Operator	Sample	Evaluates
Equals	==	`100 == 50;`	false
		`50 == 50;`	true
Not Equals	!=	`100 != 50;`	true
		`50 != 50;`	false
Greater Than	>	`100 > 50;`	true
		`50 > 50;`	false
Greater Than or Equals	>=	`100 >= 50;`	true
		`50 >= 50;`	true
Less Than	<	`100 < 50;`	false
		`50 < 50;`	false
Less Than or Equals	<=	`100 <= 50;`	false
		`50 <= 50;`	true

The `if` Statement

Normally, your program flows along line by line in the order that it appears in your source code. The `if` statement enables you to test for a condition (such as whether two variables are equal) and branch to different parts of your code depending on the result.

The simplest form of an `if` statement is this:

```
if (expression)
    statement;
```

The expression in the parentheses can be any expression at all, but it usually contains one of the relational expressions. If the expression has the value zero, it is considered false, and the statement is skipped. If it has any nonzero value, it is considered true, and the statement is executed. Look at this example:

```
if (bigNumber > smallNumber)
    bigNumber = smallNumber;
```

This code compares `bigNumber` and `smallNumber`. If `bigNumber` is larger, the second line sets its value to the value of `smallNumber`.

The `else` Clause

Often your program will want to take one branch if your condition is true, another if it is false.

The method shown so far, testing first one condition and then the other, works fine but is a bit cumbersome. The keyword else can make for far more readable code:

```
if (expression)
     statement;
else
     statement;
```

Listing 4.3 demonstrates the use of the keyword else.

LISTING 4.3   Demonstrating the else Keyword

```
0:  // Listing 4.3 - Demonstrating the else keyword
1:  #include <iostream>
2:
3:  int main()
4:  {
5:      int firstNumber, secondNumber;
6:      std::cout << "Please enter a big number: ";
7:      std::cin >> firstNumber;
8:      std::cout << "\nPlease enter a smaller number: ";
9:      std::cin >> secondNumber;
10:     if (firstNumber > secondNumber)
11:         std::cout << "\nThanks!\n";
12:     else
13:         std::cout << "\nOops. The second is bigger!";14:
15:     return 0;
16: }
```

OUTPUT
```
Please enter a big number: 10
Please enter a smaller number: 12
Oops. The second is bigger!
```

ANALYSIS The if statement on line 10 is evaluated. If the condition is true, the statement on line 11 is run; if it is false, the statement on line 13 is run. If the else clause on line 12 were removed, the statement on line 13 would run whether or not the if statement were true. Remember, the if statement ends after line 11. If the else was not there, line 13 would just be the next line in the program.

Remember that either or both of these statements can be replaced with a block of code in braces.

```
if Statement
Form 1
        if (expression)
            statement;
        next statement;
```

If the expression is evaluated as true, the statement is executed and the program continues with the next statement. If the expression is not true, the statement is ignored and the program jumps to the next statement.

Remember that the statement can be a single statement ending with a semicolon or a compound statement enclosed in braces.

Advanced `if` Statements

It is worth noting that any statement can be used in an `if` or `else` clause, even another `if` or `else` statement. Thus, you might see complex `if` statements in the following form:

```
if (expression1)
{
    if (expression2)
        statement1;
    else
    {
        if (expression3)
            statement2;
        else
            statement3;
    }
}
else
    statement4;
```

This cumbersome `if` statement says, "If expression1 is true and expression2 is true, execute statement1. If expression1 is true but expression2 is not true, then if expression3 is true, execute statement2. If expression1 is true but expression2 and expression3 are false, execute statement3. Finally, if expression1 is not true, execute statement4." As you can see, complex `if` statements can be confusing!

Listing 4.4 gives an example of such a complex `if` statement.

LISTING 4.4   A Complex, Nested `if` Statement

```
0:  // Listing 4.4 - A complex, nested if tatement
1:  #include <iostream>
2:
3:  int main()
4:  {
5:      // Ask for two numbers
6:      // Assign the numbers to bigNumber and littleNumber
7:      // If bigNumber is bigger than littleNumber,
8:      // see if they are evenly divisible
9:      // If they are, see if they are the same number
```

LISTING 4.4   continued

```
10:
11:        int firstNumber, secondNumber;
12:        std::cout << "Enter two numbers.\nFirst: ";
13:        std::cin >> firstNumber;
14:        std::cout << "\nSecond: ";
15:        std::cin >> secondNumber;
16:        std::cout << "\n\n";
17:
18:        if (firstNumber >= secondNumber)
19:        {
20:            if ( (firstNumber % secondNumber) == 0) // evenly divisible?
21:            {
22:                if (firstNumber == secondNumber)
23:                    std::cout << "They are the same!\n";
24:                else
25:                    std::cout << "They are evenly divisible!\n";
26:            }
27:            else
28:                std::cout << "They are not evenly divisible!\n";
29:        }
30:        else
31:            std::cout << "Hey! The second one is larger!\n";
32:        return 0;
33:    }
```

OUTPUT

```
Enter two numbers.
First: 10
Second: 2
They are evenly divisible!
```

ANALYSIS   Two numbers are prompted for and then compared. The first if statement, on line 18, checks to ensure that the first number is greater than or equal to the second. If not, the else clause on line 30 is executed.

If the first if is true, the block of code beginning on line 19 is executed, and the second if statement is tested on line 20. This checks to see whether the first number modulo the second number yields no remainder. If so, the numbers are either evenly divisible or equal. The if statement on line 22 checks for equality and displays the appropriate message either way.

If the if statement on line 20 fails, the else statement on line 27 is executed.

Use Braces in Nested if Statements

It is legal to leave out the braces on if statements that are only a single statement, and it is legal to nest if statements, such as the following:

```
if (x > y)              // if x is bigger than y
    if (x < z)          // and if x is smaller than z
        x = y;          // then set x to the value in y
```

However, when you are writing large nested statements, this practice can cause enormous confusion. Remember, whitespace and indentation are a convenience for the programmer; they make no difference to the compiler. It is easy to confuse the logic and inadvertently assign an else statement to the wrong if statement. Listing 4.5 illustrates this problem.

LISTING 4.5   Demonstrates Why Braces Help Clarify Which else Statement Goes with Which if Statement

```
0:  // Listing 4.5 - Demonstrates why braces
1:  // help clarify which else statement goes with which if statement
2:  #include <iostream>
3:
4:  int main()
5:  {
6:      int x;
7:      std::cout << "Enter a number less than 10 or greater than 100: ";
8:      std::cin >> x;
9:      std::cout << "\n";
10:
11:     if (x > 10)
12:         if (x > 100)
13:             std::cout << "More than 100, Thanks!\n";
14:     else                            // not the else intended!
15:         std::cout << "Less than 10, Thanks!\n";
16:
17:     return 0;
18: }
```

OUTPUT   Enter a number less than 10 or greater than 100: 20
Less than 10, Thanks!

ANALYSIS   The programmer intended to ask for a number between 10 and 100, check for the correct value, and then print a thank you note.

If the if statement on line 11 evaluates true, the following statement (line 12) is executed. In this case, line 12 executes when the number entered is greater than 10. Line 12 contains an if statement also. This if statement evaluates true if the number entered is greater than 100. If the number is greater than 100, the statement on line 13 is executed.

If the number entered is less than or equal to 10, the if on line 11 evaluates to false.

Program control goes to the next line following the `if`, in this case line 16. If you enter a number less than 10, the output is as follows:

```
Enter a number less than 10 or greater than 100: 9
```

The `else` clause on line 14 was clearly intended to be attached to the `if` statement on line 11, and thus is indented accordingly. Unfortunately, the `else` statement is really attached to the `if` on line 12, and thus this program has a subtle bug.

It is a subtle bug because the compiler will not complain. This is a legal C++ program, but it just doesn't do what was intended. Further, most of the time the programmer tests this program, it will appear to work. As long as a number that is greater than 100 is entered, the program will seem to work just fine.

Listing 4.6 fixes the problem by putting in the necessary braces.

LISTING 4.6   Demonstrates the Proper Use of Braces with an `if` Statement

```
0:  // Listing 4.6 - demonstrates proper use of braces
1:  // with an  if statement
2:  #include <iostream>
3:
4:  int main()
5:  {
6:      int x;
7:      std::cout << "Enter a number less than 10 or greater than 100: ";
8:      std::cin >> x;
9:      std::cout << "\n";
10:
11:     if (x > 10)
12:     {
13:         if (x > 100)
14:             std::cout << "More than 100, Thanks!\n";
15:     }
16:     else        // now works as intended!
17:         std::cout << "Less than 10, Thanks!\n";
18:     return 0;
19: }
```

OUTPUT   `Enter a number less than 10 or greater than 100: 20`

ANALYSIS   The braces on lines 12 and 15 make everything between them into one statement, and now the `else` on line 16 applies to the `if` on line 11 as intended.

The user typed 20, so the `if` statement on line 11 is true; however, the `if` statement on line 13 is false, so nothing is printed. It would be better if the programmer put another `else` clause after line 14 so that errors would be caught and a message printed.

The programs shown in this book are written to demonstrate the particular issues being discussed. They are intentionally kept simple; there is no attempt to "bulletproof" the code to protect against user error. In professional-quality code, every possible user error is anticipated and handled gracefully.

Logical Operators

Often you want to ask more than one relational question at a time. "Is it true that x is greater than y, and also true that y is greater than z?" A program might need to determine that both of these conditions are true, or that some other condition is true, in order to take an action.

Imagine a sophisticated alarm system that has this logic: "If the door alarm sounds AND it is after six p.m. AND it is NOT a holiday, OR if it is a weekend, then call the police." The three logical operators of C++ are used to make this kind of evaluation. These operators are listed in Table 4.2.

TABLE 4.2 The Logical Operators

Operator	Symbol	Example
AND	&&	expression1 && expression2
OR	||	expression1 || expression2
NOT	!	!expression

Logical AND

A logical AND statement evaluates two expressions, and if both expressions are true, the logical AND statement is true as well. If it is true that you are hungry, AND it is true that you have money, THEN it is true that you can buy lunch. Thus,

```
if ( (x == 5) && (y == 5) )
```

would evaluate true if both x and y are equal to 5, and it would evaluate false if either one is not equal to 5. Note that both sides must be true for the entire expression to be true.

Note that the logical AND is two && symbols.

Logical OR

A logical OR statement evaluates two expressions. If either one is true, the expression is true. If you have money OR you have a credit card, you can pay the bill. You don't need both money and a credit card; you need only one, although having both would be fine as well. Thus,

```
if ( (x == 5) || (y == 5) )
```

evaluates true if either x or y is equal to 5, or if both are equal to five. In fact, if x is equal to five, the compiler will never check on y at all!

Note that the logical OR is two || symbols.

Logical NOT

A logical NOT statement evaluates true if the expression being tested is false. Again, if the expression being tested is false, the value of the test is true! Thus

```
if ( !(x == 5) )
```

is true only if x is not equal to 5. This is exactly the same as writing

```
if (x != 5)
```

Relational Precedence

Relational operators and logical operators, being C++ expressions, each return a value: 1 (true) or 0 (false). Like all expressions, they have a precedence order that determines which relations are evaluated first. This fact is important when determining the value of the statement

```
if ( x > 5 && y > 5 || z > 5)
```

It might be that the programmer wanted this expression to evaluate true if both x and y are greater than 5 or if z is greater than 5. On the other hand, the programmer might have wanted this expression to evaluate true only if x is greater than 5 and if it is also true that either y is greater than 5 or z is greater than 5.

If x is 3, and y and z are both 10, the first interpretation will be true (z is greater than 5, so ignore x and y), but the second will be false. (It is not true that x is greater than 5, so it does not matter that y or z are greater than 5.)

Although precedence will determine which relation is evaluated first, parentheses can both change the order and make the statement clearer:

```
if ( (x > 5) && (y > 5 || z > 5) )
```

Using the values given earlier, this statement is false. Because it is not true that x is greater than 5, the left side of the AND statement fails, and thus the entire statement is false. Remember that an AND statement requires that both sides be true—something isn't both "good tasting" AND "good for you" if it isn't good tasting.

 It is often a good idea to use extra parentheses to clarify what you want to group. Remember, the goal is to write programs that work and that are easy to read and understand.

More About Truth and Falsehood

In C++ zero is false, and any other value is true. Because expressions always have a value, many C++ programmers take advantage of this feature in their if statements. A statement such as

```
if (x)           // if x is true (nonzero)
    x = 0;
```

can be read as "If x has a nonzero value, set it to 0." This is a bit of a cheat; it would be clearer if written

```
if (x != 0)      // if x is nonzero
    x = 0;
```

Both statements are legal, but the latter is clearer. It is good programming practice to reserve the former method for true tests of logic, rather than for testing for nonzero values.

These two statements are also equivalent:

```
if (!x)          // if x is false (zero)
if (x == 0)      // if x is zero
```

The second statement, however, is somewhat easier to understand and is more explicit.

Summary

In this hour you learned what a statement is. You also learned that an expression is any statement that returns a value. You learned that whitespace can be used to make your program more readable, and you saw how to use the mathematical, logical, and assignment operators. You saw how to replace a single statement with a block of statements using braces.

You also learned how to use the prefix and postfix operators, as well as the relational operators. You learned how to use the `if` statement, how to use `else`, and how to create complex and nested `if` statements.

Q&A

Q Why use unnecessary parentheses when precedence will determine which operators are acted on first?

A Although it is true that the compiler will know the precedence and that a programmer can look up the precedence order, code that is easy to understand is easier to maintain.

Q If the relational operators always return 1 or 0, why are other values considered true?

A The relational operators return 1 or 0, but every expression returns a value, and those values can also be evaluated in an `if` statement. Here's an example:

```
if ( (x = a + b) == 35 )
```

This is a perfectly legal C++ statement. It evaluates to a value even if the sum of a and b is not equal to 35. Also note that x is assigned the value that is the sum of a and b in any case.

Q What effect do tabs, spaces, and new lines have on the program?

A Tabs, spaces, and new lines (known as whitespace) have no effect on the program, although whitespace can make the program easier to read.

Q Are negative numbers true or false?

A All nonzero numbers, positive and negative, are true.

HOUR 5

Functions

When people talk about C++ they mention objects first. Yet objects rely on functions to get their work done. This hour you learn

- What a function is and what its parts are
- How to declare and define functions
- How to pass parameters into functions
- How to return a value from a function

What Is a Function?

A function is, in effect, a subprogram that can act on data and return a value. Every C++ program has at least one function, main(). When your program starts, main() is called automatically. main() might call other functions, some of which might call still others.

Each function has its own name, and when that name is encountered, the execution of the program branches off to the first statement of that function and continues until a return statement or the end of that function. When the function returns, execution resumes on the next line of the calling function. This flow is illustrated in Figure 5.1.

FIGURE 5.1

When a program calls a function, execution switches to the function and then resumes at the line after the function call.

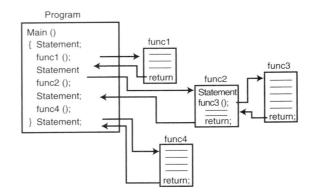

A well-designed function will perform a specific task. That means it does one thing, does it well, and then returns.

Complicated tasks should be broken down into multiple functions, and then each can be called in turn. This makes your code easier to understand and easier to maintain.

You will find throughout this book that I talk a lot about making your program easy to maintain. The big cost in programming is not *writing* the program, it is keeping it useful and reliable throughout its shelf-life.

Declaring and Defining Functions

Before you can call a function, you must first *declare* the function and then *define* the function.

NEW TERM The *function declaration* tells the compiler the name, return type, and types of the parameters of the function. The declaration of a function is called its prototype.

NEW TERM The *definition* tells the compiler how the function works. No function can be called from any other function unless the called function has first been declared.

Declaring the Function

The built-in functions supplied by your compiler vendor will have their function prototypes already written. You just #include the appropriate file and you're all set.

NEW TERM The function prototype is a statement, which means it ends with a semicolon. It consists of the function's return type, name, and parameter list.

The parameter list is a list of all the parameters and their types, separated by commas. Figure 5.2 illustrates the parts of the function prototype.

FIGURE 5.2

Parts of a function prototype.

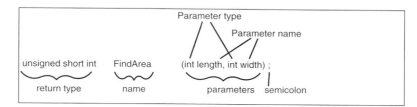

The function prototype and the function definition must agree exactly about the return type, the name, and the parameter list. If they do not agree, you will get a compile-time error. Note, however, that the function prototype does not need to contain the names of the parameters, just their types. A prototype that looks like this is perfectly legal:

```
long Area(int, int);
```

This prototype declares a function named `Area()` that returns a `long` and that has two parameters, both integers. Although this is legal, it is not a good idea. Adding parameter names makes your prototype clearer. The same function with named parameters might be:

```
long Area(int length, int width);
```

It is now obvious what this function does and what the parameters are.

Note that all functions have a return type. Listing 5.1 demonstrates a program that includes a function prototype for the `Area()` function.

Listing 5.1 Shows a Function Declaration and the Definition and Use of That Function

```
0:  // Listing 5.1 - demonstrates the use of function prototypes
1:  #include <iostream>
2:
3:  int FindArea(int length, int width); //function prototype
4:
5:  int main()
6:  {
7:      int lengthOfYard;
8:      int widthOfYard;
9:      int areaOfYard;
10:
```

Listing 5.1 continued

```
11:        std::cout << "\nHow wide is your yard? ";
12:        std::cin >> widthOfYard;
13:        std::cout << "\nHow long is your yard? ";
14:        std::cin >> lengthOfYard;
15:
16:        areaOfYard= FindArea(lengthOfYard,widthOfYard);
17:
18:        std::cout << "\nYour yard is ";
19:        std::cout << areaOfYard;
20:        std::cout << " square feet\n\n";
21:        return 0;
22:    }
23:
24:    int FindArea(int l, int w)
25:    {
26:        return l * w;
27:    }
```

OUTPUT

```
How wide is your yard? 100
How long is your yard? 200
Your yard is 20000 square feet
```

ANALYSIS   The prototype for the FindArea() function is on line 3. Compare the prototype with the definition of the function on line 24. Note that the name, the return type, and the parameter types are the same.

If they are different, a compiler error is generated. In fact, the only required difference is that the function prototype ends with a semicolon and has no body.

Also note that the parameter names in the prototype are length and width, but the parameter names in the definition are l and w. It turns out that the names in the prototype are not used; they are there as information to the programmer. The arguments are passed in to the function in the order in which they are declared and defined.

You are free to place the definition (lines 24-27) before its invocation; that is, you could move these lines above line 16. In that case, you would no longer need the prototype. While this is a fine solution for small programs, it is poor programming practice to depend on the order of the definition of functions. As your program becomes more complex, and as functions call one another, it becomes difficult to ensure that all programs are defined in the correct order. It is generally preferable to declare all the functions with prototypes, which frees you from order dependency.

Defining the Function

The definition of a function consists of the function header and its body. The header is exactly like the function prototype, except that the parameters must be named and there is no terminating semicolon.

The body of the function is a set of statements enclosed in braces. Figure 5.3 shows the header and body of a function.

FIGURE 5.3
The header and body of a function.

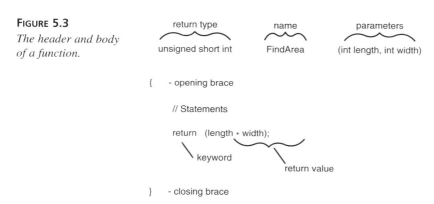

Functions

A function prototype tells the compiler the function's name, return value, and parameters.

```
return_type function_name ( [type [parameterName]]...);
```

The function definition tells the compiler how the function works.

```
return_type function_name ( [type parameterName]...)
{
    statements;
}
```

A function prototype tells the compiler the return type, name, and parameter list. Functions are not required to have parameters, and if they do, the prototype is not required to list their names, only their types. A prototype always ends with a semicolon (;).

A function definition must agree with its prototype in return type and parameter list. It must provide names for all the parameters, and the body of the function definition must be surrounded by braces. All statements within the body of the function must be terminated with semicolons, but the function itself is not ended with a semicolon; it ends with a closing brace.

If the function returns a value, it should end with a return statement, although return statements can legally appear anywhere in the body of the function.

Every function has a return type. If one is not explicitly designated, the return type will be int. Be sure to give every function an explicit return type. If a function does not return a value, its return type will be void.

Here are some examples of function prototypes:

```
long FindArea(long length, long width); // returns long, has two parameters
void PrintMessage(int messageNumber);   // returns void, has one parameter
int GetChoice();                        // returns int, has no parameters
BadFunction();                          // returns int, has no parameters
```

Here are some examples of function definitions:

```
long Area(long l, long w)
{
    return l * w;
}

void PrintMessage(int whichMsg)
{
    if (whichMsg == 0)
        std::cout << "Hello.\n";
    if (whichMsg == 1)
        std::cout << "Goodbye.\n";
    if (whichMsg > 1)
        std::cout << "I'm confused.\n";
}
```

Local Variables

NEW TERM   Not only can you pass in variables to the function, but you also can declare variables within the body of the function. This is done using *local variables*, so named because they exist only locally within the function itself. When the function returns, the local variables are no longer available.

Local variables are defined like any other variables. The parameters passed in to the function are also considered local variables and can be used exactly as if they had been defined within the body of the function. Listing 5.2 is an example of using parameters and locally defined variables within a function. The output reflects running the program three times, providing different values with each invocation.

Listing 5.2 Demonstrates Use of Local Variables and Parameters

```
0:   #include <iostream>
1:
2:   float Convert(float);
3:
4:   int main()
5:   {
6:       float TempFer;
7:       float TempCel;
8:
9:       std::cout << "Please enter the temperature in Fahrenheit: ";
10:      std::cin >> TempFer;
11:      TempCel = Convert(TempFer);
12:      std::cout << "\nHere's the temperature in Celsius: ";
13:      std::cout << TempCel << std::endl;
14:      return 0;
15:  }
16:
17:  float Convert(float TempFer)
18:  {
19:      float TempCel;
20:      TempCel = ((TempFer - 32) * 5) / 9;
21:      return TempCel;
22:  }
```

OUTPUT

```
Please enter the temperature in Fahrenheit: 212
Here's the temperature in Celsius: 100

Please enter the temperature in Fahrenheit: 32
Here's the temperature in Celsius: 0

Please enter the temperature in Fahrenheit: 85
Here's the temperature in Celsius: 29.4444
```

ANALYSIS The output reflects running the program three times, providing the values 212, 32 and 85, respectively. On lines 6 and 7, two float variables are declared, one to hold the temperature in Fahrenheit and one to hold the temperature in degrees Celsius. The user is prompted to enter a Fahrenheit temperature on line 9, and that value is passed to the function Convert().

Execution jumps to the first line of the function Convert() on line 19, where a local variable, also named TempCel, is declared. Note that this local variable is not the same as the variable TempCel on line 7. This variable exists only within the function Convert(). The value passed as a parameter, TempFer, is also just a local copy of the variable passed in by main().

This function could have named the parameter FerTemp and the local variable CelTemp, and the program would work equally well. You can reenter these names and recompile the program to see this work.

The local function variable Tempcel is assigned the value that results from subtracting 32 from the parameter TempFer, multiplying by 5, and then dividing by 9. This value is then returned as the return value of the function, and on line 11 it is assigned to the variable TempCel in the main() function. It is printed on line 13.

The program is run three times. The first time the value 212 is passed in to ensure that the boiling point of water in degrees Fahrenheit (212) generates the correct answer in degrees Celsius (100). The second test is the freezing point of water. The third test is a random number chosen to generate a fractional result.

As an exercise, try reentering the program with other variable names as illustrated here in Listing 5.3:

Listing 5.3   Demonstrates Use of Local Variables and Parameters

```
 0:  #include <iostream>
 1:
 2:  float Convert(float);
 3:
 4:  int main()
 5:  {
 6:      float TempFer;
 7:      float TempCel;
 8:
 9:      std::cout << "Please enter the temperature in Fahrenheit: ";
10:      std::cin >> TempFer;
11:      TempCel = Convert(TempFer);
12:      std::cout << "\nHere's the temperature in Celsius: ";
13:      std::cout << TempCel << std::endl;
14:      return 0;
15:  }
16:
17:  float Convert(float Fer)
18:  {
19:      float Cel;
20:      Cel = ((Fer - 32) * 5) / 9;
21:      return Cel;
22:  }
```

You should get the same results.

A variable has *scope*, which determines how long it is available to your program and where it can be accessed. Variables declared within a block are scoped to that block; they can be accessed only within that block and "go out of existence" when that block ends. Global variables have global scope and are available anywhere within your program.

Global Variables

 Variables defined outside of any function have *global* scope and thus are available from any function in the program, including `main()`.

In C++, global variables are avoided because they can create very confusing code that is hard to maintain. You won't see global variables in any code in this book, nor in any programs I write.

Function Statements

There is virtually no limit to the number or types of statements that can be in a function body.

On the other hand, well-designed functions tend to be small. The vast majority of functions will be just a handful of lines of code.

Function Arguments

Function arguments do not have to all be of the same type. It is perfectly reasonable to write a function that takes an integer, two longs, and a character as its arguments.

Any valid C++ expression can be a function argument, including constants, mathematical and logical expressions, and other functions that return a value. For example, if you have a function declared as

```
int MyFunction(int theIntegerParam, bool theBoolean);
```

you can legally invoke this function with any of the following function calls:

```
int z, x = 3, y = 5; // declare the variables
z = MyFunction(x,y); // pass in an int and a bool variable
z = MyFunction(32,true); // pass in two constants
z = MyFunction(23+9, 100>5); // expressions which equate to 32, true
```

The last function call is identical in its effect to the second function call. Finally, if you declare the following two functions

```
int MyIntFunction(int x, int y);
bool MyBoolFunction(int x, int y);
```

you can invoke MyFunction as follows:

```
z = MyFunction(MyIntFunction(3,5), MyBoolFunction(2,4));
```

In this final invocation, you are effectively passing in as parameters the integer value returned by calling MyIntFunction(3,5) and the bool value returned by calling MyBoolFunction(2,4).

Using Functions as Parameters to Functions

Although it is legal to use a function that returns a value as a parameter to another function, it can create code that is hard to read and hard to debug.

As an example, each of the functions `doubler()`, `tripler()`, `square()`, and `cube()` returns a value. You could write

```
Answer = (doubler(tripler(square(cube(myValue)))));
```

This statement takes a variable, `myValue`, and passes it as an argument to the function `cube()`, whose return value is passed as an argument to the function `square()`, whose return value is in turn passed to `tripler()`, and that return value is passed to `doubler()`. The return value of this doubled, tripled, squared, and cubed number is now passed to `Answer`.

It is difficult to be certain what this code does (was the value tripled before or after it was squared?), and if the answer is wrong it will be hard to figure out which function failed.

An alternative is to assign each step to its own intermediate variable:

```
unsigned long myValue = 2;
unsigned long cubed   =   cube(myValue);       // cubed = 8
unsigned long squared = square(cubed);         // squared = 64
unsigned long tripled = tripler(squared);       // tripled = 192
unsigned long Answer  =  doubler(tripled);      // Answer = 384
```

Now each intermediate result can be examined, and the order of execution is explicit.

Parameters Are Local Variables

The arguments passed in to the function are local to the function. Changes made to the arguments do not affect the values in the calling function. This is known as *passing by value*, which means a local copy of each argument is made in the function. These local copies are treated just as any other local variables. Listing 5.4 illustrates this point.

Listing 5.4 Demonstrates Passing by Value

```
0:   // Listing 5.4 - demonstrates passing by value
1:   #include <iostream>
2:
3:   void swap(int x, int y);
4:
5:   int main()
6:   {
7:       int x = 5, y = 10;
8:       std::cout << "Main. Before swap, x: " << x
9:                                   << " y: " << y << "\n";
10:      swap(x,y);
11:      std::cout << "Main. After swap, x: " << x
12:                                  << " y: " << y << "\n";
13:      return 0;
14:  }
15:
16:  void swap (int x, int y)
17:  {
18:      int temp;
19:      std::cout << "Swap. Before swap, x: " << x
20:                                  << " y: " << y << "\n";
21:      temp = x;
22:      x = y;
23:      y = temp;
24:      std::cout << "Swap. After swap, x: " << x
25:                                  << " y: " << y << "\n";
26:  }
```

OUTPUT
```
Main. Before swap. x: 5 y: 10
Swap. Before swap. x: 5 y: 10
Swap. After swap. x: 10 y: 5
Main. After swap. x: 5 y: 10
```

5

ANALYSIS This program initializes two variables in main() and then passes them to the swap() function, which appears to swap them. When they are examined again in main(), however, they are unchanged!

The variables are initialized on line 7, and their values are displayed on lines 8 and 9. swap() is called, and the variables are passed in.

Execution of the program switches to the swap() function, where on lines 19 and 20 the values are printed again. They are in the same order as they were in main(), as expected. On lines 21 to 23 the values are swapped, and this action is confirmed by the printout on lines 24 and 25. Indeed, while in the swap() function, the values are swapped.

Execution then returns to line 11, back in main(), where the values are no longer swapped.

As you've figured out, the values passed in to the swap() function are passed by value, meaning that copies of the values are made that are local to swap(). These local variables are swapped in lines 21 to 23, but the variables back in main() are unaffected.

Later in the book, you'll see alternatives to passing by value that will allow the values in main() to be changed.

Return Values

Functions return a value or return void. void is a signal to the compiler that no value will be returned.

To return a value from a function, write the keyword return followed by the value you want to return. The value might itself be an expression that returns a value. For example:

```
return 5;
return (x > 5);
return (MyFunction());
```

These are all legal return statements, assuming that the function MyFunction() itself returns a value. The value in the second statement return (x > 5), will be false if x is not greater than 5, or it will be true. What is returned is the value of the expression, false or true, not the value of x.

When the return keyword is encountered, the expression following return is returned as the value of the function. Program execution returns immediately to the calling function, and any statements following the return are not executed.

It is legal to have more than one return statement in a single function. However, keep in mind that as soon as a return statement is executed, the function ends. Listing 5.5 illustrates this idea.

Listing 5.5   Demonstrates Multiple Return Statements

```
 0:  // Listing 5.5 - demonstrates multiple return
 1:  // statements
 2:  #include <iostream>
 3:
 4:  int Doubler(int AmountToDouble);
 5:
 6:  int main()
 7:  {
 8:      int result = 0;
 9:      int input;
10:
11:      std::cout << "Enter a number between 0 and "
```

Listing 5.5 continued

```
12:                    << "10,000 to double: ";
13:       std::cin >> input;
14:
15:       std::cout << "\nBefore doubler is called...";
16:       std::cout << "\ninput: " << input
17:                    << " doubled: " << result << "\n";
18:
19:       result = Doubler(input);
20:
21:       std::cout << "\nBack from Doubler...";
22:       std::cout << "\ninput: " << input
23:                    << " doubled: " << result << "\n\n";
24:
25:       return 0;
26:   }
27:
28:   int Doubler(int original)
29:   {
30:       if (original <= 10000)
31:           return original * 2;
32:       else
33:           return -1;
34:       std::cout << "You can't get here!\n";
35:   }
```

OUTPUT

```
Enter a number between 0 and 10,000 to double: 9000

Before doubler is called...
input: 9000 doubled: 0

Back from doubler...
input: 9000 doubled: 18000


Enter a number between 0 and 10,000 to double: 11000

Before doubler is called...
input: 11000 doubled: 0

Back from doubler...
input: 11000 doubled: -1
```

ANALYSIS A number is requested on lines 11, 12 and 13 and printed on lines 16 and 17, along with the local variable result. The function Doubler() is called on line 19, and the input value is passed as a parameter. The result will be assigned to the local variable result, and the values will be reprinted on lines 21, 22 and 23.

On line 30, in the function `Doubler()`, the parameter is tested to see whether it is greater than 10,000. If it is not, the function returns twice the original number. If it is greater than 10,000, the function returns -1 as an error value.

The statement on line 34 is never reached, because whether or not the value is greater than 10,000, the function returns before it gets to line 34, on either line 31 or line 33. Many compilers will warn that this statement cannot be executed.

Default Parameters

For every parameter you declare in a function prototype and definition, the calling function must pass in a value. The value passed in must be of the declared type. Thus, if you have a function declared as

```
long myFunction(int);
```

the function must, in fact, take an integer variable. If the function definition differs, or if you fail to pass in an integer, you will get a compiler error.

The one exception to this rule is if the function prototype declares a default value for the parameter. A default value is a value to use if none is supplied. The preceding declaration could be rewritten as

```
long myFunction (int x = 50);
```

This prototype says "`myFunction()` returns a `long` and takes an integer parameter. If an argument is not supplied, use the default value of 50." Because parameter names are not required in function prototypes, this declaration could have been written as

```
long myFunction (int = 50);
```

The function definition is not changed by declaring a default parameter. The function definition header for this function would be

```
long myFunction (int x)
```

If the calling function did not include a parameter, the compiler would fill x with the default value of 50. The name of the default parameter in the prototype need not be the same as the name in the function header; the default value is assigned by position, not name.

Any or all the function's parameters can be assigned default values. The one restriction is this: If any of the parameters does not have a default value, no previous parameter may have a default value.

If the function prototype looks like

```
long myFunction (int Param1, int Param2, int Param3);
```

you can assign a default value to Param2 only if you have assigned a default value to Param3. You can assign a default value to Param1 only if you've assigned default values to both Param2 and Param3. Listing 5.6 demonstrates the use of default values.

Listing 5.6   Demonstrates Default Parameter Values

```
0:   // Listing 5.6 - demonstrates use
1:   // of default parameter values
2:   #include <iostream>
3:
4:   int AreaCube(int length, int width = 25, int height = 1);
5:
6:   int main()
7:   {
8:       int length = 100;
9:       int width = 50;
10:      int height = 2;
11:      int area;
12:
13:      area = AreaCube(length, width, height);
14:      std::cout << "First time area equals " << area << "\n";
15:
16:      area = AreaCube(length, width);
17:      std::cout << "Second time area equals " << area << "\n";
18:
19:      area = AreaCube(length);
20:      std::cout << "Third time area equals " << area << "\n";
21:      return 0;
22:  }
23:
24:  int AreaCube(int length, int width, int height)
25:  {
26:      return (length * width * height);
27:  }
```

OUTPUT
```
First area equals: 10000
Second time area equals: 5000
Third time area equals: 2500
```

On line 4, the AreaCube() prototype specifies that the AreaCube() function takes three integer parameters. The last two have default values.

This function computes the area of the cube whose dimensions are passed in. If no width is passed in, a width of 25 is used and a height of 1 is used. If the width, but not the height is passed in, a height of 1 is used. It is not possible to pass in the height without passing in a width.

On lines 8–10, the dimensions length, height, and width are initialized, and they are passed to the AreaCube() function on line 13. The values are computed, and the result is printed on line 14.

Execution then goes to line 16, where AreaCube() is called again, but with no value for height. The default value is used, and again the dimensions are computed and printed.

Execution continues at line 19, and this time neither the width nor the height is passed in. Execution branches off for a third time to line 26. The default values are used. The area is computed and then printed.

Overloading Functions

C++ enables you to create more than one function with the same name. This is called function overloading. The functions must differ in their parameter list, with a different type of parameter, a different number of parameters, or both. Here's an example:

```
int myFunction (int, int);
int myFunction (long, long);
int myFunction (long);
```

myFunction() is overloaded with three different parameter lists. The first and second versions differ in the types of the parameters, and the third differs in the number of parameters.

The return types can be the same or different on overloaded functions, as long as the parameter list is different. You can't overload just on return type, however.

Function overloading is also called function polymorphism. *Poly* means many, and *morph* means form: A polymorphic function is many-formed.

Function polymorphism refers to the capability to "overload" a function with more than one meaning. By changing the number or type of the parameters, you can give two or more functions the same function name, and the right one will be called by matching the parameters used. This enables you to create a function that can average integers, doubles, and other values without having to create individual names for each function, such as AverageInts(), AverageDoubles(), and so on.

Suppose you write a function that doubles whatever input you give it. You would like to be able to pass in an int, a long, a float, or a double. Without function overloading, you would have to create four function names:

```
int DoubleInt(int);
long DoubleLong(long);
float DoubleFloat(float);
double DoubleDouble(double);
```

With function overloading, you make this declaration:

```
int Double(int);
long Double(long);
float Double(float);
double Double(double);
```

This is easier to read and easier to use. You don't have to worry about which one to call; you just pass in a variable, and the right function is called automatically.

Inline Functions

When you define a function, normally the compiler creates just one set of instructions in memory. When you call the function, execution of the program jumps to those instructions, and when the function returns, execution jumps back to the next line in the calling function. If you call the function 10 times, your program jumps to the same set of instructions each time. This means there is only one copy of the function, not 10.

There is some performance overhead in jumping in and out of functions. It turns out that some functions are very small, just a line or two of code. You can gain some efficiency if the program can avoid making these jumps just to execute one or two instructions. When programmers speak of efficiency, they usually mean speed: The program runs faster if the function call can be avoided.

If a function is declared with the keyword inline, the compiler does not create a real function: It copies the code from the inline function directly into the calling function. No jump is made; it is just as if you had written the statements of the function right into the calling function.

Note that inline functions can bring a heavy cost. If the function is called 10 times, the inline code is copied into the calling functions each of those 10 times. The tiny improvement in speed you might achieve is more than swamped by the increase in size of the executable program. Even the speed increase might be illusory. First, today's optimizing compilers do a terrific job on their own, and there is almost never a big gain from declaring a function inline. More important, the increased size brings its own performance cost.

What's the rule of thumb? If you have a small function, one or two statements, it is a candidate for inline. When in doubt, though, leave it out. Listing 5.7 demonstrates an inline function.

Listing 5.7   Demonstrates an Inline Function

```
0:   // Listing 5.7 - demonstrates inline functions
1:   #include <iostream>
2:
3:   inline int Doubler(int);
4:   5:  int main()
6:   {
7:       int target;
8:
9:       std::cout << "Enter a number to work with: ";
10:      std::cin >> target;
11:      std::cout << "\n";
12:
13:      target = Doubler(target);
14:      std::cout << "Target: " << target << std::endl;
15:
16:      target = Doubler(target);
17:      std::cout << "Target: " << target << std::endl;
18:
19:      target = Doubler(target);
20:      std::cout << "Target: " << target << std::endl;
21:      return 0;
22:  }
23:
24:  int Doubler(int target)
25:  {
26:      return 2*target;
27:  }
```

OUTPUT

```
Enter a number to work with: 20

Target: 40
Target: 80
Target: 160
```

ANALYSIS   On line 3, `Doubler()` is declared to be an inline function taking an int parameter and returning an int. The declaration is just like any other prototype except that the keyword inline is prepended just before the return value.

This compiles into code that is the same as if you had written the following:

```
target = 2 * target;
```

everywhere you entered

```
target = Doubler(target);
```

By the time your program executes, the instructions are already in place, compiled into the OBJ file. This saves a jump in the execution of the code, at the cost of a larger program.

> Inline is a hint to the compiler that you would like the function to be inlined. The compiler is free to ignore the hint and make a real function call.

How Functions Work—A Look Under the Hood

When you call a function, the code branches to the called function, parameters are passed in, and the body of the function is executed. When the function completes, a value is returned (unless the function returns `void`), and control returns to the calling function. How does this work?

The Stack

New Term When you begin your program the compiler creates a *stack*. The stack is a special area of memory allocated for your program to hold the data required by each of the functions in your program. It is called a stack because it is a last-in-first-out queue, much like a stack of dishes at a cafeteria, as shown in Figure 5.4.

Last-in first-out means that whatever is added to the stack last will be the first thing taken off. Most queues are like a line at a theater: The first one on line is the first one off. A stack is more like a stack of coins: If you stack 10 pennies on a tabletop and then take some back, the last three you put on will be the first three you take off.

When data is "pushed" onto the stack, the stack grows; as data is "popped" off the stack, the stack shrinks. It isn't possible to pop a dish off of the stack without first popping off all the dishes placed on after that dish.

A stack of dishes is the common analogy. It is fine as far as it goes, but it is wrong in a fundamental way. A more accurate mental picture is of a series of cubbyholes aligned top to bottom. The top of the stack is whatever cubby the stack pointer happens to be pointing to.

Each of the cubbies has a sequential address, and one of those addresses is kept in the stack pointer register. Everything below that magic address, known as the top of the stack, is considered to be on the stack. Everything above the top of the stack is considered to be off the stack and invalid. Figure 5.5 illustrates this idea.

5

FIGURE 5.4
A stack.

FIGURE 5.5
The stack pointer.

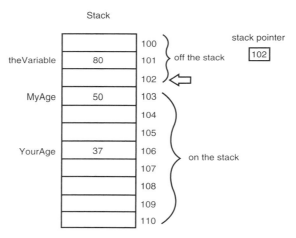

When data is put on the stack, it is placed into a cubby above the stack pointer, and then the stack pointer is moved to the new data. When data is popped off the stack, the address of the stack pointer is changed by moving it down the stack. Figure 5.6 makes this rule clear.

The Stack and Functions

When your program calls a function, a "stack frame" is established. A stack frame is an area of the stack set aside to manage that function. This is very complex and different on different computers, but here are the essential steps:

1. The return address of the function is put on the stack. When your function returns, it will resume executing at this address.

2. Room is made on the stack for the return type you've declared.

3. All the arguments to the function are placed on the stack.

4. The program branches to your function.

5. Local variables are pushed onto the stack as they are defined.

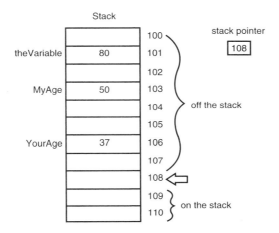

FIGURE 5.6

Moving the stack pointer.

Summary

This chapter introduced functions. A function is, in effect, a subprogram into which you can pass parameters and from which you can return a value. Every C++ program starts in the `main()` function, and `main()` in turn can call other functions.

A function is declared with a function prototype, which describes the return value, the function name, and its parameter types. A function can optionally be declared inline. A function prototype can also declare default variables for one or more of the parameters.

The function definition must match the function prototype in return type, name, and parameter list. Function names can be overloaded by changing the number or type of parameters; the compiler finds the right function based on the argument list.

Local function variables, and the arguments passed in to the function, are local to the block in which they are declared. Parameters passed by value are copies and cannot affect the value of variables in the calling function.

Q&A

Q Why not make all variables global?

A There was a time when this was exactly how programming was done. As programs became more complex, however, it became very difficult to find bugs in programs because data could be corrupted by any of the functions--global data can be changed anywhere in the program. Years of experience have convinced programmers that data should be kept as local as possible, and access to changing that data should be narrowly defined.

Q Why aren't changes to the value of function arguments reflected in the calling function?

A Arguments passed to a function are passed by value. That means that the argument in the function is actually a copy of the original value.

Q What happens if I have the following two functions?

```
int Area (int width, int length = 1);
int Area (int size);
```

Will these overload? There are a different number of parameters, but the first one has a default value.

A The declarations will compile, but if you invoke `Area` with one parameter you will receive a compile-time error: `ambiguity between Area(int, int) and Area(int)`.

HOUR 6

Program Flow

Programs accomplish most of their work by branching and looping. In this hour you will learn

- What loops are and how they are used
- How to build various loops
- An alternative to deeply-nested if...else statements

Looping

Many programming problems are solved by repeatedly acting on the same data.

NEW TERM *Iteration* means doing the same thing again and again. The principal method of iteration is the loop.

The Roots of Looping goto

In the primitive days of early computer science, loops consisted of a label, some statements, and a jump.

In C++, a label is just a name followed by a colon (:). The label is placed to the left of a legal C++ statement, and a jump is accomplished by writing goto followed by the label name.

Why goto Isn't Used

goto is generally not used in C++, and for good reason. goto statements can cause a jump to any location in your source code, backward or forward. The indiscriminate use of goto statements has caused tangled, miserable, impossible-to-read programs known as *spaghetti code*.

To avoid the use of goto, more sophisticated, tightly controlled looping commands have been introduced: for, while, and do...while. Using these commands makes programs that are more easily understood, and goto is generally avoided.

while Loops

Demonstrated in Listing 6.1, a while loop causes your program to repeat a sequence of statements as long as the starting condition remains true.

LISTING 6.1   while Loops

```
0:  // Listing 6.1
1:  // Looping with while
2:  #include <iostream>
3:
4:  int main()
5:  {
6:      int counter = 0;            // initialize the condition
7:
8:      while(counter < 5)          // test condition still true
9:      {
10:         counter++;              // body of the loop
11:         std::cout << "counter: " << counter << "\n";
12:     }
13:
14:     std::cout << "Complete. counter: " << counter << ".\n";
15:     return 0;
16: }
```

OUTPUT
```
counter: 1
counter: 2
counter: 3
counter: 4
counter: 5
Complete. counter: 5
```

ANALYSIS This simple program demonstrates the fundamentals of the while loop. A condition is tested, and if it is true, the body of the while loop is executed. In this case, the condition tested on line 8 is whether counter is less than 5. If the condition is true, the body of the loop is executed. On line 10, the counter is incremented, and on line 11 the value is printed. When the conditional statement on line 8 fails (when counter is no longer less than 5), the entire body of the while loop (on lines 9–12) is skipped. Program execution falls through to line 14.

More Complicated while Statements

The condition tested by a while loop can be as complex as any legal C++ expression. This can include expressions produced using the logical && (and), || (or), and ! (not) operators. Listing 6.2 is a somewhat more complicated while statement.

LISTING 6.2   Complex while Loops

```
0:  // Listing 6.2
1:  // Complex while statements
2:  #include <iostream>
3:
4:  int main()
5:  {
6:      unsigned short small;
7:      unsigned long  large;
8:      const unsigned short MAXSMALL=65535;
9:
10:     std::cout << "Enter a small number: ";
11:     std::cin >> small;
12:     std::cout << "Enter a large number: ";
13:     std::cin >> large;
14:
15:     std::cout << "small: " << small << "...";
16:
17:      // for each iteration, test three conditions
18:     while (small < large && large > 0 && small < MAXSMALL)
19:
20:     {
21:         if (small % 5000 == 0)  // write a dot every 5k lines
22:             std::cout << ".";
23:
24:         small++;
25:
26:         large-=2;
27:     }
28:
29:     std::cout << "\nSmall: " << small
30:               << " Large: "  << large << std::endl;
31:     return 0;
32: }
```

6

OUTPUT
```
Enter a small number: 2
Enter a large number: 100000
Small:2........
Small:33335 Large: 33334
```

ANALYSIS This program is a game. Enter two numbers, one small and one large. The smaller number will count up by ones; the larger number will count down by twos. The goal of the game is to guess when they'll meet. On lines 10–13, the numbers are entered. Line 18 sets up a `while` loop, which will continue only as long as three conditions are met:

- `small` is not bigger than `large`.
- `large` isn't negative.
- `small` doesn't overrun the size of a small integer (`MAXSMALL`).

On line 21 the value in `small` is calculated modulo 5,000. Since the modulo is the remainder, it only returns the value 0 when `small` is an exact multiple of 5,000. Remember that this does not change the value in `small`. Each time the value is 0, a dot (`.`) is printed to the screen to show progress. On line 24, `small` is incremented, and on line 26 `large` is decremented by 2.

When any of the three conditions in the `while` loop fails, the loop ends and execution of the program continues after the `while` loop's closing brace, on line 29.

continue and break

At times, you'll want to return to the top of a `while` loop before the entire set of statements in the `while` loop is executed. The `continue` statement jumps back to the top of the loop.

At other times, you might want to exit the loop before the exit conditions are met. The `break` statement immediately exits the `while` loop, and program execution resumes after the closing brace.

Listing 6.3 demonstrates the use of these statements. This time the game has become more complicated. The user is invited to enter a `small` number, a `large` number, a `skip` number, and a `target` number. The `small` number will be incremented by 1, and the `large` number will be decremented by 2. The decrement will be skipped each time the `small` number is a multiple of the `skip`. The game ends if `small` becomes larger than `large`. If the `large` number reaches the `target` exactly, a statement is printed and the game stops.

The user's goal is to put in a target number for the `large` number that will stop the game.

LISTING 6.3   break and continue

```
0:  // Listing 6.3
1:  // Demonstrates break and continue
2:  #include <iostream>
3:  using namespace std;// this file uses std::cout,
4:                      //  std::cin, std::endl, etc.
5:
6:  int main()
7:  {
8:      unsigned short small;
9:      unsigned long  large;
10:      unsigned long  skip;
11:      unsigned long target;
12:      const unsigned short MAXSMALL=65535;
13:
14:      cout << "Enter a small number: ";
15:      cin >> small;
16:      cout << "Enter a large number: ";
17:      cin >> large;
18:      cout << "Enter a skip number: ";
19:      cin >> skip;
20:      cout << "Enter a target number: ";
21:      cin >> target;
22:
23:      cout << "\n";
24:
25:      // set up 3 stop conditions for the loop
26:      while (small < large && large > 0 && small < 65535)
27:      {
28:          small++;
29:
30:          if (small % skip == 0)// skip the decrement?
31:          {
32:              cout << "skipping on " << small << endl;
33:              continue;
34:          }
35:
36:          if (large == target)  // exact match for the target?
37:          {
38:              cout << "Target reached!";
39:              break;
40:          }
41:
42:          large-=2;
43:      }                            // end of while loop
44:
45:      cout << "\nSmall: " << small << " Large: " << large << endl;
46:      return 0;
47:  }
```

OUTPUT
```
Enter a small number: 2
Enter a large number: 20
Enter a skip number: 4
Enter a target number: 6
skipping on 4
skipping on 8
Small: 10 Large: 8
```

ANALYSIS   In this play, the user lost; `small` became larger than `large` before the `target` number of 6 was reached.

On line 26, the `while` conditions are tested. If `small` continues to be smaller than `large`, `large` is larger than 0, and `small` hasn't overrun the maximum value for an unsigned short `int`, the body of the `while` loop is entered.

On line 30, the `small` value is taken modulo the `skip` value. If `small` is a multiple of `skip`, the `continue` statement is reached and program execution jumps to the top of the loop at line 26. This effectively skips over the test for the `target` and the decrement of `large`.

On line 36, `target` is tested against the value for `large`. If they are the same, the user has won. A message is printed, and the `break` statement is reached. This causes an immediate break out of the `while` loop, and program execution resumes on line 45.

Both `continue` and `break` should be used with caution. Programs that suddenly branch from within the middle of loops are harder to understand, and liberal use of `continue` and `break` can render even a small `while` loop unreadable.

while(1) Loops

The condition tested in a `while` loop can be any valid C++ expression. As long as that condition remains `true`, the `while` loop will continue. You can create a loop that will never end by using the number 1 for the condition to be tested. Because 1 is always `true`, the loop will never end, unless a `break` statement is reached. Listing 6.4 demonstrates counting to 10 using this construct.

LISTING 6.4   while(1) Loops

```
0:  // Listing 6.4
1:  // Demonstrates a while true loop
2:  #include <iostream>
3:
4:  int main()
5:  {
6:      int counter = 0;
7:
```

LISTING 6.4   continued

```
 8:     while (1)
 9:     {
10:         counter ++;
11:         if (counter > 10)
12:             break;
13:     }
14:     std::cout << "counter: " << counter << "\n";
15:     return 0;
16:  }
```

OUTPUT   counter: 11

ANALYSIS   On line 8, a while loop is set up with a condition that can never be false. The loop increments the counter variable on line 10 and then on line 11 tests to see if counter has gone past 10. If it hasn't, the while loop iterates. If counter is greater than 10, the break on line 12 ends the while loop, and program execution falls through to line 14 where the results are printed.

This program works, but it isn't pretty. This is a good example of using the wrong tool for the job. The same thing can be accomplished by putting the test of counter's value where it belongs—in the while condition.

> Infinite loops such as while(1) can cause your computer to hang up if the exit condition is never reached. Use these with caution and test them thoroughly.

C++ gives you many different ways to accomplish the same task. The real trick is picking the right tool for the particular job.

Do
DO use while loops to iterate while a condition is true.
DO exercise caution when using continue and break statements.
DO make sure your loop will eventually end.

6

do...while Loops

It is possible that the body of a while loop will never execute. The while statement checks its condition before executing any of its statements, and if the condition evaluates false, the entire body of the while loop is skipped. Listing 6.5 illustrates this.

LISTING 6.5   Skipping the Body of the while Loop

```
0:  // Listing 6.5
1:   // Demonstrates skipping the body of
2:   // the while loop when the condition is false.
3:  #include <iostream>
4:
5:  int main()
6:  {
7:      int counter;
8:      std::cout << "How many hellos?: ";
9:      std::cin >> counter;
10:     while (counter > 0)
11:     {
12:         std::cout << "Hello!\n";
13:         counter--;
14:     }
15:     std::cout << "counter is OutPut: " << counter;
16:     return 0;
17: }
```

OUTPUT
```
How many hellos?: 2
Hello!
Hello!
counter is OutPut:0

How many hellos?: 0
counter is 0
```

ANALYSIS The user is prompted for a starting value on line 8, which is stored in the integer variable counter. The value of counter is tested on line 10 and decremented in the body of the while loop. The first time through counter was set to 2, so the body of the while loop ran twice. The second time through, however, the user typed in 0. The value of counter was tested on line 10 and the condition was false; counter was not greater than 0. The entire body of the while loop was skipped, and hello was never printed.

What if you want to ensure that hello is always printed at least once? The while loop can't accomplish this because the if condition is tested before any printing is done. You can force the issue with an if statement just before entering the while:

```
if (counter < 1)  // force a minimum value
counter = 1;
```

but that is what programmers call a *kludge*, an ugly and inelegant solution.

The do...while loop executes the body of the loop before its condition is tested, and ensures that the body always executes at least one time. Listing 6.6 demonstrates this program rewritten with a do...while loop.

LISTING 6.6 Demonstrating a do...while Loop

```
0:   // Listing 6.6
1:   // Demonstrates do while
2:   #include <iostream>
3:
4:   int main()
5:   {
6:       int counter;
7:       std::cout << "How many hellos? ";
8:       std::cin >> counter;
9:       do
10:      {
11:          std::cout << "Hello\n";
12:          counter--;
13:      } while (counter >0 );
14:      std::cout << "counter is: " << counter << std::endl;
15:      return 0;
16:  }
```

OUTPUT

```
How many hellos? 2
Hello
Hello
counter is: 0
```

ANALYSIS The user is prompted for a starting value on line 7, which is stored in the integer variable counter. In the do...while loop, the body of the loop is entered before the condition is tested, and therefore is guaranteed to be executed at least once. On line 11 the message is printed, on line 12 the counter is decremented, and on line 13 the condition is tested. If the condition evaluates true, execution jumps to the top of the loop on line 11; otherwise it falls through to line 14.

The continue and break statements work in the do...while loop exactly as they do in the while loop. The only difference between a while loop and a do...while loop is when the condition is tested.

for Loops

When programming while loops, you'll often find yourself setting up a starting condition, testing to see if the condition is true, and incrementing or otherwise changing a variable each time through the loop. Listing 6.7 demonstrates this.

LISTING 6.7 while Loop Reexamined

```
0:   // Listing 6.7
1:   // Looping with while
```

6

LISTING 6.7 continued

```
2:   #include <iostream>
3:
4:   int main()
5:   {
6:       int counter = 0;
7:
8:       while(counter < 5)
9:       {
10:          counter++;
11:          std::cout << "Looping!   ";
12:      }
13:
14:      std::cout << "\nCounter: " << counter << ".\n";
15:      return 0;
16:  }
```

OUTPUT

```
Looping!  Looping!  Looping!  Looping!  Looping!
counter: 5.
```

ANALYSIS The condition is set on line 6: counter is initialized to 0. On line 8 counter is tested to see if it is less than 5. counter is incremented on line 10. On line 11, a simple message is printed, but you can imagine that more important work could be done for each increment of the counter.

Initialization, Test, and Increment

A for loop combines the three steps of initialization, test, and increment into one statement. A for statement consists of the keyword for followed by a pair of parentheses. Within the parentheses are three statements separated by semicolons.

The first statement is the initialization. Any legal C++ statement can be put here, but typically this is used to create and initialize a counting variable. Statement two is the test, and any legal C++ expression can be used there. This serves the same role as the condition in the while loop. Statement three is the action. Typically a value is incremented or decremented, although any legal C++ statement can be put there. Note that statements one and three can be any legal C++ statement, but statement two must be an expression—a C++ statement that returns a value. Listing 6.8 demonstrates the for loop.

LISTING 6.8 Demonstrating the for Loop

```
0:   // Listing 6.8
1:   // Looping with for
2:   #include <iostream>
3:
```

LISTING 6.8 continued

```
4:  int main()
5:  {
6:      int counter;
7:      for (counter = 0; counter < 5; counter++)
8:          std::cout << "Looping! ";
9:
10:     std::cout << "\nCounter: " << counter << ".\n";
11:     return 0;
12: }
```

OUTPUT
```
Looping!  Looping!  Looping!  Looping!  Looping!
counter: 5.
```

ANALYSIS The `for` statement on line 7 combines the initialization of `counter`, the test that `counter` is less than 5, and the action to increment to `counter` all into one line. The body of the `for` statement is on line 8. Of course, a block could be used here as well.

Advanced `for` Loops

`for` statements are powerful and flexible. The three independent statements (initialization, test, and action) lend themselves to a number of variations. A `for` loop works in the following sequence:

1. Performs the operations in the initialization.
2. Evaluates the condition.
3. If the condition is `true`, executes the loop and then the action statement.

After each time through the loop, it repeats steps 2 and 3.

Multiple Initialization and Increments

It is not uncommon to initialize more than one variable, to test a compound logical expression, and to execute more than one statement. The initialization and action statements can be replaced by multiple C++ statements, each separated by a comma. Listing 6.9 demonstrates the initialization and incrementing of two variables.

LISTING 6.9 Demonstrating Multiple Statements in `for` Loops

```
0:  //listing 6.9
1:  // demonstrates multiple statements in
2:  // for loops
3:  #include <iostream>
4:
```

LISTING 6.9   continued

```
 5:  int main()
 6:  {
 7:      for (int i=0, j=0; i<3; i++, j++)
 8:          std::cout << "i: " << i << " j: " << j << std::endl;
 9:      return 0;
10:  }
```

OUTPUT
```
i: 0  j: 0
i: 1  j: 1
i: 2  j: 2
```

ANALYSIS On line 7, two variables, i and j, are each initialized with the value 0. The test (i<3) is evaluated, and because it is true, the body of the for statement is executed and the values are printed. Finally, the third clause in the for statement is executed, and i and j are incremented.

After line 8 completes, the condition is evaluated again, and if it remains true the actions are repeated (i and j are again incremented), and the body of the loop is executed again. This continues until the test fails, in which case the action statement is not executed, and control falls out of the loop.

Null Statements in for Loops

Any or all of the statements in a for loop can be null. To accomplish this, use the semi-colon to mark where the statement would have been. To create a for loop that acts exactly like a while loop, leave out the first and third statement. Listing 6.10 illustrates this idea.

LISTING 6.10   Null Statements in for Loops

```
 0:  // Listing 6.10
 1:  // For loops with null statements
 2:  #include <iostream>
 3:
 4:  int main()
 5:  {
 6:      int counter = 0;
 7:
 8:      for( ; counter < 5; )
 9:      {
10:          counter++;
11:          std::cout << "Looping!   ";
12:      }
13:
14:      std::cout << "\nCounter: " << counter << ".\n";
15:      return 0;
16:  }
```

Looping! Looping! Looping! Looping! Looping!
counter: 5.

You might recognize this as being exactly like the while loop illustrated previously. On line 6, the counter variable is initialized. The for statement on line 8 does not initialize any values, but it does include a test for counter < 5. There is no increment statement, so this loop behaves exactly as if it had been written like this:

```
while (counter < 5)
```

Once again, C++ gives you a number of ways to accomplish the same thing. No experienced C++ programmer would use a for loop in this way, but it does illustrate the flexibility of the for statement. In fact, it is possible, using break and continue, to create a for loop with none of the three statements. Listing 6.11 illustrates how.

LISTING 6.11   Illustrating an Empty for Loop Statement

```
0:   //Listing 6.11 illustrating
1:   //empty for loop statement
2:   #include <iostream>
3:
4:   int main()
5:   {
6:       int counter=0;        // initialization
7:       int max;
8:       std::cout << "How many hellos?";
9:       std::cin >> max;
10:      for (;;)              // a for loop that doesn't end
11:      {
12:          if (counter < max)        // test
13:          {
14:              std::cout << "Hello!\n";
15:              counter++;            // increment
16:          }
17:          else
18:              break;
19:      }
20:      return 0;
21:  }
```

How many hellos? 3
Hello!
Hello!
Hello!

The for loop has now been pushed to its absolute limit. Initialization, test, and action have all been taken out of the for statement. The initialization is done on line 6, before the for loop begins. The test is done in a separate if statement on line 12, and if the test succeeds, the action—an increment to `counter`—is performed on line 15. If the test fails, breaking out of the loop occurs on line 18.

Although this particular program is somewhat absurd, there are times when a `for(;;)` loop or a `while(1)` loop is just what you'll want. You'll see an example of a more reasonable use of such loops when `switch` statements are discussed.

Empty `for` Loops

So much can be done in the header of a `for` statement that there are times you won't need the body to do anything at all. In that case, be sure to put a `null` statement (`;`) as the body of the loop. The semicolon can be on the same line as the header, but this is easy to overlook. Listing 6.12 illustrates how this is done.

LISTING 6.12   Illustrating a `null` Statement in a `for` Loop

```
0:   //Listing 6.12
1:   //Demonstrates null statement
2:   // as body of for loop
3:   #include <iostream>
4:
5:   int main()
6:   {
7:       for (int i = 0; i<5; std::cout << "i: " << i++ << std::endl)
8:           ;
9:       return 0;
10: }
```

OUTPUT
```
i: 0
i: 1
i: 2
i: 3
i: 4
```

ANALYSIS   The `for` loop on line 7 includes three statements. The initialization statement establishes the counter `i` and initializes it to `0`. The condition statement tests for `i<5`, and the action statement prints the value in `i` and increments it.

There is nothing left to do in the body of the `for` loop, so the `null` statement (`;`) is used. Note that this is not a well-designed `for` loop; the action statement is doing far too much. This would be better rewritten as

```
8:           for (int i = 0; i<5; i++)
9:               std::cout << "i: " << i << endl;
```

Although both do exactly the same thing, this example is easier to understand. Keep in mind that when you create a variable inside a `for` loop, it is local to that loop and only exists while the loop is executing.

Nested Loops

Loops can be *nested*, with one loop sitting in the body of another. The inner loop will be executed in full for every execution of the outer loop. Listing 6.13 illustrates writing marks into a matrix using nested for loops.

LISTING 6.13   Nested for Loops

```
0:   //Listing 6.13
1:   //Illustrates nested for loops
2:   #include <iostream>
3:
4:   int main()
5:   {
6:       int rows, columns;
7:       char theChar;
8:       std::cout << "How many rows? ";
9:       std::cin >> rows;
10:      std::cout << "How many columns? ";
11:      std::cin >> columns;
12:      std::cout << "What character? ";
13:      std::cin >> theChar;
14:      for (int i = 0; i<rows; i++)
15:      {
16:          for (int j = 0; j < columns; j++)
17:              std::cout << theChar;
18:          std::cout << "\n";
19:      }
20:      return 0;
21:  }
```

OUTPUT
```
How many rows? 4
How many columns?  12
What character?  x
xxxxxxxxxxxx
xxxxxxxxxxxx
xxxxxxxxxxxx
xxxxxxxxxxxx
```

ANALYSIS   The user is prompted for the number of rows and columns and for a character to print. The first for loop, on line 14, initializes a counter (i) to 0, and then the body of the outer for loop is run.

On line 16, the first line of the body of the outer for loop, another for loop, is established. A second counter (j) is also initialized to 0, and the body of the inner for loop is executed. On line 17, the chosen character is printed, and control returns to the header of the inner for loop. Note that the inner for loop is only one statement (the printing of the

6

character). The condition is tested (j < columns); if it evaluates to true, j is incremented and the next character is printed. This continues until j equals the number of columns.

When the inner for loop fails its test, in this case after 12 xs are printed, execution falls through to line 18, and a new line is printed. The outer for loop now returns to its header, where its condition (i < rows) is tested. If this evaluates to true, i is incremented and the body of the loop is executed.

In the second iteration of the outer for loop, the inner for loop is started over. Thus j is reinitialized to 0 (!), and the entire inner loop is run again.

The important idea here is that by using a nested loop, the inner loop is executed for each iteration of the outer loop. Thus the character is printed columns times for each row.

switch Statements

if and else...if combinations can become quite confusing when nested too deeply, and C++ offers an alternative. Unlike if, which evaluates one value, switch statements enable you to branch on any of a number of different values. The general form of the switch statement is

```
switch (expression)
{
case valueOne: statement;
                    break;
case valueTwo: statement;
                    break;
....
case valueN:   statement;
                    break;
default:       statement;
}
```

expression is any legal C++ expression, and the *statements* are any legal C++ statements or block of statements. switch evaluates *expression* and compares the result to each of the case values. Note, however, that the evaluation is only for equality; relational operators cannot be used here, nor can Boolean operations. If one of the case values matches the expression, execution jumps to those statements and continues to the end of the switch block unless a break statement is encountered. If nothing matches, execution branches to the optional default statement. If there is no default and no matching value, execution falls through the switch statement and the statement ends.

It is almost always a good idea to have a default case in switch statements. If you have no other need for the default, use it to test for the supposedly impossible case and print out an error message; this can be a tremendous aid in debugging.

It is important to note that if there is no break statement at the end of a case statement, execution will fall through to the next case. This is sometimes necessary, but usually is an error. If you decide to let execution fall through, be sure to put a comment indicating that you didn't just forget the break.

Listing 6.14 illustrates the use of the switch statement.

LISTING 6.14 Demonstrating the switch Statement

```
0:   //Listing 6.14
1:   // Demonstrates switch statement
2:   #include <iostream>
3:
4:   int main()
5:   {
6:       unsigned short int number;
7:       std::cout << "Enter a number between 1 and 5: ";
8:       std::cin >> number;
9:       switch (number)
10:      {
11:      case 0:
12:          std::cout << "Too small, sorry!";
13:          break;
14:      case 5:
15:          std::cout << "Good job!\n";  // fall through
16:      case 4:
17:          std::cout << "Nice Pick!\n"; // fall through
18:      case 3:
19:          std::cout << "Excellent!\n"; // fall through
20:      case 2:
21:          std::cout << "Masterful!\n"; // fall through
22:      case 1:
23:          std::cout << "Incredible!\n";
24:          break;
25:      default:
26:          std::cout << "Too large!\n";
27:          break;
28:      }
29:      std::cout << "\n\n";
30:      return 0;
31:  }
```

6

OUTPUT

```
Enter a number between 1 and 5:   3
Excellent!
Masterful!
Incredible!

Enter a number between 1 and 5: 8
Too large!
```

ANALYSIS The user is prompted for a number. That number is given to the `switch` statement. If the number is `0`, the `case` statement on line 11 matches, the message `Too small, sorry!` is printed, and the `break` statement ends the `switch`. If the value is `5`, execution switches to line 14 where a message is printed and then falls through to line 17 where another message is printed, and so forth until hitting the `break` on line 24.

The net effect of these statements is that, for a number `0–5`, many messages are printed. If the value of a number is not `0–5` it is assumed to be too large, and the `default` statement is invoked on line 25.

Summary

There are a number of different ways of causing a C++ program to loop. `while` loops check a condition, and if it is `true`, execute the statements in the body of the loop. `do...while` loops execute the body of the loop and then test the condition. `for` loops initialize a value and then test an expression. If *expression* is `true`, the body of the loop is executed, as is the final statement in the `for` header. Each subsequent time through the loop, the expression is tested again. The `goto` statement is generally avoided, because it causes an unconditional jump to a seemingly arbitrary location in the code, thus making source code difficult to understand and maintain. `continue` causes `while`, `do...while`, and `for` loops to start over, and `break` causes `while`, `do...while`, `for`, and `switch` statements to end.

Q&A

Q How do you choose between `if...else` and `switch`?

A If there are more than just one or two `else` clauses, and all are testing the same value, consider using a `switch` statement.

Q How do you choose between `while` and `do...while`?

A If the body of the loop should always execute at least once, consider a `do...while` loop; otherwise try to use the `while` loop.

Q **How do you choose between `while` and `for`?**

A If you are initializing a counting variable, testing that variable and incrementing it each time through the loop, consider the `for` loop. If your variable is already initialized and is not incremented on each loop, a `while` loop might be the better choice.

Q **Is it better to use `while(1)` or `for(;;)`?**

A There is no significant difference.

6

PART II
Classes

Hour

HOUR 7

Basic Classes

Classes extend the existing capabilities of C++ to assist you in representing and solving complex, real-world problems. These are referred to as built-in capabilities. In this hour you will learn

- What types are
- What classes and objects are
- How to define a new class and create objects of that class

What Is a Type?

A *type* is a category. One of the things that distinguishes humans is our ability to categorize. We don't see hundreds of shapes on the savanna; we see animals and trees. And we don't just see animals; we see gazelles, giraffes, elephants, water buffalo, and so forth. Humans created taxonomies, classifications, orders, groupings, divisions, and classes. In short, we think in terms of *types* of things.

An orange is a type of citrus. A citrus is a type of fruit. A fruit is a type of plant. A plant is a type of living thing.

Familiar types include car, house, person, and shape. In C++, a type is an object with a size, a state, and a set of abilities.

A C++ programmer can create any type needed, and each of these new types can have all the functionality and power of the built-in types predefined by C++ such as int, long and double.

Why Create a New Type?

Programs are usually written to solve real-world problems, such as keeping track of employee records or simulating the workings of a heating system. Although it is possible to solve complex problems by using programs written with only integers and characters, it is far easier to grapple with large, complex problems if you can create representations of the objects that you are talking about. In other words, simulating the workings of a heating system is easier if you can create variable types that represent rooms, heat sensors, thermostats, and boilers. The closer these variables correspond to reality, the easier it is to write the program.

Creating New Types

You've already learned about the C++ built-in types, including `int` (integers) and `char` (characters). The type of a variable tells you quite a bit about it. For example, if you declare `Height` and `Width` to be unsigned short integers, you know that each one can hold a number between 0 and 65,535 (assuming an unsigned short integer is 2 bytes).

In addition to telling you the size, the type tells you the capabilities of the variable. For example, short integers can be added together. Thus, just by declaring `Height` and `Width` to be unsigned short integers, you know that it is possible to add `Height` to `Width` and to assign that number to another number.

The type of these variables tells you

- Their size in memory
- What information they can hold
- What actions can be performed on them

In C++ you can also define your own types to model the problem you are trying to solve. The mechanism for declaring a new type in is to create a class. A class is a definition of a new type.

Classes and Members

NEW TERM You make a new type by declaring a class. A *class* is a collection of variables—often of different types—combined with a set of related functions.

One way to think about a car is as a collection of wheels, doors, seats, windows, and so forth. Another way is to think about what a car can do: It can move, speed up, slow down, stop, park, and so on.

NEW TERM *Encapsulation* is bundling together all the information, capabilities, and responsibilities of an entity into a single object.

Encapsulating everything you know about a car into one class has a number of advantages for a programmer. Everything is in one place, which makes it easy to refer to, copy, and manipulate the data.

NEW TERM *Clients* of your class are other classes or functions that make use of your class. Encapsulation allows the clients of your class to use it without knowing or caring about how it works. You can drive a car without understanding how the internal combustion engine operates, and clients of your class can use your class without knowing how your class does what it does. They only need to know *what* it does, not *how* it does it.

A class can consist of any combination of the variable types and also other class types. The variables in the class are referred to as the *member variables* or *data members*. A Car class might have member variables representing the seats, radio type, tires, and so forth.

NEW TERM *Member variables*, also known as *data members*, are the variables in your class. Member variables are part of your class, just like the wheels and engine are part of your car.

NEW TERM The functions in the class typically manipulate the member variables. They are referred to as *member functions* or *methods* of the class. Methods of the Car class might include Start() and Brake(). A Cat class might have data members that represent age and weight; its methods might include Sleep(), Meow(), and ChaseMice().

Member functions are the functions in your class. Member functions are as much a part of your class as the member variables. They determine what the objects of your class can do.

Declaring a Class

To declare a class, you use the class keyword followed by an opening brace and then list the data members and methods of that class. End the declaration with a closing brace and a semicolon. Here's the declaration of a class called Cat:

```
class Cat
{
public:
    unsigned int  itsAge;
    unsigned int  itsWeight;
    Meow();
};
```

Declaring this class does not allocate memory for a Cat. It just tells the compiler what the Cat class is— what data it contains (itsAge and itsWeight) and what it can do (Meow()). It also tells the compiler how big it is—that is, how much room the compiler must set aside for each of the Cat classes that you create. In this example, if an integer is 4 bytes, Cat is only 8 bytes big: itsAge is 4 bytes, and itsWeight is another 4. Meow() takes up no room because no storage space is set aside for member functions.

A Word on Naming Conventions

As programmer, you must name all your member variables, member functions, and classes. As you learned in Hour 3, "Variables and Constants," these should be easily understood and meaningful names. Cat, Rectangle, and Employee are good class names. Meow(), ChaseMice(), and StopEngine() are good function names because they tell you what the functions do. Many programmers name the member variables with the prefix its, as in itsAge, itsWeight, and itsSpeed. This helps to distinguish member variables from nonmember variables.

C++ is case sensitive, and all class names should follow the same pattern. If they do, you never have to check how to spell your class name—was it Rectangle, rectangle or REC-TANGLE? Some programmers like to prefix every class name with a particular letter (for example, cCat or cPerson), whereas others put the name in all uppercase or all lower-case. The convention that I use is to name all classes with initial-capitalization, as in Cat and Person.

Similarly, many programmers begin all functions with capital letters and all variables with lowercase. Words are usually separated with an underscore (as in Chase_Mice) or by capitalizing each word (for example, ChaseMice or DrawCircle).

The important idea is that you should pick one style and stay with it through each program. Over time, your style will evolve to include not only naming conventions, but also indentation, alignment of braces, and commenting style.

Defining an Object

You define an object of your new type just as you define an integer variable:

```
unsigned int GrossWeight;        // define an unsigned integer
Cat Frisky;                      // define a Cat
```

This code defines a variable called Gross Weight whose type is an unsigned integer. It also defines Frisky, which is an object whose class (or type) is Cat.

Classes Versus Objects

You never pet the definition of a cat; you pet individual cats. You draw a distinction between the idea of a cat and the particular cat that right now is shedding all over your living room. In the same way, C++ differentiates between the class Cat, which is the idea of a cat, and each individual Cat object. Thus, Frisky is an object of type Cat in the same way in which GrossWeight is a variable of type unsigned int.

An object is simply an individual instance of a class.

Accessing Class Members

After you define an actual Cat object (for example, Frisky), you use the dot operator (.) to access the member functions of that object. Therefore, to assign 50 to Frisky's itsWeight member variable, you would write

```
Frisky.itsWeight = 50;
```

In the same way, to call the Meow() function, you would write

```
Frisky.Meow();
```

Assign to Objects, Not to Classes

In C++ you don't assign values to types; you assign values to variables. For example, you would never write

```
int = 5;                // wrong
```

The compiler would flag this as an error because you can't assign 5 to an integer. Rather, you must define an integer variable and assign 5 to that variable. For example:

```
int  x;                 // define x to be an int
x = 5;                  // set x's value to 5
```

This is a shorthand way of saying, "Assign 5 to the variable x, which is of type int." In the same way, you wouldn't write

```
Cat.age=5;
```

You must define a Cat object and assign 5 to that object. For example,

```
Cat Frisky;             // just like  int x;
Frisky.itsAge = 5;      // just like  x = 5;
```

7

Private Versus Public

NEW TERM Other keywords are used in the declaration of a class. Two of the most important are public and private.

All member data and functions are private by default. Private members can be accessed only within methods of the class itself. Public members can be accessed through any object of the class. This distinction is important, but can be confusing. To make it a bit clearer, consider an example from earlier in this chapter:

```
class Cat
{
    unsigned int  itsAge;
    unsigned int  itsWeight;
    Meow();
};
```

In this declaration, itsAge, itsWeight, and Meow() are all private, because all members of a class are private by default. This means that unless you specify otherwise, they are private.

However, if you write

```
Cat  Boots;
Boots.itsAge=5;     // error! can't access private data!
```

the compiler flags this as an error. In effect, you've said to the compiler, "I'll access the members itsAge, itsWeight, and Meow() from only within member functions of the Cat class." Yet here you've tried to access it from outside a Cat method. Just because Boots is an object of class Cat, that doesn't mean that you can access the parts of Boots that are private.

The way to use a class so that you can access the data members is to declare a section of the class to be public:

```
class Cat
{
public:
    unsigned int  itsAge;
    unsigned int  itsWeight;
    Meow();
};
```

Now itsAge, itsWeight, and Meow() are all public. Boots.itsAge=5 compiles without a problem.

Make Member Data Private

NEW TERM   As a general rule of design, you should keep the member data of a class private. Therefore, you must create public methods known as *accessor* methods to set and get the private member variables. These accessor methods are the member functions that other parts of your program call to get and set your private member variables.

Accessor methods enable you to separate the details of how the data is stored from how it is used. This enables you to change how the data is stored without having to rewrite functions that use the data.

You use the access control keywords to declare sections of the class as public or private. Each use of public or private changes the access control from that point on to the end of the class or until the next access control keyword. Class declarations end with a closing brace and a semicolon.

Take a look at the following example:

```
class Cat
{
public:
    unsigned int Age;
    unsigned int Weight;
    void Meow();
};

Cat  Frisky;
Frisky.Age = 8;
Frisky.Weight = 18;
Frisky.Meow();
```

Now look at this example:

```
class Car
{
public:                         // the next five are public

    void Start();
    void Accelerate();
    void Brake();
    void SetYear(int year);
    int GetYear();

private:                        // the last two are private

    int Year;
    Char Model [255];
};                              // end of class declaration
```

7

```
Car OldFaithful;            // make an instance of Car
int bought;                 // a local variable of type int
OldFaithful.SetYear(84) ;   // assign 84 to the year
bought = OldFaithful.GetYear();  // set bought to 84
OldFaithful.Start();        // call the start method
```

Implementing Class Methods

Every class method that you declare must also be defined.

> A member method (or member function) definition begins with the name of the class and is then followed by two colons, the name of the function, and its parameters.

NEW TERM A member *method (or member function) definition* begins with the name of the class followed by two colons, the name of the function, and its parameters.

Listing 7.1 shows the complete declaration of a simple Cat class and the implementation of its accessor function and one general class member function.

LISTING 7.1   Implementing the Methods of a Simple Class

```
 0:  // Demonstrates declaration of a class and
 1:  // definition of class methods,
 2:
 3:  #include <iostream>       // for std::cout
 4:
 5:  class Cat                 // begin declaration of the class
 6:  {
 7:  public:                   // begin public section
 8:      int GetAge();         // accessor function
 9:      void SetAge (int age); // accessor function
10:      void Meow();          // general function
11:  private:                  // begin private section
12:      int itsAge;           // member variable
13:  };
14:
15:  // GetAge, Public accessor function
16:  // returns value of itsAge member
17:  int Cat::GetAge()
18:  {
19:      return itsAge;
20:  }
21:
22:  // definition of SetAge, public
```

LISTING 7.1 continued

```
23:    // accessor function
24:    // sets itsAge member
25:    void Cat::SetAge(int age)
26:    {
27:        // set member variable its age to
28:        // value passed in by parameter age
29:        itsAge = age;
30:    }
31:
32:    // definition of Meow method
33:    // returns: void
34:    // parameters: None
35:    // action: Prints "meow" to screen
36:    void Cat::Meow()
37:    {
38:        std::cout << "Meow.\n";
39:    }
40:
41:    // create a cat, set its age, have it
42:    // meow, tell us its age, then meow again.
43:    int main()
44:    {
45:        Cat Frisky;
46:        Frisky.SetAge(5);
47:        Frisky.Meow();
48:        std::cout << "Frisky is a cat who is " ;
49:        std::cout << Frisky.GetAge() << " years old.\n";
50:        Frisky.Meow();
51:        return 0;
52:    }
```

OUTPUT

```
Meow.
Frisky is a cat who is 5 years old.
Meow.
```

ANALYSIS Lines 5–13 contain the definition of the Cat class. Line 7 contains the keyword public, which tells the compiler that what follows is a set of public members. Line 8 has the declaration of the public accessor method GetAge(). GetAge() provides access to the private member variable itsAge, which is declared in line 12. Line 9 has the public accessor function SetAge(). SetAge() takes an integer as an argument and sets itsAge to the value of that argument.

Line 11 begins the private section, which includes only the declaration in line 12 of the private member variable itsAge. The class declaration ends with a closing brace and semicolon in line 13.

7

Lines 17–20 contain the definition of the member function `GetAge()`. This method takes no parameters; it returns an integer. Note that class methods include the class name followed by two colons and the function's name (line 17). This syntax tells the compiler that the `GetAge()` function you are defining here is the one that you declared in the `Cat` class. With the exception of this header line, the `GetAge()` function is created like any other function.

The `GetAge()` function takes only one line; it returns the value in `itsAge`. Note that the `main()` function cannot access `itsAge` because `itsAge` is private to the `Cat` class. The `main()` function has access to the public method `GetAge()`. Because `GetAge()` is a member function of the `Cat` class, it has full access to the `itsAge` variable. This access enables `GetAge()` to return the value of `itsAge` to `main()`.

Line 25 contains the definition of the `SetAge()` member function. It takes an integer parameter and sets the value of `itsAge` to the value of that parameter in line 29. Because it is a member of the `Cat` class, `SetAge()` has direct access to the member variable `itsAge`.

Line 36 begins the definition, or implementation, of the `Meow()` method of the `Cat` class. It is a one-line function that prints the word `Meow` to the screen, followed by a new line. (Remember that the `\n` character prints a new line to the screen.)

Line 44 begins the body of the program with the familiar `main()` function. In this case, it takes no arguments and returns `void`. In line 45, `main()` declares a `Cat` named `Frisky`. In line 46, the value `5` is assigned to the `itsAge` member variable by way of the `SetAge()` accessor method. Note that the method is called by using the class name (`Frisky`) followed by the member operator (`.`) and the method name (`SetAge()`). In this same way, you can call any of the other methods in a class.

Line 47 calls the `Meow()` member function, and lines 48 and 49 print a message using the `GetAge()` accessor. Line 50 calls `Meow()` again.

Constructors and Destructors

There are two ways to define an integer variable. You can define the variable and then assign a value to it later in the program. For example:

```
int Weight;              // define a variable
...                      // other code here
Weight = 7;              // assign it a value
```

Or you can define the integer and immediately initialize it. For example:

```
int Weight = 7;          // define and initialize to 7
```

Initialization combines the definition of the variable with its initial assignment. Nothing stops you from changing that value later. Initialization ensures that your variable is never without a meaningful value.

How do you initialize the member data of a class? Classes have a special member function called a *constructor* that is called when an object of the class is instantiated. The job of the constructor is to create a valid instance of the class. Creating a valid instance of the class often includes initializing its member data. The constructor is a class method with the same name as the class itself but with no return value. Constructors may or may not have parameters, just like any other method of the class.

Whenever you declare a constructor, you'll also want to declare a *destructor*. Just as constructors create and initialize objects of your class, destructors clean up after your object and free any memory you might have allocated. A destructor always has the name of the class preceded by a tilde (~). Destructors take no arguments and have no return value. To write a destructor for the Cat class, you would write:

```
~Cat();
```

Default Constructors

 When you write

```
Cat Frisky(5);
```

you invoke the constructor for Cat that takes one parameter (in this case, the value 5). If, however, you write

```
Cat Frisky;
```

the compiler allows you to leave the parentheses off and calls the *default constructor*. The default constructor is a constructor with no parameters.

Constructors Provided by the Compiler

If you declare no constructors at all, the compiler will create a default constructor for you. (Remember, the default constructor is the constructor that takes no parameters.)

The default constructor the compiler provides takes no action; it is as if you had declared a constructor that took no parameters and whose body was empty.

There are two important points to note about this:

- The default constructor is any constructor that takes no parameters, whether you define it or you get it as a default from the compiler.

7

- If you define *any* constructor (with or without parameters), the compiler will *not* provide a default constructor for you. In that case, if you want a default constructor, you must define it yourself.

If you fail to define a destructor, the compiler will also give you one of those, and this too will have an empty body and will do nothing.

As a matter of form, if you define a constructor, be sure to define a destructor, even if your destructor does nothing. Although it is true that the default destructor would work correctly, it doesn't hurt to define your own, and it makes your code clearer.

Listing 7.2 rewrites the Cat class to use a constructor to initialize the Cat object, setting its age to whatever initial age you provide. It also demonstrates where the destructor is called.

LISTING 7.2   Using Constructors and Destructors

```
0:    // Demonstrates declaration of a constructor and
1:    // destructor for the Cat class
2:    #include <iostream>      // for std::cout
3:    using std::cout;         // always use std::cout in this file
4:
5:    class Cat                // begin declaration of the class
6:    {
7:    public:                  // begin public section
8:        Cat(int initialAge); // constructor
9:        ~Cat();              // destructor
10:       int GetAge();        // accessor function
11:       void SetAge(int age);// accessor function
12:       void Meow();
13:   private:                 // begin private section
14:       int itsAge;          // member variable
15:   };
16:
17:   // constructor of Cat,
18:   Cat::Cat(int initialAge)
19:   {
20:       itsAge = initialAge;
21:   }
22:
23:   // destructor, takes no action
24:   Cat::~Cat()
25:   {
26:
27:   }
28:
29:   // GetAge, Public accessor function
30:   // returns value of itsAge member
```

LISTING 7.2 continued

```
31:  int Cat::GetAge()
32:  {
33:      return itsAge;
34:  }
35:
36:  // Definition of SetAge, public
37:  // accessor function
38:  void Cat::SetAge(int age)
39:  {
40:      // set member variable itsAge to
41:      // value passed in by parameter age
42:      itsAge = age;
43:  }
44:
45:  // definition of Meow method
46:  // returns: void
47:  // parameters: None
48:  // action: Prints "meow" to screen
49:  void Cat::Meow()
50:  {
51:      cout << "Meow.\n";
52:  }
53:
54:  // create a cat, set its age, have it
55:  // meow, tell us its age, then meow again.
56:  int main()
57:  {
58:      Cat Frisky(5);
59:      Frisky.Meow();
60:      cout << "Frisky is a cat who is " ;
61:      cout << Frisky.GetAge() << " years old.\n";
62:      Frisky.Meow();
63:      Frisky.SetAge(7);
64:      cout << "Now Frisky is " ;
65:      cout << Frisky.GetAge() << " years old.\n";
66:      return 0;
67:  }
```

OUTPUT

```
Meow,
Frisky is a cat who is 5 years old.
Meow.
Now Frisky is 7 years old.
```

ANALYSIS   Listing 7.2 is similar to 7.1, except that line 8 adds a constructor that takes an integer. Line 9 declares the destructor, which takes no parameters. Destructors never take parameters, and neither constructors nor destructors return a value—not even void.

Lines 18–21 show the implementation of the constructor, which is similar to the implementation of the SetAge() accessor function. There is no return value.

Lines 24–27 show the implementation of the destructor ~Cat(). This function does nothing, but you must include the definition of the function if you define it in the class declaration.

Line 58 contains the definition of a Cat object, Frisky. The value 5 is passed in to Frisky's constructor. There is no need to call SetAge(), because Frisky was created with the value 5 in its member variable itsAge, as shown in line 61. In line 63, Frisky's itsAge variable is reassigned to 7. Line 65 prints the new value.

Summary

In this hour you learned how to create new data types called classes. You learned how to define variables of these new types, which are called objects.

A class has data members, which are variables of various types, including other classes. A class also includes member functions, also known as methods. You use these member functions to manipulate the member data and to perform other services.

Class members—both data and functions—can be public or private. Public members are accessible to any part of your program. Private members are accessible only to the member functions of the class.

Q&A

Q How big is a class object?

A A class object's size in memory is determined by the sum of the sizes of its member variables. Class methods don't take up room as part of the memory set aside for the object.

Some compilers align variables in memory in such a way that 2-byte variables actually consume somewhat more than 2 bytes. Check your compiler manual to be sure, but at this point there is no reason to be concerned with these details.

Q Why shouldn't I make all the member data public?

A Making member data private enables the client of the class to use the data without worrying about how it is stored or computed. For example, if the Cat class has a method GetAge(), clients of the Cat class can ask for the cat's age without knowing or caring if the cat stores its age in a member variable or computes its age on-the-fly.

HOUR 8

More About Classes

In Hour 7, "Basic Classes," you learned how to declare new types by declaring classes. In this hour you'll learn how to manage your classes and how to enlist the compiler in helping you find and avoid bugs. In this hour you learn

- What constant member functions are
- How to separate the class interface from its implementation

const Member Functions

NEW TERM If you declare a class member function to be const, you are promising that the method won't change the value of any of the members of the class. To declare a class method as constant, put the keyword const after the parentheses, but before the semicolon. The declaration of the *constant member function* SomeFunction() takes no arguments and returns void. It looks like this:

```
void SomeFunction() const;
```

Get accessor functions (some programmers call them "getter functions") are often declared as constant functions by using the const modifier. The Cat class has two accessor functions:

```
void SetAge(int anAge);
int GetAge();
```

SetAge() cannot be const because it changes the member variable itsAge. GetAge(), on the other hand, can and should be const because it doesn't change the class at all. It simply returns the current value of the member variable itsAge. Therefore, the declaration of these functions should be written like this:

```
void SetAge(int anAge);
int GetAge() const;
```

If you declare a function to be const and then the implementation of that function changes the object (by changing the value of any of its members), the compiler will flag it as an error. For example, if you wrote GetAge() so that it kept count of the number of times that Cat was asked its age, it would generate a compiler error. You would be changing the Cat object by calling this method.

> Use const whenever possible. Declare member functions to be const whenever they should not change the object. This lets the compiler help you find errors; it's faster and less expensive than doing it yourself.

It is good programming practice to declare as many methods to be const as possible. Each time you do, you enable the compiler to catch your errors, instead of letting your errors become bugs that will show up when your program is running.

Interface Versus Implementation

As you've learned, clients are the parts of the program that create and use objects of your class. You can think of the interface to your class—the class declaration—as a contract with these clients. The contract tells what data your class has available and how your class will behave.

For example, in the Cat class declaration, you create a contract that every Cat will know and be able to retrieve its own age, that you can initialize that age at construction and set it or retrieve it later, and that every Cat will know how to Meow().

If you make GetAge() a const function (as you should), the contract also promises that GetAge() won't change the Cat on which it is called.

Why Use the Compiler to Catch Errors?

The harsh reality of programming is that none of us writes perfectly bug-free code. What separates the professional from the hobbyist is not that the professional's code is perfect; it is that the bugs are found *before* the product ships, not after.

Compile-time errors—that is, errors found while you are compiling—are far better than runtime errors— errors found while you are executing the program.

Compile-time errors can be found much more reliably. It is possible to run a program many times without going down every possible code path. Therefore, a runtime error can hide for quite awhile. Compile-time errors are found every time you compile, so they are easier to identify and fix. It is the goal of quality programming to ensure that the code has no runtime bugs. One tried-and-true technique to accomplish this is to use the compiler to catch your mistakes early in the development process.

Of course, your code can be perfectly legal but not do what you intend. That is why you still need a Quality Assurance team.

Where to Put Class Declarations and Method Definitions

Each function that you declare for your class must have a definition. The definition is also called the function *implementation*. Like other functions, the definition of a class method has a function header and a function body.

The definition must be in a file that the compiler can find. Most C++ compilers want that file to end with .C, or .CPP. This book uses .CPP, but check your compiler to see what it prefers.

Many compilers assume that files ending with .C are C programs, and that C++ program files end with .CPP. You can use any extension, but .CPP will minimize confusion.

You will need to add these .CPP files to your project or makefile. How you do this will depend on your compiler. If you are using an integrated development environment, look for a command such as "add files to project." Every .CPP file for your program must be added to the project so that it will be compiled and linked into the final executable.

Put Class Declarations in Header Files

Although you are free to put the declaration in the source code file, it is not good programming practice. The convention that most programmers adopt is to put the

declaration into what is called a header file, usually with the same name but ending in
.H, .HP, or .HPP. This book names the header files with .HPP, but check your compiler to
see what it prefers.

For example, I put the declaration of the Cat class into a file named CAT.HPP, and I put
the definition of the class methods into a file called CAT.CPP. I then incorporate the
header file into the .CPP file by putting the following code at the top of CAT.CPP:

```
#include "Cat.hpp"
```

This tells the compiler to read CAT.HPP into the file, just as if I had typed its contents into
the file at this point. Why bother separating them if you're just going to read them back
in? Most of the time, clients of your class don't care about the implementation specifics.
Reading the header file tells them everything they need to know; they can ignore the
implementation files.

> The declaration of a class tells the compiler what the class is, what data it
> holds, and what functions it has. The declaration of the class is called its
> *interface* because it tells the user how to interact with the class. The inter-
> face is usually stored in an .HPP file, which is referred to as a *header file*.
>
> The function definition tells the compiler how the function works. The func-
> tion definition is called the *implementation* of the class method, and it is
> kept in a .CPP file. The implementation details of the class are of concern
> only to the author of the class. Clients of the class—that is, the parts of the
> program that use the class—don't need to know (and don't care) how the
> functions are implemented.

Inline Implementation

Just as you can ask the compiler to make a regular function inline, you can make class
methods inline. The keyword inline appears before the return value. The inline implementation of the GetWeight() function, for example, looks like this:

```
inline int Cat::GetWeight()
{
    return itsWeight;          // return the Weight data member
}
```

You can also put the definition of a function into the declaration of the class, which automatically makes that function inline. For example:

```
class Cat
{
public:
```

```
    int GetWeight() const { return itsWeight; }    // inline
    void SetWeight(int aWeight);
};
```

Note the syntax of the `GetWeight()` definition. The body of the inline function begins immediately after the declaration of the class method; there is no semicolon after the parentheses. Like any function, the definition begins with an opening brace and ends with a closing brace. As usual, whitespace doesn't matter; you could have written the declaration as

```
class Cat
{
public:
    int GetWeight() const
    {
        return itsWeight;
    }                               // inline
    void SetWeight(int aWeight);
};
```

Listings 8.1 and 8.2 re-create the `Cat` class, but they put the declaration in CAT.HPP and the implementation of the functions in CAT.CPP. Listing 8.1 also changes both the accessor functions and the `Meow()` function to inline.

LISTING 8.1   `Cat` Class Declaration in CAT.HPP

```
 0:   #include <iostream>
 1:
 2:   class Cat
 3:   {
 4:   public:
 5:       Cat (int initialAge);
 6:       ~Cat();
 7:       int GetAge() { return itsAge;}          // inline!
 8:       void SetAge (int age) { itsAge = age;}  // inline!
 9:       void Meow() { std::cout << "Meow.\n";}  // inline!
10:   private:
11:       int itsAge;
12:   };
```

LISTING 8.2   `Cat` Implementation in CAT.CPP

```
 0:   // Demonstrates inline functions
 1:   // and inclusion of header files
 2:   #include "cat.hpp"  // be sure to include the header files!
 3:
 4:   Cat::Cat(int initialAge)    //constructor
```

LISTING 8.2 continued

```
 5:  {
 6:      itsAge = initialAge;
 7:  }
 8:
 9:  Cat::~Cat()                 //destructor, takes no action
10:  {
11:  }
12:
13:  // Create a cat, set its age, have it
14:  // meow, tell us its age, then meow again.
15:  int main()
16:  {
17:      Cat Frisky(5);
18:      Frisky.Meow();
19:      std::cout << "Frisky is a cat who is " ;
20:      std::cout << Frisky.GetAge() << " years old.\n";
21:      Frisky.Meow();
22:      Frisky.SetAge(7);
23:      std::cout << "Now Frisky is " ;
24:      std::cout << Frisky.GetAge() << " years old.\n";
25:      return 0;
26:  }
```

OUTPUT
```
Meow.
Frisky is a cat who is 5 years old.
Meow.
Now Frisky is 7 years old.
```

ANALYSIS GetAge() is declared in line 7 of Listing 8.1, and its inline implementation is provided. Lines 8 and 9 provide more inline functions, but the functionality of these functions is unchanged from the previous "outline" implementations.

Line 2 of Listing 8.2 shows #include "cat.hpp", which brings in the listings from CAT.HPP. IOSTREAM, which is needed for cout, is included on line 5.

Classes with Other Classes as Member Data

It is not uncommon to build up a complex class by declaring simpler classes and including them in the declaration of the more complicated class. For example, you might declare a Wheel class, a Motor class, a Transmission class, and so forth, and then combine them into a Car class. This declares a *has-a* relationship: A car has a motor, it has wheels, and it has a transmission.

Consider a second example. A rectangle is composed of lines. A line is defined by two points. A point is defined by an x coordinate and a y coordinate. Listing 8.3 shows a complete declaration of a `Rectangle` class as it might appear in `RECTANGLE.HPP`. Because a rectangle is defined as four lines connecting four points, and each point refers to a coordinate on a graph, a `Point` class is first declared to hold the x,y coordinates of each point. Listing 8.4 shows a complete declaration of both classes.

LISTING 8.3   Declaring a Complete Class

```
0:  // Begin Rect.hpp
1:  #include <iostream>
2:
3:  class Point      // holds x,y coordinates
4:  {
5:      // no constructor, use default
6:  public:
7:      void SetX(int x) { itsX = x; }
8:      void SetY(int y) { itsY = y; }
9:      int GetX()const { return itsX;}
10:     int GetY()const { return itsY;}
11: private:
12:     int itsX;
13:     int itsY;
14: };// end of Point class declaration
15:
16:
17: class  Rectangle
18: {
19: public:
20:     Rectangle (int top, int left, int bottom, int right);
21:     ~Rectangle () {}
22:
23:     int GetTop() const { return itsTop; }
24:     int GetLeft() const { return itsLeft; }
25:     int GetBottom() const { return itsBottom; }
26:     int GetRight() const { return itsRight; }
27:
28:     Point  GetUpperLeft() const { return itsUpperLeft; }
29:     Point  GetLowerLeft() const { return itsLowerLeft; }
30:     Point  GetUpperRight() const { return itsUpperRight; }
31:     Point  GetLowerRight() const { return itsLowerRight; }
32:
33:     void SetUpperLeft(Point Location);
34:     void SetLowerLeft(Point Location);
35:     void SetUpperRight(Point Location);
36:     void SetLowerRight(Point Location);
37:
38:     void SetTop(int top);
39:     void SetLeft (int left);
40:     void SetBottom (int bottom);
41:     void SetRight (int right);
```

LISTING 8.3   continued

```
42:
43:        int GetArea() const;
44:
45:    private:
46:        Point  itsUpperLeft;
47:        Point  itsUpperRight;
48:        Point  itsLowerLeft;
49:        Point  itsLowerRight;
50:        int    itsTop;
51:        int    itsLeft;
52:        int    itsBottom;
53:        int    itsRight;
54:    };
55:    // end Rect.hpp
```

LISTING 8.4. RECT.CPP.

```
0:    // Begin rect.cpp
1:    #include "rect.hpp"
2:
3:    Rectangle::Rectangle(int top, int left, int bottom, int right)
4:    {
5:        itsTop = top;
6:        itsLeft = left;
7:        itsBottom = bottom;
8:        itsRight = right;
9:
10:        itsUpperLeft.SetX(left);
11:        itsUpperLeft.SetY(top);
12:
13:        itsUpperRight.SetX(right);
14:        itsUpperRight.SetY(top);
15:
16:        itsLowerLeft.SetX(left);
17:        itsLowerLeft.SetY(bottom);
18:
19:        itsLowerRight.SetX(right);
20:        itsLowerRight.SetY(bottom);
21:    }
22:
23:    void Rectangle::SetUpperLeft(Point Location)
24:    {
25:        itsUpperLeft = Location;
26:        itsUpperRight.SetY(Location.GetY());
27:        itsLowerLeft.SetX(Location.GetX());
28:        itsTop = Location.GetY();
29:        itsLeft = Location.GetX();
30:    }
```

LISTING 8.4. continued

```
31:
32:  void Rectangle::SetLowerLeft(Point Location)
33:  {
34:      itsLowerLeft = Location;
35:      itsLowerRight.SetY(Location.GetY());
36:      itsUpperLeft.SetX(Location.GetX());
37:      itsBottom = Location.GetY();
38:      itsLeft = Location.GetX();
39:  }
40:
41:  void Rectangle::SetLowerRight(Point Location)
42:  {
43:      itsLowerRight = Location;
44:      itsLowerLeft.SetY(Location.GetY());
45:      itsUpperRight.SetX(Location.GetX());
46:      itsBottom = Location.GetY();
47:      itsRight = Location.GetX();
48:  }
49:
50:  void Rectangle::SetUpperRight(Point Location)
51:  {
52:      itsUpperRight = Location;
53:      itsUpperLeft.SetY(Location.GetY());
54:      itsLowerRight.SetX(Location.GetX());
55:      itsTop = Location.GetY();
56:      itsRight = Location.GetX();
57:  }
58:
59:  void Rectangle::SetTop(int top)
60:  {
61:      itsTop = top;
62:      itsUpperLeft.SetY(top);
63:      itsUpperRight.SetY(top);
64:  }
65:
66:  void Rectangle::SetLeft(int left)
67:  {
68:      itsLeft = left;
69:      itsUpperLeft.SetX(left);
70:      itsLowerLeft.SetX(left);
71:  }
72:
73:  void Rectangle::SetBottom(int bottom)
74:  {
75:      itsBottom = bottom;
76:      itsLowerLeft.SetY(bottom);
77:      itsLowerRight.SetY(bottom);
78:  }
79:
```

LISTING 8.4. continued

```
80:   void Rectangle::SetRight(int right)
81:   {
82:       itsRight = right;
83:       itsUpperRight.SetX(right);
84:       itsLowerRight.SetX(right);
85:   }
86:
87:   int Rectangle::GetArea() const
88:   {
89:       int Width = itsRight-itsLeft;
90:       int Height = itsTop - itsBottom;
91:       return (Width * Height);
92:   }
93:
94:   // compute area of the rectangle by finding corners,
95:   // establish width and height and then multiply
96:   int main()
97:   {
98:       //initialize a local Rectangle variable
99:       Rectangle MyRectangle (100, 20, 50, 80 );
100:
101:      int Area = MyRectangle.GetArea();
102:
103:      std::cout << "Area: " << Area << "\n";
104:      std::cout << "Upper Left X Coordinate: ";
105:      std::cout << MyRectangle.GetUpperLeft().GetX();
106:      return 0;
107:  }
```

OUTPUT
```
Area: 3000
Upper Left X Coordinate: 20
```

ANALYSIS Lines 3–14 in Listing 8.3 declare the class Point, which is used to hold a specific *x,y* coordinate on a graph. As it is written, this program doesn't use Points much. However, other drawing methods require Points.

Within the declaration of the class Point, you declare two member variables—itsX and itsY—on lines 12 and 13. These variables hold the values of the coordinates. As the x coordinate increases, you move to the right on the graph. As the y coordinate increases, you move upward on the graph. Other graphs use different systems. Some windowing programs, for example, increase the y coordinate as you move down in the window.

The Point class uses inline accessor functions to get and set the X and Y points declared on lines 7–10. Points use the default constructor and destructor; therefore, you must set their coordinates explicitly.

8

Line 17 begins the declaration of a `Rectangle` class. A `Rectangle` consists of four points that represent the corners of the `Rectangle`.

The constructor for the `Rectangle` (line 20) takes four integers, known as `top`, `left`, `bottom`, and `right`. The four parameters to the constructor are copied into four member variables, and then the four `Point`s are established.

In addition to the accessor functions, `Rectangle` has a function named `GetArea()` declared in line 43. Instead of storing the area as a variable, the `GetArea()` function computes the area on lines 89–91 of Listing 8.4. To do this, it computes the width and the height of the rectangle and then multiplies those two values.

Getting the x coordinate of the upper-left corner of the rectangle requires that you access the `UpperLeft` point and ask that point for its `X` value. Because `GetUpperLeft()`is a method of `Rectangle`, it can directly access the private data of `Rectangle`, including its`UpperLeft`. Because `itsUpperLeft` is a `Point`, and `Point`'s `itsX` value is private, `GetUpperLeft()` cannot directly access this data. Rather, it must use the public accessor function `GetX()` to obtain the value.

Line 96 of Listing 8.4 is the beginning of the body of the actual program. Until line 99, no memory has been allocated, and nothing has really happened. The only thing I've done is to tell the compiler how to make a `Point` and how to make a `Rectangle`, in case one is ever needed.

In line 99, I define a `Rectangle` by passing in values for `top`, `left`, `bottom`, and `right`.

In line 101, I make a local variable, `Area`, of type `int`. This variable holds the area of the `Rectangle` that I've created. `Area` is initialized with the value returned by `Rectangle`'s `GetArea()` function.

A client of `Rectangle` could create a `Rectangle` object and get its area without ever looking at the implementation of `GetArea()`.

Just by looking at the header file, which contains the declaration of the `Rectangle` class, the programmer knows that `GetArea()` returns an `int`. How `GetArea()` does its magic is not of concern to the user of class `Rectangle`. In fact, the author of `Rectangle` could change `GetArea()` without affecting the programs that use the `Rectangle` class.

Summary

In this hour you learned more about creating classes.

You learned how to create constant member functions, and the differences between a class's interface and the implementation of a class's methods.

It is good programming practice to isolate the interface—or declaration—of the class in a header file. You usually do this in a file with an .HPP extension. The implementation of the class methods is written in a file with a .CPP extension.

Q&A

Q **If using a** const **function to change the class causes a compiler error, why shouldn't I just leave out the word** const **and be sure to avoid errors?**

A If your member function logically shouldn't change the class, using the keyword const is a good way to enlist the compiler in helping you find silly mistakes. For example, GetAge() might have no reason to change the Cat class, but if your implementation has this line

```
if (itsAge = 100) std::cout << "Hey! You're 100 years old\n";
```

declaring GetAge() to be const causes this code to be flagged as an error. You meant to check whether itsAge is equal to 100, but instead you inadvertently assigned 100 to itsAge. Because this assignment changes the class, and you said this method would not change the class, the compiler is able to find the error.

This kind of mistake can be hard to find just by scanning the code—the eye often sees only what it expects to see. More importantly, the program might appear to run correctly, but itsAge has now been set to a bogus number. This will cause problems sooner or later.

Q **Is there ever a reason to use a structure in a C++ program?**

A Many C++ programmers reserve the struct keyword for classes that have no functions. This is a throwback to the old C structures, which could not have functions. Frankly, I find it confusing and poor programming practice. Today's methodless structure might need methods tomorrow. Then you'll be forced either to change the type to class or to break your rule and end up with a structure with methods.

PART III
Memory Management

Hour

HOUR 9

Pointers

One of the most powerful tools available to a C++ programmer is a pointer. Pointers provide the capability to manipulate computer memory directly. Pointers, however, are also considered one of the most confusing aspects of C++.

I believe pointers can be understood without confusion if we spend just a little time understanding what pointers really are. In this hour you will learn

- What pointers are
- How to declare and use pointers
- What the heap is and how to manipulate memory

This chapter explains how pointers work, step by step. Please note, however, that you will fully understand the need for pointers only as the book progresses.

What Is a Pointer?

NEW TERM A *pointer* is a variable that holds a memory address.

Stop. Read that again. A pointer is a variable. You know what a variable is; it is an object that can hold a value. An integer variable holds a number. A character variable holds a letter. A pointer is a variable that holds a memory address.

Okay, so what is a memory address? To fully understand this, you must know a little about computer memory. Don't panic; it isn't very difficult.

Computer memory is where variable values are stored. By convention, computer memory is divided into sequentially numbered memory locations. Each of these locations is a memory address.

Every variable of every type is located at a unique address in memory. Figure 9.1 shows a schematic representation of the storage of an unsigned long integer variable, the Age.

FIGURE 9.1

A schematic representation of the Age.

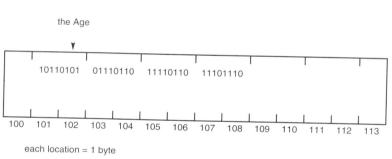

Memory

the Age

| 10110101 | 01110110 | 11110110 | 11101110 |

100 101 102 103 104 105 106 107 108 109 110 111 112 113

each location = 1 byte
unsigned long int theAge = 4 bytes = 32 bits
variable name theAge points to 1st byte
the address of theAge is 102

Different computers number the memory using different complex schemes. Usually, programmers don't need to know the particular address of any given variable because the compiler handles the details. If you want this information, though, you can use the address of operator (&), which is illustrated in Listing 9.1.

LISTING 9.1   Demonstrating the Addresses of Variables

```
0:  // Listing 9.1 Demonstrates address of operator
1:  // and addresses of local variables
2:  #include <iostream>
3:
```

LISTING 9.1 continued

```
 4:  int main()
 5:  {
 6:      unsigned short shortVar=5;
 7:      unsigned long  longVar=65535;
 8:      long sVar = -65535;
 9:
10:      std::cout << "shortVar:\t" << shortVar;
11:      std::cout << "\tAddress of shortVar:\t" << &shortVar << "\n";
12:      std::cout << "longVar:\t"  << longVar;
13:      std::cout << "\tAddress of longVar:\t"  << &longVar  << "\n";
14:      std::cout << "sVar:\t\t"   << sVar;
15:      std::cout << "\tAddress of sVar:\t"      << &sVar      << "\n";
16:
17:      return 0;
18:  }
```

OUTPUT

```
shortVar: 5        Address of shortVar: 0x8fc9:fff4
longVar:  65535    Address of longVar:  0x8fc9:fff2
sVar:     -65535   Address of sVar:     0x8fc9:ffee
```

(Your printout may look different because each computer will store variables at different addresses, depending on what else is in memory and how much memory is available.)

ANALYSIS Three variables are declared and initialized: a short in line 6, an unsigned long in line 7, and a long in line 8. Their values and addresses are printed in lines 10–15, by using the address of operator (&).

The value of shortVar is 5 (as expected), and its address is 0x8fc9:fff4 when run on my 80386-based computer. This complicated address is computer specific and can change slightly each time the program is run. Your results will be different. What doesn't change, however, is that the difference in the first two addresses is 2 bytes if your computer uses 2-byte short integers. The difference between the second and third is 4 bytes if your computer uses 4-byte long integers. Figure 9.2 illustrates how the variables in this program would be stored in memory. (Note that on some computers the difference will be 4 bytes on both, depending on how your compiler is configured.)

There is no reason why you would need to know the actual numeric value of the address of each variable. What you care about is that each one *has* an address and that the right amount of memory is set aside.

How does the compiler know how much memory each variable needs? You tell the compiler how much memory to allow for your variables by declaring the variable type.

FIGURE 9.2

Illustration of variable storage.

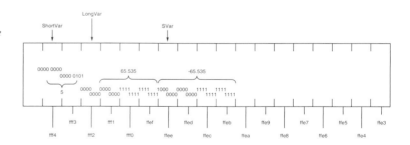

Therefore, if you declare your variable to be of type `unsigned long`, the compiler knows to set aside 4 bytes of memory because every `unsigned long` takes 4 bytes. The compiler takes care of assigning the actual address.

Storing the Address in a Pointer

Every variable has an address. Even without knowing the specific address of a given variable, you can store that address in a pointer.

For example, suppose that `howOld` is an integer. To declare a pointer called `pAge` to hold its address, you would write

```
int *pAge = 0;
```

This declares `pAge` to be a pointer to `int`. That is, `pAge` is declared to hold the address of an `int`.

Note that `pAge` is a variable like any of the variables. When you declare an integer variable (of type `int`), it is set up to hold an integer. When you declare a pointer variable like `pAge`, it is set up to hold an address. A pointer is just a special type of variable that is set up to hold the address of some object in memory; in this case, `pAge` is holding the address of an integer variable.

In this example, `pAge` is initialized to `0`. A pointer whose value is `0` is called a *null pointer*. All pointers, when they are created, should be initialized to something. If you don't know what you want to assign to the pointer, assign `0`. A pointer that is not initialized is called a *wild pointer*. Wild pointers are very dangerous.

 Practice safe computing: initialize your pointers!

If you initialize the pointer to `0`, you must specifically assign the address of `howOld` to `pAge`. Here's an example that shows how to do that:

```
int howOld = 50;        // make a variable
int * pAge = 0;         // make a pointer
pAge = &howOld;                      // put howOld's address in pAge
```

The first line creates a variable—howOld, whose type is unsigned short int—and initializes it with the value 50. The second line declares pAge to be a pointer to type unsigned short int and initializes it to 0. You know that pAge is a pointer because of the asterisk (*) after the variable type and before the variable name.

The third and final line assigns the address of howOld to the pointer pAge. You can tell that the address of howOld is being assigned to the pointer because of the address of operator (&). If the address of operator were not used, the value of howOld would be assigned instead of its address. That value might—or might not—be a valid address somewhere in memory, but if it were, it would be entirely a coincidence.

At this point, pAge has as its value the address of howOld. howOld, in turn, has the value 50. You could have accomplished this with fewer steps, as in

```
unsigned short int howOld = 50;         // make a variable
unsigned short int * pAge = &howOld;  // make pointer to howOld
```

pAge is a pointer that now contains the address of the howOld variable. Using pAge, you can actually determine the value of howOld, which in this case is 50. Accessing howOld by using the pointer pAge is called *indirection* because you are indirectly accessing howOld by means of pAge. Later this hour you will see how to use indirection to access a variable's value.

NEW TERM *Indirection* means accessing the value at the address held by a pointer. The pointer provides an indirect way to get the value held at that address.

Pointer Names

Pointers can have any name that is legal for other variables. This book follows the convention of naming all pointers with an initial p, as in pAge and pNumber.

The Indirection Operator

The indirection operator (*) is also called the *dereference operator*. When a pointer is dereferenced, the value at the address stored by the pointer is retrieved.

```
unsigned short int howOld = 50;
unsigned short int yourAge;
yourAge = howOld;
```

A pointer provides indirect access to the value of the variable whose address it stores. To assign the value in howOld to the new variable yourAge by way of the pointer pAge, you would write

```
unsigned short int howOld = 50;        // create the variable howOld
unsigned short int * pAge = &howOld;   // pAge points to the address of howOld
unsigned short int yourAge;            // create another variable
yourAge = *pAge;                       // assign value at pAge (50) to yourAge
```

The indirection operator (*) in front of the variable pAge means "the value stored at." This assignment says, "Take the value stored at the address in pAge and assign it to yourAge."

> The indirection operator (*) is used in two distinct ways with pointers: declaration and dereference. When a pointer is declared, the star indicates that it is a pointer, not a normal variable. For example:
>
> ```
> unsigned short * pAge = 0; // make a pointer to an unsigned short
> ```
>
> When the pointer is dereferenced, the indirection operator indicates that the value at the memory location stored in the pointer is to be accessed, rather than the address itself:
>
> ```
> *pAge = 5; // assign 5 to the value at pAge
> ```
>
> Also note that this same character (*) is used as the multiplication operator. The compiler knows which operator to call based on context.

Pointers, Addresses, and Variables

It is important to distinguish between a pointer, the address that the pointer holds, and the value at the address held by the pointer. This is the source of much of the confusion about pointers.

Consider the following code fragment:

```
int theVariable = 5;
int * pPointer = &theVariable ;
```

theVariable is declared to be an integer variable initialized with the value 5. pPointer is declared to be a pointer to an integer; it is initialized with the address of theVariable. The address that pPointer holds is the address of theVariable. The value at the address that pPointer holds is 5. Figure 9.3 shows a schematic representation of theVariable and pPointer.

Manipulating Data by Using Pointers

After a pointer is assigned the address of a variable, you can use that pointer to access the data in that variable. Listing 9.2 demonstrates how the address of a local variable is assigned to a pointer and how the pointer manipulates the values in that variable.

FIGURE 9.3

A schematic represen-
tation of memory.

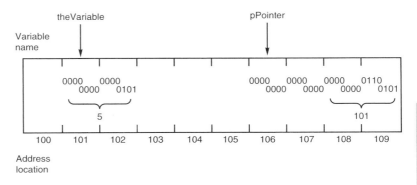

LISTING 9.2   Manipulating Data by Using Pointers

```
0:   // Listing 9.2 Using pointers
1:   #include <iostream>
2:   using std::cout; // this file uses std::cout
3:
4:   int main()
5:   {
6:       int myAge;            // a variable
7:       int * pAge = 0;       // a pointer
8:
9:       myAge = 5;
10:      pAge = &myAge;        // assign address of myAge to pAge
11:      cout << "myAge: " << myAge << "\n";
12:      cout << "*pAge: " << *pAge << "\n\n";
13:
14:      cout << "*pAge = 7\n";
15:      *pAge = 7;            // sets myAge to 7
16:      cout << "*pAge: " << *pAge << "\n";
17:      cout << "myAge: " << myAge << "\n\n";
18:
19:      cout << "myAge = 9\n";
20:      myAge = 9;
21:      cout << "myAge: " << myAge << "\n";
22:      cout << "*pAge: " << *pAge << "\n";
23:
24:      return 0;
25:  }
```

OUTPUT

```
myAge: 5
*pAge: 5

*pAge = 7
*pAge: 7
myAge: 7
```

```
myAge =9
myAge: 9
*pAge: 9
```

ANALYSIS This program declares two variables: an `int`, `myAge`; and a pointer `pAge`, which is a pointer to `int` and which holds the address of `myAge`. `myAge` is assigned the value 5 in line 9; this is verified by the printout in line 11.

In line 10, `pAge` is assigned the address of `myAge`. In line 12, `pAge` is dereferenced and printed, showing that the value at the address that `pAge` stores is the 5 stored in `myAge`. In line 15, the value 7 is assigned to the variable at the address stored in `pAge`. This sets `myAge` to 7, and the printouts in lines 16 and 17 confirm this.

In line 20, the value 9 is assigned to the variable `myAge`. This value is obtained directly in line 21 and indirectly—by dereferencing `pAge`—in line 22.

Examining the Address

Pointers enable you to manipulate addresses without ever knowing their real value. After this hour, you'll take it on faith that when you assign the address of a variable to a pointer, the pointer really has the address of that variable as its value. But just this once, why not check to make sure? Listing 9.3 illustrates this idea.

LISTING 9.3   Finding Out What Is Stored in Pointers

```
0:   // Listing 9.3 What is stored in a pointer.
1:   #include <iostream>
2:
3:   int main()
4:   {
5:       unsigned short int myAge = 5, yourAge = 10;
6:       unsigned short int * pAge = &myAge;  // a pointer
7:
8:       std::cout << "myAge:\t" << myAge;
9:       std::cout << "\t\tyourAge:\t" << yourAge << "\n";
10:      std::cout << "&myAge:\t" << &myAge;
11:      std::cout << "\t&yourAge:\t" << &yourAge <<"\n";
12:
13:      std::cout << "pAge:\t" << pAge << "\n";
14:      std::cout << "*pAge:\t" << *pAge << "\n\n";
15:
16:      pAge = &yourAge;         // reassign the pointer
17:
18:      std::cout << "myAge:\t" << myAge;
19:      std::cout << "\t\tyourAge:\t" << yourAge << "\n";
20:      std::cout << "&myAge:\t" << &myAge;
21:      std::cout << "\t&yourAge:\t" << &yourAge <<"\n";
```

LISTING 9.3   continued

```
22:
23:        std::cout << "pAge:\t" << pAge << "\n";
24:        std::cout << "*pAge:\t" << *pAge << "\n\n";
25:
26:        std::cout << "&pAge:\t" << &pAge << "\n";
27:        return 0;
28:    }
```

OUTPUT

```
myAge:      5               yourAge:   10
&myAge:     0x355C          &yourAge:  0x355E
pAge:       0x355C
*pAge:      5

myAge:      5               yourAge:   10
&myAge:     0x355C          &yourAge:  0x355E
pAge:       0x355E
*pAge:      10

&pAge:      0x355A
```

(Again, your output may look different because each computer will store variables at different addresses, depending on what else is in memory and how much memory is available.)

ANALYSIS In line 5, myAge and yourAge are declared to be variables of type unsigned short integer. In line 6, pAge is declared to be a pointer to an unsigned short integer, and it is initialized with the address of the variable myAge.

Lines 8—11 print the values and the addresses of myAge and yourAge. Line 13 prints the contents of pAge, which is the address of myAge. Line 14 prints the result of dereferencing pAge, which prints the value at pAge—the value in myAge, or 5.

This is the essence of pointers. Line 13 shows that pAge stores the address of myAge, and line 14 shows how to get the value stored in myAge by dereferencing the pointer pAge. Make sure that you understand this fully before you go on. Study the code and look at the output.

In line 16, pAge is reassigned to point to the address of yourAge. The values and addresses are printed again. The output shows that pAge now has the address of the variable yourAge, and that dereferencing obtains the value in yourAge.

Line 26 prints the address of pAge itself. Like any variable, it too has an address, and that address can be stored in a pointer. (Assigning the address of a pointer to another pointer will be discussed shortly.)

Do

DO use the indirection operator (*) to access the data stored at the address in a pointer.

DO initialize all pointers either to a valid address or to null (0).

DO remember the difference between the address in a pointer and the value at that

---

Why Would You Use Pointers?

So far you've seen step-by-step details of assigning a variable's address to a pointer. In practice, though, you would never do this. After all, why bother with a pointer when you already have a variable with access to that value? The only reason for this kind of pointer manipulation of a variable is to demonstrate how pointers work.

Now that you are comfortable with the syntax of pointers, you can put them to good use. Pointers are used, most often, for three tasks:

- Managing data on the heap
- Accessing class member data and functions
- Passing variables by reference to functions

The rest of this chapter focuses on managing data on the heap and accessing class member data and functions. In Hour 11, "References," you will learn about passing variables by reference.

The Stack and the Heap

Programmers generally deal with five areas of memory:

Global name space

The heap

Registers

Code space

The stack

Local variables are on the stack, along with function parameters. Code is in code space, of course, and global variables are in global name space. The registers are used for internal housekeeping functions, such as keeping track of the top of the stack and the instruction pointer. Just about all remaining memory is given over to the heap, which is sometimes referred to as the free store.

The problem with local variables is that they don't persist. When the function returns, the local variables are thrown away. Global variables solve that problem at the cost of unrestricted access throughout the program, which leads to the creation of code that is difficult to understand and maintain. Putting data in the heap solves both of these problems.

You can think of the heap as a massive section of memory in which thousands of sequentially numbered cubbyholes lie waiting for your data. You can't label these cubbyholes, though, as you can with the stack. You must ask for the address of the cubbyhole that you reserve and then stash that address away in a pointer.

One way to think about this is with an analogy: A friend gives you the 800 number for Acme Mail Order. You go home and program your telephone with that number, and then you throw away the piece of paper with the number on it. When you push the button, a telephone rings somewhere, and Acme Mail Order answers. You don't remember the number, and you don't know where the other telephone is located, but the button gives you access to Acme Mail Order. Acme Mail Order is your data on the heap. You don't know where it is, but you know how to get to it. You access it by using its address—in this case, the telephone number. You don't have to know that number; you just have to put it into a pointer—the button. The pointer gives you access to your data without bothering you with the details.

The stack is cleaned automatically when a function returns. All the local variables go out of scope, and they are removed from the stack. The heap is not cleaned until your program ends, and it is your responsibility to free any memory that you've reserved when you are done with it.

The advantage to the heap is that the memory you reserve remains available until you explicitly free it. If you reserve memory on the heap while in a function, the memory is still available when the function returns.

The advantage of accessing memory in this way, rather than using global variables, is that only functions with access to the pointer have access to the data. This provides a tightly controlled interface to that data, and it eliminates the problem of one function changing that data in unexpected and unanticipated ways.

For this to work, you must be able to create a pointer to an area on the heap. The following sections describe how to do this.

new

You allocate memory on the heap in C++ by using the `new` keyword. `new` is followed by the type of the object that you want to allocate so that the compiler knows how much memory is required. Therefore, `new unsigned short int` allocates 2 bytes in the heap, and `new long` allocates 4.

The return value from new is a memory address. It must be assigned to a pointer. To create an unsigned short on the heap, you might write

```
unsigned short int * pPointer;
pPointer = new unsigned short int;
```

You can, of course, initialize the pointer at its creation with

```
unsigned short int * pPointer = new unsigned short int;
```

In either case, pPointer now points to an unsigned short int on the heap. You can use this like any other pointer to a variable and assign a value into that area of memory by writing

```
*pPointer = 72;
```

This means, "Put 72 at the value in pPointer," or "Assign the value 72 to the area on the heap to which pPointer points."

If new cannot create memory on the heap—memory is, after all, a limited resource—it throws an exception.

Exceptions are error-handling objects covered in detail in Hour 24.

Some older compilers return the null pointer. If you have an older compiler, check your pointer for null each time you request new memory; but all modern compilers can be counted on to throw an exception.

delete

When you are finished with your area of memory, you must call delete on the pointer. delete returns the memory to the heap. Remember that the pointer itself—as opposed to the memory to which it points—is a local variable. When the function in which it is declared returns, that pointer goes out of scope and is lost. The memory allocated with the new operator is not freed automatically, however. That memory becomes unavailable—a situation called a *memory leak*. It's called a memory leak because that memory can't be recovered until the program ends. It is as though the memory has leaked out of your computer.

To restore the memory to the heap, you use the keyword delete. For example:

```
delete pPointer;
```

When you delete the pointer, what you are really doing is freeing up the memory whose address is stored in the pointer. You are saying, "Return to the heap the memory that this pointer points to." The pointer is still a pointer, and it can be reassigned. Listing 9.4 demonstrates allocating a variable on the heap, using that variable, and deleting it.

> When you call delete on a pointer, the memory it points to is freed. Calling delete on that pointer again will crash your program! When you delete a pointer, set it to 0 (null). Calling delete on a null pointer is guaranteed to be safe. For example:
>
> ```
> Animal *pDog = new Animal;
> delete pDog; //frees the memory
> pDog = 0; //sets pointer to null
> //...
> delete pDog; //harmless
> ```

LISTING 9.4   Allocating and Deleting a Pointer

```
0:   // Listing 9.4
1:   // Allocating and deleting a pointer
2:   #include <iostream>
3:
4:   int main()
5:   {
6:       int localVariable = 5;
7:       int * pLocal= &localVariable;
8:       int * pHeap = new int;
9:       if (pHeap == NULL)
10:      {
11:          std::cout << "Error! No memory for pHeap!!";
12:          return 1;
13:      }
14:      *pHeap = 7;
15:      std::cout << "localVariable: " << localVariable << "\n";
16:      std::cout << "*pLocal: " << *pLocal << "\n";
17:      std::cout << "*pHeap: " << *pHeap << "\n";
18:      delete pHeap;
19:      pHeap = new int;
20:      if (pHeap == NULL)
21:      {
22:          std::cout << "Error! No memory for pHeap!!";
23:          return 1;
24:      }
25:      *pHeap = 9;
26:      std::cout << "*pHeap: " << *pHeap << "\n";
27:      delete pHeap;
28:      return 0;
29:   }
```

OUTPUT
```
localVariable: 5
*pLocal: 5
*pHeap: 7
*pHeap: 9
```

ANALYSIS   Line 6 declares and initializes a local variable. Line 7 declares and initializes a pointer with the address of the local variable. Line 8 declares another pointer but initializes it with the result obtained from calling `new int`. This allocates space on the heap for an `int`. Line 14 assigns the value 7 to the newly allocated memory. Line 15 prints the value of the local variable, and line 16 prints the value pointed to by `pLocal`. As expected, these are the same. Line 17 prints the value pointed to by `pHeap`. It shows that the value assigned in line 14 is, in fact, accessible.

In line 18, the memory allocated in line 8 is returned to the heap by a call to `delete`. This frees the memory and disassociates the pointer from that memory location. `pHeap` is now free to point to other memory. It is reassigned in lines 19—25, and line 26 prints the result. Line 27 again restores that memory to the heap.

Although line 27 is redundant (the end of the program would have returned that memory), it is a good idea to free this memory explicitly. If the program changes or is extended, it will be beneficial that this step was already taken care of.

Memory Leaks

Another way you might inadvertently create a memory leak is by reassigning your pointer before deleting the memory to which it points. Consider this code fragment:

```
1:    unsigned short int * pPointer = new unsigned short int;
2:    *pPointer = 72;
3:    pPointer = new unsigned short int;
4:    *pPointer = 84;
```

Line 1 creates `pPointer` and assigns it the address of an area on the heap. Line 2 stores the value 72 in that area of memory. Line 3 reassigns `pPointer` to another area of memory. Line 4 places the value 84 in that area. The original area—in which the value 72 is now held—is unavailable because the pointer to that area of memory has been reassigned. There is no way to access that original area of memory, nor is there any way to free it before the program ends.

The code should have been written like this:

```
1: unsigned short int * pPointer = new unsigned short int;
2: *pPointer = 72;
3: delete pPointer;
4: pPointer = new unsigned short int;
5: *pPointer = 84;
```

Now the memory originally pointed to by pPointer is deleted—and thus freed—in line 3.

For every time in your program that you call new, there should be a call to delete. It is important to keep track of which pointer owns an area of memory and to ensure that the memory is returned to the heap when you are done with it.

Summary

Pointers provide a powerful way to access data by indirection. Every variable has an address, which can be obtained using the address of operator (&). The address can be stored in a pointer.

Pointers are declared by writing the type of object that they point to, followed by the indirection operator (*) and the name of the pointer. Pointers should be initialized to point to an object or to NULL (0). You access the value at the address stored in a pointer by using the indirection operator (*).

To create new objects on the heap, you use the new keyword and assign the address that is returned to a pointer. You free that memory by calling the delete keyword on the pointer. delete frees the memory, but it doesn't destroy the pointer. Therefore, you must reassign the pointer after its memory has been freed.

Q&A

Q Why are pointers so important?

A During this hour you saw how pointers are used to hold the address of objects on the heap and how they are used to pass arguments by reference. In addition, in Hour 13, "Advanced Functions," you'll see how pointers are used in class polymorphism.

Q Why should I bother to declare anything on the heap?

A Objects on the heap persist after the return of a function. Additionally, the capability to store objects on the heap enables you to decide at runtime how many objects you need, instead of having to declare this in advance. This is explored in greater depth in Hour 10.

HOUR **10**

Advanced Pointers

One of the most powerful tools available to a C++ programmer is the capability to directly manipulate computer memory by using pointers. In this hour, you will learn

- How to create objects on the heap
- How to use pointers effectively
- How to prevent memory problems when using pointers

Creating Objects on the Heap

Just as you can create a pointer to an integer, you can create a pointer to any object. If you have declared an object of type Cat, you can declare a pointer to that class and instantiate a Cat object on the heap, just as you can make one on the stack. The syntax is the same as for integers:

```
Cat *pCat = new Cat;
```

This calls the default constructor—the constructor that takes no parameters. The constructor is called whenever an object is created—on the stack or on the heap.

Deleting Objects

When you call delete on a pointer to an object on the heap, that object's destructor is called before the memory is released. This gives your class a chance to clean up, just as it does for objects destroyed on the stack. Listing 10.1 illustrates creating and deleting objects on the heap.

LISTING **10.1**   Creating and Deleting Objects on the Heap

```
0:  // Listing 10.1
1:  // Creating objects on the heap
2:  #include <iostream>
3:
4:  class SimpleCat
5:  {
6:  public:
7:      SimpleCat();
8:      ~SimpleCat();
9:  private:
10:      int itsAge;
11:  };
12:
13:  SimpleCat::SimpleCat()
14:  {
15:      std::cout << "Constructor called.\n";
16:      itsAge = 1;
17:  }
18:
19:  SimpleCat::~SimpleCat()
20:  {
21:      std::cout << "Destructor called.\n";
22:  }
23:
24:  int main()
25:  {
26:      std::cout << "SimpleCat Frisky...\n";
27:      SimpleCat Frisky;
28:
29:      std::cout << "SimpleCat *pRags = new SimpleCat...\n";
30:      SimpleCat * pRags = new SimpleCat;
31:
32:      std::cout << "delete pRags...\n";
33:      delete pRags;
34:
35:      std::cout << "Exiting, watch Frisky go...\n";
36:      return 0;
37:  }
```

OUTPUT
```
SimpleCat Frisky...
Constructor called.
SimpleCat * pRags = new SimpleCat..
Constructor called.
delete pRags...
Destructor called.
Exiting, watch Frisky go...
Destructor called.
```

ANALYSIS Lines 4–11 declare the stripped-down class SimpleCat. On line 27, Frisky is created on the stack, which causes the constructor to be called. In line 30, the SimpleCat pointed to by pRags is created on the heap; the constructor is called again. In line 33, delete is called on pRags, and the destructor is called. When the function ends, Frisky goes out of scope, and the destructor is called.

Accessing Data Members Using Pointers

You accessed data members and functions by using the dot (.) operator for Cat objects created locally. To access the Cat object on the heap, you must dereference the pointer and call the dot operator on the object pointed to by the pointer. Therefore, to access the GetAge member function, you would write

```
(*pRags).GetAge();
```

Parentheses are used to assure that pRags is dereferenced before GetAge() is accessed.

Because this is cumbersome, C++ provides a shorthand operator for indirect access: the points-to operator (->), which is created by typing the dash (-) immediately followed by the greater-than symbol (>). C++ treats this as a single symbol. Listing 10.2 demonstrates accessing member variables and functions of objects created on the heap.

LISTING 10.2   Accessing Member Data of Objects on the Heap

```
0:  // Listing 10.2
1:  // Accessing members of objects on the heap
2:  #include <iostream>
3:
4:  class SimpleCat
5:  {
6:  public:
7:      SimpleCat() {itsAge = 2; }
8:      ~SimpleCat() {}
9:      int GetAge() const { return itsAge; }
10:     void SetAge(int age) { itsAge = age; }
11: private:
12:     int itsAge;
```

LISTING 10.2   continued

```
13:  };
14:
15:  int main()
16:  {
17:      SimpleCat * Frisky = new SimpleCat;
18:      std::cout << "Frisky is " << Frisky->GetAge()
19:                << " years old\n";
20:
21:      Frisky->SetAge(5);
22:      std::cout << "Frisky is " << Frisky->GetAge()
23:                << " years old\n";
24:
25:      delete Frisky;
26:      return 0;
27:  }
```

OUTPUT   Frisky is 2 years old
               Frisky is 5 years old

ANALYSIS   In line 17, a SimpleCat object is instantiated on the heap. The default construc-
               tor sets its age to 2, and the GetAge() method is called in line 18. Because this is
a pointer, the points-to operator (->) is used to access the member data and functions. In
line 21, the SetAge() method is called, and GetAge() is accessed again in line 22.

Member Data on the Heap

One or more of the data members of a class can be a pointer to an object on the heap.
The memory can be allocated in the class constructor or in one of its methods, and it can
be deleted in its destructor, as Listing 10.3 illustrates.

LISTING 10.3   Pointers as Data Members

```
0:  // Listing 10.3
1:  // Pointers as data members
2:  #include <iostream>
3:
4:  class SimpleCat
5:  {
6:  public:
7:      SimpleCat();
8:      ~SimpleCat();
9:      int GetAge() const { return *itsAge; }
10:     void SetAge(int age) { *itsAge = age; }
11:
```

LISTING 10.3   continued

```
12:        int GetWeight() const { return *itsWeight; }
13:        void setWeight (int weight) { *itsWeight = weight; }
14:
15:    private:
16:        int * itsAge;
17:        int * itsWeight;
18:    };
19:
20:    SimpleCat::SimpleCat()
21:    {
22:        itsAge = new int(2);
23:        itsWeight = new int(5);
24:    }
25:
26:    SimpleCat::~SimpleCat()
27:    {
28:        delete itsAge;
29:        delete itsWeight;
30:    }
31:
32:    int main()
33:    {
34:        SimpleCat *Frisky = new SimpleCat;
35:        std::cout << "Frisky is " << Frisky->GetAge()
36:                  << " years old\n";
37:
38:        Frisky->SetAge(5);
39:        std::cout << "Frisky is " << Frisky->GetAge()
40:                  << " years old\n";
41:
42:        delete Frisky;
43:        return 0;
44:    }
```

OUTPUT   Frisky is 2 years old
              Frisky is 5 years old

ANALYSIS   The class SimpleCat has two member variables—both of which are pointers to integers. The constructor (lines 20–24) initializes the pointers to memory on the heap and to the default values.

The destructor (lines 26–30) cleans up the allocated memory. Because this is the destructor, there is no point in assigning these pointers to null, because they will no longer be accessible. This is one of the safe places to break the rule that deleted pointers should be assigned to null, although following the rule doesn't hurt.

The calling function—in this case, main()—is unaware that itsAge and itsWeight are pointers to memory on the heap. main() continues to call GetAge() and SetAge(), and the details of the memory management are hidden in the implementation of the class—as they should be.

When Frisky is deleted in line 42, its destructor is called. The destructor deletes each of its member pointers. If these, in turn, point to objects of other user-defined classes, their destructors are called as well.

The this Pointer

Every class member function has a hidden parameter: the this pointer. this points to the individual object. Therefore, in each call to GetAge() or SetAge(), the this pointer for the object is included as a hidden parameter.

The job of the this pointer is to point to the individual object whose method has been invoked. Usually, you don't need this; you just call methods and set member variables. Occasionally, however, you'll need to access the object itself (perhaps to return a pointer to the current object). It is at that point that the this pointer becomes so helpful.

Normally, you don't need to use the this pointer to access the member variables of an object from within methods of that object. You can, however, explicitly call the this pointer if you want to. This is done in Listing 10.4 to illustrate that the this pointer exists and works.

LISTING 10.4   Using the this Pointer

```
0:  // Listing 10.4
1:  // Using the this pointer
2:  #include <iostream>
3:
4:  class Rectangle
5:  {
6:  public:
7:      Rectangle();
8:      ~Rectangle();
9:      void SetLength(int length) { this->itsLength = length; }
10:     int GetLength() const { return this->itsLength; }
11:     void SetWidth(int width) { itsWidth = width; }
12:     int GetWidth() const { return itsWidth; }
13:
14: private:
15:     int itsLength;
16:     int itsWidth;
17: };
```

LISTING 10.4 continued

```
18:
19:    Rectangle::Rectangle()
20:    {
21:        itsWidth = 5;
22:        itsLength = 10;
23:    }
24:
25:    Rectangle::~Rectangle()
26:    {}
27:
28:    int main()
29:    {
30:        Rectangle theRect;
31:        std::cout << "theRect is " << theRect.GetLength()
32:                  << " feet long.\n";
33:        std::cout << "theRect is " << theRect.GetWidth()
34:                  << " feet wide.\n";
35:
36:        theRect.SetLength(20);
37:        theRect.SetWidth(10);
38:        std::cout << "theRect is " << theRect.GetLength()
39:                  << " feet long.\n";
40:        std::cout << "theRect is " << theRect.GetWidth()
41:                  << " feet wide.\n";
42:
43:        return 0;
44:    }
```

OUTPUT
```
theRect is 10 feet long
theRect is 5 feet wide
theRect is 20 feet long
theRect is 10 feet wide
```

ANALYSIS The SetLength() and GetLength() accessor functions explicitly use the this pointer to access the member variables of the Rectangle object. The SetWidth and GetWidth accessors do not. There is no difference in their behavior, although the method without the this pointer may be easier to read.

What's the this Pointer For?

If that's all there is to the this pointer, there would be little point in bothering you with it. The this pointer, however, is a pointer, which means it stores the memory address of an object. As such, it can be a powerful tool.

You'll see a practical use for the `this` pointer later in the book, when operator overloading is discussed (in Hour 14). For now, your goal is to know about the `this` pointer and to understand what it is: a pointer to the object itself.

You don't have to worry about creating or deleting the `this` pointer. The compiler takes care of that.

Stray or Dangling Pointers

One source of bugs that are nasty and difficult to find is stray pointers. A *stray pointer* is created when you call `delete` on a pointer—thereby freeing the memory that it points to—and later try to use that pointer again without reassigning it.

It is as though the Acme Mail Order company moved away, and you still pressed the programmed button on your phone. It is possible that nothing terrible happens—a telephone rings in a deserted warehouse. Another possibility is that the telephone number has been reassigned to a munitions factory, and your call detonates an explosive and blows up your whole city!

In short, be careful not to use a pointer after you have called `delete` on it. The pointer still points to the old area of memory, but the compiler is free to put other data there; using the pointer can cause your program to crash. Worse, your program might proceed merrily on its way and crash several minutes later. This is called a *time bomb*, and it is no fun. To be safe, after you delete a pointer, set it to `null` (`0`). This disarms the pointer.

Stray pointers are often called *wild pointers* or *dangling pointers*.

const Pointers

You can use the keyword `const` for pointers before the type, after the type, or in both places. For example, all the following are legal declarations:

```
const int * pOne;
int * const pTwo;
const int * const pThree;
```

pOne is a pointer to a constant integer. The value that is pointed to can't be changed using this pointer. That means you can't write

```
*pOne = 5
```

If you try to do so, the compiler will object with an error.

pTwo is a constant pointer to an integer. The integer can be changed, but pTwo can't point to anything else. A constant pointer can't be reassigned. That means you can't write

pTwo = &x

pThree is a constant pointer to a constant integer. The value that is pointed to can't be changed, and pThree can't be changed to point to anything else.

Draw an imaginary line just to the right of the asterisk. If the word const is to the left of the line, that means the object is constant. If the word const is to the right of the line, the pointer itself is constant.

```
const int * p1;   // the int pointed to is constant
int * const p2;   // p2 is constant, it can't point to anything else
```

const Pointers and const Member Functions

In Hour 7, "Basic Classes," you learned that you can apply the keyword const to a member function. When a function is declared as const, the compiler flags as an error any attempt to change data in the object from within that function.

If you declare a pointer to a const object, the only methods that you can call with that pointer are const methods. Listing 10.5 illustrates this.

LISTING 10.5   Using Pointers to const Objects

```
 0: // Listing 10.5
 1: // Using pointers with const methods
 2: #include <iostream>
 3:
 4: class Rectangle
 5: {
 6: public:
 7:     Rectangle();
 8:     ~Rectangle();
 9:     void SetLength(int length) { itsLength = length; }
10:     int GetLength() const { return itsLength; }
11:
12:     void SetWidth(int width) { itsWidth = width; }
13:     int GetWidth() const { return itsWidth; }
14:
15: private:
16:     int itsLength;
17:     int itsWidth;
18: };
19:
20: Rectangle::Rectangle():
21: itsWidth(5),
```

LISTING 10.5   continued

```
22:    itsLength(10)
23:    {}
24:
25:    Rectangle::~Rectangle()
26:    {}
27:
28:    int main()
29:    {
30:        Rectangle* pRect =  new Rectangle;
31:        const Rectangle * pConstRect = new Rectangle;
32:        Rectangle * const pConstPtr = new Rectangle;
33:
34:        std::cout << "pRect width: "
35:                  << pRect->GetWidth() << " feet\n";
36:        std::cout << "pConstRect width: "
37:                  << pConstRect->GetWidth() << " feet\n";
38:        std::cout << "pConstPtr width: "
39:                  << pConstPtr->GetWidth() << " feet\n";
40:
41:        pRect->SetWidth(10);
42:        // pConstRect->SetWidth(10);
43:        pConstPtr->SetWidth(10);
44:
45:        std::cout << "pRect width: "
46:                  << pRect->GetWidth() << " feet\n";
47:        std::cout << "pConstRect width: "
48:                  << pConstRect->GetWidth() << " feet\n";
49:        std::cout << "pConstPtr width: "
50:                  << pConstPtr->GetWidth() << " feet\n";
51:        return 0;
52:    }
```

OUTPUT

```
pRect width:      5 feet
pConstRect width: 5 feet
pConstPtr width:  5 feet
pRect width:      10 feet
pConstRect width: 5 feet
pConstPtr width:  10 feet
```

ANALYSIS   Lines 4–18 declare `Rectangle`. Line 13 declares the `GetWidth()` member method `const`. Line 30 declares a pointer to a `Rectangle`. Line 31 declares `pConstRect`, which is a pointer to a constant `Rectangle`. Line 32 declares `pConstPtr`, which is a constant pointer to `Rectangle`.

Lines 34–39 print the value of the widths.

In line 41, pRect is used to set the width of the rectangle to 10. In line 42, pConstRect would be used, but it was declared to point to a constant Rectangle. Therefore, it cannot legally call a non-const member function; it is commented out. On line 32, pConstPtr is declared to be a constant pointer to a rectangle. In other words, the pointer is constant and cannot point to anything else, but the rectangle is not constant.

const this Pointers

When you declare an object to be const, you are, in effect, declaring that the this pointer is a pointer to a const object. A const this pointer can be used only with const member functions.

Constant objects and constant pointers will be discussed again in the next hour, when references to constant objects are discussed.

Summary

Pointers can be a powerful technique for managing objects on the heap. They bring risks of memory leaks and stray pointers; but, if you are careful, they are safe and effective to use in your programs.

You can declare pointers to be constant, and enlist the compiler in helping you find those places in which you use your pointers in ways you had not intended. The this pointer is a hidden parameter to every member method and provides a pointer to the object itself. Const pointers allow you to refer to an object's address without allowing you to use the pointer to modify the object. Const member functions are member functions that promise they will not alter the state of the object. Const member functions have a constant this pointer.

Q&A

Q Why should I declare an object as const if it limits what I can do with it?

A As a programmer, you want to enlist the compiler in helping you find bugs. One serious bug that is difficult to find is a function that changes an object in ways that aren't obvious to the calling function. Declaring an object const prevents such changes.

Q Why should I bother to declare anything on the heap?

A Objects on the heap persist after the return of a function. In addition, objects declared on the heap can be used to create complex data structures as explored in Hour 19, "Linked Lists."

Hour **11**

References

In the past two hours, you learned how to use pointers to manipulate objects on the heap and how to refer to those objects indirectly. References, the topic of this hour's chapter, give you almost all the power of pointers but with a much easier syntax. In this hour you will learn

- What references are
- How references differ from pointers
- How to create and use references
- What the limitations of references are
- How to pass values and objects into and out of functions by reference

What Is a Reference?

NEW TERM   A *reference* is an alias. When you create a reference, you initialize it with the name of another object, the *target*. From that moment on, the reference acts as an alternative name for the target, and anything you do to the reference is really done to the target.

That's it. You might read in some sources that references are pointers, but that is not correct. Although references are often implemented using pointers, that is a matter of concern only to creators of compilers; as a programmer you must keep these two ideas distinct.

Pointers are variables that hold the address of another object. References are aliases to an object.

Creating a Reference

You create a reference by writing the type of the target object, followed by the reference operator (&), followed by the name of the reference. References can use any legal variable name, but for this book we'll prefix all reference names with r. So, if you have an integer variable named someInt, you can make a reference to that variable by writing the following:

```
int &rSomeRef = someInt;
```

This is read as "rSomeRef is a reference to an integer that is initialized to refer to someInt." Listing 11.1 shows how references are created and used.

> The reference operator (&) is the same symbol as the one used for the address of the operator.

LISTING 11.1 Creating and Using References

```
0:  //Listing 11.1
1:  // Creating and Using References
2:  #include <iostream>
3:
4:  int main()
5:  {
6:      int  intOne;
7:      int &rSomeRef = intOne;
8:
9:      intOne = 5;
10:     std::cout << "intOne: " << intOne << std::endl;
11:     std::cout << "rSomeRef: " << rSomeRef << std::endl;
12:
13:     rSomeRef = 7;
14:     std::cout << "intOne: " << intOne << std::endl;
15:     std::cout << "rSomeRef: " << rSomeRef << std::endl;
16:     return 0;
17: }
```

```
intOne: 5
rSomeRef: 5
intOne: 7
rSomeRef: 7
```

ANALYSIS On line 6, a local int variable, intOne, is declared. On line 7, a reference to an int, rSomeRef, is declared and initialized to refer to intOne. If you declare a reference but don't initialize it, you will get a compile-time error. References must be initialized.

On line 9, intOne is assigned the value 5. On lines 10 and 11, the values in intOne and rSomeRef are printed, and are (of course) the same, because rSomeRef is simply the reference to intOne.

On line 13, 7 is assigned to rSomeRef. Because this is a reference, it is an alias for intOne, thus the 7 is really assigned to intOne, as is shown by the display on lines 14 and 15.

Using the Address of Operator on References

If you ask a reference for its address, it returns the address of its target. That is the nature of references—they are aliases for the target. Listing 11.2 demonstrates this.

LISTING 11.2 Taking the Address of a Reference

```
1:  // Demonstrating the use of References
2:  #include <iostream>
3:
4:  int main()
5:  {
6:      int  intOne;
7:      int &rSomeRef = intOne;
8:
9:      intOne = 5;
10:     std::cout << "intOne: " << intOne << std::endl;
11:     std::cout << "rSomeRef: " << rSomeRef << std::endl;
12:
13:     std::cout << "&intOne: "  << &intOne << std::endl;
14:     std::cout << "&rSomeRef: " << &rSomeRef << std::endl;
15:
16:     return 0;
17:  }
```

OUTPUT
```
intOne: 5
rSomeRef: 5
&intOne: 0x0012FF7C
&rSomeRef: 0x0012FF7C
```

ANALYSIS   Once again, rSomeRef is initialized as a reference to intOne. This time the addresses of the two variables are displayed, and they are identical. C++ gives you no way to access the address of the reference itself because it is not meaningful, as it would be if you were using a pointer or other variable. References are initialized when created and always act as a synonym for their target, even when the address of operator is applied.

For example, if you had a class called President, you might declare an instance of that class as follows:

```
President  George_W._Bush;
```

You might then declare a reference to President and initialize it with this object:

```
President &Dubya = George_W._Bush;
```

There is only one President; both identifiers refer to the same object of the same class. Any action you take on Dubya will be taken on George_W._Bush as well.

Be careful to distinguish between the & symbol on line 7 of Listing 11.2, which declares a reference to int named rSomeRef, and the & symbols on lines 13 and 14, which return the addresses of the integer variable intOne and the reference rSomeRef.

Normally, when you use a reference, you do not use the address of operator. You simply use the reference as you would use the target variable. This is shown on line 11.

Even experienced C++ programmers, who know the rule that references cannot be reassigned and are always aliases for their target, can be confused by what happens when you try to reassign a reference. What appears to be a reassignment turns out to be the assignment of a new value to the target. Listing 11.3 illustrates this fact.

LISTING 11.3   Assigning to a Reference

```
0:  //Listing 11.3
1:  //Reassigning a reference
2:  #include <iostream>
3:  using namespace std; // use std:: objects in this file
4:
5:  int main()
6:  {
7:      int  intOne;
8:      int &rSomeRef = intOne;
```

LISTING 11.3 continued

```
 9:
10:        intOne = 5;
11:        cout << "intOne:\t" << intOne << endl;
12:        cout << "rSomeRef:\t" << rSomeRef << endl;
13:        cout << "&intOne:\t"  << &intOne << endl;
14:        cout << "&rSomeRef:\t" << &rSomeRef << endl;
15:
16:        int intTwo = 8;
17:        rSomeRef = intTwo;  // not what you think!
18:        cout << "\nintOne:\t" << intOne << endl;
19:        cout << "intTwo:\t" << intTwo << endl;
20:        cout << "rSomeRef:\t" << rSomeRef << endl;
21:        cout << "&intOne:\t"  << &intOne << endl;
22:        cout << "&intTwo:\t"  << &intTwo << endl;
23:        cout << "&rSomeRef:\t" << &rSomeRef << endl;
24:        return 0;
25:    }
```

OUTPUT

```
intOne:     5
rSomeRef:   5
&intOne:    0x0012FF7C
&rSomeRef:  0x0012FF7C

intOne:     8
intTwo:     8
rSomeRef:   8
&intOne:    0x0012FF7C
&intTwo:    0x0012FF74
&rSomeRef:  0x0012FF7C
```

ANALYSIS Once again, an integer variable and a reference to an integer are declared, on lines 7 and 8. The integer is assigned the value 5 on line 10, and the values and their addresses are printed on lines 11–14.

On line 16 a new variable, intTwo, is created and initialized with the value 8. On line 17 the programmer tries to reassign rSomeRef to now be an alias to the variable intTwo, but that is not what happens. What actually happens is that rSomeRef continues to act as an alias for intOne, so this assignment is exactly equivalent to the following:

```
intOne = intTwo;
```

Sure enough, when the values of intOne and rSomeRef are printed (lines 18–20) they are the same as intTwo. In fact, when the addresses are printed on lines 21–23, you see that rSomeRef continues to refer to intOne and not intTwo.

Do	Don't

DO use references to create an alias to an object.

DO initialize all references.

DON'T try to reassign a reference.

DON'T confuse the address of operator with the reference operator.

What Can Be Referenced?

Any object can be referenced, including user-defined objects. Note that you create a reference to an object, not to a class. You do not write this:

```
int & rIntRef = int;    // wrong
```

You must initialize rIntRef to a particular integer, such as this:

```
int howBig = 200;
int & rIntRef = howBig;
```

In the same way, you don't initialize a reference to a CAT:

```
CAT & rCatRef = CAT;    // wrong
```

You must initialize rCatRef to a particular CAT object:

```
CAT frisky;
CAT & rCatRef = frisky;
```

References to objects are used just like the object itself. Member data and methods are accessed using the normal class member access operator (.), and just as with the built-in types, the reference acts as an alias to the object.

Null Pointers and Null References

When pointers are not initialized, or when they are deleted, they ought to be assigned to null (0). This is not true for references. In fact, a reference cannot be null, and a program with a reference to a null object is considered an invalid program. When a program is invalid, just about anything can happen. It can appear to work, or it can erase all the files on your disk. Both are possible outcomes of an invalid program.

Most compilers will support a null reference without much complaint, crashing only if you try to use the reference in some way. Taking advantage of this, however, is not a good idea. When you move your program to another machine or compiler, mysterious bugs might develop if you have null references.

Passing Function Arguments by Reference

In Hour 5, "Functions," you learned that functions have two limitations: Arguments are passed by value, and the return statement can return only one value.

Passing values to a function by reference can overcome both of these limitations. In C++, passing by reference is accomplished in two ways: using pointers and using references. The syntax is different, but the net effect is the same: Rather than a copy being created within the scope of the function, the actual original object is passed into the function.

Passing an object by reference enables the function to change the object being referred to.

Listing 11.4 creates a swap function and passes in its parameters by value.

LISTING 11.4 Demonstrating Pass by Value

```
0:   //Listing 11.4 Demonstrates passing by value
1:   #include <iostream>
2:
3:   void swap(int x, int y);
4:
5:   int main()
6:   {
7:       int x = 5, y = 10;
8:
9:       std::cout << "Main. Before swap, x: " << x
10:                             << " y: " << y << "\n";
11:      swap(x,y);
12:      std::cout << "Main. After swap, x: " << x
13:                             << " y: " << y << "\n";
14:      return 0;
15:  }
16:
17:  void swap (int x, int y)
18:  {
19:      int temp;
20:
21:      std::cout << "Swap. Before swap, x: " << x
22:                             << " y: " << y << "\n";
23:
24:      temp = x;
25:      x = y;
26:      y = temp;
27:
28:      std::cout << "Swap. After swap, x: " << x
29:                             << " y: " << y << "\n";
30:
31:  }
```

11

OUTPUT Main. Before swap. x: 5 y: 10
Swap. Before swap. x: 5 y: 10
Swap. After swap. x: 10 y: 5
Main. After swap. x: 5 y: 10

ANALYSIS This program initializes two variables in main() and then passes them to the swap() function, which appears to swap them. But when they are examined again in main(), they are unchanged!

The problem here is that x and y are being passed to swap() by value. That is, local copies were made in the function. What you want is to pass x and y by reference.

There are two ways to solve this problem in C++: You can make the parameters of swap() pointers to the original values, or you can pass in references to the original values.

Making swap() Work with Pointers

When you pass in a pointer, you pass in the actual address of the object, and thus the function can manipulate the value at that address. To make swap() change the actual values using pointers, the function, swap(), should be declared to accept two int pointers. Then, by dereferencing the pointers, the values of x and y will, in fact, be swapped. Listing 11.5 demonstrates this idea.

LISTING 11.5   Passing by Reference Using Pointers

```
0:  //Listing 11.5 Demonstrates passing by reference
1:  #include <iostream>
2:
3:  void swap(int *x, int *y);
4:
5:  int main()
6:  {
7:      int x = 5, y = 10;
8:
9:      std::cout << "Main. Before swap, x: " << x
10:                                 << " y: " << y << "\n";
11:     swap(&x,&y);
12:     std::cout << "Main. After swap, x: " << x
13:                                 << " y: " << y << "\n";
14:     return 0;
15: }
16:
17: void swap (int *px, int *py)
18: {
19:     int temp;
20:
```

LISTING 11.5   continued

```
21:        std::cout << "Swap. Before swap, *px: " << *px
22:                              << " *py: " << *py << "\n";
23:
24:        temp = *px;
25:        *px = *py;
26:        *py = temp;
27:
28:        std::cout << "Swap. After swap, *px: " << *px
29:                              << " *py: " << *py << "\n";
30:    }
```

OUTPUT
```
Main. Before swap. x: 5 y: 10
Swap. Before swap. *px: 5 *py: 10
Swap. After swap. *px: 10 *py: 5
Main. After swap. x: 10 y: 5
```

ANALYSIS   Success! On line 3, the prototype of swap() is changed to indicate that its two parameters will be pointers to int rather than int variables. When swap() is called on line 11, the addresses of x and y are passed as the arguments.

On line 19, a local variable, temp, is declared in the swap() function. Temp need not be a pointer; it will just hold the value of *px (that is, the value of x in the calling function) for the life of the function. After the function returns, temp will no longer be needed.

On line 24, temp is assigned the value at px. On line 25, the value at px is assigned to the value at py. On line 26, the value stashed in temp (that is, the original value at px) is put into py.

The net effect of this is that the values in the calling function, whose address was passed to swap(), are in fact swapped.

Implementing swap() with References

The preceding program works, but the syntax of the swap() function is cumbersome in two ways. First, the repeated need to dereference the pointers within the swap() function makes it error-prone and hard to read. Second, the need to pass the address of the variables in the calling function makes the inner workings of swap() overly apparent to its users.

It is a goal of C++ to prevent the user of a function from worrying about how it works. Passing by pointers puts the burden on the calling function which is not where it belongs. The calling function must know to pass in the address of the object it wants to swap.

The burden of understanding the reference semantics should be on the function implementing the swap. To accomplish this, you use references. Listing 11.6 rewrites the swap() function using references. Now the calling function just passes in the object, and because the parameters are declared to be references, the semantics are pass by reference. The calling function doesn't need to do anything special.

LISTING 11.6   swap() Rewritten with References

```
0:  //Listing 11.6 Demonstrates passing by reference
1:  // using references!
2:  #include <iostream>
3:
4:  void swap(int &x, int &y);
5:
6:  int main()
7:  {
8:      int x = 5, y = 10;
9:
10:     std::cout << "Main. Before swap, x: " << x
11:                           << " y: " << y << "\n";
12:     swap(x,y);
13:     std::cout << "Main. After swap, x: " << x
14:                           << " y: " << y << "\n";
15:     return 0;
16: }
17:
18: void swap (int &rx, int &ry)
19: {
20:     int temp;
21:
22:     std::cout << "Swap. Before swap, rx: " << rx
23:                           << " ry: " << ry << "\n";
24:
25:     temp = rx;
26:     rx = ry;
27:     ry = temp;
28:
29:     std::cout << "Swap. After swap, rx: " << rx
30:                           << " ry: " << ry << "\n";
31: }
```

OUTPUT
```
Main. Before swap, x:5 y: 10
Swap. Before swap, rx:5 ry:10
Swap. After swap, rx:10 ry:5
Main. After swap, x:10, y:5
```

ANALYSIS   Just as in the example with pointers, two variables are declared on line 8, and their values are printed on lines 10 and 11. On line 12 the function swap() is called, but note that x and y are passed, not their addresses. The calling function simply passes the variables.

When swap() is called, program execution jumps to line 18, where the variables are identified as references. Their values are printed on lines 22 and 23, but note that no special operators are required. These are aliases for the original values, and can be used as such.

On lines 25–27 the values are swapped, and then they're printed on lines 29 and 30. Program execution jumps back to the calling function, and on lines 13 and 14 the values are printed in main(). Because the parameters to swap() are declared to be references, the values from main() are passed by reference, and thus are changed in main() as well.

References provide the convenience and ease of use of normal variables, with the power and pass-by-reference capability of pointers!

Understanding Function Headers and Prototypes

Listing 11.7 shows swap() using pointers, and Listing 11.8 shows it using references. Using the function that takes references is easier, and the code is easier to read; but how does the calling function know if the values are passed by reference or by value? As a client (or user) of swap(), the programmer must ensure that swap() will in fact change the parameters.

This is another use for the function prototype. By examining the parameters declared in the prototype, which is typically in a header file along with all the other prototypes, the programmer knows that the values passed into swap() are passed by reference, and thus will be swapped properly.

If swap() had been a member function of a class, the class declaration, also available in a header file, would have supplied this information.

In C++, clients of classes (that is any other class's method using the class) rely on the header file to tell all that is needed; it acts as the interface to the class or function. The actual implementation is hidden from the client. This enables the programmer to focus on the problem at hand and to use the class or function without concern for how it is implemented.

Returning Multiple Values

As discussed, functions can only return one value. What if you need to get two values back from a function? One way to solve this problem is to pass two objects into the function, by reference. The function can then fill the objects with the correct values. Because passing by reference enables a function to change the original objects, this effectively lets the function return two pieces of information. This approach bypasses the return value of the function, which can then be reserved for reporting errors.

Once again, this can be done with references or pointers. Listing 11.7 demonstrates a function that returns three values, two as pointer parameters and one as the return value of the function.

LISTING 11.7 Returning Values with Pointers

```
0:  //Listing 11.7
1:  // Returning multiple values from a function
2:  #include <iostream>
3:
4:  short Factor(int, int*, int*);
5:
6:  int main()
7:  {
8:      int number, squared, cubed;
9:      short error;
10:
11:     std::cout << "Enter a number (0 - 20): ";
12:     std::cin >> number;
13:
14:     error = Factor(number, &squared, &cubed);
15:
16:     if (!error)
17:     {
18:         std::cout << "number: " << number << "\n";
19:         std::cout << "square: " << squared << "\n";
20:         std::cout << "cubed: "  << cubed   << "\n";
21:     }
22:     else
23:         std::cout << "Error encountered!!\n";
24:     return 0;
25: }
26:
27: short Factor(int n, int *pSquared, int *pCubed)
28: {
29:     short Value = 0;
30:     if (n > 20)
31:         Value = 1;
32:     else
33:     {
34:         *pSquared = n*n;
35:         *pCubed = n*n*n;
36:         Value = 0;
37:     }
38:     return Value;
39: }
```

OUTPUT

```
Enter a number (0-20): 3
number: 3
square: 9
cubed: 27
```

ANALYSIS On line 8, number, squared, and cubed are defined as int. number is assigned a value based on user input. This number and the addresses of squared and cubed are passed to the function Factor().

Factor() examines the first parameter, which is passed by value. If it is greater than 20 (the maximum value this function can handle), it sets return Value to a simple error value. Note that the return value from Function() is reserved for either this error value or the value 0, indicating all went well; also note that the function returns this value on line 38.

The actual values needed, the square and cube of number, are returned not by using the return mechanism, but rather by changing the values directly using the pointers that were passed into the function.

On lines 34 and 35, the pointers are assigned their return values. On line 36, return Value is assigned a success value. On line 38, return Value is returned.

One improvement to this program might be to declare the following:

```
enum ERROR_VALUE { SUCCESS, FAILURE};
```

Then, rather than returning 0 or 1, the program could return SUCCESS or FAILURE. As you saw earlier, the first enumerated value (SUCCESS) will be given the value 0 and the second will be given the value 1.

Returning Values by Reference

Although Listing 11.7 works, it can be made easier to read and maintain by using references rather than pointers. Listing 11.8 shows the same program rewritten to use references and to incorporate the ERROR enumeration.

LISTING 11.8 Listing 11.7 Rewritten Using References

```
0:  //Listing 11.8
1:  // Returning multiple values from a function
2:  // using references
3:  #include <iostream>
4:
5:  enum ERR_CODE { SUCCESS, ERROR };
6:
7:  ERR_CODE Factor(int, int&, int&);
```

LISTING **11.8**   continued

```
 8:
 9:  int main()
10:  {
11:      int number, squared, cubed;
12:      ERR_CODE result;
13:
14:      std::cout << "Enter a number (0 - 20): ";
15:      std::cin >> number;
16:
17:      result = Factor(number, squared, cubed);
18:
19:      if (result == SUCCESS)
20:      {
21:          std::cout << "number: " << number << "\n";
22:          std::cout << "square: " << squared << "\n";
23:          std::cout << "cubed: "  << cubed   << "\n";
24:      }
25:      else
26:          std::cout << "Error encountered!!\n";
27:      return 0;
28:  }
29:
30:  ERR_CODE Factor(int n, int &rSquared, int &rCubed)
31:  {
32:      if (n > 20)
33:          return ERROR;   // simple error code
34:      else
35:      {
36:          rSquared = n*n;
37:          rCubed = n*n*n;
38:          return SUCCESS;
39:      }
40:  }
```

OUTPUT   Enter a number

```
 (0-20): 3
number: 3
square: 9
cubed: 27
```

ANALYSIS   Listing 11.8 is identical to 11.7, with two exceptions. The ERR_CODE enumeration
            makes the error reporting a bit more explicit on lines 33 and 38, as well as the
error handling on line 19.

The larger change, however, is that Factor() is now declared to take references to
squared and cubed rather than pointers. This makes the manipulation of these parameters far simpler and easier to understand.

Summary

In this hour, you learned what references are and how they compare to pointers. You saw that references must be initialized to refer to an existing object, and cannot be reassigned to refer to anything else. Any action taken on a reference is, in fact, taken on the reference's target object. Proof of this is that taking the address of a reference returns the address of the target.

In this hour you also examined null pointers and null references, and learned why null pointers are useful, but null references are disastrous. You went on to learn about how pass by reference semantics differ from pass by value. Finally, you saw how to use references to return multiple values from function calls.

Q&A

Q Why use references if pointers can do everything references can?

A References are easier to use and understand. The indirection is hidden, and there is no need to repeatedly dereference the variable.

Q Why use pointers if references are easier?

A References cannot be null, and they cannot be reassigned. Pointers offer greater flexibility, but are slightly more difficult to use.

11

Hour **12**

Advanced References and Pointers

In the past three hours, you learned how to use references and pointers. In this hour you'll learn

- How to use pass by reference to make your programs more efficient
- How to decide when to use references and when to use pointers
- How to avoid memory problems when using pointers
- How to avoid the pitfalls of using references

Passing by Reference for Efficiency

Each time you pass an object into a function by value, a copy of the object is made. Each time you return an object from a function by value, another copy is made.

With larger, user-created objects, the cost of these copies is substantial. You'll use more memory than you need to, and ultimately your program will run more slowly.

The size of a user-created object on the stack is the sum of each of its member variables. These, in turn, can each become user-created objects. Passing such a massive structure by copying it onto the stack can be very expensive in terms of performance and memory consumption.

There is another cost as well. With the classes you create, each of these temporary copies is created when the compiler calls a special constructor: the copy constructor. In Hour 13, "Advanced Functions," you will learn how copy constructors work and how you can make your own, but for now it is enough to know that the copy constructor is called each time a temporary copy of the object is put on the stack. When the temporary object is destroyed, which happens when the function returns, the object's destructor is called. If an object is returned by value, a copy of that object must be made and destroyed as well.

With large objects, these constructor and destructor calls can be expensive in speed and use of memory. To illustrate this idea, Listing 12.1 creates a stripped-down, user-created object: SimpleCat. A real object would be larger and more expensive, but this is sufficient to show how often the copy constructor and destructor are called.

Listing 12.1 creates the SimpleCat object and then calls two functions. The first function receives the Cat by value and then returns it by value. The second one takes its argument by reference, meaning it receives a pointer to the object, rather than the object itself, and returns a pointer to the object. Passing by reference avoids creating the copy and calling the copy constructor, and thus is generally more efficient. On the other hand, it also passes the object itself, and thus exposes that object to change in the called function.

LISTING 12.1   Passing Objects by Reference

```
0:  //Listing 12.1
1:  // Passing pointers to objects
2:  #include <iostream>
3:
4:  class SimpleCat
5:  {
6:  public:
7:      SimpleCat ();                    // constructor
8:      SimpleCat(SimpleCat&);    // copy constructor
9:      ~SimpleCat();                    // destructor
10: };
11:
12: SimpleCat::SimpleCat()
13: {
14:     std::cout << "Simple Cat Constructor...\n";
15: }
16:
17: SimpleCat::SimpleCat(SimpleCat&)
```

LISTING 12.1   continued

```
18:  {
19:      std::cout << "Simple Cat Copy Constructor...\n";
20:  }
21:
22:  SimpleCat::~SimpleCat()
23:  {
24:      std::cout << "Simple Cat Destructor...\n";
25:  }
26:
27:  SimpleCat FunctionOne (SimpleCat theCat);
28:  SimpleCat* FunctionTwo (SimpleCat *theCat);
29:
30:  int main()
31:  {
32:      std::cout << "Making a cat...\n";
33:      SimpleCat Frisky;
34:      std::cout << "Calling FunctionOne...\n";
35:      FunctionOne(Frisky);
36:      std::cout << "Calling FunctionTwo...\n";
37:      FunctionTwo(&Frisky);
38:      return 0;
39:  }
40:
41:  // FunctionOne, passes by value
42:  SimpleCat FunctionOne(SimpleCat theCat)
43:  {
44:      std::cout << "Function One. Returning...\n";
45:      return theCat;
46:  }
47:
48:  // functionTwo, passes by reference
49:  SimpleCat* FunctionTwo (SimpleCat  *theCat)
50:  {
51:      std::cout << "Function Two. Returning...\n";
52:      return theCat;
53:  }
```

OUTPUT

```
1:  Making a cat...
2:  Simple Cat Constructor...
3:  Calling FunctionOne...
4:  Simple Cat Copy Constructor...
5:  Function One. Returning...
6:  Simple Cat Copy Constructor...
7:  Simple Cat Destructor...
8:  Simple Cat Destructor...
9:  Calling FunctionTwo...
10: Function Two. Returning...
11: Simple Cat Destructor...
```

12

> The line numbers shown here will not print. They were added to aid in the analysis.

ANALYSIS A very simplified SimpleCat class is declared on lines 4–10. The constructor, copy constructor, and destructor all print an informative message so you can tell when they've been called.

On line 32, main() prints out a message; you can see it on output line 1. On line 33, a SimpleCat object is instantiated. This causes the constructor to be called, and the output from the constructor is shown on output line 2.

On line 34, main() reports that it is calling FunctionOne(), which creates output line 3. Because FunctionOne() is called passing the SimpleCat object by value, a copy of the SimpleCat object is made on the stack as an object local to the called function. This causes the copy constructor to be called, which creates output line 4.

Program execution jumps to line 44 in the called function, which prints an informative message, output line 5. The function then returns, returning the SimpleCat object by value. This creates yet another copy of the object, calling the copy constructor and producing line 6.

The return value from FunctionOne() is not assigned to any object, so the temporary object created for the return is thrown away, calling the destructor, which produces output line 7. Because FunctionOne() has ended, its local copy goes out of scope and is destroyed, calling the destructor and producing line 8.

Program execution returns to main(), and FunctionTwo() is called, but the parameter is passed by reference. No copy is produced, so there's no output. FunctionTwo() prints the message that appears as output line 10 and then returns the SimpleCat object, again by reference, and so again produces no calls to the constructor or destructor.

Finally, the program ends and Frisky goes out of scope, causing one final call to the destructor and printing output line 11.

The net effect of this is that the call to FunctionOne(), because it passed the cat by value, produced two calls to the copy constructor and two to the destructor, although the call to FunctionTwo() produced none.

Passing a const Pointer

Although passing a pointer to FunctionTwo() is more efficient, it is dangerous. FunctionTwo() is not supposed to change the SimpleCat object it is passed, yet it is given the address of the `SimpleCat`. This exposes the object to impermissible change and defeats the protection offered in passing by value.

Passing by value is like giving a museum a photograph of your masterpiece instead of the real thing. If vandals mark it up, there is no harm done to the original. Passing by reference is like sending your home address to the museum and inviting guests to come over and look at the real thing.

If you wish to provide the security of pass by value, and the efficiency of pass by reference, the solution is to pass a `const` pointer to `SimpleCat`. Doing so prevents calling any non-const method on `SimpleCat`, and thus protects the object from change. Listing 12.2 demonstrates this idea.

LISTING 12.2   Passing const Pointers

```
0:  //Listing 12.2
1:  // Passing pointers to objects
2:  #include <iostream>
3:
4:  class SimpleCat
5:  {
6:  public:
7:      SimpleCat();
8:      SimpleCat(SimpleCat&);
9:      ~SimpleCat();
10:
11:     int GetAge() const { return itsAge; }
12:     void SetAge(int age) { itsAge = age; }
13:
14:  private:
15:      int itsAge;
16:  };
17:
18:  SimpleCat::SimpleCat()
19:  {
20:      std::cout << "Simple Cat Constructor...\n";
21:      itsAge = 1;
22:  }
23:
24:  SimpleCat::SimpleCat(SimpleCat&)
25:  {
26:      std::cout << "Simple Cat Copy Constructor...\n";
27:  }
28:
29:  SimpleCat::~SimpleCat()
30:  {
31:      std::cout << "Simple Cat Destructor...\n";
32:  }
```

12

LISTING 12.2   continued

```
33:
34:   const SimpleCat * const
35:   FunctionTwo (const SimpleCat * const theCat);
36:
37:   int main()
38:   {
39:       std::cout << "Making a cat...\n";
40:       SimpleCat Frisky;
41:       std::cout << "Frisky is ";
42:       std::cout << Frisky.GetAge() << " years old\n";
43:       int age = 5;
44:       Frisky.SetAge(age);
45:       std::cout << "Frisky is ";
46:       std::cout << Frisky.GetAge() << " years old\n";
47:       std::cout << "Calling FunctionTwo...\n";
48:       FunctionTwo(&Frisky);
49:       std::cout << "Frisky is ";
50:       std::cout << Frisky.GetAge() << " years old\n";
51:       return 0;
52:   }
53:
54:   // functionTwo, passes a const pointer
55:   const SimpleCat * const
56:   FunctionTwo (const SimpleCat * const theCat)
57:   {
58:       std::cout << "Function Two. Returning...\n";
59:       std::cout << "Frisky is now " << theCat->GetAge();
60:       std::cout << " years old \n";
61:       // theCat->SetAge(8);    const!
62:       return theCat;
63:   }
```

OUTPUT

```
Making a cat...
Simple Cat Constructor...
Frisky is 1 years old
Frisky is 5 years old
Calling FunctionTwo...
Function Two. Returning...
Frisky is now 5 years old
Frisky is 5 years old
Simple Cat Destructor...
```

ANALYSIS   SimpleCat has added two accessor functions: GetAge() on line 11, which is a const function; and SetAge() on line 12, which is not. It has also added the member variable itsAge on line 15.

The constructor, copy constructor, and destructor are still defined to print their messages. The copy constructor is never called, however, because the object is passed by reference (because the object is passed by reference no copies are made). On line 40, an object is created, and its default age is printed on lines 41 and 42.

On line 44, itsAge is set using the accessor SetAge, and the result is printed on lines 45 and 46. FunctionOne() is not used in this program, but FunctionTwo() is called. FunctionTwo() has changed slightly; the parameter and return value are now declared, on lines 34 and 35, to take a constant pointer to a constant object and to return a constant pointer to a constant object.

Because the parameter and return value are still passed by reference, no copies are made and the copy constructor is not called. The pointer in FunctionTwo(), however, is now constant and, thus, cannot call the non-const method, SetAge(). If the call to SetAge() on line 61 were not commented out, the program would not compile.

Note that the object created in main() is not constant, and Frisky can call SetAge(). The address of this non-constant object is passed to FunctionTwo(), but because FunctionTwo()'s declaration declares the pointer to be a constant pointer, the object is treated as if it were constant!

References as an Alternative to Pointers

Listing 12.2 solves the problem of making extra copies and, thus, saves the calls to the copy constructor and destructor. It uses constant pointers to constant objects, thereby solving the problem of the called function making impermissible changes to the objects passed in as parameters. The method is still somewhat cumbersome, however, because the objects passed to the function are pointers.

Because you know the parameters will never be null, it would be easier to work with the function if references were passed in rather than pointers. Listing 12.3 rewrites Listing 12.2 to use references rather than pointers.

Listing 12.3   Passing References to Objects

```
 0:   //Listing 12.3
 1:   // Passing references to objects
 2:   #include <iostream>
 3:
 4:   class SimpleCat
 5:   {
 6:   public:
 7:       SimpleCat();
 8:       SimpleCat(SimpleCat&);
 9:       ~SimpleCat();
10:
```

Listing 12.3 continued

```
11:        int GetAge() const { return itsAge; }
12:        void SetAge(int age) { itsAge = age; }
13:
14:   private:
15:        int itsAge;
16:   };
17:
18:   SimpleCat::SimpleCat()
19:   {
20:        std::cout << "Simple Cat Constructor...\n";
21:        itsAge = 1;
22:   }
23:
24:   SimpleCat::SimpleCat(SimpleCat&)
25:   {
26:        std::cout << "Simple Cat Copy Constructor...\n";
27:   }
28:
29:   SimpleCat::~SimpleCat()
30:   {
31:        std::cout << "Simple Cat Destructor...\n";
32:   }
33:
34:   const SimpleCat & FunctionTwo (const SimpleCat & theCat);
35:
36:   int main()
37:   {
38:        std::cout << "Making a cat...\n";
39:        SimpleCat Frisky;
40:        std::cout << "Frisky is " << Frisky.GetAge()
41:                  << " years old\n";
42:
43:        int age = 5;
44:        Frisky.SetAge(age);
45:        std::cout << "Frisky is " << Frisky.GetAge()
46:                  << " years old\n";
47:
48:        std::cout << "Calling FunctionTwo...\n";
49:        FunctionTwo(Frisky);
50:        std::cout << "Frisky is " << Frisky.GetAge()
51:                  << " years old\n";
52:        return 0;
53:   }
54:
55:   // functionTwo passes a ref to a const object
56:   const SimpleCat & FunctionTwo (const SimpleCat & theCat)
57:   {
58:        std::cout << "Function Two. Returning...\n";
59:        std::cout << "Frisky is now " << theCat.GetAge()
```

Listing 12.3 continued

```
60:                    << " years old \n";
61:        // theCat.SetAge(8);   const!
62:        return theCat;
63:  }
```

OUTPUT

```
Making a cat...
Simple Cat constructor...
Frisky is 1 years old
Frisky is 5 years old
Calling FunctionTwo
FunctionTwo. Returning...
Frisky is now 5 years old
Frisky is 5 years old
Simple Cat Destructor...
```

The output is identical to that produced by Listing 12.2. The only significant change is that FunctionTwo() now takes and returns a reference to a constant object. Once again, working with references is somewhat simpler than working with pointers; and the same savings and efficiency, as well as the safety provided by using const, is achieved.

When to Use References and When to Use Pointers

Generally, C++ programmers strongly prefer references to pointers because they are cleaner and easier to use. References cannot be reassigned, however. If you need to point first to one object and then to another, you must use a pointer. References cannot be null, so if there is any chance that the object in question might be null, you must not use a reference. You must use a pointer.

12

Don't Return a Reference to an Object That Isn't in Scope!

After C++ programmers learn to pass by reference, they have a tendency to go hog-wild. It is possible, however, to overdo it. Remember that a reference is always an alias that refers to some other object. If you pass a reference into or out of a function, be sure to ask yourself, "What is the object I'm aliasing, and will it still exist every time it's used?"

Listing 12.4 illustrates the danger of returning a reference to an object that no longer exists.

Listing 12.4   Returning a Reference to a Nonexistent Object

```
0:  // Listing 12.4
1:  // Returning a reference to an object
2:  // which no longer exists
3:  #include <iostream>
4:
5:  class SimpleCat
6:  {
7:  public:
8:      SimpleCat (int age, int weight);
9:      ~SimpleCat() {}
10:     int GetAge() { return itsAge; }
11:     int GetWeight() { return itsWeight; }
12: private:
13:     int itsAge;
14:     int itsWeight;
15: };
16:
17: SimpleCat::SimpleCat(int age, int weight):
18: itsAge(age), itsWeight(weight) {}
19:
20: SimpleCat &TheFunction();
21:
22: int main()
23: {
24:     SimpleCat &rCat = TheFunction();
25:     int age = rCat.GetAge();
26:     std::cout << "rCat is " << age << " years old!\n";
27:     return 0;
28: }
29:
30: SimpleCat &TheFunction()
31: {
32:     SimpleCat Frisky(5,9);
33:     return Frisky;
34: }
```

OUTPUT   Compile error: Attempting to return a reference to a local object!

> Some compilers are smart enough to see the reference to a null object and
> report a compile error as shown in the output. Other compilers will compile
> and even run; however, it should be noted that this is a bad coding practice
> and you should not take advantage of it when using a compiler that will
> allow you to do this.

ANALYSIS On lines 5–15, `SimpleCat` is declared. On line 24, a reference to `SimpleCat` is initialized with the results of calling `TheFunction()`, which is declared on line 20 to return a reference to a `SimpleCat`.

The body of `TheFunction()` declares a local object of type `SimpleCat` and initializes its age and weight. It then returns that local object by reference. Some compilers are smart enough to catch this error and won't let you run the program. Others will let you run the program, but with unpredictable results. When `TheFunction()` returns, the local object, `Frisky`, will be destroyed (painlessly, I assure you). The reference returned by this function will be to a nonexistent object, and this is a bad thing.

Returning a Reference to an Object on the Heap

You might be tempted to solve the problem in Listing 12.4 by having `TheFunction()` create `Frisky` on the heap. That way, when you return from `TheFunction()`, `Frisky` will still exist.

The problem with this approach is: What do you do with the memory allocated for `Frisky` when you are done with it? Listing 12.5 illustrates this problem.

Listing 12.5 Memory Leaks

```
0:  // Listing 12.5
1:  // Resolving memory leaks
2:  #include <iostream>
3:
4:  class SimpleCat
5:  {
6:  public:
7:      SimpleCat (int age, int weight);
8:      ~SimpleCat() {}
9:      int GetAge() { return itsAge; }
10:     int GetWeight() { return itsWeight; }
11:
12: private:
13:     int itsAge;
14:     int itsWeight;
15: };
16:
17: SimpleCat::SimpleCat(int age, int weight):
18: itsAge(age), itsWeight(weight) {}
19:
20: SimpleCat & TheFunction();
```

12

Listing 12.5   continued

```
21:
22:   int main()
23:   {
24:       SimpleCat & rCat = TheFunction();
25:       int age = rCat.GetAge();
26:       std::cout << "rCat is " << age << " years old!\n";
27:       std::cout << "&rCat: " << &rCat << std::endl;
28:       // How do you get rid of that memory?
29:       SimpleCat * pCat = &rCat;
30:       delete pCat;
31:       // Uh oh, rCat now refers to ??
32:       return 0;
33:   }
34:
35:   SimpleCat &TheFunction()
36:   {
37:       SimpleCat * pFrisky = new SimpleCat(5,9);
38:       std::cout << "pFrisky: " << pFrisky << std::endl;
39:       return *pFrisky;
40:   }
```

OUTPUT
```
pFrisky: 0x00431CA0
rCat is 5 years old!
&rCat: 0x00431CA0
```

> This compiles, links, and appears to work. But it is a time bomb waiting to go off.

ANALYSIS   The function TheFunction() has been changed so that it no longer returns a reference to a local variable. Memory is allocated on the heap and assigned to a pointer on line 37. The address that pointer holds is printed, and then the pointer is dereferenced and the SimpleCat object is returned by reference.

On line 24, the return of TheFunction() is assigned to a reference to a SimpleCat, and that object is used to obtain the cat's age, which is printed on line 26.

To prove that the reference declared in main() is referring to the object put on the heap in TheFunction(), the address of operator is applied to rCat. Sure enough, it displays the address of the object it refers to, and this matches the address of the object on the heap.

So far, so good. But how will that memory be freed? You can't call `delete` on the reference. One clever solution is to create another pointer and initialize it with the address obtained from `rCat`. This does delete the memory and plugs the memory leak. One small problem, though: What is `rCat` referring to after line 31? As stated earlier, a reference must always be an alias for an actual object; if it references a null object (as this does now), the program is invalid.

It cannot be overemphasized that a program with a reference to a null object might compile, but it is invalid and its performance is unpredictable.

There are actually two solutions to this problem. The first is to return a pointer to the memory created on line 37. Then the calling function can delete the pointer when it is done. To do this, change the return value of `TheFunction` to pointer (rather than reference) and return the pointer, rather than the dereferenced pointer:

```
SimpleCat * TheFunction()
{
    SimpleCat * pFrisky = new SimpleCat(5,9);
    std::cout << "pFrisky: " << pFrisky << std::endl;
    return pFrisky;  // return the pointer
}
```

The alternative and more desirable solution is to declare the object in the calling function and then to pass it to `TheFunction()` by reference. The advantage of this alternative is that the function that allocates the memory (the calling function) is also the function that is responsible for de-allocating it, which, as you'll see in the next section, is preferable.

Pointer, Pointer, Who Has the Pointer?

When your program allocates memory on the heap, a pointer is returned. It is imperative that you keep a pointer to that memory, because after the pointer is lost, the memory cannot be deleted and becomes a memory leak.

As you pass this block of memory between functions, one of the functions will "own" the pointer. Typically the value in the block will be passed using references, and the function that created the memory block is the one that deletes it. But this is a general rule, not an ironclad one.

It is dangerous for one function to create space in memory and another to free it, however. Ambiguity about which owns the pointer can lead to one of two problems: forgetting to delete a pointer or deleting it twice. Either one can cause serious problems in your program. It is safer to build your functions so that they delete the memory spaces they created.

If you write a function that needs to create a block of memory and then pass it back to the calling function, consider changing your interface. Have the calling function allocate the memory and then pass it into your function by reference. This moves all memory management out of your program and back to the function that is prepared to delete it.

Do	Don't
DO pass parameters by value when you must.	
DO return by value when you must.	
DON'T pass by reference if the item referred to might go out of scope.	
DON'T use references to null objects.	

Summary

In this hour, you learned that passing objects by reference can be more efficient than passing by value. Passing by reference also enables the called function to change the value in the arguments back in the calling function.

You saw that arguments to functions and values returned from functions can be passed by reference, and that this can be implemented with pointers or with references.

You learned how to use const pointers and const references to safely pass values between functions while achieving the efficiency of passing by reference.

Q&A

Q Why have pointers if references are easier?

A References cannot be null, and they cannot be reassigned. Pointers offer greater flexibility, but are slightly more difficult to use.

Q Why would you ever return by value from a function?

A If the object being returned is local, you must return by value or you will be returning a reference to a nonexistent object.

Q Given the danger in returning by reference, why not always return by value?

A There is far greater efficiency in returning by reference. Memory is saved, and the program runs faster.

PART IV
Power Tools

Hour

Hour 13

Advanced Functions

In Hour 5, "Functions," you learned the fundamentals of working with functions. Now that you know how pointers and references work, there is more you can learn to do with functions. In this hour you will learn the following:

- How to overload member functions
- How to write functions to support classes with dynamically allocated variables

Overloaded Member Functions

In Hour 5, you learned how to implement function polymorphism, or function overloading, by writing two or more functions with the same name but with different parameters. Class member functions can also be overloaded.

The Rectangle class, demonstrated in Listing 13.1, has two DrawShape() functions. One, which takes no parameters, draws the Rectangle based on the class's current values. The other takes two values, a width and a length, and draws the Rectangle based on those values, ignoring the current class values.

LISTING 13.1   An Illustration of Overloading Member Functions

```
0:   //Listing 13.1 Overloading class member functions
1:   #include <iostream>
2:
3:   // Rectangle class declaration
4:   class Rectangle
5:   {
6:   public:
7:       // constructors
8:       Rectangle(int width, int height);
9:       ~Rectangle(){}
10:
11:       // overloaded class function DrawShape
12:       void DrawShape() const;
13:       void DrawShape(int aWidth, int aHeight) const;
14:
15:   private:
16:       int itsWidth;
17:       int itsHeight;
18:   };
19:
20:   //Constructor implementation
21:   Rectangle::Rectangle(int width, int height)
22:   {
23:       itsWidth = width;
24:       itsHeight = height;
25:   }
26:
27:
28:   // Overloaded DrawShape - takes no values
29:   // Draws based on current class member values
30:   void Rectangle::DrawShape() const
31:   {
32:       DrawShape( itsWidth, itsHeight);
33:   }
34:
35:
36:   // overloaded DrawShape - takes two values
37:   // draws shape based on the parameters
38:   void Rectangle::DrawShape(int width, int height) const
39:   {
40:       for (int i = 0; i<height; i++)
41:       {
42:           for (int j = 0; j< width; j++)
43:           {
44:               std::cout << "*";
45:           }
46:           std::cout << "\n";
47:       }
```

LISTING 13.1 continued

```
48:   }
49:
50:   // Driver program to demonstrate overloaded functions
51:   int main()
52:   {
53:       // initialize a rectangle to 30,5
54:       Rectangle theRect(30,5);
55:       std::cout << "DrawShape(): \n";
56:       theRect.DrawShape();
57:       std::cout << "\nDrawShape(40,2): \n";
58:       theRect.DrawShape(40,2);
59:       return 0;
60:   }
```

OUTPUT

```
DrawShape():
*****************************
*****************************
*****************************
*****************************
*****************************

DrawShape(40,2):
*****************************************
*****************************************
```

This listing passes width and height values to several functions. You should note that sometimes width is passed first and, at other times, height is passed first.

ANALYSIS The important code in this listing is on lines 12 and 13, where DrawShape() is overloaded. The implementation for these overloaded class methods is on lines 28–48. Note that the version of DrawShape() that takes no parameters simply calls the version that takes two parameters, passing in the current member variables. Try very hard to avoid duplicating code in two functions. Otherwise, when you make changes to one or the other, keeping the two of them in synch will be difficult and error-prone.

The driver program, on lines 50–60, creates a Rectangle object and then calls DrawShape(), first passing in no parameters and then passing in two integers.

The compiler decides which method to call based on the number and type of parameters entered. You can imagine a third overloaded function named DrawShape() that takes one dimension and an enumeration for whether it is the width or height, at the user's choice.

13

Using Default Values

Just as non-class functions can have one or more default values, so can each member function of a class. The same rules apply for declaring the default values, as illustrated in Listing 13.2.

LISTING 13.2   Using Default Values

```
 0:  //Listing 13.2 Default values in member functions
 1:  #include <iostream>
 2:
 3:  // Rectangle class declaration
 4:  class Rectangle
 5:  {
 6:  public:
 7:      // constructors
 8:      Rectangle(int width, int height);
 9:      ~Rectangle(){}
10:      void DrawShape(int aWidth, int aHeight,
11:      bool UseCurrentVals = false) const;
12:  private:
13:      int itsWidth;
14:      int itsHeight;
15:  };
16:
17:  //Constructor implementation
18:  Rectangle::Rectangle(int width, int height):
19:  itsWidth(width),        // initializations
20:  itsHeight(height)
21:  {}                      // empty body
22:
23:  // default values used for third parameter
24:  void Rectangle::DrawShape(
25:      int width,
26:      int height,
27:      bool UseCurrentValue
28:      ) const
29:  {
30:      int printWidth;
31:      int printHeight;
32:
33:      if (UseCurrentValue == true)
34:      {
35:          printWidth = itsWidth;        // use current class values
36:          printHeight = itsHeight;
37:      }
38:      else
39:      {
40:          printWidth = width;           // use parameter values
```

LISTING 13.2 Using Default Values

```
41:             printHeight = height;
42:         }
43:
44:     for (int i = 0; i<printHeight; i++)
45:     {
46:         for (int j = 0; j< printWidth; j++)
47:         {
48:             std::cout << "*";
49:         }
50:         std::cout << "\n";
51:     }
52: }
53:
54: // Driver program to demonstrate overloaded functions
55: int main()
56: {
57:     // initialize a rectangle to 10,20
58:     Rectangle theRect(30,5);
59:     std::cout << "DrawShape(0,0,true)...\n";
60:     theRect.DrawShape(0,0,true);
61:     std::cout <<"DrawShape(40,2)...\n";
62:     theRect.DrawShape(40,2);
63:     return 0;
64: }
```

OUTPUT

```
DrawShape(0,0,true)...
******************************
******************************
******************************
******************************
******************************

DrawShape(40,2)...
****************************************************************
****************************************************************
```

ANALYSIS Listing 13.2 replaces the overloaded DrawShape() function with a single function with default parameters. The function is declared on lines 10 and 11 to take three parameters. The first two, aWidth and aHeight, are ints; the third, UseCurrentValue, is a bool (true or false) that defaults to false.

ANALYSIS The implementation for this function begins on line 29. The third parameter, UseCurrentValue, is evaluated. If it is true, the member variables itsWidth and itsHeight are used to set the local variables printWidth and printHeight, respectively.

If UseCurrentValue is false, either because it has defaulted false or was set by the user, the first two parameters are used for setting printWidth and printHeight.

13

Note that if `UseCurrentValue` is `true`, the values of the other two parameters are completely ignored.

Choosing Between Default Values and Overloaded Functions

Listings 13.1 and 13.2 accomplish the same thing, but the overloaded functions in 13.1 are simpler to understand and more natural to use. Also, if a third variation is needed—perhaps the user wants to supply either the width or the height, but not both—it is easy to extend the overloaded functions. The default value, however, will quickly become too complex to use as new variations are added.

How do you decide whether to use function overloading or default values? Here's a rule of thumb:

Look to function overloading when

- There is no reasonable default value.
- You need different algorithms.
- You need to support differing types in your parameter list.

Overloading Constructors

Constructors, like all member functions, can be overloaded. The capability to overload constructors is very powerful and very flexible.

For example, you might have a rectangle object that has two constructors: The first takes a length and a width and makes a rectangle of that size. The second takes no values and makes a default-sized rectangle. The compiler chooses the right constructor just as it does any overloaded function: based on the number and type of the parameters.

While you can overload constructors, you *cannot* overload destructors. Destructors, by definition, always have exactly the same signature: the name of the class prepended by a tilde (~) and no parameters.

Initializing Objects

Until now, you've been setting the member variables of objects in the body of the constructor. Constructors, however, are created in two stages: the initialization stage followed by the body of the constructor.

Most variables can be set in either stage, either by initializing in the initialization stage or by assigning in the body of the constructor. It is cleaner and often more efficient to initialize member variables at the initialization stage. The following example shows how to initialize member variables:

```
CAT():          // constructor name and parameters
itsAge(5),      // initialization list
itsWeight(8)
{ }             // body of constructor
```

After the closing parentheses on the constructor's parameter list, put a colon. Then put the name of the member variable and a pair of parentheses. Inside the parentheses, put the expression to be used to initialize that member variable. If there is more than one initialization, separate each one with a comma.

Remember that references and constants *must* be initialized and cannot be assigned to. If you have references or constants as member data, these must be initialized as shown in the initialization list above.

Earlier, I said it is more efficient to initialize member variables rather than to assign to them. To understand this, you must first understand the copy constructor.

The Copy Constructor

In addition to providing a default constructor and destructor, the compiler provides a default copy constructor. The copy constructor is called every time a copy of an object is made.

When you pass an object by value, either into a function or as a function's return value, a temporary copy of that object is made. If the object is a user-defined object, the class's copy constructor is called.

All copy constructors take one parameter: a reference to an object of the same class. It is a good idea to make it a constant reference, because the constructor will not have to alter the object passed in. For example:

```
CAT(const CAT & theCat);
```

Here the CAT constructor takes a constant reference to an existing CAT object. The goal of the copy constructor is to make a copy of theCat.

The default copy constructor simply copies each member variable from the object passed as a parameter to the member variables of the new object. This is called a shallow (or member-wise) copy, and although this is fine for most member variables, it does not work as intended for member variables that are pointers to objects on the heap.

NEW TERM   A *shallow* or member-wise copy copies the exact values of one object's member variables into another object. Pointers in both objects end up pointing to the same memory. A *deep copy*, on the other hand, copies the values allocated on the heap to newly allocated memory.

If the CAT class includes a member variable, itsAge, that points to an integer on the heap, the default copy constructor will copy the passed-in CAT's itsAge member variable to the new CAT's itsAge member variable. The two objects will then point to the same memory, as illustrated in Figure 13.1.

FIGURE 13.1

Using the default copy constructor.

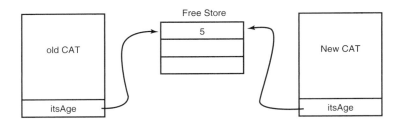

This will lead to a disaster when either CAT goes out of scope. When the object goes out of scope, the destructor is called, and it will attempt to clean up the allocated memory.

In this case, if the original CAT goes out of scope, its destructor will free the allocated memory. The copy will still be pointing to that memory, however, and if it tries to access that memory it will crash your program. Figure 13.2 illustrates this problem.

FIGURE 13.2

Creating a stray pointer.

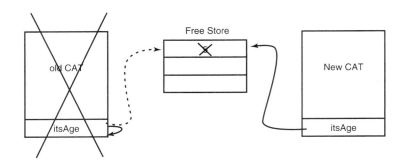

The solution to this problem caused by a shallow copy is to define your own copy constructor and to allocate memory as required in the copy. Creating a deep copy allows you to copy the existing values into new memory. Listing 13.3 illustrates how to do this.

Listing 13.3 Copy Constructors

```
0:    // Listing 13.3
1:    // Copy constructors
2:    #include <iostream>
3:
4:    class CAT
5:    {
6:    public:
7:        CAT();                              // default constructor
8:        CAT (const CAT &);       // copy constructor
9:        ~CAT();                              // destructor
10:       int GetAge() const { return *itsAge; }
11:       int GetWeight() const { return *itsWeight; }
12:       void SetAge(int age) { *itsAge = age; }
13:
14:   private:
15:       int *itsAge;
16:       int *itsWeight;
17:   };
18:
19:   CAT::CAT()
20:   {
21:       itsAge = new int;
22:       itsWeight = new int;
23:       *itsAge = 5;
24:       *itsWeight = 9;
25:   }
26:
27:   CAT::CAT(const CAT & rhs)
28:   {
29:       itsAge = new int;
30:       itsWeight = new int;
31:       *itsAge = rhs.GetAge();
32:       *itsWeight = rhs.GetWeight();
33:   }
34:
35:   CAT::~CAT()
36:   {
37:       delete itsAge;
38:       itsAge = 0;
39:       delete itsWeight;
40:       itsWeight = 0;
41:   }
42:
43:   int main()
44:   {
45:       CAT frisky;
46:       std::cout << "frisky's age: " << frisky.GetAge() << "\n";
47:       std::cout << "Setting frisky to 6...\n";
```

13

Listing 13.3 continued

```
48:        frisky.SetAge(6);
49:        std::cout << "Creating boots from frisky\n";
50:        CAT boots(frisky);
51:        std::cout << "frisky's age: " << frisky.GetAge() << "\n";
52:        std::cout << "boots' age: " << boots.GetAge() << "\n";
53:        std::cout << "setting frisky to 7...\n";
54:        frisky.SetAge(7);
55:        std::cout << "frisky's age: " << frisky.GetAge() << "\n";
56:        std::cout << "boot's age: " << boots.GetAge() << "\n";
57:        return 0;
58:   }
```

OUTPUT

```
frisky's age: 5
Setting frisky to 6...
Creating boots from frisky
frisky's age: 6
boots' age:  6
setting frisky to 7...
frisky's age: 7
boots' age: 6
```

ANALYSIS On lines 4–17, the CAT class is declared. Note that on line 7 a default constructor is declared and on line 8 a copy constructor is declared.

On lines 15 and 16, two member variables are declared, each as a pointer to an integer. Typically, there'd be little reason for a class to store int member variables as pointers, but this was done to illustrate how to manage member variables on the heap.

The default constructor, on lines 19–25, allocates room on the heap for two int variables and then assigns values to them.

The copy constructor begins on line 27. Note that the parameter is rhs. It is common to refer to the parameter to a copy constructor as rhs, which stands for right-hand side. When you look at the assignments in lines 31 and 32, you'll see that the object passed in as a parameter is on the right-hand side of the equal sign. Here's how it works:

- On lines 29 and 30, memory is allocated on the heap. Then, on lines 31 and 32, the value at the new memory location is assigned the values from the existing CAT.

- The parameter rhs is a CAT that is passed into the copy constructor as a constant reference. The member function rhs.GetAge() returns the value stored in the memory pointed to by rhs's member variable itsAge. As a CAT object, rhs has all the member variables of any other CAT.

- When the copy constructor is called to create a new CAT, an existing CAT is passed in as a parameter.

Figure 13.3 diagrams what is happening here. The values pointed to by the existing CAT are copied to the memory allocated for the new CAT.

On line 45, a CAT is created, called frisky. frisky's age is printed, and then his age is set to 6 on line 48. On line 50, a new CAT is created, boots, using the copy constructor and passing in frisky. Had frisky been passed as a parameter to a function, this same call to the copy constructor would have been made by the compiler.

On lines 51 and 52, the ages of both CATs are printed. Sure enough, boots has frisky's age, 6, not the default age of 5. On line 54, frisky's age is set to 7, and then the ages are printed again. This time frisky's age is 7 but boots' age is still 6, demonstrating that they are stored in separate areas of memory.

FIGURE 13.3

An illustration of a deep copy.

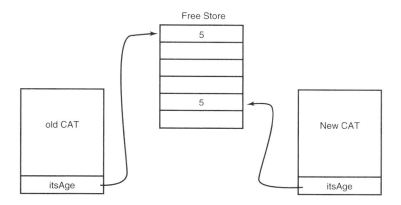

When the CATs fall out of scope, their destructors are automatically invoked. The implementation of the CAT destructor is shown on lines 37–43. delete is called on both pointers, itsAge and itsWeight, returning the allocated memory to the heap. Also, for safety, the pointers are reassigned to NULL.

Summary

In this hour you learned how to overload member functions of your classes. You also learned how to supply default values to functions, how to decide when to use default values, and when to overload.

Overloading class constructors enables you to create flexible classes that can be created from other objects. The initialization of objects happens at the initialization stage of construction, which is more efficient than assigning values in the body of the constructor.

13

The copy constructor is supplied by the compiler if you don't create your own, but it creates a shallow copy of the class. In classes in which member data includes pointers to the heap, this method must be overridden so that you allocate memory for the target object.

Q&A

Q Why would you ever use default values when you can overload a function?

A It is easier to maintain one function than two, and often easier to understand a function with default parameters than to study the bodies of two functions. Furthermore, updating one of the functions and neglecting to update the second is a common source of bugs.

Q Given the problems with overloaded functions, why not always use default values instead?

A Overloaded functions supply capabilities not available with default variables, such as varying the list of parameters by type rather than just by number.

Q When writing a class constructor, how do you decide what to put in the initialization and what to put in the body of the constructor?

A A simple rule of thumb is to do as much as possible in the initialization phase; that is, initialize all member variables there. Some things, like computations and `print` statements, must be in the body of the constructor.

Q Can an overloaded function have a default parameter?

A Yes. There is no reason not to combine these powerful features. One or more of the overloaded functions can have their own default values, following the normal rules for default variables in any function.

HOUR 14

Operator Overloading

In the previous hour you learned how to overload member methods and how to create a copy constructor to provide deep copies. In this hour you will learn

- How to overload member functions
- How to overload the assignment operator to manage memory
- How to write functions to support classes with dynamically allocated variables

Operator Overloading

C++ has a number of built-in types, including int, real, char, and so forth. Each of these has a number of built-in operators, such as addition (+) and multiplication (*). C++ enables you to add these operators to your own classes as well.

In order to explore operator overloading fully, Listing 14.1 creates a new class, Counter. A Counter object will be used in counting (surprise!) in loops and other applications where a number must be incremented, decremented, or otherwise tracked.

Listing 14.1   The Counter Class

```
0:  // Listing 14.1
1:  // The Counter class
2:  #include <iostream>
3:
4:  class Counter
5:  {
6:  public:
7:      Counter();
8:      ~Counter(){}
9:      int GetItsVal()const { return itsVal; }
10:     void SetItsVal(int x) {itsVal = x; }
11:
12: private:
13:     int itsVal;
14: };
15:
16: Counter::Counter():
17: itsVal(0)
18: {}
19:
20: int main()
21: {
22:     Counter i;
23:     std::cout << "The value of i is " << i.GetItsVal()
24:         << std::endl;
25:     return 0;
26: }
```

OUTPUT   The value of i is 0.

ANALYSIS   As it stands, this is a pretty useless class. It is defined on lines 4–14. Its only member variable is an int. The default constructor, which is declared on line 7 and whose implementation is on line 18, initializes the one member variable, itsVal, to 0.

Unlike a real, built-in, honest, red-blooded int, the counter object cannot be incremented, decremented, added, assigned, or otherwise manipulated. In exchange for this, it makes printing its value far more difficult!

Writing an Increment Function

Operator overloading provides much of the functionality that would otherwise be missing in user-defined classes such as Counter. When you implement an operator for your class, you are said to be "overloading" that operator. Listing 14.2 illustrates how to overload the increment operator.

Listing 14.2   Overloading the Increment Operator

```
0:   // Listing 14.2
1:   // Overloading the increment operator
2:   #include <iostream>
3:
4:   class Counter
5:   {
6:   public:
7:       Counter();
8:       ~Counter(){}
9:       int GetItsVal()const { return itsVal; }
10:      void SetItsVal(int x) {itsVal = x; }
11:      void Increment() { ++itsVal; }
12:      const Counter& operator++ ();
13:
14:  private:
15:      int itsVal;
16:  };
17:
18:  Counter::Counter():
19:  itsVal(0)
20:  {}
21:
22:  const Counter& Counter::operator++()
23:  {
24:      ++itsVal;
25:      return *this;
26:  }
27:
28:  int main()
29:  {
30:      Counter i;
31:      std::cout << "The value of i is " << i.GetItsVal()
32:          << std::endl;
33:      i.Increment();
34:      std::cout << "The value of i is " << i.GetItsVal()
35:          << std::endl;
36:      ++i;
37:      std::cout << "The value of i is " << i.GetItsVal()
38:          << std::endl;
39:      Counter a = ++i;
40:      std::cout << "The value of a: " << a.GetItsVal();
41:      std::cout << " and i: " << i.GetItsVal() << std::endl;
42:      return 0;
43:  }
```

14

OUTPUT
```
The value of i is 0
The value of i is 1
The value of i is 2
The value of a: 3 and i: 3
```

On line 36 you can see that the increment operator is invoked

```
++i;
```

This is interpreted by the compiler as a call to the implementation of operator++ shown on lines 22–26, which increments its member variable itsValue and then dereferences the this pointer to return the current object. This provides a Counter object to be assigned to a. If the Counter object allocated memory, it would be important to override the copy constructor. In this case, the default copy constructor works fine.

Note that the value returned is a Counter reference, thereby avoiding the creation of an extra temporary object. It is a const reference because the value should not be changed by the function using this Counter.

Overloading the Postfix Operator

What if you want to overload the postfix increment operator? Here the compiler has a problem. How is it to differentiate between prefix and postfix? By convention, an integer variable is supplied as a parameter to the operator declaration. The parameter's value is ignored; it is just a signal that this is the postfix operator.

The Difference Between Prefix and Postfix

Before you can write the postfix operator, you must understand how it is different from the prefix operator. To review, prefix says *increment and then fetch* while postfix says *fetch and then increment*.

Therefore, while the prefix operator can simply increment the value and then return the object itself, the postfix must return the value that existed *before* it was incremented. To do this, a temporary object must be created. This temporary object will hold the original value while the value of the original object is incremented. The temporary object is returned, however, because the postfix operator asks for the *original* value, not the incremented value.

Let's go over that again. If you write

```
a = x++;
```

Then x is 5, after this statement a is 5, but x is 6. The value in x is returned and assigned to a, which increases the value of x. If x is an object, its postfix increment operator must stash away the original value (5) in a temporary object, increment x's value to 6, and then return that temporary object to assign its value to a.

Note that because the temporary object is being returned, it must be returned by value and not by reference, because it will go out of scope as soon as the function returns.

Listing 14.3 demonstrates the use of both the prefix and the postfix operators.

Listing 14.3   Prefix and Postfix Operators

```
0:  // Listing 14.3
1:  // Returning the dereferenced this pointer
2:  #include <iostream>
3:
4:  class Counter
5:  {
6:  public:
7:      Counter();
8:      ~Counter(){}
9:      int GetItsVal()const { return itsVal; }
10:     void SetItsVal(int x) {itsVal = x; }
11:     const Counter& operator++ ();      // prefix
12:     const Counter operator++ (int); // postfix
13:
14: private:
15:     int itsVal;
16: };
17:
18: Counter::Counter():
19: itsVal(0)
20: {}
21:
22: const Counter& Counter::operator++()
23: {
24:     ++itsVal;
25:     return *this;
26: }
27:
28: const Counter Counter::operator++(int)
29: {
30:     Counter temp(*this);
31:     ++itsVal;
32:     return temp;
33: }
34:
35: int main()
36: {
37:     Counter i;
38:     std::cout << "The value of i is " << i.GetItsVal()
39:         << std::endl;
40:     i++;
41:     std::cout << "The value of i is " << i.GetItsVal()
42:         << std::endl;
43:     ++i;
44:     std::cout << "The value of i is " << i.GetItsVal()
45:         << std::endl;
```

14

Listing 14.3   continued

```
46:        Counter a = ++i;
47:        std::cout << "The value of a: " << a.GetItsVal();
48:        std::cout << " and i: " << i.GetItsVal() << std::endl;
49:        a = i++;
50:        std::cout << "The value of a: " << a.GetItsVal();
51:        std::cout << " and i: " << i.GetItsVal() << std::endl;
52:        return 0;
53:    }
```

OUTPUT

```
The value of i is 0
The value of i is 1
The value of i is 2
The value of a: 3 and i: 3
The value of a: 4 and i: 4
```

ANALYSIS   The postfix operator is declared on line 12 and implemented on lines 28–33. Note that the call to the prefix operator on line 43 does not include the flag integer (x), but is used with its normal syntax. The postfix operator uses a flag value (x) to signal that it is the postfix and not the prefix. The flag value (x) is never used, however.

operator+

NEW TERM   The Increment operator is a *unary* operator, which means that it takes only one term. The addition operator (+) is a binary operator; two terms are used by the addition operator (a+b). How do you implement overloading the + operator for Count?

The goal is to be able to declare two Counter variables and then add them, as in this example:

```
Counter varOne, varTwo, varThree;
VarThree = VarOne + VarTwo;
```

Once again, you could start by writing a function, Add(), that would take a Counter as its argument, add the values, and then return a Counter with the result. Listing 14.4 illustrates this approach.

Listing 14.4   The Add() Function

```
0:  // Listing 14.4
1:  // Add function
2:  #include <iostream>
3:
4:  class Counter
5:  {
6:  public:
```

Listing 14.4 continued

```
7:          Counter();
8:          Counter(int initialValue);
9:          ~Counter(){}
10:         int GetItsVal()const { return itsVal; }
11:         void SetItsVal(int x) {itsVal = x; }
12:         Counter Add(const Counter &);
13:
14:  private:
15:         int itsVal;
16:
17:  };
18:
19:  Counter::Counter(int initialValue):
20:  itsVal(initialValue)
21:  {}
22:
23:  Counter::Counter():
24:  itsVal(0)
25:  {}
26:
27:  Counter Counter::Add(const Counter & rhs)
28:  {
29:         return Counter(itsVal+ rhs.GetItsVal());
30:  }
31:
32:  int main()
33:  {
34:         Counter varOne(2), varTwo(4), varThree;
35:         varThree = varOne.Add(varTwo);
36:         std::cout << "varOne: " << varOne.GetItsVal()<< std::endl;
37:         std::cout << "varTwo: " << varTwo.GetItsVal() << std::endl;
38:         std::cout << "varThree: " << varThree.GetItsVal()
39:             << std::endl;
40:         return 0;
41:  }
```

OUTPUT

```
varOne: 2
varTwo: 4
varThree: 6
```

ANALYSIS The Add() function is declared on line 12. It takes a constant Counter reference, which is the number to add to the current object. It returns a Counter object, which is the result to be assigned to the left side of the assignment statement, as shown on line 35. That is: varOne is the object, varTwo is the parameter to the Add() function, and the result is assigned to varThree.

14

In order to create varThree without having to initialize a value for it, a default constructor is required. The default constructor initializes itsVal to 0, as shown on lines 23–25. Because varOne and varTwo need to be initialized to a non-zero value, another constructor is created, as shown on lines 19–21. Another solution to this problem is to provide the default value 0 to the constructor declared on line 8.

Overloading operator+

The Add() function itself is shown on lines 29–32. It works, but its use is unnatural. Overloading the operator + is a more natural use of the Counter class. Listing 14.5 illustrates this.

Listing 14.5   Operator+

```
0:  // Listing 14.5
1:  //Overload operator plus (+)
2:  #include <iostream>
3:
4:  class Counter
5:  {
6:  public:
7:      Counter();
8:      Counter(int initialValue);
9:      ~Counter(){}
10:     int GetItsVal()const { return itsVal; }
11:     void SetItsVal(int x) {itsVal = x; }
12:     Counter operator+ (const Counter &);
13: private:
14:     int itsVal;
15: };
16:
17: Counter::Counter(int initialValue):
18: itsVal(initialValue)
19: {}
20:
21: Counter::Counter():
22: itsVal(0)
23: {}
24:
25: Counter Counter::operator+ (const Counter & rhs)
26: {
27:     return Counter(itsVal + rhs.GetItsVal());
28: }
29:
30: int main()
31: {
32:     Counter varOne(2), varTwo(4), varThree;
33:     varThree = varOne + varTwo;
```

LISTING 14.5   continued

```
34:        std::cout << "varOne: " << varOne.GetItsVal()<< std::endl;
35:        std::cout << "varTwo: " << varTwo.GetItsVal() << std::endl;
36:        std::cout << "varThree: " << varThree.GetItsVal()
37:            << std::endl;
38:        return 0;
39:    }
```

OUTPUT
```
varOne: 2
varTwo: 4
varThree: 6
```

ANALYSIS   When the addition operator is invoked on line 33

```
varThree = varOne + varTwo;
```

the compiler interprets this as if you had written

```
varThree = varOne.operator+(varTwo);
```

and invokes the `operator+` method declared on line 12 and defined on lines 25–28. Compare these with the declaration and definition of the `Add()` function in the previous listing; they are nearly identical. The syntax of their use, however, is quite different. It is more natural to say this:

```
varThree = varOne + varTwo;
```

than it is to say this:

```
varThree = varOne.Add(varTwo);
```

Not a big change, but enough to make the program easier to use and understand.

Limitations on Operator Overloading

NEW TERM   Operators on built-in types (such as `int`) cannot be overloaded. The precedence order cannot be changed, and the *arity* of the operator, that is whether it is unary, binary, or trinary cannot be changed. You cannot make up new operators, so you cannot declare `**` to be the "power of" operator.

What to Overload

Operator overloading is one of the aspects of C++ most overused and abused by new programmers. It is tempting to create new and interesting uses for some of the more obscure operators, but these invariably lead to code that is confusing and difficult to read.

Of course, making the + operator subtract and the * operator add can be fun, but no pro-

14

fessional programmer would do that. The greater danger lies in the well-intentioned but idiosyncratic use of an operator—using + to mean concatenate a series of letters, or / to mean split a string. There is good reason to consider these uses, but there is even better reason to proceed with caution. Remember, the goal of overloading operators is to increase usability and understanding.

operator=

Remember that the compiler provides a default constructor, destructor, and copy constructor. The fourth and final function that is supplied by the compiler, if you don't specify one, is the assignment operator (operator=()).

This operator is called whenever you assign to an object. For example:

```
CAT catOne(5,7);
CAT catTwo(3,4);
// ... other code here
catTwo = catOne;
```

Here, catOne is created and in the constructor, the parameters (5,7) will be used to initialize the member variables itsAge and itsWeight respectively. catTwo is then created, assigned, and initialized with the values 3 and 4. Finally, you see the assignment operator (operator =)

```
catTwo = catOne;
```

The result of this assignment is that catTwo's itsAge and itsWeight values are assigned the values from catOne. Thus, after this statement executes, catTwo.itsAge will have the value 5 and catTwo.itsWeight will have the value 7.

Note, in this case the copy constructor is not called. catTwo already exists; there is no need to construct it, and so the compiler is smart enough to call the assignment operator.

In Hour 13, "Advanced Functions," I discussed the difference between a shallow (member-wise) copy and a deep copy. A shallow copy just copies the members, and both objects end up pointing to the same area on the heap. A deep copy allocates the necessary memory. You saw an illustration of the default copy constructor in Figure 13.1; refer back to that figure if you need to refresh your memory.

You see the same issue here with assignment as you did with the copy constructor. There is an added wrinkle with the assignment operator, however. The object catTwo already exists and already has memory allocated. That memory must be deleted if there is to be no memory leak. So the first thing you must do when implementing the assignment operator is delete the memory assigned to its pointers. But what happens if you assign catTwo to itself, like this:

```
catTwo = catTwo;
```

No one is likely to do this on purpose, but the program must be able to handle it. More important, it is possible for this to happen by accident when references and dereferenced pointers hide the fact that the object's assignment is to itself.

If you did not handle this problem carefully, catTwo would delete its own memory allocation. Then, when it was ready to copy in the memory from the right-hand side of the assignment, it would have a very big problem: The memory would be gone.

To protect against this, your assignment operator must check to see if the right-hand side of the assignment operator is the object itself. It does this by examining the this pointer. Listing 14.6 shows a class with an assignment operator.

Listing 14.6 An Assignment Operator

```
0:  // Listing 14.6
1:  // Copy constructors
2:  #include <iostream>
3:
4:  class CAT
5:  {
6:  public:
7:      CAT(); // default constructor
8:      // copy constructor and destructor elided!
9:      int GetAge() const { return *itsAge; }
10:     int GetWeight() const { return *itsWeight; }
11:     void SetAge(int age) { *itsAge = age; }
12:     CAT operator=(const CAT &);
13:
14: private:
15:     int *itsAge;
16:     int *itsWeight;
17: };
18:
19: CAT::CAT()
20: {
21:     itsAge = new int;
22:     itsWeight = new int;
23:     *itsAge = 5;
24:     *itsWeight = 9;
25: }
26:
```

14

Listing 14.6   continued

```
27:
28:   CAT CAT::operator=(const CAT & rhs)
29:   {
30:       if (this == &rhs)
31:           return *this;
32:       delete itsAge;
33:       delete itsWeight;
34:       itsAge = new int;
35:       itsWeight = new int;
36:       *itsAge = rhs.GetAge();
37:       *itsWeight = rhs.GetWeight();
38:       return *this;
39:   }
40:
41:
42:   int main()
43:   {
44:       CAT frisky;
45:       std::cout << "frisky's age: " << frisky.GetAge()
46:           << std::endl;
47:       std::cout << "Setting frisky to 6...\n";
48:       frisky.SetAge(6);
49:       CAT whiskers;
50:       std::cout << "whiskers' age: " << whiskers.GetAge()
51:           << std::endl;
52:       std::cout << "copying frisky to whiskers...\n";
53:       whiskers = frisky;
54:       std::cout << "whiskers' age: " << whiskers.GetAge()
55:           << std::endl;
56:       return 0;
57:   }
```

OUTPUT

```
frisky's age: 5
Setting frisky to 6;
whiskers' age: 5
copying frisky to whiskers...
whiskers' age: 6
```

Listing 14.6 brings back the CAT class, and leaves out the copy constructor and destructor to save room. On line 12, the assignment operator is declared, and on lines 28–39, it is defined.

On line 30, the current object (the CAT being assigned to) is tested to see if it is the same as the CAT being assigned. This is done by checking if the address of rhs is the same as the address stored in the this pointer.

Of course, the equality operator (==) can be overloaded as well, enabling you to determine for yourself what it means for your objects to be equal.

> On lines 32–35 the member variables are deleted and then re-created on the heap. While this is not strictly necessary, it is good, clean programming practice and will save you from memory leaks when working with variable length objects that do not overload their assignment operator.

Conversion Operators

What happens when you try to assign a variable of a built-in type, such as int or unsigned short, to an object of a user-defined class? Listing 14.7 brings back the Counter class and attempts to assign a variable of type int to a Counter object.

> Listing 14.7 will not compile!

Listing 14.7   Attempting to Assign a Counter to an int

```
0:   // Listing 14.7
1:   // This code won't compile!
2:   #include <iostream>
3:
4:   class Counter
5:   {
6:   public:
7:       Counter();
8:       ~Counter(){}
9:       int GetItsVal()const { return itsVal; }
10:      void SetItsVal(int x) {itsVal = x; }
11:  private:
12:      int itsVal;
13:  };
14:
15:  Counter::Counter():
16:  itsVal(0)
17:  {}
18:
19:  int main()
20:  {
21:      int theShort = 5;
22:      Counter theCtr = theShort;
```

14

Listing 14.7   continued

```
23:        std::cout << "theCtr: " << theCtr.GetItsVal()
24:            << std::endl;
25:        return 0;
26:   }
```

OUTPUT   Compiler error! Unable to convert int to Counter

ANALYSIS   The Counter class declared on lines 4–13 has only a default constructor. It declares no particular method for turning an int into a Counter object, so line 22 causes a compile error. The compiler cannot figure out, unless you tell it, that given an int it should assign that value to the member variable itsVal.

Listing 14.8 corrects this by creating a conversion operator: a constructor that takes an int and produces a Counter object.

Listing 14.8   Converting int to Counter

```
0:   // Listing 14.8
1:   // Constructor as conversion operator
2:   #include <iostream>
3:
4:   class Counter
5:   {
6:   public:
7:       Counter();
8:       Counter(int val);
9:       ~Counter(){}
10:      int GetItsVal()const { return itsVal; }
11:      void SetItsVal(int x) {itsVal = x; }
12:  private:
13:      int itsVal;
14:  };
15:
16:  Counter::Counter():
17:  itsVal(0)
18:  {}
19:
20:  Counter::Counter(int val):
21:  itsVal(val)
22:  {}
23:
24:  int main()
25:  {
26:      int theShort = 5;
27:      Counter theCtr = theShort;
```

Listing 14.8   continued

```
28:        std::cout << "theCtr: " << theCtr.GetItsVal() << std::endl;
29:        return 0;
30:    }
```

OUTPUT   theCtr: 5

The important change is on line 8, where the constructor is overloaded to take an `int`, and on lines 20–22, where the constructor is implemented. The effect of this constructor is to create a `Counter` out of an `int`.

Given this, the compiler is able to call the constructor that takes an `int` as its argument. What happens, however, if you try to reverse the assignment with the following:

```
1:   Counter theCtr(5);
2:   int theShort = theCtr;
3:   cout << "theShort : " << theShort  << endl;
```

Once again, this will generate a compile error. Although the compiler now knows how to create a `Counter` out of an `int`, it does not know how to reverse the process.

The `int()` Operator

To solve the problem of creating an `int` from a `Counter`, and similar problems, C++ provides conversion operators that can be added to your class. These conversion operators enable your class to specify how to do implicit conversions to built-in types. Listing 14.9 illustrates this. One note, however: Conversion operators do not specify a return value, even though they do, in effect, return a converted value.

Listing 14.9   Converting from `Counter` to `int()`

```
0:   // Listing 14.9
1:   // conversion operator
2:   #include <iostream>
3:
4:   class Counter
5:   {
6:   public:
7:       Counter();
8:       Counter(int val);
9:       ~Counter(){}
10:      int GetItsVal()const { return itsVal; }
11:      void SetItsVal(int x) {itsVal = x; }
12:      operator unsigned short();
13:   private:
14:       int itsVal;
```

14

Listing 14.9   continued

```
15:  };
16:
17:  Counter::Counter():
18:  itsVal(0)
19:  {}
20:
21:  Counter::Counter(int val):
22:  itsVal(val)
23:  {}
24:
25:  Counter::operator unsigned short ()
26:  {
27:      return ( int (itsVal) );
28:  }
29:
30:  int main()
31:  {
32:      Counter ctr(5);
33:      int theShort = ctr;
34:      std::cout << "theShort: " << theShort << std::endl;
35:      return 0;
36:  }
```

OUTPUT   theShort: 5

ANALYSIS   On line 12 the conversion operator is declared. Note that it has no return value. The implementation of this function is on lines 25–28. Line 27 returns the value of itsVal converted to an int.

Now the compiler knows how to turn ints into Counter objects and vice versa, and they can be assigned to one another freely.

Summary

In this hour you learned about operator overloading.

The copy constructor and operator= are supplied by the compiler if you don't create your own, but they create a shallow copy of the class. In classes in which member data includes pointers to the heap, methods must be overridden so that you allocate memory for the target object.

Almost all C++ operators can be overloaded, although you want to be cautious not to create operators whose use is counterintuitive. You cannot change the arity of operators, nor can you invent new operators.

The `this` pointer refers to the current object and is an invisible parameter to all member functions. The dereferenced `this` pointer is often returned by overloaded operators.

Conversion operators enable you to create classes that can be used in expressions that expect a different type of object. They are exceptions to the rule that all functions return an explicit value; like constructors and destructors, they have no return type.

Q&A

Q Why would you overload an operator when you can just create a member method?

A It is easier to use overloaded operators when their behavior is well understood. It enables your class to mimic the functionality of the built-in types.

Q What is the difference between the copy constructor and the assignment operator?

A The copy constructor creates a *new* object with the same values as an existing object. The assignment operator changes an *existing* object so that it has the same values as another object.

Q What happens to the `int` used in the postfix operators?

A Nothing. That `int` is never used except as a flag to overload the postfix and prefix operators.

14

Hour 15

Arrays

In previous chapters, you declared a single `int`, `char`, or other object. You often want to declare a collection of objects, such as 20 `ints` or a litter of `CAT`s. In this hour, you learn

- What arrays are and how to declare them
- What strings are and how to use character arrays to make them
- The relationship between arrays and pointers
- How to use pointer arithmetic with arrays

What Is an Array?

NEW TERM An *array* is a collection of objects, all of the same type. An array can be envisioned as a series of data storage locations; each storage location is called an element of the array.

NEW TERM You declare an array by writing the type, followed by the array name, a left brace, the subscript, and a right brace. The *subscript* is the number of elements in the array surrounded by square brackets. For example,

```
long LongArray[25];
```

declares an array of 25 long integers, named LongArray. When the compiler sees this declaration, it sets aside enough memory to hold all 25 elements. Because each long integer requires 4 bytes, this declaration sets aside 100 contiguous bytes of memory, as illustrated in Figure 15.1.

FIGURE 15.1
Declaring an array.

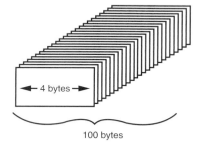

Array Elements

You access each of the array elements by referring to an offset from the array name followed by subscript within the braces. Array elements are counted from 0; therefore, the first array element is arrayName[0]. In the LongArray example, LongArray[0] is the first array element, LongArray[1] the second, and so forth.

This can be somewhat confusing. The array SomeArray[3] has three elements: SomeArray[0], SomeArray[1], and SomeArray[2]. More Generally, SomeArray[n] has n elements that are numbered SomeArray[0] through SomeArray[n-1].

Therefore, LongArray[25] is numbered from LongArray[0] through LongArray[24]. Listing 15.1 shows how to declare an array of five integers and fill each with a value.

LISTING 15.1   Using an Integer Array

```
0:  //Listing 15.1 - Arrays
1:  #include <iostream>
2:
3:  int main()
4:  {
5:      int myArray[5];
6:      for (int i=0; i<5; i++)   // 0-4
7:      {
8:          std::cout << "Value for myArray[" << i << "]: ";
9:          std::cin >> myArray[i];
10:     }
11:     for (int i = 0; i<5; i++)
12:         std::cout << i << ": " << myArray[i] << "\n";
13:     return 0;
14: }
```

```
Value for myArray[0]:   3
Value for myArray[1]:   6
Value for myArray[2]:   9
Value for myArray[3]:   12
Value for myArray[4]:   15

0: 3
1: 6
2: 9
3: 12
4: 15
```

ANALYSIS Line 5 declares an array called `myArray`, which holds five integer variables. Line 6 establishes a loop that counts from 0 through 4, which is the proper set of offsets for a five-element array. The user is prompted for a value, and that value is saved at the correct element of the array.

The first value is saved at `myArray[0]`, the second at `myArray[1]`, and so forth. The second `for` loop prints each value to the screen.

> Arrays count from 0, not from 1. This is the cause of many bugs in programs written by C++ novices. Whenever you use an array, remember that an array with 10 elements counts from `ArrayName[0]` to `ArrayName[9]`. There is no `ArrayName[10]`.

Writing Past the End of an Array

When you write a value to an element in an array, the compiler computes where to store the value based on the size of each element and the subscript. Suppose that you ask to write over the value at `LongArray[5]`, which is the sixth element. The compiler multiplies the offset—5—by the size of each element—in this case, 4. It then moves that many bytes—20—from the beginning of the array and writes the new value at that location.

If you ask to write at `LongArray[50]`, the compiler ignores the fact that there is no such element. It computes how far past the first element it should be—200 bytes—and then writes over whatever is at that location. This can be virtually any data, and writing your new value there might have unpredictable results. If you're lucky, your program will crash immediately. If you're unlucky, you'll get strange results much later in your program, and you'll have a difficult time figuring out what went wrong.

The compiler is like a blind man pacing off the distance from a house. He starts out at the first house, `MainStreet[0]`. When you ask him to go to the sixth house on Main

Street, he says to himself, "I must go five more houses. Each house is four big paces. I must go an additional 20 steps." If you ask him to go to MainStreet[100], and Main Street is only 25 houses long, he will pace off 400 steps. Long before he gets there, he will, no doubt, step in front of a moving bus. So be careful where you send him.

Fence Post Errors

It is so common to write to one element past the end of an array that this bug has its own name. It is called a *fence post error*. This refers to the problem of counting how many fence posts you need for a 10-foot fence if you need one post for every foot. Most people answer 10, but of course you need 11. Figure 15.2 makes this clear.

FIGURE 15.2
Fence post errors.

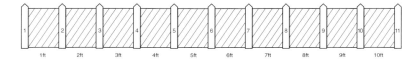

This sort of "off by one" counting can be the bane of any programmer's life. Over time, however, you'll get used to the idea that a 25-element array counts only to element 24, and that everything counts from 0. (Programmers are often confused why office buildings don't have a floor zero. Indeed, some have been known to push the 4 elevator button when they want to get to the fifth floor.)

Initializing Arrays

You can initialize a simple array of built-in types, such as integers and characters, when you first declare the array. After the array name, you put an equal sign (=) and a list of comma-separated values enclosed in braces. For example,

```
int IntegerArray[5] = { 10, 20, 30, 40, 50 };
```

declares IntegerArray to be an array of five integers. It assigns IntegerArray[0] the value 10, IntegerArray[1] the value 20, and so forth.

If you omit the size of the array, an array just big enough to hold the initialization is created. Therefore, if you write

```
int IntegerArray[] = { 10, 20, 30, 40, 50 };
```

you will create exactly the same array as you did in the previous example.

If you need to know the size of the array, you can use the `sizeof()` function to calculate it. For example,

```
const int IntegerArrayLength =
sizeof(IntegerArray)/sizeof(IntegerArray[0]);
```

sets the constant `int` variable `IntegerArrayLength` to the result obtained from dividing the size of the entire array by the size of an individual element in the array. That quotient is the number of members in the array.

You cannot initialize more elements than you've declared for the array. Therefore,

```
int IntegerArray[5] = { 10, 20, 30, 40, 50, 60};
```

generates a compiler error because you've declared a five-member array and initialized six values. It is legal, however, to write

```
int IntegerArray[5] = { 10, 20};
```

Arrays of Objects

Any object, whether built-in or user defined, can be stored in an array. When you declare the array, you tell the compiler the type of object to store and the number of objects for which to allocate room. The compiler knows how much room is needed for each object based on the class declaration. The class must have a default constructor that takes no arguments so that the objects can be created when the array is defined.

> Remember that the default constructor is *not* the constructor provided by the compiler, but rather is a constructor with no parameters that is either created by the compiler or created by the programmer.

Accessing member data in an array of objects is a two-step process. You identify the member of the array by using the index operator (`[ ]`), and then you add the member operator (`.`) to access the particular member variable. Listing 15.2 demonstrates how you would create an array of five CATs.

LISTING 15.2 Creating an Array of Objects

```
0:   // Listing 15.2 - An array of objects
1:   #include <iostream>
2:
```

LISTING 15.2 continued

```
 3:   class CAT
 4:   {
 5:   public:
 6:       CAT() { itsAge = 1; itsWeight=5; } // default constructor
 7:       ~CAT() {}                          // destructor
 8:       int GetAge() const { return itsAge; }
 9:       int GetWeight() const { return itsWeight; }
10:       void SetAge(int age) { itsAge = age; }
11:
12:   private:
13:       int itsAge;
14:       int itsWeight;
15:   };
16:
17:   int main()
18:   {
19:       CAT Litter[5];
20:       int i;
21:       for (i = 0; i < 5; i++)
22:           Litter[i].SetAge(2*i +1);
23:
24:       for (i = 0; i < 5; i++)
25:           std::cout << "Cat #" << i+1<< ": "
26:               << Litter[i].GetAge() << std::endl;
27:       return 0;
28:   }
```

OUTPUT

```
cat #1: 1
cat #2: 3
cat #3: 5
cat #4: 7
cat #5: 9
```

ANALYSIS Lines 3–15 declare the CAT class. The CAT class must have a default constructor so that CAT objects can be created in an array. The default constructor is on line 6. Remember that if you create any other constructor, the compiler-supplied default constructor is not created; you must create your own.

The first for loop (lines 21 and 22) sets the age of each of the five CATs in the array. The second for loop (lines 24–26) accesses each member of the array and calls GetAge().

Each individual CAT's GetAge() method is called by accessing the member in the array, Litter[i], followed by the dot operator (.) and the member function.

Multidimensional Arrays

An array can be thought of as a row of data. You can imagine a grid of data, with rows and columns. This is a two-dimensional array of data, with one dimension representing each row and the second dimension representing each column. A three-dimensional array would be a cube, with one dimension representing width, a second dimension representing height, and a third dimension representing depth. You can even have arrays of more than three dimensions, though they are harder to imagine as objects in space.

When you declare arrays, each dimension is represented as a subscript in the array. Therefore, a two-dimensional array has two subscripts, a three-dimensional array has three subscripts, and so on. Arrays can have any number of dimensions, although it is likely that most of the arrays you create will have one or two dimensions.

A good example of a two-dimensional array is a chessboard. One dimension represents the eight rows; other dimension represents the eight columns. Figure 15.3 illustrates this idea.

FIGURE 15.3

A chessboard and a two-dimensional array.

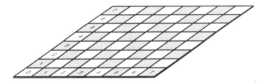

Suppose that you have a class named SQUARE. The declaration of an array named Board that represents it would be

```
SQUARE Board[8][8];
```

You could also represent the same data with a one-dimensional, 64-square array. For example:

```
SQUARE Board[64]
```

This doesn't correspond as closely to the real-world object as the two-dimensional array, however. When the game begins, the king is located in the fourth position in the first row. Counting from zero, that position corresponds to

```
Board[0][3];
```

assuming that the first subscript corresponds to row, and the second to column. The layout of positions for the entire board is illustrated in Figure 15.3.

Initializing Multidimensional Arrays

You can initialize multidimensional arrays. You assign the list of values to array elements in order, with the last array subscript changing and each of the former ones holding steady. Therefore, if you have an array

```
int theArray[5][3]
```

the first three elements go into theArray[0], the next three into theArray[1], and so forth.

You initialize this array by writing

```
int theArray[5][3] = { 1,2,3,4,5,6,7,8,9,10,11,12,13,14,15 }
```

For the sake of clarity, you could group the initializations with braces. For example:

```
int theArray[5][3] = {  {1,2,3},
{4,5,6},
{7,8,9},
{10,11,12},
{13,14,15} };
```

The compiler ignores the inner braces, which just make it easier for the programmer to understand how the numbers are distributed.

Each value must be separated by a comma, without regard to the braces. The entire initialization set must be within braces, and it must end with a semicolon.

Listing 15.3 creates a two-dimensional array. The first dimension is the set of numbers from 0 to 4. However, unlike the previous example, the values are set so the second dimension consists of the double of each value in the first dimension.

LISTING **15.3**   Creating a Multidimensional Array

```
0:  // Listing 15.3 - Creating A Multidimensional Array
1:  #include <iostream>
2:
3:  int main()
4:  {
5:      int SomeArray[5][2] = { {0,0}, {1,2}, {2,4}, {3,6}, {4,8}};
6:      for (int i = 0; i<5; i++)
7:          for (int j=0; j<2; j++)
8:              {
9:                  std::cout << "SomeArray[" << i << "][" << j << "]: ";
```

LISTING 15.3   continued

```
10:                std::cout << SomeArray[i][j]<< std::endl;
11:          }
12:     return 0;
13: }
```

OUTPUT
```
SomeArray[0][0]: 0
SomeArray[0][1]: 0
SomeArray[1][0]: 1
SomeArray[1][1]: 2
SomeArray[2][0]: 2
SomeArray[2][1]: 4
SomeArray[3][0]: 3
SomeArray[3][1]: 6
SomeArray[4][0]: 4
SomeArray[4][1]: 8
```

ANALYSIS   Line 5 declares SomeArray to be a two-dimensional array. The first dimension consists of five integers; the second dimension consists of two integers. This creates a 5×2 grid, as Figure 15.4 shows.

FIGURE 15.4
A 5×2 array.

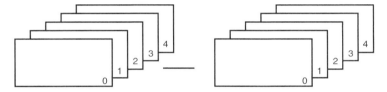

Some Array [5] [2]

The values are initialized in pairs, although they could be computed as well. Lines 6 and 7 create a nested for loop. The outer for loop ticks through each member of the first dimension. For every member in that dimension, the inner for loop ticks through each member of the second dimension. This is consistent with the printout; SomeArray[0][0] is followed by SomeArray[0][1]. The first dimension is incremented only after the second dimension is incremented by 1. Then the second dimension starts over.

A Word About Memory

When you declare an array, you tell the compiler exactly how many objects you expect to store in it. The compiler sets aside memory for all the objects, even if you never need to use it. This isn't a problem with arrays for which you can estimate how many objects you'll need. For example, a chessboard has 64 squares, and CATs generally have between

1 and 10 kittens. When you have no idea of how many objects you'll need, however, you must use more advanced data structures.

This book looks at arrays of pointers, arrays built on the heap, and various other collections. More advanced data structures that solve large data-storage problems are beyond the scope of this book. Two great things about programming are that there are always more things to learn and that there are always more books from which to learn.

Arrays of Pointers

The arrays discussed so far store all their members on the stack. Usually stack memory is severely limited, whereas heap memory is far larger. It is possible to declare each object on the heap and then to store only a pointer to the object in the array. This dramatically reduces the amount of stack memory used. Listing 15.4 rewrites the array from Listing 11.4, but it stores all the objects on the heap. As an indication of the greater memory that this makes possible, the array is expanded from 5 to 500, and the name is changed from Litter to Family.

LISTING 15.4   Storing an Array on the Heap

```
0:   // Listing 15.4 - An array of pointers to objects
1:   #include <iostream>
2:
3:   class CAT
4:   {
5:   public:
6:       CAT() { itsAge = 1; itsWeight=5; } // default constructor
7:       ~CAT() {}                          // destructor
8:       int GetAge() const { return itsAge; }
9:       int GetWeight() const { return itsWeight; }
10:      void SetAge(int age) { itsAge = age; }
11:
12:  private:
13:      int itsAge;
14:      int itsWeight;
15:  };
16:
17:  int main()
18:  {
19:      CAT * Family[500];
20:      int i;
21:      CAT * pCat;
22:      for (i = 0; i < 500; i++)
```

LISTING 15.4 continued

```
23:     {
24:         pCat = new CAT;
25:         pCat->SetAge(2*i +1);
26:         Family[i] = pCat;
27:     }
28:
29:     for (i = 0; i < 500; i++)
30:         std::cout << "Cat #" << i+1 << ": "
31:             << Family[i]->GetAge() << std::endl;
32:
33:     for (i = 0; i < 500; i++)
34:     {
35:         delete Family[i];
36:         Family[i] = NULL;
37:     }
38:
39:     return 0;
40: }
```

OUTPUT

```
Cat #1: 1
Cat #2: 3
Cat #3: 5
...
Cat #499: 997
Cat #500: 999
```

ANALYSIS The CAT object declared in lines 3–15 is identical to the CAT object declared in Listing 15.3. This time, however, the array declared in line 19 is named Family, and it is declared to hold 500 pointers to CAT objects.

In the initial loop (lines 22–27), 500 new CAT objects are created on the heap, and each one has its age set to twice the index plus one. Therefore, the first CAT is set to 1, the second CAT to 3, the third CAT to 5, and so on. Finally, the pointer is added to the array.

Because the array has been declared to hold pointers, the pointer—rather than the dereferenced value in the pointer—is added to the array.

The second loop (lines 29–31) prints each of the values. The pointer is accessed by using the index, Family[i]. That address is then used to access the GetAge() method.

In this example, the array Family and all its pointers are stored on the stack, but the 500 CATs that are created are stored on the heap.

The third loop deletes the CATs from the heap and sets all elements of Family to null.

Declaring Arrays on the Heap

It is possible to put the entire array on the heap, also known as the *heap*. You do this by calling new and using the subscript operator. The result is a pointer to an area on the heap that holds the array. For example:

```
CAT *Family = new CAT[500];
```

declares Family to be a pointer to the first in an array of 500 CATs. In other words, Family points to—or has the address of—Family[0].

The advantage of using Family in this way is that you can use pointer arithmetic to access each member of Family. For example, you can write

```
CAT *Family = new CAT[500];
CAT *pCat = Family;              // pCat points to Family[0]
pCat->SetAge(10);               // set Family[0] to 10
pCat++;                         // advance to Family[1]
pCat->SetAge(20);               // set Family[1] to 20
```

This declares a new array of 500 CATs and a pointer to point to the start of the array. Using that pointer, the first CAT's SetAge() function is called with the value 10. The pointer is then incremented to point to the next CAT, and the second CAT's SetAge() method is then called.

A Pointer to an Array Versus an Array of Pointers

Examine these three declarations:

```
1:  Cat    FamilyOne[500]
2:  CAT * FamilyTwo[500];
3:  CAT * FamilyThree = new CAT[500];
```

FamilyOne is an array of 500 CATs. FamilyTwo is an array of 500 pointers to CATs. FamilyThree is a pointer to an array of 500 CATs.

The differences among these three code lines dramatically affect how these arrays operate. What is perhaps even more surprising is that FamilyThree is a variant of FamilyOne, but it is very different from FamilyTwo.

This raises the thorny issue of how pointers relate to arrays. FamilyThree is a pointer to an array. That is, the address in the pointer FamilyThree is the address of the first item in that array. This is exactly the case for FamilyOne; it is the actual address for the pointer FamilyThree.

Pointers and Array Names

In C++ an array name is a constant pointer to the first element of the array. Therefore, in the declaration

```
CAT Family[50];
```

Family is a pointer to &Family[0], which is the address of the first element of the array Family.

It is legal to use array names as constant pointers, and vice versa. Therefore, Family + 4 is a legitimate way of accessing the data at Family[4].

The compiler does all the arithmetic when you add to, increment, and decrement pointers. The address accessed when you write Family + 4 isn't 4 bytes past the address of Family—it is four objects past it. If each object is 4 bytes long, Family + 4 is 16 bytes. If each object is a CAT that has four long member variables of 4 bytes each and two short member variables of 2 bytes each, each CAT is 20 bytes, and Family + 4 is 80 bytes past the start of the array.

Listing 15.5 illustrates declaring and using an array on the heap.

LISTING 15.5   Creating an Array by Using new

```
0:  // Listing 15.5 - An array on the heap
1:  #include <iostream>
2:
3:  class CAT
4:  {
5:  public:
6:      CAT() { itsAge = 1; itsWeight=5; }      // default constructor
7:      ~CAT();                                  // destructor
8:      int GetAge() const { return itsAge; }
9:      int GetWeight() const { return itsWeight; }
10:     void SetAge(int age) { itsAge = age; }
11:
12: private:
13:     int itsAge;
14:     int itsWeight;
15: };
16:
17: CAT :: ~CAT()
18: {
19: //  std::cout << "Destructor called!\n";
20: }
21:
22: int main()
23: {
```

LISTING 15.5   continued

```
24:        CAT * Family = new CAT[500];
25:        int i;
26:        CAT * pCat;
27:        for (i = 0; i < 500; i++)
28:        {
29:            pCat = new CAT;
30:            pCat->SetAge(2*i +1);
31:            Family[i] = *pCat;
32:            delete pCat;
33:        }
34:
35:        for (i = 0; i < 500; i++)
36:            std::cout << "Cat #" << i+1 << ": "
37:                << Family[i].GetAge() << std::endl;
38:
39:        delete [] Family;
40:
41:        return 0;
42:    }
```

```
Cat #1: 1
Cat #2: 3
Cat #3: 5
...
Cat #499: 997
Cat #500: 999
```

   Line 24 declares the array `Family`, which holds 500 CAT objects. The entire array is created on the heap with the call to new `CAT[500]`.

> Technically, line 24 declares an unnamed array on the heap and returns the address of its first element to the pointer Family. It is customary to refer to that pointer as the array itself. In fact, whenever you declare an array (even on the stack) the array name is really just a pointer to the first element.

Each CAT object added to the array also is created on the heap (line 29). Note, however, that the pointer isn't added to the array this time; the object itself is. This array isn't an array of pointers to CATs—it is an array of CATs.

Deleting Arrays on the Heap

`Family` is a pointer—a pointer to the new CAT array on the heap. When, on line 33, the pointer pCat is dereferenced, the CAT object itself is stored in the array. (Why not? The array is on the heap.) But pCat is used again in the next iteration of the loop. Isn't there a danger that there is now no pointer to that CAT object, and a memory leak is created?

This would be a big problem, except that deleting Family returns all the memory set aside for the array. The compiler is smart enough to destroy each object in the array and to return its memory to the heap.

To see this, change the size of the array from 500 to 10 in lines 24, 27, and 35. Then uncomment the cout statement in line 19. When line 39 is reached and the array is destroyed, each CAT object destructor is called.

When you create an item on the heap by using new, you always delete that item and free its memory with delete[] followed by the name of the array. Similarly, when you create an array by using new <class>[size], you delete that array and free all its memory with delete[] <class>. The empty brackets signal to the compiler that this entire array is being deleted.

If you leave the brackets off, only the first object in the array will be deleted. You can prove this to yourself by removing the brackets on line 39. If you edited line 21 so that the destructor prints, you should then see only one CAT object destroyed. Congratulations! You just created a memory leak.

Do	**Don't**
DO remember that an array of *n* items is numbered from 0 through *n*–1. **DO** use array indexing with pointers that point to arrays. **DON'T** write or read past the end of an array. **DON'T** confuse an array of pointers with a pointer to an array.	

char Arrays

 A *string* is a series of characters. The only strings you've seen until now have been unnamed string constants used in cout statements, such as

```
cout << "hello world.\n";
```

In C++, a string is an array of chars ending with a null character. You can declare and initialize a string just as you would any other array. For example:

```
char Greeting[] = { 'H', 'e', 'l', 'l', 'o', ' ',
'W','o','r','l','d', '\0' };
```

The last character, '\0', is the null character, which many C++ functions recognize as the terminator for a string. Although this character-by-character approach works, it is difficult to type and admits too many opportunities for error. C++ enables you to use a shorthand form of the previous line of code:

```
char Greeting[] = "Hello World";
```

You should note two things about this syntax:

- Instead of single quoted characters separated by commas and surrounded by braces, you have a double-quoted string, no commas, and no braces.
- You don't need to add the null character because the compiler adds it for you.

The string Hello World is 12 bytes: Hello is 5 bytes, the space is 1, World is 5, and the null character is 1 byte.

You can also create uninitialized character arrays, often referred to as a buffer. As with all arrays, it is important to ensure that you don't put more into the buffer than there is room for.

Listing 15.6 demonstrates the use of an uninitialized buffer.

LISTING 15.6   Filling an Array

```
 0:   //Listing 15.6 char array buffers
 1:   #include <iostream>
 2:
 3:   int main()
 4:   {
 5:       char buffer[80];
 6:       std::cout << "Enter the string: ";
 7:       std::cin >> buffer;
 8:       std::cout << "Here's the buffer:  " << buffer << std::endl;
 9:       return 0;
10:   }
```

OUTPUT
```
Enter the string: Hello World
Here's the buffer: Hello
```

ANALYSIS On line 5 a buffer is declared to hold 80 characters. This is large enough to hold a 79-character string and a terminating null character.

On line 6 the user is prompted to enter a string, which is entered into the buffer on line 7. cin writes a terminating null to the buffer automatically after it writes the string.

There are two problems with the program in Listing 15.6. First, if the user enters more than 79 characters, cin writes past the end of the buffer. Second, if the user enters a space, cin thinks that it is the end of the string, and it stops writing to the buffer.

To solve these problems, you must call a special method on `cin`: `get()`. `Cin.get()` takes three parameters:

- The buffer to fill
- The maximum number of characters to get
- The delimiter that terminates input

The default delimiter is `newline`. Listing 15.7 illustrates its use.

LISTING 15.7   Filling an Array

```
 0:   //Listing 15.7 using cin.get()
 1:   #include <iostream>
 2:
 3:   int main()
 4:   {
 5:       char buffer[80];
 6:       std::cout << "Enter the string: ";
 7:       std::cin.get(buffer, 79);       // get up to 79 or newline
 8:       std::cout << "Here's the buffer:  " << buffer << std::endl;
 9:       return 0;
10:   }
```

OUTPUT
```
Enter the string: Hello World
Here's the buffer: Hello World
```

ANALYSIS Line 7 calls the method `get()` of `cin`. The buffer declared in line 5 is passed in as the first argument. The second argument is the maximum number of characters to get. In this case, it must be 79 to allow for the terminating `null`. There is no need to provide a terminating character because the default value of `newline` is sufficient. `cin` and all its variations are covered in Hour 21, "The Preprocessor."

strcpy() and strncpy()

C++ inherits from C a library of functions for dealing with strings. Among the many functions provided are two for copying one string into another: `strcpy()` and `strncpy()`. `strcpy()` copies the entire contents of one string into a designated buffer. Listing 15.8 demonstrates its use.

LISTING 15.8   Using `strcpy()`

```
 0:   // Listing 15.8 - Using strcpy()
 1:   #include <iostream>
 2:   #include <string.h>
```

LISTING 15.8   continued

```
 3:
 4:  int main()
 5:  {
 6:      char String1[] = "No man is an island";
 7:      char String2[80];
 8:
 9:      strcpy(String2,String1);
10:
11:      std::cout << "String1: " << String1 << std::endl;
12:      std::cout << "String2: " << String2 << std::endl;
13:      return 0;
14:  }
```

OUTPUT String1: No man is an island
String2: No man is an island

ANALYSIS The header file STRING.H is included in line 2. This file contains the prototype of the strcpy() function. strcpy() takes two character arrays—a destination followed by a source. If the source were larger than the destination, strcpy() would overwrite past the end of the buffer.

To protect against this, the standard library also includes strncpy(). This variation allows you to enter the maximum number of characters to copy. strncpy() copies up to the first null character or the maximum number of characters specified into the destination buffer.

Listing 15.9 illustrates the use of strncpy().

LISTING 15.9   Using strncpy()

```
 0:  // Listing 15.9 Using strncpy()
 1:  #include <iostream>
 2:  #include <string.h>
 3:
 4:  int main()
 5:  {
 6:      const int MaxLength = 80;
 7:      char String1[] = "No man is an island";
 8:      char String2[MaxLength+1];
 9:
10:      strncpy(String2,String1,MaxLength);
11:      String2[strlen(String1)] = '\0'; // add a null to the end
12:      std::cout << "String1: " << String1 << std::endl;
13:      std::cout << "String2: " << String2 << std::endl;
14:      return 0;
15:  }
```

OUTPUT
```
String1: No man is an island
String2: No man is an island
```

ANALYSIS In line 10, the call to strcpy() has been changed to a call to strncpy(), which takes a third parameter: the maximum number of characters to copy. The buffer String2 is declared to take MaxLength+1 characters. The extra character is for the null, which must terminate the string.

String Classes

Most C++ compilers come with a class library that includes a large set of classes for data manipulation. A standard component of a class library is a String class.

C++ inherited the null-terminated string and the library of functions that includes strcpy() from C, but these functions aren't integrated into an object-oriented framework. A String class provides an encapsulated set of data and functions for manipulating that data, as well as accessor functions so that the data itself is hidden from the clients of the String class.

If you are not using the compiler that came with this book, the compiler you are using might not provide a String class; and perhaps even if it does, you might want to write your own.

At a minimum, a String class should overcome the basic limitations of character arrays. Like all arrays, character arrays are static. You define how large they are. They always take up that much room in memory, even if you don't need it all. Writing past the end of the array is disastrous.

A good String class allocates only as much memory as it needs and always enough to hold whatever it is given. If it can't allocate enough memory, it should fail gracefully.

Summary

In this hour, you learned how to create arrays in C++. An array is a fixed-size collection of objects that are all the same type.

Arrays don't do bounds checking. Therefore, it is legal—even if disastrous—to read or write past the end of an array. Arrays count from 0. A common mistake is to write to offset n of an array of n members.

Arrays can be one-dimensional or multidimensional. In either case, the members of the array can be initialized, as long as the array contains either built-in types, such as int, or objects of a class that has a default constructor.

Arrays and their contents can be on the heap or on the stack. If you want to delete an array on the heap, remember to use the brackets in the call to delete or you will only delete the first element, not the entire array.

Array names are constant pointers to the first elements of the array. Pointers and arrays use pointer arithmetic to find the next element of an array.

Strings are arrays of characters, or chars. C++ provides special features for managing char arrays, including the capability to initialize them with quoted strings.

Q&A

Q What happens if I write to element 25 in a 24-member array?

A You will write to other memory, with potentially disastrous effects on your program.

Q What is in an uninitialized array element?

A An array element that has not been assigned a value. The value is whatever happens to be in memory at a given time. The results of using this member without assigning a value are unpredictable.

Q Can I combine arrays?

A Yes. With simple arrays you can use pointers to combine them into a new, larger array. With strings you can use some of the built-in functions, such as strcat, to combine strings.

PART V

Inheritance and Polymorphism

Hour

Hour **16**

Inheritance

It is a fundamental aspect of human intelligence to seek out, recognize, and create relationships among concepts. We build hierarchies, matrices, networks, and other interrelationships to explain and understand the ways in which things interact. C++ attempts to capture this in inheritance hierarchies. In this hour, you will learn

- What inheritance is
- How to derive one class from another
- What protected access is and how to use it

What Is Inheritance?

What is a dog? When you look at your pet, what do you see? A biologist sees a network of interacting organs; a physicist sees atoms and forces at work; a taxonomist sees a representative of the species canine *domesticus*; and my mother sees dog hair and saliva.

It is the taxonomist's perspective that interests us at the moment (sorry, Mom). To a taxonomist, a dog is a canine. A canine is a kind of mammal.

A mammal is a kind of animal, and so forth. Taxonomists divide the world of living things into kingdom, phyla, class, order, family, genus, and species. You can remember this by remembering that King Philip Came Over From Great Spain. I'm not sure why this is easier, who King Philip was, why he came over, or where exactly Great Spain is; but that's what my ninth-grade teacher told me, and I've remembered it ever since.

The taxonomist's hierarchy establishes an *is-a* relationship. A dog is a canine. We see the *is-a* relationships everywhere: A Toyota is a kind of car, which is a kind of vehicle. A sundae is a kind of dessert, which is a kind of food.

What exactly do we mean when we say something is a kind of something else? We mean that it is a specialization of that thing. That is, a car is a special kind of vehicle. Cars and buses are both vehicles. They are distinguished by their specific characteristics of car-ness or bus-ness, but to the extent that they are vehicles they are identical. Their vehicle-ness is shared.

Inheritance and Derivation

The concept *dog* inherits (automatically gets) all the features of a mammal. Because it is a mammal, we know that it moves and that it breathes air—by definition all mammals move and breathe air. The concept of a dog adds the idea of barking, a wagging tail, and so forth, to that definition. The dog-ness is specialized, but the mammal-ness is universal to all mammals.

We can further divide dogs into hunting dogs and terriers; we can divide terriers into Yorkshire Terriers, Dandie Dinmont Terriers, and so forth.

A Yorkshire Terrier is a kind of terrier; therefore, it is a kind of dog; therefore, a kind of mammal; therefore, a kind of animal; and, therefore, a kind of living thing. This hierarchy is represented in Figure 16.1.

C++ attempts to represent these relationships by defining classes that derive from one another. Derivation is a way of expressing the *is-a* relationship. You derive a new class, Dog, from the class Mammal. You don't have to state explicitly that dogs move because they inherit that from Mammal. Because it derives from Mammal, Dog *automatically* moves.

A class that adds new functionality to an existing class is said to *derive* from that original class. The original class is said to be the new class's *base class*.

If the Dog class derives from the Mammal class, then Mammal is a base class of Dog. Derived classes are supersets of their base classes. Just as dog adds certain features to the idea of a mammal, the Dog class will add certain methods or data to the Mammal class.

Typically, a base class will have more than one derived class. Just as dogs, cats, and horses are all types of mammals, their classes would all derive from the Mammal class.

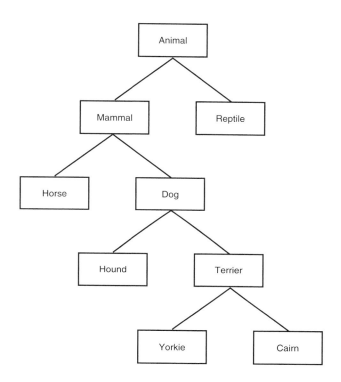

FIGURE 16.1
Hierarchy of animals.

The Animal Kingdom

To facilitate the discussion of derivation and inheritance, this chapter focuses on the relationships among a number of classes representing animals. You can imagine that you have been asked to design a children's game—a simulation of a farm.

In time, you will develop a whole set of farm animals, including horses, cows, dogs, cats, sheep, and so forth. You will create methods for these classes so that they can act in the ways the child might expect, but for now you'll stub out each method with a simple `print` statement.

NEW TERM *Stubbing out* a function means you'll write only enough to show that the function was called, leaving the details for later when you have more time. I've been stubbing out functions for years, just saving up for that glorious day when I have more time.

Please feel free to extend the minimal code provided in this chapter to enable the animals to act more realistically (when you have more time…).

The Syntax of Derivation

When you declare a class, you indicate what class it derives from by writing a colon after the class name, the type of derivation (public or otherwise), and the class from which it derives. For now, always use `public`. The following is an example:

```
class Dog : public Mammal
```

The type of derivation is discussed later in this chapter. The class from which you derive must already be declared, or you will get a compiler error. Listing 16.1 illustrates how to declare a `Dog` class that is derived from a `Mammal` class.

Listing 16.1   Simple Inheritance

```
0:   //Listing 16.1 Simple inheritance
1:   #include <iostream>
2:
3:   enum BREED { YORKIE, CAIRN, DANDIE, SHETLAND, DOBERMAN, LAB };
4:
5:   class Mammal
6:   {
7:   public:
8:       // constructors
9:       Mammal();
10:      ~Mammal();
11:
12:      // accessors
13:      int GetAge() const;
14:      void SetAge(int);
15:      int GetWeight() const;
16:      void SetWeight();
17:
18:      // Other methods
19:      void Speak();
20:      void Sleep();
21:
22:
23:   protected:
24:       int itsAge;
25:       int itsWeight;
26:   };
27:
28:   class Dog : public Mammal
29:   {
30:   public:
31:       // Constructors
32:       Dog();
33:       ~Dog();
```

Listing 16.1   continued

```
34:
35:        // Accessors
36:        BREED GetBreed() const;
37:        void SetBreed(BREED);
38:
39:        // Other methods
40:        // WagTail();
41:        // BegForFood();
42:
43:   protected:
44:        BREED itsBreed;
45:   };
46: int main()
47: {
48:        return 0;
   }
```

This program has no output because it is only a set of class declarations without their implementations. Nonetheless, there is much to see here.

ANALYSIS On lines 5–26, the Mammal class is declared. Note that in this example, Mammal does not derive from any other class. In the real world, mammals do derive—that is, mammals are kinds of animals. In a C++ program you can represent only a fraction of the information you have about any given object. Reality is far too complex for a program to capture all of it, so every C++ hierarchy is an arbitrary representation of the data available. The trick of a good design is to represent the areas that you care about in a way that maps back to reality in a reasonably faithful way.

The hierarchy has to begin somewhere; this program begins with Mammal. Because of this decision, some member variables that might properly belong in a higher base class are now represented here. For example, certainly all animals have an age and weight; so if Mammal derived from Animal, we might expect it to inherit those attributes. As it is, the attributes appear in the Mammal class.

To keep the program reasonably simple and manageable, only six methods have been put in the Mammal class—four accessor methods, Speak(), and Sleep().

The Dog class inherits from Mammal, as indicated on line 28. Every Dog object will have three member variables: itsAge, itsWeight, and itsBreed. Note that the class declaration for Dog does not include the member variables itsAge and itsWeight. Dog objects inherit these variables from the Mammal class, along with all Mammal's methods except the copy operator, the constructors, and the destructor.

Private Versus Protected

You may have noticed that a new access keyword, protected, has been introduced on lines 23 and 43 of Listing 16.1. Previously, class data had been declared private. However, private members are not available to derived classes. You could make itsAge and itsWeight public, but that is not desirable. You don't want other classes accessing these data members directly.

What you want is a designation that says, "Make these visible to this class and to classes that derive from this class." That designation is protected. Protected data members and functions are fully visible to derived classes, but are otherwise private.

There are, in total, three access specifiers: public, protected, and private. If a function has an instance of a class, it can access all of the public member data and functions of that class. The member functions of a class, however, can access all the private data members and functions of any class from which they derive.

Therefore, the function Dog::WagTail() can access the private data itsBreed and can access the protected data in the Mammal class.

Even if other classes are layered between Mammal and Dog (for example, DomesticAnimals), the Dog class will still be able to access the protected members of Mammal, assuming that these other classes all use public inheritance.

Listing 16.2 demonstrates how to create objects of type Dog and access the data and functions of that type.

Listing 16.2   Using a Derived Object

```
 0:  //Listing 16.2 Using a derived object
 1:  #include <iostream>
 2:
 3:  enum BREED { YORKIE, CAIRN, DANDIE, SHETLAND, DOBERMAN, LAB };
 4:
 5:  class Mammal
 6:  {
 7:  public:
 8:      // constructors
 9:      Mammal():itsAge(2), itsWeight(5){}
10:      ~Mammal(){}
11:
12:      //accessors
13:      int GetAge()const { return itsAge; }
14:      void SetAge(int age) { itsAge = age; }
15:      int GetWeight() const { return itsWeight; }
16:      void SetWeight(int weight) { itsWeight = weight; }
17:
18:      //Other methods
```

Listing 16.2   continued

```
19:        void Speak()const { std::cout << "Mammal sound!\n"; }
20:        void Sleep()const { std::cout << "shhh. I'm sleeping.\n"; }
21:
22:
23:    protected:
24:        int itsAge;
25:        int itsWeight;
26:    };
27:
28:    class Dog : public Mammal
29:    {
30:    public:
31:        // Constructors
32:        Dog():itsBreed(YORKIE){}
33:        ~Dog(){}
34:
35:        // Accessors
36:        BREED GetBreed() const { return itsBreed; }
37:        void SetBreed(BREED breed) { itsBreed = breed; }
38:
39:        // Other methods
40:        void WagTail() { std::cout << "Tail wagging...\n"; }
41:        void BegForFood() { std::cout << "Begging for food...\n"; }
42:
43:    private:
44:        BREED itsBreed;
45:    };
46:
47:    int main()
48:    {
49:        Dog fido;
50:        fido.Speak();
51:        fido.WagTail();
52:        std::cout << "Fido is " << fido.GetAge() << " years old\n";
53:        return 0;
54:    }
```

OUTPUT
```
Mammal sound!
Tail wagging...
Fido is 2 years old
```

ANALYSIS   On lines 5–26, the Mammal class is declared (all its functions are inline to save space here). On lines 28–45, the Dog class is declared as a derived class of Mammal. Thus, by these declarations, all Dogs have an age, a weight, and a breed.

On line 49 a Dog is declared, Fido. Fido inherits all the attributes of a Mammal, as well as all the attributes of a Dog. Thus Fido knows how to WagTail(), but also knows how to Speak() and Sleep().

Constructors and Destructors

Dog objects are `Mammal` objects. This is the essence of the *is-a* relationship. When `Fido` is created, his base constructor is called first, creating a `Mammal`. Then the `Dog` constructor is called, completing the construction of the `Dog` object. Because we gave `Fido` no parameters, the default constructor was called in each case. `Fido` doesn't exist until he is completely constructed, which means that both his `Mammal` part and his `Dog` part must be constructed. Thus, both constructors must be called.

When `Fido` is destroyed, first the `Dog` destructor will be called and then the destructor for the `Mammal` part of `Fido`. Each destructor is given an opportunity to clean up after its own part of `Fido`. Remember to clean up after your `Dog`! Listing 16.3 demonstrates this.

Listing 16.3 Constructors and Destructors Called

```
0:    //Listing 16.3 Constructors and destructors called.
1:    #include <iostream>
2:
3:    enum BREED { YORKIE, CAIRN, DANDIE, SHETLAND, DOBERMAN, LAB };
4:
5:    class Mammal
6:    {
7:    public:
8:        // constructors
9:        Mammal();
10:       ~Mammal();
11:
12:       //accessors
13:       int GetAge() const { return itsAge; }
14:       void SetAge(int age) { itsAge = age; }
15:       int GetWeight() const { return itsWeight; }
16:       void SetWeight(int weight) { itsWeight = weight; }
17:
18:       //Other methods
19:       void Speak() const { std::cout << "Mammal sound!\n"; }
20:       void Sleep() const { std::cout << "shhh. I'm sleeping.\n"; }
21:
22:    protected:
23:        int itsAge;
24:        int itsWeight;
25:    };
26:
27:    class Dog : public Mammal
28:    {
29:    public:
```

Listing 16.3   continued

```
30:        // Constructors
31:        Dog();
32:        ~Dog();
33:
34:        // Accessors
35:        BREED GetBreed() const { return itsBreed; }
36:        void SetBreed(BREED breed) { itsBreed = breed; }
37:
38:        // Other methods
39:        void WagTail() { std::cout << "Tail wagging...\n"; }
40:        void BegForFood() { std::cout << "Begging for food...\n"; }
41:
42:    private:
43:        BREED itsBreed;
44:    };
45:
46:    Mammal::Mammal():
47:    itsAge(1),
48:    itsWeight(5)
49:    {
50:        std::cout << "Mammal constructor...\n";
51:    }
52:
53:    Mammal::~Mammal()
54:    {
55:        std::cout << "Mammal destructor...\n";
56:    }
57:
58:    Dog::Dog():
59:    itsBreed(YORKIE)
60:    {
61:        std::cout << "Dog constructor...\n";
62:    }
63:
64:    Dog::~Dog()
65:    {
66:        std::cout << "Dog destructor...\n";
67:    }
68:
69:    int main()
70:    {
71:        Dog fido;
72:        fido.Speak();
73:        fido.WagTail();
74:        std::cout << "Fido is " << fido.GetAge() << " years old\n";
75:        return 0;
76:    }
```

```
Mammal constructor...
Dog constructor...
Mammal sound!
Tail wagging...
Fido is 1 years old
Dog destructor...
Mammal destructor...
```

Listing 16.3 is just like Listing 16.2, except that the constructors and destructors now print to the screen when called. Mammal's constructor is called, and then Dog's. At that point the Dog fully exists, and its methods can be called. When Fido goes out of scope, Dog's destructor is called, followed by a call to Mammal's destructor.

Passing Arguments to Base Constructors

It is possible that you'll want to overload the constructor of Mammal to take a specific age, and that you'll want to overload the Dog constructor to take a breed. How do you get the age and weight parameters passed up to the right constructor in Mammal? What if Dogs want to initialize weight but Mammals don't?

Base class initialization can be performed during class initialization by writing the base class name followed by the parameters expected by the base class. Listing 16.4 demonstrates this.

Listing 16.4   Overloading Constructors in Derived Classes

```
0:  //Listing 16.4 Overloading constructors in derived classes
1:  #include <iostream>
2:
3:  enum BREED { YORKIE, CAIRN, DANDIE, SHETLAND, DOBERMAN, LAB };
4:
5:  class Mammal
6:  {
7:  public:
8:      // constructors
9:      Mammal();
10:     Mammal(int age);
11:     ~Mammal();
12:
13:     //accessors
14:     int GetAge() const { return itsAge; }
15:     void SetAge(int age) { itsAge = age; }
16:     int GetWeight() const { return itsWeight; }
17:     void SetWeight(int weight) { itsWeight = weight; }
18:
19:     //Other methods
20:     void Speak() const { std::cout << "Mammal sound!\n"; }
```

Listing 16.4 continued

```
21:        void Sleep() const { std::cout << "shhh. I'm sleeping.\n"; }
22:
23:    protected:
24:        int itsAge;
25:        int itsWeight;
26:    };
27:
28:    class Dog : public Mammal
29:    {
30:    public:
31:        // Constructors
32:        Dog();
33:        Dog(int age);
34:        Dog(int age, int weight);
35:        Dog(int age, BREED breed);
36:        Dog(int age, int weight, BREED breed);
37:        ~Dog();
38:
39:        // Accessors
40:        BREED GetBreed() const { return itsBreed; }
41:        void SetBreed(BREED breed) { itsBreed = breed; }
42:
43:        // Other methods
44:        void WagTail() { std::cout << "Tail wagging...\n"; }
45:        void BegForFood() { std::cout << "Begging for food...\n"; }
46:
47:    private:
48:        BREED itsBreed;
49:    };
50:
51:    Mammal::Mammal():
52:    itsAge(1),
53:    itsWeight(5)
54:    {
55:        std::cout << "Mammal constructor...\n";
56:    }
57:
58:    Mammal::Mammal(int age):
59:    itsAge(age),
60:    itsWeight(5)
61:    {
62:        std::cout << "Mammal(int) constructor...\n";
63:    }
64:
65:    Mammal::~Mammal()
66:    {
67:        std::cout << "Mammal destructor...\n";
68:    }
69:
```

Listing 16.4   continued

```
70:   Dog::Dog():
71:   Mammal(),
72:   itsBreed(YORKIE)
73:   {
74:       std::cout << "Dog constructor...\n";
75:   }
76:
77:   Dog::Dog(int age):
78:   Mammal(age),
79:   itsBreed(YORKIE)
80:   {
81:       std::cout << "Dog(int) constructor...\n";
82:   }
83:
84:   Dog::Dog(int age, int weight):
85:   Mammal(age),
86:   itsBreed(YORKIE)
87:   {
88:       itsWeight = weight;
89:       std::cout << "Dog(int, int) constructor...\n";
90:   }
91:
92:   Dog::Dog(int age, int weight, BREED breed):
93:   Mammal(age),
94:   itsBreed(breed)
95:   {
96:       itsWeight = weight;
97:       std::cout << "Dog(int, int, BREED) constructor...\n";
98:   }
99:
100:  Dog::Dog(int age, BREED breed):
101:  Mammal(age),
102:  itsBreed(breed)
103:  {
104:      std::cout << "Dog(int, BREED) constructor...\n";
105:  }
106:
107:  Dog::~Dog()
108:  {
109:      std::cout << "Dog destructor...\n";
110:  }
111:
112:  int main()
113:  {
114:      Dog fido;
115:      Dog rover(5);
116:      Dog buster(6,8);
117:      Dog yorkie (3,YORKIE);
118:      Dog dobbie (4,20,DOBERMAN);
```

Listing 16.4 continued

```
119:      fido.Speak();
120:      rover.WagTail();
121:      std::cout << "Yorkie is "
122:          << yorkie.GetAge() << " years old\n";
123:      std::cout << "Dobbie weighs "
124:          << dobbie.GetWeight() << " pounds\n";
125:      return 0;
126:  }
```

16

The output has been numbered so that each line can be referred to in the analysis. These numbers do not print in the actual output.

OUTPUT

```
1:  Mammal constructor...
2:  Dog constructor...
3:  Mammal(int) constructor...
4:  Dog(int) constructor...
5:  Mammal(int) constructor...
6:  Dog(int, int) constructor...
7:  Mammal(int) constructor...
8:  Dog(int, BREED) constructor....
9:  Mammal(int) constructor...
10: Dog(int, int, BREED) constructor...
11: Mammal sound!
12: Tail wagging...
13: Yorkie is 3 years old.
14: Dobie weighs 20 pounds.
15: Dog destructor. . .
16: Mammal destructor...
17: Dog destructor...
18: Mammal destructor...
19: Dog destructor...
20: Mammal destructor...
21: Dog destructor...
22: Mammal destructor...
23: Dog destructor...
24: Mammal destructor...
```

ANALYSIS In Listing 16.4, Mammal's constructor has been overloaded on line 10 to take an integer, the Mammal's age. The implementation on lines 58–63 initializes itsAge with the value passed into the constructor, and itsWeight with the value 5.

Dog has overloaded five constructors on lines 32–36. The first is the default constructor. The second takes the age, which is the same parameter that the Mammal constructor takes.

The third constructor takes both the age and the weight; the fourth takes the age and breed; and the fifth takes the age, weight, and breed.

Note that on line 71 Dog's default constructor calls Mammal's default constructor. Although it is not strictly necessary to do this, it serves as documentation that you intended to call the base constructor, which takes no parameters. The base constructor would be called in any case, but actually doing so makes your intentions explicit.

The implementation for the Dog constructor, which takes an integer, is on lines 77–82. In its initialization phase (lines 78–79), Dog initializes its base class, passing in the parameter; and then it initializes its breed.

Another Dog constructor is on lines 84–90. This one takes two parameters. Once again, it initializes its base class by calling the appropriate constructor, but this time it also assigns weight to its base class's variable itsWeight. Note that you cannot assign to the base class variable in the initialization phase. That is, you can not write

```
Dog::Dog(int age, int weight):
Mammal(age),
itsBreed(YORKIE),
itsWeight(weight)        // error!
{
    std::cout << "Dog(int, int) constructor...\n";
}
```

because you are not allowed to initialize a value in the base class. Similarly, you may not write

```
Dog::Dog(int age, int weight):
Mammal(age, weight),     // error!
itsBreed(YORKIE)
{
    std::cout << "Dog(int, int) constructor...\n";
}
```

because Mammal does not have a constructor that takes the weight parameter; you must do this assignment within the body of the Dog's constructor.

```
Dog::Dog(int age, int weight):
Mammal(age),          // base constructor
itsBreed(YORKIE)      // initialization
{
    itsWeight = weight;   // assignment
```

Walk through the remaining constructors to make sure you are comfortable with how they work. Note what is initialized and what must wait for the body of the constructor.

The output has been numbered so that each line can be referred to in this analysis. The first two lines of output represent the instantiation of Fido, using the default constructor.

In the output, lines 3 and 4 represent the creation of rover. Lines 5 and 6 represent buster. Note that the Mammal constructor that was called is the constructor that takes one integer, but the Dog constructor is the constructor that takes two integers.

After all the objects are created, they are used and then go out of scope. As each object is destroyed, first the Dog destructor and then the Mammal destructor is called; there are five of each in total.

Overriding Functions

A Dog object has access to all the member functions in class Mammal, as well as to any member functions, such as WagTail(), that the declaration of the Dog class might add. It can also override a base class function. Overriding a function means changing the implementation of a base class function in a derived class. When you make an object of the derived class, the correct function is called.

NEW TERM   When a derived class creates a member function with the same return type and signature as a member function in the base class, but with a new implementation, it is said to be *overriding* that method.

When you override a function, it must agree in return type and in signature with the function in the base class. The signature is the function prototype other than the return type: that is, the name, the parameter list, and the keyword const, if used.

NEW TERM   The *signature* of a function is its name, as well as the number and type of its parameters. The signature does not include the return type.

Listing 16.5 illustrates what happens if the Dog class overrides the speak() method in Mammal. To save room, the accessor functions have been left out of these classes.

Listing 16.5   Overriding a Base Class Method in a Derived Class

```
0:   //Listing 16.5 Overriding a base class method in a derived class
1:   #include <iostream>
2:
3:   enum BREED { YORKIE, CAIRN, DANDIE, SHETLAND, DOBERMAN, LAB };
4:
5:   class Mammal
6:   {
7:   public:
8:       // constructors
9:       Mammal() { std::cout << "Mammal constructor...\n"; }
10:      ~Mammal() { std::cout << "Mammal destructor...\n"; }
11:
12:      //Other methods
```

Listing 16.5   continued

```
13:        void Speak()const { std::cout << "Mammal sound!\n"; }
14:        void Sleep()const { std::cout << "shhh. I'm sleeping.\n"; }
15:
16:    protected:
17:        int itsAge;
18:        int itsWeight;
19:    };
20:
21:    class Dog : public Mammal
22:    {
23:    public:
24:        // Constructors
25:        Dog(){ std::cout << "Dog constructor...\n"; }
26:        ~Dog(){ std::cout << "Dog destructor...\n"; }
27:
28:        // Other methods
29:        void WagTail() { std::cout << "Tail wagging...\n"; }
30:        void BegForFood() { std::cout << "Begging for food...\n"; }
31:        void Speak()const { std::cout << "Woof!\n"; }
32:
33:    private:
34:        BREED itsBreed;
35:    };
36:
37:    int main()
38:    {
39:        Mammal bigAnimal;
40:        Dog fido;
41:        bigAnimal.Speak();
42:        fido.Speak();
43:        return 0;
44:    }
```

OUTPUT
```
Mammal constructor...
Mammal constructor...
Dog constructor...
Mammal sound!
Woof!
Dog destructor...
Mammal destructor...
Mammal destructor...
```

ANALYSIS   On line 31, the Dog class overrides the Speak() method, causing Dog objects to
say Woof! when the Speak() method is called. On line 39, a Mammal object,
bigAnimal, is created, causing the first line of output when the Mammal constructor is
called. On line 40, a Dog object, fido, is created, causing the next two lines of output,
where the Mammal constructor and then the Dog constructor are called.

On line 41, the `Mammal` object calls its `Speak()` method; then on line 42 the `Dog` object calls its `Speak()` method. The output reflects that the correct methods were called. Finally, the two objects go out of scope, and the destructors are called.

Overloading Versus Overriding

These terms are similar, and they do similar things. When you overload a method, you create more than one method with the same name but with different signatures. When you override a method, you create a method in a derived class with the same name as a method in the base class and with the same signature.

Hiding the Base Class Method

In the previous listing, the `Dog` class's method `Speak()` hides the base class's method. This is just what is wanted, but it can have unexpected results. If `Mammal` has a `Move()` method that is overloaded, and `Dog` overrides that method, the `Dog` method will hide all the `Mammal` methods with that name.

If `Mammal` overloads `Move()` as three methods—one that takes no parameters, one that takes an integer, and one that takes an integer and a direction—and `Dog` overrides just the `Move()` method, which takes no parameters, it will not be easy to access the other two methods using a `Dog` object. Listing 16.6 illustrates this problem.

Listing 16.6 Hiding Methods

```
 0:  //Listing 16.6 Hiding methods
 1:
 2:  #include <iostream>
 3:
 4:  class Mammal
 5:  {
 6:  public:
 7:      void Move() const { std::cout << "Mammal move one step\n"; }
 8:      void Move(int distance) const
 9:          { std::cout << "Mammal move " << distance <<" steps.\n"; }
10:  protected:
11:      int itsAge;
12:      int itsWeight;
13:  };
14:
15:  class Dog : public Mammal
16:  {
17:  public:
18:      void Move() const { std::cout << "Dog move 5 steps.\n"; }
19:  }; // You may receive a warning that you are hiding a function!
20:
```

Listing 16.6   continued

```
21:   int main()
22:   {
23:       Mammal bigAnimal;
24:       Dog fido;
25:       bigAnimal.Move();
26:       bigAnimal.Move(2);
27:       fido.Move();
28:       // fido.Move(10);
29:       return 0;
30:   }
```

OUTPUT

```
Mammal move one step
Mammal move 2 steps
Dog move 5 steps
```

ANALYSIS All the extra methods and data have been removed from these classes. On lines 7 and 8, the Mammal class declares the overloaded Move() methods. On line 18, Dog overrides the version of Move() with no parameters. These are invoked on lines 25–27, and the output reflects this as executed.

Line 28, however, is commented out, as it causes a compile-time error. Although the Dog class could have called the Move(int) method if it had not overridden the version of Move() without parameters, now that it has done so it must override both if it wants to use both. This is reminiscent of the rule that states if you supply any constructor, the compiler will no longer supply a default constructor.

It is a common mistake to hide a base class method, when you intend to override it, by forgetting to include the keyword const. const is part of the signature, and leaving it off changes the signature and thus hides the method rather than overriding it.

Calling the Base Method

If you have overridden the base method, it is still possible to call it by fully qualifying the name of the method. You do this by writing the base name, followed by two colons and then the method name. For example:

```
Mammal::Move()
```

It would have been possible to rewrite line 28 in Listing 16.6 so that it would compile:

```
28:    fido.Mammal::Move(10);
```

This calls the Mammal method explicitly. Listing 16.7 fully illustrates this idea.

Listing 16.7 Calling the Base Method from the Overridden Method

```
0:  //Listing 16.7 Calling base method from overridden method.
1:  #include <iostream>
2:
3:  class Mammal
4:  {
5:  public:
6:      void Move() const { std::cout << "Mammal move one step\n"; }
7:      void Move(int distance) const
8:          { std::cout << "Mammal move "
9:              << distance << " steps.\n"; }
10: protected:
11:     int itsAge;
12:     int itsWeight;
13: };
14:
15: class Dog : public Mammal
16: {
17: public:
18:     void Move()const;
19: };
20:
21: void Dog::Move() const
22: {
23:     std::cout << "In dog move...\n";
24:     Mammal::Move(3);
25: }
26:
27: int main()
28: {
29:     Mammal bigAnimal;
30:     Dog fido;
31:     bigAnimal.Move(2);
32:     fido.Mammal::Move(6);
33:     return 0;
34: }
```

OUTPUT
```
Mammal move 2_steps
Mammal move 6_steps
```

ANALYSIS On line 29, a Mammal, bigAnimal, is created; and on line 30, a Dog, Fido, is created. The method call on line 31 invokes the Move() method of Mammal, which takes an int.

The programmer wants to invoke Move(int) on the Dog object, but has a problem. Dog overrides the Move() method, but does not overload it and does not provide a version that takes an int. This is solved by the explicit call to the base class Move(int) method on line 32.

> **DO** extend the functionality of tested classes by deriving.
>
> **DO** change the behavior of certain functions in the derived class by overriding the base class methods.
>
> **DON'T** hide a base class function by changing the function signature.

Summary

In this hour, you learned how derived classes inherit from base classes. Classes inherit all the public and protected data and functions from their base classes.

Protected access is public to derived classes and private to all other objects. Even derived classes cannot access private data or functions in their base classes.

Member variables can be initialized before the body of the constructor. It is at this time that base constructors are invoked and parameters can be passed to the base class.

Methods in the base class can be invoked by explicitly naming the function with the prefix of the base class name and two colons. For example, if Dog inherits from `Mammal`, `Mammal`'s `walk()` method can be called with `Mammal::Walk()`.

Q&A

Q Are inherited members and functions passed along to subsequent generations? If Dog derives from `Mammal` and `Mammal` derives from `Animal` does Dog inherit `Animal`'s functions and data?

A Yes. As derivation continues, derived classes inherit the sum of all the functions and data in all their base classes.

Q Can a derived class make a public base function private?

A Yes, and it will then remain private for all subsequent derivations.

HOUR 17

Polymorphism and Derived Classes

In the previous hour, you learned about inheritance and how derived classes can create an inheritance hierarchy. You also saw how methods in the base class can be overridden in the derived class. In this hour, you will learn how virtual methods enable you to use your base classes polymorphically. The following topics are covered:

- What virtual methods are
- How to use virtual destructors and copy constructors
- The costs and dangers in using virtual methods

Polymorphism Implemented With Virtual Methods

The previous chapter emphasized the fact that a Dog object is a Mammal object. So far that has meant only that the Dog object has inherited the attributes (data) and capabilities (methods) of its base class. In C++, the *is-a* relationship runs deeper than that, however.

Polymorphism allows you to treat derived objects as if they were base objects. For example, suppose you create a number of specialized Mammal types: Dog, Cat, Horse, and so forth. All of these derive from Mammal, and Mammal has a number of methods which are factored out of the derived classes. One such method might be Speak(). All mammals can make noise.

You'd like to teach each of the derived types to specialize how they speak. A Dog says "bow wow," a cat says "meow," and so forth. Each class must be able to override how it implements the Speak() method.

At the same time, when you have a collection of Mammal objects (for example, a Farm with Dog, Cat, Horse and Cow objects), you want the Farm simulation to be able to tell each of these objects to Speak() without knowing or caring about the details of how they implement the Speak() method. When you treat these objects as if they are all Mammals, by calling the Mammal.Speak() method, you are treating them polymorphically. Poly means many, morph means form; you are dealing with Mammal in all its many forms.

You can, for example, declare a pointer to Mammal, and assign to it the address of a Dog object you create on the heap. Since a Dog *is-a* Mammal, the following is perfectly legal:

```
Mammal* pMammal = new Dog;
```

You can then use this pointer to invoke any method on Mammal. What you would like is for those methods that are overridden in Dog to call the correct function. Virtual member functions let you do that. When you treat these objects polymorphically, you call the method on the Mammal pointer and you don't know or care what the actual object (in this case Dog) is or how it implements its method.

Listing 17.1 illustrates how virtual functions implement polymorphism.

LISTING 17.1   Using Virtual Methods

```
0:  //Listing 17.1 Using virtual methods
1:  #include <iostream>
2:
3:  class Mammal
4:  {
5:  public:
6:      Mammal():itsAge(1) { std::cout << "Mammal constructor...\n"; }
7:      ~Mammal() { std::cout << "Mammal destructor...\n"; }
8:      void Move() const { std::cout << "Mammal move one step\n"; }
```

LISTING 17.1 continued

```
 9:        virtual void Speak() const { std::cout << "Mammal speak!\n"; }
10:
11:    protected:
12:        int itsAge;
13:    };
14:
15:    class Dog : public Mammal
16:    {
17:    public:
18:        Dog() { std::cout << "Dog constructor...\n"; }
19:        ~Dog() { std::cout << "Dog destructor...\n"; }
20:        void WagTail() { std::cout << "Wagging Tail...\n"; }
21:        void Speak()const { std::cout << "Woof!\n"; }
22:        void Move()const { std::cout << "Dog moves 5 steps...\n"; }
23:    };
24:
25:    int main()
26:    {
27:        Mammal *pDog = new Dog;
28:        pDog->Move();
29:        pDog->Speak();
30:        return 0;
31:    }
```

OUTPUT

```
Mammal constructor...
Dog Constructor...
Mammal move one step
Woof!
```

ANALYSIS On line 9, Mammal is provided a virtual method—Speak(). The designer of this class thereby signals that he expects this class to eventually be another class's base type. The derived class will probably want to override this function.

On line 27, a pointer to Mammal is created, pDog, but it is assigned the address of a new Dog object. Because a Dog is a Mammal, this is a legal assignment. The pointer is then used to call the Move() function. Because the compiler knows pDog only to be a Mammal, it looks to the Mammal object to find the Move() method.

On line 29, the pointer then calls the Speak() method. Because Speak() is virtual, the Speak() method overridden in Dog is invoked.

This is almost magical—as far as the calling function knew, it had a Mammal pointer, but here a method on Dog was called. In fact, if you have an array of pointers to Mammal, each of which points to a subclass of Mammal, you can call each in turn and the correct function is called. Listing 17.2 illustrates this idea.

LISTING 17.2   Multiple Virtual Member Functions Called in Turn

```
0:  //Listing 17.2 Multiple virtual member functions called in turn
1:  #include <iostream>
2:
3:  class Mammal
4:  {
5:  public:
6:      Mammal():itsAge(1) {  }
7:      ~Mammal() { }
8:      virtual void Speak() const { std::cout << "Mammal speak!\n"; }
9:  protected:
10:     int itsAge;
11: };
12:
13: class Dog : public Mammal
14: {
15: public:
16:     void Speak()const { std::cout << "Woof!\n"; }
17: };
18:
19:
20: class Cat : public Mammal
21: {
22: public:
23:     void Speak()const { std::cout << "Meow!\n"; }
24: };
25:
26:
27: class Horse : public Mammal
28: {
29: public:
30:     void Speak()const { std::cout << "Winnie!\n"; }
31: };
32:
33: class Pig : public Mammal
34: {
35: public:
36:     void Speak()const { std::cout << "Oink!\n"; }
37: };
38:
39: int main()
40: {
41:     Mammal* theArray[5];
42:     Mammal* ptr;
43:     int choice, i;
44:     for ( i = 0; i<5; i++)
45:     {
46:         std::cout << "(1)dog (2)cat (3)horse (4)pig: ";
47:         std::cin >> choice;
```

LISTING 17.2 continued

```
48:          switch (choice)
49:          {
50:          case 1:
51:              ptr = new Dog;
52:              break;
53:          case 2:
54:              ptr = new Cat;
55:              break;
56:          case 3:
57:              ptr = new Horse;
58:              break;
59:          case 4:
60:              ptr = new Pig;
61:              break;
62:          default:
63:              ptr = new Mammal;
64:              break;
65:          }
66:          theArray[i] = ptr;
67:      }
68:      for (i=0;i<5;i++)
69:          theArray[i]->Speak();
70:      return 0;
71:  }
```

OUTPUT
```
(1)dog (2)cat (3)horse (4)pig: 1
(1)dog (2)cat (3)horse (4)pig: 2
(1)dog (2)cat (3)horse (4)pig: 3
(1)dog (2)cat (3)horse (4)pig: 4
(1)dog (2)cat (3)horse (4)pig: 5
Woof!
Meow!
Winnie!
Oink!
Mammal Speak!
```

ANALYSIS This stripped-down program, which provides only the barest functionality to each class, illustrates virtual member functions in their purest form. Four classes are declared, Dog, Cat, Horse, and Pig, all derived from Mammal.

On line 8, Mammal's Speak() function is declared to be virtual. On lines 16, 23, 30, and 36, the four derived classes override the implementation of Speak().

The user is prompted to pick which objects to create, and the pointers are added to the array in lines 44–65.

Note that at compile time it is impossible to know which objects will be created, and therefore, which `Speak()` methods will be invoked. The pointer `ptr` is bound to its object at runtime. This is called *late binding*, or sometimes *runtime binding*, as opposed to static binding, or compile-time binding.

How Virtual Member Functions Work

When a derived object, such as a `Dog` object, is created, first the constructor for the base class is called and then the constructor for the derived class is called. Figure 17.1 shows what the `Dog` object looks like after it is created. Note that the `Mammal` part of the object is contiguous in memory with the `Dog` part.

FIGURE 17.1

The Dog *object after it is created.*

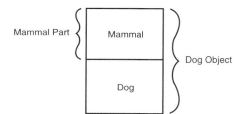

When a virtual function is created in an object, the object must keep track of that function. Many compilers build a virtual function table, called a *v-table*. One of these is kept for each type, and each object of that type keeps a virtual table pointer (called a `vptr` or *v-pointer*), which points to that table.

Although implementations vary, all compilers must accomplish the same thing, so you won't be too wrong with this description.

Each object's `vptr` points to the v-table that, in turn, has a pointer to each of the virtual member functions. When the `Mammal` part of the `Dog` is created, the `vptr` is initialized to point to the virtual methods for Mammal, as shown in Figure 17.2.

When the `Dog` constructor is called and the `Dog` part of this object is added, the `vptr` is adjusted to point to the virtual function overrides (if any) in the `Dog` object, as illustrated in Figure 17.3.

When a pointer to a `Mammal` is used, the `vptr` continues to point to the correct function, depending on the real type of the object. Thus, when `Speak()` is invoked, the correct function is invoked.

FIGURE 17.2
The v-table of a Mammal.

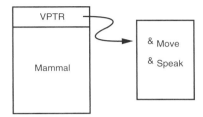

FIGURE 17.3
The v-table of a Dog.

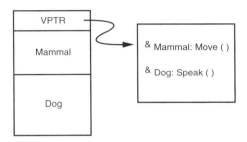

You Can't Get There from Here

If the Dog object had a method, WagTail(), that was not in the Mammal, you could not use the pointer to Mammal to access that method (unless you cast it to be a pointer to Dog). Because WagTail() is not a virtual function, and because it is not in a Mammal object, you can't get there without either a Dog object or a Dog pointer.

Although you can transform the Mammal pointer into a Dog pointer, there are usually far better and safer ways to call the WagTail() method. C++ frowns on explicit casts because they are error-prone. This subject is addressed in depth when multiple-inheritance is covered in Hour 18, "Advanced Polymorphism," and again when templates are covered in Hour 24, "Exceptions and Error Handling."

Slicing

Note that the virtual function magic only operates on pointers and references. Passing an object by value will not enable the virtual member functions to be invoked. Listing 17.3 illustrates this problem.

LISTING 17.3 Data Slicing when Passing by Value

```
0:  //Listing 17.3 Data slicing with passing by value
1:  #include <iostream>
2:
```

LISTING 17.3   continued

```
 3:  class Mammal
 4:  {
 5:  public:
 6:      Mammal():itsAge(1) {  }
 7:      ~Mammal() { }
 8:      virtual void Speak() const { std::cout << "Mammal speak!\n"; }
 9:  protected:
10:      int itsAge;
11:  };
12:
13:  class Dog : public Mammal
14:  {
15:  public:
16:      void Speak()const { std::cout << "Woof!\n"; }
17:  };
18:
19:  class Cat : public Mammal
20:  {
21:  public:
22:      void Speak()const { std::cout << "Meow!\n"; }
23:  };
24:
25:  void ValueFunction (Mammal);
26:  void PtrFunction   (Mammal*);
27:  void RefFunction   (Mammal&);
28:
29:  int main()
30:  {
31:      Mammal* ptr=0;
32:      int choice;
33:      while (1)
34:      {
35:          bool fQuit = false;
36:          std::cout << "(1)dog (2)cat (0)Quit: ";
37:          std::cin >> choice;
38:          switch (choice)
39:          {
40:          case 0:
41:              fQuit = true;
42:              break;
43:          case 1:
44:              ptr = new Dog;
45:              break;
46:          case 2:
47:              ptr = new Cat;
48:              break;
49:          default:
50:              ptr = new Mammal;
51:              break;
```

LISTING **17.3**   continued

```
52:             }
53:             if (fQuit)
54:                 break;
55:             PtrFunction(ptr);
56:             RefFunction(*ptr);
57:             ValueFunction(*ptr);
58:         }
59:     return 0;
60: }
61:
62: void ValueFunction (Mammal MammalValue)
63: {
64:     MammalValue.Speak();
65: }
66:
67: void PtrFunction (Mammal * pMammal)
68: {
69:     pMammal->Speak();
70: }
71:
72: void RefFunction (Mammal & rMammal)
73: {
74:     rMammal.Speak();
75: }
```

OUTPUT

```
 (1)dog (2)cat (0)Quit: 1
Woof
Woof
Mammal Speak!
 (1)dog (2)cat (0)Quit: 2
Meow!
Meow!
Mammal Speak!
 (1)dog (2)cat (0)Quit: 0
```

ANALYSIS On lines 3–23, stripped-down versions of the Mammal, Dog, and Cat classes are declared. Three functions are declared—PtrFunction(), RefFunction(), and ValueFunction(). They take a pointer to a Mammal, a Mammal reference, and a Mammal object, respectively. All three functions then do the same thing—they call the Speak() method.

The user is prompted to choose a Dog or Cat; based on the choice he makes, a pointer to the correct type is created on lines 38–52.

In the first line of the output, the user chooses Dog. The Dog object is created on the heap in line 44. The Dog is then passed as a pointer, as a reference, and by value to the three functions. The pointer and references all invoke the virtual member functions, and the Dog->Speak() member function is invoked. This is shown on the first two lines of output after the user's choice.

The dereferenced pointer, however, is passed by value. The function expects a Mammal object, so the compiler slices down the Dog object to just the Mammal part. At that point, the Mammal Speak() method is called, as reflected in the third line of output after the user's choice.

This experiment is then repeated for the Cat object, with similar results.

Virtual Destructors

It is legal and common to pass a pointer to a derived object when a pointer to a base object is expected. What happens when that pointer to a derived subject is deleted? If the destructor is virtual, as it should be, the right thing happens—the derived class's destructor is called. Because the derived class's destructor will automatically invoke the base class's destructor, the entire object will be properly destroyed.

The rule of thumb is this: If any of the functions in your class are virtual, the destructor should be virtual as well.

Virtual Copy Constructors

As previously stated, no constructor can be virtual. Nonetheless, there are times when your program desperately needs to be able to pass in a pointer to a base object and have a copy of the correct derived object that is created. A common solution to this problem is to create a clone method in the base class and to make it virtual. A *clone method* creates a new copy of the current object and returns that object.

Because each derived class overrides the clone method, a copy of the derived class is created. Listing 17.4 illustrates how this is used.

LISTING 17.4 A Virtual Copy Constructor

```
0:  //Listing 17.4 Virtual copy constructor
1:  #include <iostream>
2:
3:  class Mammal
4:  {
5:  public:
6:      Mammal():itsAge(1) { std::cout << "Mammal constructor...\n"; }
7:      virtual ~Mammal() { std::cout << "Mammal destructor...\n"; }
8:      Mammal (const Mammal & rhs);
9:      virtual void Speak() const { std::cout << "Mammal speak!\n"; }
10:     virtual Mammal* Clone() { return new Mammal(*this); }
```

LISTING **17.4**   continued

```
11:        int GetAge()const { return itsAge; }
12:
13:    protected:
14:        int itsAge;
15:    };
16:
17:    Mammal::Mammal (const Mammal & rhs):itsAge(rhs.GetAge())
18:    {
19:        std::cout << "Mammal Copy Constructor...\n";
20:    }
21:
22:    class Dog : public Mammal
23:    {
24:    public:
25:        Dog() { std::cout << "Dog constructor...\n"; }
26:        virtual ~Dog() { std::cout << "Dog destructor...\n"; }
27:        Dog (const Dog & rhs);
28:        void Speak()const { std::cout << "Woof!\n"; }
29:        virtual Mammal* Clone() { return new Dog(*this); }
30:    };
31:
32:    Dog::Dog(const Dog & rhs):
33:    Mammal(rhs)
34:    {
35:        std::cout << "Dog copy constructor...\n";
36:    }
37:
38:    class Cat : public Mammal
39:    {
40:    public:
41:        Cat() { std::cout << "Cat constructor...\n"; }
42:        virtual ~Cat() { std::cout << "Cat destructor...\n"; }
43:        Cat (const Cat &);
44:        void Speak()const { std::cout << "Meow!\n"; }
45:        virtual Mammal* Clone() { return new Cat(*this); }
46:    };
47:
48:    Cat::Cat(const Cat & rhs):
49:    Mammal(rhs)
50:    {
51:        std::cout << "Cat copy constructor...\n";
52:    }
53:
54:    enum ANIMALS { MAMMAL, DOG, CAT};
55:    const int NumAnimalTypes = 3;
56:    int main()
57:    {
58:        Mammal *theArray[NumAnimalTypes];
59:        Mammal* ptr;
60:        int choice,i;
```

LISTING **17.4**   continued

```
61:        for (i = 0; i<NumAnimalTypes; i++)
62:        {
63:            std::cout << "(1)dog (2)cat (3)Mammal: ";
64:            std::cin >> choice;
65:            switch (choice)
66:            {
67:            case DOG:
68:                ptr = new Dog;
69:                break;
70:            case CAT:
71:                ptr = new Cat;
72:                break;
73:            default:
74:                ptr = new Mammal;
75:                break;
76:            }
77:            theArray[i] = ptr;
78:        }
79:        Mammal *OtherArray[NumAnimalTypes];
80:        for (i=0;i<NumAnimalTypes;i++)
81:        {
82:            theArray[i]->Speak();
83:            OtherArray[i] = theArray[i]->Clone();
84:        }
85:        for (i=0;i<NumAnimalTypes;i++)
86:            OtherArray[i]->Speak();
87:        return 0;
88:    }
```

OUTPUT

```
1:  (1)dog (2)cat (3)Mammal: 1
2:  Mammal constructor...
3:  Dog Constructor...
4:  (1)dog (2)cat (3)Mammal: 2
5:  Mammal constructor...
6:  Cat constructor...
7:  (1)dog (2)cat (3)Mammal: 3
8:  Mammal constructor...
9:  Woof!
10: Mammal copy constructor...
11: Dog copy constructor...
12: Meow!
13: Mammal copy constructor...
14: Cat copy constructor...
15: Mammal speak!
16: Mammal copy constructor...
17: Woof!
18: Meow!
19: Mammal speak!
```

ANALYSIS Listing 17.4 is very similar to the previous two listings, except that a new virtual method has been added to the `Mammal` class: `clone()`. This method returns a pointer to a new `Mammal` object by calling the copy constructor, passing in itself (`*this`) as a `const` reference.

`Dog` and `Cat` both override the `clone()` method, initializing their data and passing in copies of themselves to their own copy constructors. Because `clone()` is virtual, this will effectively create a virtual copy constructor, as shown on line 83.

The user is prompted to choose dogs, cats, or mammals, and these are created on lines 65–76. A pointer to each choice is stored in an array on line 77.

As the program iterates over the array, each object has its `Speak()` and its `Clone()` method called, in turn, on lines 82 and 83. The result of the `Clone()` call is a pointer to a copy of the object, which is then stored in a second array on line 83.

On line 1 of the output, the user is prompted and responds with 1, choosing to create a dog. The `Mammal` and `Dog` constructors are invoked. This is repeated for `Cat` and for `Mammal` on lines 4–8 of the output.

Line 9 of the output represents the call to `Speak` on the first object, the `Dog`. The virtual `Speak()` method is called, and the correct version of `Speak()` is invoked. The `Clone()` function is then called, and as this is also virtual, `Dog`'s `Clone` method is invoked, causing the `Mammal` constructor and the `Dog` copy constructor to be called.

The same is repeated for `Cat` on lines 12–14 of the output, and then for `Mammal` on lines 15 and 16. Finally, the new array is iterated, and each of the new objects has `Speak()` invoked.

The Cost of Virtual Methods

Because objects with virtual methods must maintain a v-table, there is some overhead in having virtual methods. If you have a very small class from which you do not expect to derive other classes, there might be no reason to have any virtual methods at all.

After you declare any methods virtual, you've paid most of the price of the v-table (although each entry does add a small memory overhead). At that point, you'll want the destructor to be virtual, and the assumption will be that all other methods probably will be virtual as well. Take a long hard look at any non-virtual methods, and be certain you understand why they are not virtual.

DO use virtual methods when you expect to derive from a class.

DO use a virtual destructor if any methods are virtual.

DON'T mark the constructor as virtual.

Summary

In this hour, you learned how to use virtual member functions to enable your derived classes to behave polymorphically with their base classes.

In classes with virtual methods, the destructor should almost always be made virtual. A virtual destructor ensures that the derived part of the object will be freed when `delete` is called on the pointer. Constructors cannot be virtual. Virtual copy constructors can be effectively created by making a virtual member function that calls the copy constructor.

Q&A

Q Why not make all class functions virtual?

A There is overhead with the first virtual function in the creation of a v-table. After that, the overhead is trivial. Many C++ programmers feel that if one function is virtual, all others should be. Other programmers disagree, feeling that there should always be a reason for what you do.

Q If a function `SomeFunc()` is virtual in a base class and is also overloaded so as to take either an integer or two integers, and the derived class overrides the form taking one integer, what is called when a pointer to a derived object calls the two-integer form?

A The overriding of the one `int` form hides the entire base class function; thus you will get a compile error complaining that the function requires only one `int`.

HOUR 18

Advanced Polymorphism

In the previous hours, you learned how to write virtual functions in derived classes. The fundamental building block of polymorphism is the capability to bind specific, derived class objects to base class pointers at runtime. Now you will learn

- What "casting down" is and why you might want to do it
- What abstract data types are
- What pure virtual functions are

Problems with Single Inheritance

In the previous chapters, I discussed treating derived objects polymorphically with their base classes. You saw that if the base class has a method Speak() that is overridden in the derived class, a pointer to a base object that is assigned to a derived object will "do the right thing." Listing 18.1 illustrates this idea.

LISTING 18.1 Virtual Methods

```
0:  // Listing 18.1 - virtual methods
1:  #include <iostream>
2:
3:  class Mammal
4:  {
5:  public:
6:      Mammal():itsAge(1) { std::cout << "Mammal constructor...\n"; }
7:      virtual ~Mammal() { std::cout << "Mammal destructor...\n"; }
8:      virtual void Speak() const { std::cout << "Mammal speak!\n"; }
9:  protected:
10:     int itsAge;
11: };
12:
13: class Cat: public Mammal
14: {
15: public:
16:     Cat() { std::cout << "Cat constructor...\n"; }
17:     ~Cat() { std::cout << "Cat destructor...\n"; }
18:     void Speak()const { std::cout << "Meow!\n"; }
19: };
20:
21: int main()
22: {
23:     Mammal *pCat = new Cat;
24:     pCat->Speak();
25:     return 0;
26: }
```

OUTPUT

```
Mammal constructor...
Cat Constructor...
Meow!
```

ANALYSIS On line 8, Speak() is declared to be a virtual method; it is overridden on line 18 and invoked on line 24. Note, again, that pCat is declared to be a pointer to Mammal, but the address of a Cat is assigned to it. This is, as discussed in Hour 17, "Polymorphism and Derived Classes," the essence of polymorphism.

What happens, however, if you want to add a method to Cat that is inappropriate for Mammal? For example, suppose you want to add a method called Purr(). Cats purr, but no other mammals do. You would declare your class like this:

```
class Cat: public Mammal
{
public:
    Cat() { std::cout << "Cat constructor...\n"; }
    ~Cat() { std::cout << "Cat destructor...\n"; }
   void Speak()const { std::cout << "Meow\n"; }
   void Purr()const { std::cout << "rrrrrrrrrrrrrrrr\n"; }
};
```

The problem is this: If you now call `Purr()` using your pointer to Mammal, you will get a compile error. When you call `Purr()`, your compiler will reply:

```
error C2039: 'Purr' : is not a member of 'Mammal'
```

> Compilers vary in their error message. The Bloodshed compiler, for example, gives this error message:
>
> ```
> No matching function for call to 'Mammal::Purr()'
> ```

When your compiler tries to resolve `Purr()` in its `Mammal` virtual table, there will be no entry. You can percolate this method up into the base class, but that is a very bad idea. Although it will work as an expedient, populating your base class with methods that are specific to derived classes is poor programming practice and a recipe for difficult-to-maintain code.

In fact, this entire problem is a reflection of bad design. Generally, if you have a pointer to a base class that is assigned to a derived class object, it is because you *intend* to use that object polymorphically, and in this case, you ought not even try to access methods that are specific to the derived class.

Let me be clear: The problem is not that you have such specific methods; it is that you are trying to get at them with the base class pointer. In an ideal world, when you have such a pointer you would not try to get at those methods.

But this is not an ideal world, and at times, you find yourself with a collection of base objects—for example, a zoo full of mammals. At one point or another, you might realize you have a `Cat` object and you want the darn thing to purr. In this case, there might be only one thing to do: cheat.

This is the way you cheat: You cast your base class pointer to your derived type. You say to the compiler, "Look, Bub, I happen to know this is really a cat, so shaddup and do what I tell you." You have to sound like a thug when you say it, because you are acting like one; you are essentially extorting `Cat` behavior out of a `Mammal` pointer.

To make this work, you'll use the `dynamic_cast` operator. This operator ensures that when you cast, you cast safely. Further, it helps you quickly find those places in your code where you have used this feature, so that you can remove it as soon as you come to your senses.

Here's how it works: If you have a pointer to a base class, such as `Mammal`, and you assign to it a pointer to a derived class, such as `Cat`, you can use the `Mammal` pointer polymorphically to access virtual functions. Then, if you need to get at the Cat object to call, for example, the purr() method, you create a Cat pointer using the dynamic_cast operator to do so. At runtime, the base pointer will be examined. If the conversion is proper, your new Cat pointer will be fine. If the conversion is improper, if you didn't really have a Cat object after all, your new pointer will be null. Listing 18.2 illustrates this.

LISTING 18.2   Dynamic Cast

```
 0:    // Listing 18.2 - dynamic cast
 1:    #include <iostream>
 2:    using std::cout; // this file uses std::cout
 3:
 4:    class Mammal
 5:    {
 6:    public:
 7:        Mammal():itsAge(1) { cout << "Mammal constructor...\n"; }
 8:        virtual ~Mammal() { cout << "Mammal destructor...\n"; }
 9:        virtual void Speak() const { cout << "Mammal speak!\n"; }
10:    protected:
11:        int itsAge;
12:    };
13:
14:    class Cat: public Mammal
15:    {
16:    public:
17:        Cat() { cout << "Cat constructor...\n"; }
18:        ~Cat() { cout << "Cat destructor...\n"; }
19:        void Speak()const { cout << "Meow\n"; }
20:        void Purr() const { cout << "rrrrrrrrrr\n"; }
21:    };
22:
23:    class Dog: public Mammal
24:    {
25:    public:
26:        Dog() { cout << "Dog Constructor...\n"; }
27:        ~Dog() { cout << "Dog destructor...\n"; }
28:        void Speak()const { cout << "Woof!\n"; }
29:    };
30:
31:
32:    int main()
33:    {
34:        const int NumberMammals = 3;
35:        Mammal* Zoo[NumberMammals];
36:        Mammal* pMammal;
37:        int choice,i;
38:        for (i=0; i<NumberMammals; i++)
39:        {
40:            cout << "(1)Dog (2)Cat: ";
```

LISTING 18.2   continued

```
41:             std::cin >> choice;
42:             if (choice == 1)
43:                 pMammal = new Dog;
44:             else
45:                 pMammal = new Cat;
46:
47:             Zoo[i] = pMammal;
48:         }
49:
50:     cout << "\n";
51:
52:     for (i=0; i<NumberMammals; i++)
53:     {
54:         Zoo[i]->Speak();
55:
56:         Cat *pRealCat =  dynamic_cast<Cat *> (Zoo[i]);
57:
58:         if (pRealCat)
59:             pRealCat->Purr();
60:         else
61:             cout << "Uh oh, not a cat!\n";
62:
63:         delete Zoo[i];
64:         cout << "\n";
65:     }
66:
67:     return 0;
68: }
```

OUTPUT

```
(1)Dog (2)Cat: 1
Mammal constructor...
Dog constructor...
(1)Dog (2)Cat: 2
Mammal constructor...
Cat constructor...
(1)Dog (2)Cat: 1
Mammal constructor...
Dog constructor...

Woof!
Uh oh, not a cat!
Mammal destructor...

Meow
rrrrrrrrrrr
Mammal destructor...

Woof!
Uh oh, not a cat!
Mammal destructor...
```

ANALYSIS On lines 38–48, the user is asked to choose to add either a Cat or a Dog object to the array of Mammal pointers. Line 52 walks through the array and, on line 54, each object's virtual speak() method is called. These methods respond polymorphically: Cats meow, and dogs say woof!

On line 60, I want the Cat objects to purr, but I don't want to call that method on Dog objects. I used the dynamic_cast operator on line 57 to ensure that the object I am calling purr() on is a Cat. If it is, the pointer will not be null and will pass the test on line 59.

Abstract Data Types

Often, you will create a hierarchy of classes together. For example, you might create a Shape class as a base class to derive a Rectangle and a Circle. From Rectangle, you might derive Square as a special case of Rectangle.

Each of the derived classes will override the Draw() method, the GetArea() method, and so forth. Listing 18.3 illustrates a bare-bones implementation of the Shape class and its derived Circle and Rectangle classes.

LISTING 18.3   Shape Classes

```
 0:  //Listing 18.3. Shape classes.
 1:  #include <iostream>
 2:
 3:  class Shape
 4:  {
 5:  public:
 6:      Shape(){}
 7:      virtual ~Shape(){}
 8:      virtual long GetArea() { return -1; } // error
 9:      virtual long GetPerim() { return -1; }
10:      virtual void Draw() {}
11:  };
12:
13:  class Circle : public Shape
14:  {
15:  public:
16:      Circle(int radius):itsRadius(radius){}
17:      ~Circle(){}
18:      long GetArea() { return 3 * itsRadius * itsRadius; }
19:      long GetPerim() { return 9 * itsRadius; }
20:      void Draw();
21:  private:
22:      int itsRadius;
23:      int itsCircumference;
24:  };
```

LISTING **18.3**   continued

```
25:
26:  void Circle::Draw()
27:  {
28:      std::cout << "Circle drawing routine here!\n";
29:  }
30:
31:
32:  class Rectangle : public Shape
33:  {
34:  public:
35:      Rectangle(int len, int width):
36:          itsLength(len), itsWidth(width){}
37:      virtual ~Rectangle(){}
38:      virtual long GetArea() { return itsLength * itsWidth; }
39:      virtual long GetPerim() {return 2*itsLength + 2*itsWidth; }
40:      virtual int GetLength() { return itsLength; }
41:      virtual int GetWidth() { return itsWidth; }
42:      virtual void Draw();
43:  private:
44:      int itsWidth;
45:      int itsLength;
46:  };
47:
48:  void Rectangle::Draw()
49:  {
50:      for (int i = 0; i<itsLength; i++)
51:      {
52:          for (int j = 0; j<itsWidth; j++)
53:              std::cout << "x ";
54:
55:          std::cout << "\n";
56:      }
57:  }
58:
59:  class Square : public Rectangle
60:  {
61:  public:
62:      Square(int len);
63:      Square(int len, int width);
64:      ~Square(){}
65:      long GetPerim() {return 4 * GetLength();}
66:  };
67:
68:  Square::Square(int len):
69:      Rectangle(len,len)
70:  {}
71:
72:  Square::Square(int len, int width):
73:      Rectangle(len,width)
74:  {
75:      if (GetLength() != GetWidth())
```

18

LISTING 18.3   continued

```
76:              std::cout << "Error, not a square... a Rectangle??\n";
77:  }
78:
79:  int main()
80:  {
81:      int choice;
82:      bool fQuit = false;
83:      Shape * sp;
84:
85:      while (1)
86:      {
87:          std::cout << "(1)Circle (2)Rectangle (3)Square (0)Quit: ";
88:          std::cin >> choice;
89:
90:          switch (choice)
91:          {
92:          case 1:
93:              sp = new Circle(5);
94:              break;
95:          case 2:
96:               sp = new Rectangle(4,6);
97:              break;
98:          case 3:
99:              sp = new Square(5);
100:              break;
101:          default:
102:              fQuit = true;
103:              break;
104:          }
105:          if (fQuit)
106:              break;
107:
108:          sp->Draw();
109:          std::cout << "\n";
110:      }
111:      return 0;
112:  }
```

OUTPUT
```
(1)Circle (2)Rectangle (3)Square (0)Quit: 2
x x x x x x
x x x x x x
x x x x x x
x x x x x x
 (1)Circle (2)Rectangle (3)Square (0)Quit:3
x x x x x
x x x x x
x x x x x
x x x x x
x x x x x
 (1)Circle (2)Rectangle (3)Square (0)Quit:0
```

ANALYSIS On lines 3–11, the Shape class is declared. The GetArea() and GetPerim() methods return an error value, and Draw() takes no action. After all, what does it mean to draw a shape? Only types of shapes (circles, rectangle, and so on) can be drawn; shapes as an abstraction cannot be drawn.

Circle derives from Shape and overrides the three virtual methods. Note that there is no reason to add the word virtual, as that is part of their inheritance. But there is no harm in doing so either, as shown in the Rectangle class on lines 38–42. It is a good idea to include the term virtual as a reminder, a form of documentation.

Square derives from Rectangle, and it too overrides the GetPerim() method, inheriting the rest of the methods defined in Rectangle.

It is troubling, though, that it is possible to instantiate a Shape object, and it might be desirable to make that impossible. The Shape class exists only to provide an interface for the classes derived from it; as such, it is an *abstract data type*, or ADT.

An abstract data type represents a concept (like *shape*) rather than an object (like *circle*). In C++, an ADT is always the base class to other classes, and it is not valid to make an instance of an ADT. Thus, if you make Shape an ADT, it will not be possible to make an instance of a Shape object.

Pure Virtual Functions

C++ supports the creation of abstract data types with pure virtual functions. A pure virtual function is a virtual function which *must* be overridden in the derived class. A virtual function is made pure by initializing it with 0, as in

```
virtual void Draw() = 0;
```

Any class with one or more pure virtual functions is an ADT, and it is illegal to instantiate an object of a class that is an ADT. Trying to do so will cause a compile-time error. Putting a pure virtual function in your class signals two things to clients of your class:

• Don't make an object of this class, derive from it.

• Make sure to override the pure virtual function.

Any class that derives from an ADT inherits the pure virtual function as pure, and so must override every pure virtual function if it wants to instantiate objects. Therefore, if Rectangle inherits from Shape, and Shape has three pure virtual functions, Rectangle must override all three or it, too, will be an ADT. Listing 18.4 rewrites the Shape class to be an abstract data type. To save space, the rest of Listing 18.3 is not reproduced here. Replace the declaration of Shape in Listing 18.3, lines 3–11, with the declaration of Shape in Listing 18.4 and run the program again.

LISTING 18.4   Abstract Data Types

```
 1:  class Shape
 2:  {
 3:  public:
 4:      Shape(){}
 5:      virtual ~Shape(){}
 6:      virtual long GetArea() = 0;
 7:      virtual long GetPerim()= 0;
 8:      virtual void Draw() = 0;
 9:  private:
10: };
```

OUTPUT

```
 (1)Circle (2)Rectangle (3)Square (0)Quit:2
x x x x x x
x x x x x x
x x x x x x
x x x x x x
 (1)Circle (2)Rectangle (3)Square (0)Quit:3
x x x x x
x x x x x
x x x x x
x x x x x
x x x x x
 (1)Circle (2)Rectangle (3)Square (0)Quit:0
```

ANALYSIS   As you can see, the workings of the program are totally unaffected. The only difference is that it is now impossible to make an object of class Shape.

Abstract Data Types

You declare a class to be an abstract data type by including one or more pure virtual functions in the class declaration. Declare a pure virtual function by writing = 0 after the function declaration.

For example:

```
class Shape
{
    virtual void Draw() = 0;    // pure virtual
};
```

Implementing Pure Virtual Functions

Typically, the pure virtual functions in an abstract base class are never implemented. Because no objects of that type are ever created, there is no reason to provide implementations, and the ADT works purely as the definition of an interface to objects that derive from it.

It is possible, however, to provide an implementation to a pure virtual function. The function can then be called by objects derived from the ADT, perhaps to provide common functionality to all the overridden functions. Listing 18.5 reproduces Listing 18.3, this time with Shape as an ADT and with an implementation for the pure virtual function Draw(). The Circle class overrides Draw(), as it must, but it then chains up to the base class function for additional functionality.

In this example, the additional functionality is simply an additional message printed, but you can imagine that the base class provides a shared drawing mechanism, perhaps setting up a window that all derived classes will use.

LISTING 18.5   Implementing Pure Virtual Functions

```
0:  //Implementing pure virtual functions
1:  #include <iostream>
2:
3:  class Shape
4:  {
5:  public:
6:      Shape(){}
7:      virtual ~Shape(){}
8:      virtual long GetArea() = 0;
9:      virtual long GetPerim()= 0;
10:     virtual void Draw() = 0;
11: private:
12: };
13:
14: void Shape::Draw()
15: {
16:     std::cout << "Abstract drawing mechanism!\n";
17: }
18:
19: class Circle : public Shape
20: {
21: public:
22:     Circle(int radius):itsRadius(radius){}
23:     ~Circle(){}
24:     long GetArea() { return 3 * itsRadius * itsRadius; }
25:     long GetPerim() { return 9 * itsRadius; }
26:     void Draw();
27: private:
28:     int itsRadius;
29:     int itsCircumference;
30: };
31:
32: void Circle::Draw()
33: {
34:     std::cout << "Circle drawing routine here!\n";
```

18

LISTING 18.5   continued

```
35:         Shape::Draw();
36:    }
37:
38:    class Rectangle : public Shape
39:    {
40:    public:
41:        Rectangle(int len, int width):
42:            itsLength(len), itsWidth(width){}
43:        virtual ~Rectangle(){}
44:        long GetArea() { return itsLength * itsWidth; }
45:        long GetPerim() {return 2*itsLength + 2*itsWidth; }
46:        virtual int GetLength() { return itsLength; }
47:        virtual int GetWidth() { return itsWidth; }
48:        void Draw();
49:    private:
50:        int itsWidth;
51:        int itsLength;
52:    };
53:
54:    void Rectangle::Draw()
55:    {
56:        for (int i = 0; i<itsLength; i++)
57:        {
58:            for (int j = 0; j<itsWidth; j++)
59:                std::cout << "x ";
60:
61:            std::cout << "\n";
62:        }
63:        Shape::Draw();
64:    }
65:
66:    class Square : public Rectangle
67:    {
68:    public:
69:        Square(int len);
70:        Square(int len, int width);
71:        ~Square(){}
72:        long GetPerim() {return 4 * GetLength();}
73:    };
74:
75:    Square::Square(int len):
76:        Rectangle(len,len)
77:    {}
78:
79:    Square::Square(int len, int width):
80:        Rectangle(len,width)
81:    {
82:        if (GetLength() != GetWidth())
83:            std::cout << "Error, not a square... a Rectangle??\n";
84:    }
```

LISTING 18.5   continued

```
85:
86:  int main()
87:  {
88:      int choice;
89:      bool fQuit = false;
90:      Shape * sp;
91:
92:      while (1)
93:      {
94:          std::cout << "(1)Circle (2)Rectangle (3)Square (0)Quit: ";
95:          std::cin >> choice;
96:
97:          switch (choice)
98:          {
99:          case 1:
100:             sp = new Circle(5);
101:             break;
102:         case 2:
103:             sp = new Rectangle(4,6);
104:             break;
105:         case 3:
106:             sp = new Square (5);
107:             break;
108:         default:
109:             fQuit = true;
110:             break;
111:         }
112:         if (fQuit)
113:             break;
114:         sp->Draw();
115:         std::cout << "\n";
116:     }
117:     return 0;
118: }
```

OUTPUT
```
 (1)Circle (2)Rectangle (3)Square (0)Quit: 2
x x x x x x
x x x x x x
x x x x x x
x x x x x x
Abstract drawing mechanism!
 (1)Circle (2)Rectangle (3)Square (0)Quit:3
x x x x x
x x x x x
x x x x x
x x x x x
x x x x x
Abstract drawing mechanism!
 (1)Circle (2)Rectangle (3)Square (0)Quit:0
```

ANALYSIS   On lines 3–12, the abstract data type Shape is declared, with all three of its accessor methods declared to be pure virtual. Note that this is not necessary. If any one were declared pure virtual, the class would have been an ADT.

The GetArea() and GetPerim() methods are not implemented, but Draw() is. Circle and Rectangle both override Draw(); and both chain up to the base method, taking advantage of shared functionality in the base class.

Complex Hierarchies of Abstraction

At times, you will derive ADTs from other ADTs. It may be that you want to make some of the derived pure virtual functions non-pure and leave others pure.

If you create the Animal class, you can make Eat(), Sleep(), Move(), and Reproduce() pure virtual functions. Perhaps you derive Mammal and Fish from Animal.

On examination, you decide that every Mammal will reproduce in the same way, and so you make Mammal::Reproduce() be non-pure, but you leave Eat(), Sleep(), and Move() as pure virtual functions.

From Mammal you derive Dog, and Dog must override and implement the three remaining pure virtual functions so that you can make objects of type Dog.

What you say, as class designer, is that no Animals or Mammals can be instantiated, but that all Mammals can inherit the provided Reproduce() method without overriding it.

Listing 18.6 illustrates this technique with a bare-bones implementation of these classes.

LISTING 18.6   Deriving ADTs from Other ADTs

```
0:  // Listing 18.6
1:  // Deriving ADTs from other ADTs
2:  #include <iostream>
3:
4:  enum COLOR { Red, Green, Blue, Yellow, White, Black, Brown } ;
5:
6:  class Animal        // common base to both horse and bird
7:  {
8:  public:
9:      Animal(int);
10:     virtual ~Animal() { std::cout << "Animal destructor...\n"; }
11:     virtual int GetAge() const { return itsAge; }
12:     virtual void SetAge(int age) { itsAge = age; }
13:     virtual void Sleep() const = 0;
14:     virtual void Eat() const = 0;
15:     virtual void Reproduce() const = 0;
16:     virtual void Move() const = 0;
```

LISTING **18.6**   continued

```
17:        virtual void Speak() const = 0;
18:    private:
19:        int itsAge;
20:    };
21:
22:    Animal::Animal(int age):
23:    itsAge(age)
24:    {
25:        std::cout << "Animal constructor...\n";
26:    }
27:
28:    class Mammal : public Animal
29:    {
30:    public:
31:        Mammal(int age):Animal(age)
32:            { std::cout << "Mammal constructor...\n";}
33:        virtual ~Mammal() { std::cout << "Mammal destructor...\n";}
34:        virtual void Reproduce() const
35:            { std::cout << "Mammal reproduction depicted...\n"; }
36:    };
37:
38:    class Fish : public Animal
39:    {
40:    public:
41:        Fish(int age):Animal(age)
42:            { std::cout << "Fish constructor...\n";}
43:        virtual ~Fish()
44:            { std::cout << "Fish destructor...\n";  }
45:        virtual void Sleep() const
46:            { std::cout << "fish snoring...\n"; }
47:        virtual void Eat() const
48:            { std::cout << "fish feeding...\n"; }
49:        virtual void Reproduce() const
50:            { std::cout << "fish laying eggs...\n"; }
51:        virtual void Move() const
52:            { std::cout << "fish swimming...\n";    }
53:        virtual void Speak() const { }
54:    };
55:
56:    class Horse : public Mammal
57:    {
58:    public:
59:        Horse(int age, COLOR color ):
60:            Mammal(age), itsColor(color)
61:            { std::cout << "Horse constructor...\n"; }
62:        virtual ~Horse()
63:            { std::cout << "Horse destructor...\n"; }
64:        virtual void Speak()const
65:            { std::cout << "Whinny!... \n"; }
```

18

LISTING 18.6   continued

```
66:        virtual COLOR GetItsColor() const
67:            { return itsColor; }
68:        virtual void Sleep() const
69:            { std::cout << "Horse snoring...\n"; }
70:        virtual void Eat() const
71:            { std::cout << "Horse feeding...\n"; }
72:        virtual void Move() const
73:            { std::cout << "Horse running...\n";}
74:
75:    protected:
76:        COLOR itsColor;
77:    };
78:
79:    class Dog : public Mammal
80:    {
81:    public:
82:        Dog(int age, COLOR color ):
83:            Mammal(age), itsColor(color)
84:            { std::cout << "Dog constructor...\n"; }
85:        virtual ~Dog()
86:            { std::cout << "Dog destructor...\n"; }
87:        virtual void Speak()const
88:            { std::cout << "Whoof!... \n"; }
89:        virtual void Sleep() const
90:            { std::cout << "Dog snoring...\n"; }
91:        virtual void Eat() const
92:            { std::cout << "Dog eating...\n"; }
93:        virtual void Move() const
94:            { std::cout << "Dog running...\n"; }
95:        virtual void Reproduce() const
96:            { std::cout << "Dogs reproducing...\n"; }
97:
98:    protected:
99:        COLOR itsColor;
100:   };
101:
102:   int main()
103:   {
104:        Animal *pAnimal=0;
105:        int choice;
106:        bool fQuit = false;
107:
108:        while (1)
109:        {
110:            std::cout << "(1)Dog (2)Horse (3)Fish (0)Quit: ";
111:            std::cin >> choice;
112:
113:            switch (choice)
114:            {
```

LISTING 18.6   continued

```
115:            case 1:
116:                pAnimal = new Dog(5,Brown);
117:                break;
118:            case 2:
119:                pAnimal = new Horse(4,Black);
120:                break;
121:            case 3:
122:                pAnimal = new Fish (5);
123:                break;
124:            default:
125:                fQuit = true;
126:                break;
127:            }
128:            if (fQuit)
129:                break;
130:
131:            pAnimal->Speak();
132:            pAnimal->Eat();
133:            pAnimal->Reproduce();
134:            pAnimal->Move();
135:            pAnimal->Sleep();
136:            delete pAnimal;
137:            std::cout << "\n";
138:        }
139:     return 0;
140: }
```

18

OUTPUT
```
(1)Dog (2)Horse (3)Bird (0)Quit: 1
Animal constructor...
Mammal constructor...
Dog constructor...
Whoof!...
Dog eating...
Dog reproducing....
Dog running...
Dog snoring...
Dog destructor...
Mammal destructor...
Animal destructor...
  (1)Dog (2)Horse (3)Bird (0)Quit: 0
```

ANALYSIS   On lines 6–20, the abstract data type Animal is declared. Animal has non-pure virtual accessors for itsAge, which are shared by all Animal objects. It has five pure virtual functions: Sleep(), Eat(), Reproduce(), Move(), and Speak().

Mammal is derived from Animal and is declared on lines 28–36. It adds no data. It overrides Reproduce(), however, providing a common form of reproduction for all Mammals.

Fish must override Reproduce(), because Fish derives directly from Animal and cannot take advantage of Mammalian reproduction (and a good thing, too!).

Mammal classes no longer have to override the Reproduce() function, but they are free to do so if they choose (as Dog does on lines 95 and 96). Fish, Horse, and Dog all override the remaining pure virtual functions so that objects of their type can be instantiated.

In the body of the program, an Animal pointer is used to point to the various derived objects in turn. The virtual methods are invoked; and, based on the runtime binding of the pointer, the correct method is called in the derived class.

It would cause a compile-time error to try to instantiate an Animal or a Mammal, as both are abstract data types.

Which Types Are Abstract?

In one program, the class Animal is abstract; in another it is not. What determines whether to make a class abstract?

The answer to this question is decided not by any real-world, intrinsic factor, but by what makes sense in your program. If you are writing a program that depicts a farm or a zoo, you may want Animal to be an abstract data type but Dog to be a class from which you can instantiate objects.

On the other hand, if you are making an animated kennel, you may want to keep Dog as an abstract data type, and only instantiate types of dogs: retrievers, terriers, and so forth. The level of abstraction is a function of how finely you need to distinguish your types.

Do	Don't
DO use abstract data types to provide common functionality for a number of related classes. **DO** override all pure virtual functions. **DO** make pure virtual any function that must be overridden. **DON'T** try to instantiate an object of an abstract data type.	

Summary

In this hour, you learned how to use the dynamic_cast operator to cast down the inheritance hierarchy. You also learned why this may be a sign of poor class design.

You also saw how to create abstract data types using pure virtual functions and how to implement the pure virtual functions so that they can be used by derived classes. Any class with a pure virtual function is abstract, and abstract classes may not be instantiated. You examined how you can create hierarchies of abstract data types to represent abstractions in your design, and how you must ultimately create non-abstract (concrete) classes which can be instantiated.

Q&A

Q **What does percolating functionality upward mean?**

A This refers to the idea of moving shared functionality upwards into a common base class. If more than one class shares a function, it is desirable to find a common base class in which that function can be stored.

Q **Is percolating upward always a good thing?**

A Yes, if you are percolating shared functionality upward; no, if all you are moving is interface. That is, if all the derived classes can't use the method, it is a mistake to move it up into a common base class. If you do, you'll have to switch on the runtime type of the object before deciding whether you can invoke the function.

Q **Why is dynamic casting bad?**

A The point of virtual functions is to let the virtual table, rather than the programmer, determine the runtime type of the object.

Q **Why bother making an abstract data type? Why not just make it non-abstract and avoid creating any objects of that type?**

A The purpose of many of the conventions in C++ is to enlist the compiler in finding bugs to avoid runtime bugs in code that you give to your customers. Making a class abstract—that is, giving it pure virtual functions—causes the compiler to flag any objects created of that abstract type as errors.

18

HOUR **19**

Linked Lists

In the previous hours, you learned about inheritance, polymorphism, and abstract data types. You also learned about arrays. Now, you will learn to improve on the array by utilizing the fundamentals of object-oriented programming: inheritance, polymorphism, and encapsulation. In this hour you will learn

- What a linked list is
- How to create a linked list
- How to encapsulate functionality through inheritance

Linked Lists and Other Structures

Arrays are much like Tupperware. They are great containers, but they are of a fixed size. If you pick a container that is too large, you waste space in your storage area. If you pick one that is too small, its contents spill all over and you have a big mess.

NEW TERM One way to solve this problem is with a linked list. A *linked list* is a data structure that consists of small containers that "snap together."

Containers, in this context, are classes that contain the objects to be held in the list. The idea is to write a class that holds one object of your data—such as one CAT or one Rectangle—and that can point at the next container in the list. You create one container for each object that you need to store, and you chain them together as needed.

These small containers are called *nodes*. The first node in the list is called the *head*, and the last node in the list is called the *tail*.

Lists come in three fundamental forms. From simplest to most complex, they are

Singly linked

Doubly linked

Trees

NEW TERM In a *singly linked list*, each node points to the next one forward, but not backward. To find a particular node, you start at the top and go from node to node, as in a treasure hunt ("The next node is under the sofa"). A *doubly linked list* enables you to move backward and forward in the chain. A *tree* is a complex structure built from nodes, each of which can point in two or three directions. Figure 19.1 shows these three fundamental structures.

Computer scientists have created even more complex and clever data structures, nearly all of which rely on interconnecting nodes.

FIGURE 19.1
Linked lists.

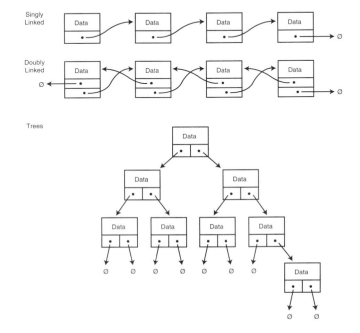

A Case Study

In this section we will examine a linked list in detail, as a case study it looks at how you create complex structures and, more important, how you use inheritance, polymorphism, and encapsulation to manage large projects.

Delegation of Responsibility

A fundamental premise of object-oriented programming is that each object does *one* thing very well and delegates to other objects anything that is not its core mission.

An automobile is a perfect example of this idea in hardware: The engine's job is to produce the power. Distribution of that power is not the engine's job; that is up to the transmission. Turning is not the job of the engine or the transmission; that is delegated to the wheels.

A well-designed machine has lots of small, well-understood parts, each doing its own job and working together to accomplish a greater good. A well-designed program is much the same: Each class sticks to its own knitting, but together they create a heck of an afghan.

The Component Parts

The linked list will consist of nodes. The node class itself will be abstract; we'll use three subtypes to accomplish the work. There will be a head node whose job is to manage the head of the list, a tail node (guess what its job is!), and zero or more internal nodes. The internal nodes will keep track of the actual data to be held in the list.

Note that the data and the list are quite distinct. You can, in theory, save any type of data you like in a list. It isn't the data that is linked together; it is the node that *holds* the data that is linked.

The program doesn't actually know about the nodes; it only works with the list. The list, however, does little work; it simply delegates to the nodes.

Listing 19.1 shows the code; we'll examine it in excruciating detail:

LISTING 19.1 Linked List

```
0:  // **************************************************
1:  //    FILE:       Listing 19.1
2:  //
3:  //    PURPOSE:    Demonstrate ilinked list
4:  //    NOTES:
```

Listing 19.1 continued

```
5:  //
6:  //  COPYRIGHT:  Copyright (C) 1997 Liberty Associates, Inc.
7:  //                  All Rights Reserved
8:  //
9:  // Demonstrates an object-oriented approach to
10: // linked lists. The list delegates to the node.
11: // The node is an abstract data type. Three types of
12: // nodes are used, head nodes, tail nodes and internal
13: // nodes. Only the internal nodes hold data.
14: //
15: // The Data class is created to serve as an object to
16: // hold in the linked list.
17: //
18: // ************************************************
19: #include <iostream>
20:
21: enum { kIsSmaller, kIsLarger, kIsSame};
22:
23: // Data class to put into the linked list
24: // Any class in this linked list must support two methods:
25: // Show (displays the value) and Compare
26: // (returns relative position)
27: class Data
28: {
29: public:
30:     Data(int val):myValue(val){}
31:     ~Data(){}
32:     int Compare(const Data &);
33:     void Show() { std::cout << myValue << std::endl; }
34: private:
35:     int myValue;
36: };
37:
38: // Compare is used to decide where in the list
39: // a particular object belongs.
40: int Data::Compare(const Data & theOtherData)
41: {
42:     if (myValue < theOtherData.myValue)
43:         return kIsSmaller;
44:     if (myValue > theOtherData.myValue)
45:         return kIsLarger;
46:     else
47:         return kIsSame;
48: }
49:
50: // forward declarations
51: class Node;
52: class HeadNode;
53: class TailNode;
```

LISTING 19.1   continued

```
54:  class InternalNode;
55:
56:  // ADT representing the node object in the list
57:  // Every derived class must override Insert and Show
58:  class Node
59:  {
60:  public:
61:      Node(){}
62:      virtual ~Node(){}
63:      virtual Node * Insert(Data * theData)=0;
64:      virtual void Show() = 0;
65:  private:
66:  };
67:
68:  // This is the node which holds the actual object
69:  // In this case the object is of type Data
70:  // We'll see how to make this more general when
71:  // we cover templates
72:  class InternalNode: public Node
73:  {
74:  public:
75:      InternalNode(Data * theData, Node * next);
76:      virtual ~InternalNode(){ delete myNext; delete myData; }
77:      virtual Node * Insert(Data * theData);
78:      virtual void Show()
79:          { myData->Show(); myNext->Show(); } // delegate!
80:
81:  private:
82:      Data * myData;  // the data itself
83:      Node * myNext;    // points to next node in the linked list
84:  };
85:
86:  // All the constructor does is to initialize
87:  InternalNode::InternalNode(Data * theData, Node * next):
88:  myData(theData),myNext(next)
89:  {
90:  }
91:
92:  // the meat of the list
93:  // When you put a new object into the list
94:  // it is passed ot the node which figures out
95:  // where it goes and inserts it into the list
96:  Node * InternalNode::Insert(Data * theData)
97:  {
98:
99:      // is the new guy bigger or smaller than me?
100:      int result = myData->Compare(*theData);
101:
102:
```

LISTING 19.1   continued

```
103:        switch(result)
104:        {
105:        // by convention if it is the same as me it comes first
106:        case kIsSame:      // fall through
107:        case kIsLarger:    // new data comes before me
108:            {
109:                InternalNode * dataNode =
110:                    new InternalNode(theData, this);
111:                return dataNode;
112:            }
113:
114:            // it is bigger than I am so pass it on to the next
115:            // node and let HIM handle it.
116:        case kIsSmaller:
117:            myNext = myNext->Insert(theData);
118:            return this;
119:        }
120:        return this;  // appease MSC
121:    }
122:
123:
124: // Tail node is just a sentinel
125: class TailNode : public Node
126: {
127: public:
128:        TailNode(){}
129:        virtual ~TailNode(){}
130:        virtual Node * Insert(Data * theData);
131:        virtual void Show() { }
132: private:
133: };
134:
135: // If data comes to me, it must be inserted before me
136: // as I am the tail and NOTHING comes after me
137: Node * TailNode::Insert(Data * theData)
138: {
139:        InternalNode * dataNode = new InternalNode(theData, this);
140:        return dataNode;
141: }
142:
143: // Head node has no data, it just points
144: // to the very beginning of the list
145: class HeadNode : public Node
146: {
147: public:
148:        HeadNode();
149:        virtual ~HeadNode() { delete myNext; }
150:        virtual Node * Insert(Data * theData);
151:        virtual void Show() { myNext->Show(); }
```

LISTING 19.1 continued

```
152:    private:
153:        Node * myNext;
154:    };
155:
156:    // As soon as the head is created
157:    // it creates the tail
158:    HeadNode::HeadNode()
159:    {
160:        myNext = new TailNode;
161:    }
162:
163:    // Nothing comes before the head so just
164:    // pass the data on to the next node
165:    Node * HeadNode::Insert(Data * theData)
166:    {
167:        myNext = myNext->Insert(theData);
168:        return this;
169:    }
170:
171:    // I get all the credit and do none of the work
172:    class LinkedList
173:    {
174:    public:
175:        LinkedList();
176:        ~LinkedList() { delete myHead; }
177:        void Insert(Data * theData);
178:        void ShowAll() { myHead->Show(); }
179:    private:
180:        HeadNode * myHead;
181:    };
182:
183:    // At birth, i create the head node
184:    // It creates the tail node
185:    // So an empty list points to the head which
186:    // points to the tail and has nothing between
187:    LinkedList::LinkedList()
188:    {
189:        myHead = new HeadNode;
190:    }
191:
192:    // Delegate, delegate, delegate
193:    void LinkedList::Insert(Data * pData)
194:    {
195:        myHead->Insert(pData);
196:    }
197:
198:    // test driver program
199:    int main()
200:    {
```

19

LISTING 19.1 continued

```
201:        Data * pData;
202:        int val;
203:        LinkedList ll;
204:
205:        // ask the user to produce some values
206:        // put them in the list
207:        for (;;)
208:        {
209:            std::cout << "What value? (0 to stop): ";
210:            std::cin >> val;
211:            if (!val)
212:                break;
213:            pData = new Data(val);
214:            ll.Insert(pData);
215:        }
216:
217:        // now walk the list and show the data
218:        ll.ShowAll();
219:        return 0;  // ll falls out of scope and is destroyed!
220:    }
```

OUTPUT

```
What value? (0 to stop): 5
What value? (0 to stop): 8
What value? (0 to stop): 3
What value? (0 to stop): 9
What value? (0 to stop): 2
What value? (0 to stop): 10
What value? (0 to stop): 0
2
3
5
8
9
10
```

ANALYSIS The first thing to note is the enumerated constant, which provides three constant values: kIsSmaller, kIsLarger, and kIsSame. Every object that may be held in this linked list must support a Compare() method. These constants will be the result value returned by the Compare() method.

For illustration purposes, the class Data is created on lines 27–36, and the Compare() method is implemented on lines 40–48. A Data object holds a value and can compare itself with other Data objects. It also supports a Show() method to display the value of the Data object.

The easiest way to understand the workings of the linked list is to step through an example of using one. On line 199 the main program is declared, on line 201 a pointer to a Data object is declared, and on line 203 a local linked list is defined.

When the linked list is created, the constructor on line 187 is called. The only work done in the constructor is to allocate a HeadNode object and to assign that object's address to the pointer held in the linked list on line 180.

This allocation of a HeadNode invokes the HeadNode constructor shown on line 158. This in turn allocates a TailNode and assigns its address to the head node's myNext pointer. The creation of the TailNode calls the TailNode constructor shown on line 128, which is inline and does nothing.

Thus, by the simple act of allocating a linked list on the stack the list is created, a head and a tail node are created, and their relationship is established, as illustrated in Figure 19.2.

FIGURE 19.2

The linked list after it is created.

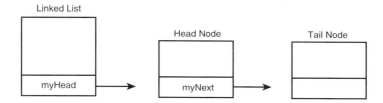

Line 207 begins an infinite loop. The user will be prompted for values to add to the linked list. He can add as many values as he likes, entering 0 when he is finished. The code on line 211 evaluates the value entered; if it is 0, it breaks out of the loop.

If the value is not 0 a new Data object is created on line 213, and that is inserted into the list on line 214. For illustration purposes, assume the user enters the value 15. This invokes the Insert method on line 193.

The linked list immediately delegates responsibility for inserting the object to its head node. This invokes the method Insert on line 165. The head node immediately passes the responsibility to whatever node its myNext is pointing to. In this (first) case, it is pointing to the tail node. (Remember, when the head node was born, it created a link to a tail node). This therefore invokes the method Insert on line 137.

TailNode::Insert knows that the object it has been handed must be inserted immediately before itself—that is, the new object will be in the list right before the tail node. Therefore, on line 139 it creates a new InternalNode object, passing in the data and a pointer to itself. This invokes the constructor for the InternalNode object, shown on line 87.

The InternalNode constructor does nothing more than initialize its Data pointer with the address of the Data object it was passed and its myNext pointer with the node's address it was passed. In this case, the node it will point to is the tail node. (Remember, the tail node passed in its own this pointer.)

Now that the InternalNode has been created, the address of that internal node is assigned to the pointer dataNode on line 139, and that address is in turn returned from the TailNode::Insert() method. This returns us to HeadNode::Insert(), where the address of the InternalNode is assigned to the HeadNode's myNext pointer (on line 167). Finally, the HeadNode's address is returned to the linked list where, on line 195, it is thrown away (nothing is done with it because the linked list already knows the address of the head node).

Why bother returning the address if it is not used? Insert is declared in the base class, Node. The return value is needed by the other implementations. If you change the return value of HeadNode::Insert(), you will get a compiler error; it is simpler just to return the HeadNode and let the linked list throw its address on the floor.

So what happened? The data was inserted into the list. The list passed it to the head. The head blindly passed the data to whatever the head happened to be pointing to. In this (first) case the head was pointing to the tail. The tail immediately created a new internal node, initializing the new node to point to the tail. The tail then returned the address of the new node to the head, which reassigned its myNext pointer to point to the new node. Hey! Presto! The data is in the list in the right place, as illustrated in Figure 19.3.

FIGURE 19.3

The linked list after the first node is inserted.

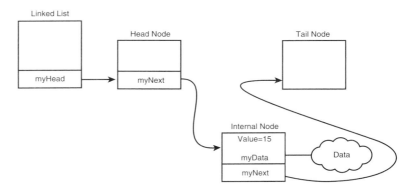

After inserting the first node, program control resumes at line 209. Once again the value is evaluated. For illustration purposes, assume that the value 3 is entered. This causes a new Data object to be created on line 213 and to be inserted into the list on line 214.

Once again, on line 195 the list passes the data to its HeadNode. The
HeadNode::Insert() method in turn passes the new value to whatever its myNext happens to be pointing to. As you know, it is now pointing to the node that contains the Data
object whose value is 15. This invokes the InternalNode::Insert() method on line 96.

On line 100, the InternalNode uses its myData pointer to tell its Data object (the one
whose value is 15) to call its Compare() method, passing in the new Data object (whose
value is 3). This invokes the Compare() method shown on line 40.

The two values are compared; and, because myValue will be 15 and
theOtherData.myValue will be 3, the returned value will be kIsLarger. This will cause
program flow to jump to line 107.

A new InternalNode is created for the new Data object. The new node will point to the
current InternalNode object, and the new InternalNode's address is returned from the
InternalNode::Insert() method to the HeadNode. Thus, the new node, whose object's
value is smaller than the current node's object's value, is inserted into the list, and the list
now looks like Figure 19.4.

FIGURE 19.4

*The linked list after the
second node is
inserted.*

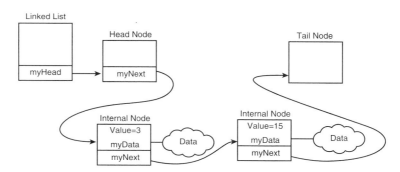

In the third invocation of the loop, the customer adds the value 8. This is larger than 3
but smaller than 15, and so should be inserted between the two existing nodes. Progress
will be exactly like the previous example except that when the node whose object's value
is 3 does the compare, rather than returning kIsLarger, it will return kIsSmaller (meaning that the object whose value is 3 is smaller than the new object, whose value is 8).

This will cause the InternalNode::Insert() method to branch to line 116. Rather than
creating a new node and inserting it, the InternalNode will just pass the new data on to
the Insert method of whatever its myNext pointer happens to be pointing to. In this
case, it will invoke InsertNode on the InternalNode whose Data object's value is 15.

The comparison will be done again, and now a new `InternalNode` will be created. This new `InternalNode` will point to the `InternalNode` whose `Data` object's value is 15, and its address will be passed back to the `InternalNode` whose `Data` object's value is 3, as shown on line 118.

The net effect is that the new node will be inserted into the list at the right location.

If at all possible, you'll want to step through the insertion of a number of nodes in your debugger. You should be able to watch these methods invoke one another, and the pointers be properly adjusted.

What Have You Learned, Dorothy?

"If I ever go looking for my heart's desire again, I won't look any further than my own backyard." While it is true there is no place like home, it is also true that this is nothing like procedural programming. In procedural programming, a controlling method would examine data and invoke functions.

In this object-oriented approach, each individual object is given a narrow and well-defined set of responsibilities. The linked list is responsible for maintaining the head node. The `HeadNode` immediately passes any new data on to whatever it currently points to, without regard for what that might be.

The `TailNode`, whenever it is handed data, creates a new node and inserts it. It knows only one thing: If this came to me, it gets inserted right before me.

Internal nodes are marginally more complicated; they ask their existing object to compare itself with the new object. Depending on the result, either they then insert or they just pass it along.

Note that the `InternalNode` has *no idea* how to do the comparison; that is properly left to the object itself. All the `InternalNode` knows is to ask the objects to compare themselves and to expect one of three possible answers. Given one answer, it inserts; otherwise it just passes it along, not knowing or caring where it will end up.

So who's in charge? In a well-designed object-oriented program, *no one* is in charge. Each object does its own little job, and the net effect is a well-running machine.

Summary

In this hour you learned about linked lists.

A linked list is a dynamically sized collection. Each data object is held in a node in the list. To get to a particular node, you must start at one end of the list and walk the list to the node you need.

You saw how to encapsulate limited functionality into each small class in the list and how these well-designed objects can work together synergistically. The node hierarchy uses inheritance to factor out common node methods such as `Insert()`. Nodes use virtual functions to allow you to treat the various kinds of Nodes polymorphically. For example, when you call `Insert()` you do not need to know if you are calling it on a head node, a tail node or an internal node.

Q&A

Q Why should I create a linked list if an array will work?

A An array must have a fixed size, whereas a linked list can be sized dynamically at runtime.

Q Why do you separate the data object from the node?

A Once you get your node objects working properly, you can reuse that code for any number of objects that might want to live in a list.

Q If I want to add other objects to the list, do I have to create a new list type and a new node type?

A For now, yes. We'll solve that when we get to templates.

19

PART VI
Special Topics

Hour

HOUR 20

Special Classes, Functions, and Pointers

C++ offers a number of ways to limit the scope and impact of variables and pointers. So far you've seen how to create global variables, local function variables, pointers to variables, and class member variables. In this hour you will learn

- What static member variables and static member functions are
- How to use static member variables and static member functions
- What friend functions and friend classes are
- How to use friend functions to solve special problems
- How to use pointers to member functions

Static Member Data

Until now, you have probably thought of the data in each object as unique to that object and not shared among objects in a class. For example, if you have five Cat objects, each has its own age, weight, and other data. The age of one does not affect the age of another.

There are times, however, when you'll want to keep track of information that is shared among the many objects of a class. For example, you might want to know how many Cats have been born so far, and how many are still in existence.

Unlike other member variables, *static* member variables are shared among all instances of a class. They are a compromise between global data, which is available to all parts of your program, and member data, which is usually available only to each object.

You can think of a static member as belonging to the class rather than to the object. Normal member data is one per object, but static members are one per class. Listing 20.1 declares a Cat object with a static data member, HowManyCats. This variable keeps track of how many Cat objects have been created. This is done by incrementing the static variable, HowManyCats, with each construction and decrementing it with each destruction.

LISTING 20.1   Static Member Data

```
0:  //Listing 20.1 static data members
1:  #include <iostream>
2:
3:  class Cat
4:  {
5:  public:
6:      Cat(int age = 1):itsAge(age){HowManyCats++; }
7:      virtual ~Cat() { HowManyCats--; }
8:      virtual int GetAge() { return itsAge; }
9:      virtual void SetAge(int age) { itsAge = age; }
10:     static int HowManyCats;
11:
12: private:
13:     int itsAge;
14:
15: };
16:
17: int Cat::HowManyCats = 0;
18:
19: int main()
20: {
21:     const int MaxCats = 5;
22:     Cat *CatHouse[MaxCats];
23:     int i;
24:     for (i = 0; i<MaxCats; i++)
25:         CatHouse[i] = new Cat(i);
26:
27:     for (i = 0; i<MaxCats; i++)
```

LISTING 20.1   continued

```
28:      {
29:          std::cout << "There are ";
30:          std::cout << Cat::HowManyCats;
31:          std::cout << " cats left!\n";
32:          std::cout << "Deleting the one which is ";
33:          std::cout << CatHouse[i]->GetAge();
34:          std::cout << " years old\n";
35:          delete CatHouse[i];
36:          CatHouse[i] = 0;
37:      }
38:      return 0;
39:  }
```

OUTPUT
```
There are 5 cats left!
Deleting the one which is 0 years old
There are 4 cats left!
Deleting the one which is 1 years old
There are 3 cats left!
Deleting the one which is 2 years old
There are 2 cats left!
Deleting the one which is 3 years old
There are 1 cats left!
Deleting the one which is 4 years old
```

ANALYSIS   On lines 3–15 the simplified class Cat is declared. On line 10, HowManyCats is declared to be a static member variable of type int.

The declaration of HowManyCats does not define an integer; no storage space is set aside. Unlike the non-static member variables, no storage space is set aside for static members as a result of instantiating a Cat object, because the HowManyCats member variable is not *in* the object. Therefore, on line 17 the variable is defined and initialized.

It is a common mistake to forget to define the static member variables of classes. Don't let this happen to you! Of course, if it does, the linker will catch it with a pithy error message such as the following:

```
undefined_reference toCat::HowManyCats
```

You don't need to do this for itsAge because it is a non-static member variable and is defined each time you make a Cat object, which is done here on line 25.

The constructor for Cat increments the static member variable on line 6. The destructor decrements it on line 7. Thus, at any moment, HowManyCats has an accurate measure of how many Cat objects were created but not yet destroyed.

20

The main program on lines 19–39 instantiates five `Cat`s and puts them in an array. This calls five `Cat` constructors; thus `HowManyCats` is incremented five times from its initial value of `0`.

The program then loops through each of the five positions in the array and prints out the value of `HowManyCats` before deleting the current `Cat` pointer. The printout reflects that the starting value is `5` (after all, five are constructed), and that each time the loop is run, one less `Cat` remains.

Note that `HowManyCats` is public and is accessed directly by `main()`. There is no reason to expose this member variable in this way. It is preferable to make it private along with the other member variables and provide a public accessor method, as long as you will always access the data through an instance of `Cat`. On the other hand, if you'd like to access this data directly without necessarily having a `Cat` object available, you have two options: keep it public or provide a static member function.

Static Member Functions

Static member functions are like static member variables: They exist not in an object but in the scope of the class. Therefore, they can be called without having an object of that class, as illustrated in Listing 20.2.

LISTING 20.2   Static Member Functions

```
 0:    //Listing 20.2 static data members
 1:    #include <iostream>
 2:
 3:    class Cat
 4:    {
 5:    public:
 6:        Cat(int age = 1):itsAge(age){HowManyCats++; }
 7:        virtual ~Cat() { HowManyCats--; }
 8:        virtual int GetAge() { return itsAge; }
 9:        virtual void SetAge(int age) { itsAge = age; }
10:        static int GetHowMany() { return HowManyCats; }
11:    private:
12:        int itsAge;
13:        static int HowManyCats;
14:    };
15:
16:    int Cat::HowManyCats = 0;
17:
18:    void TelepathicFunction();
19:
20:    int main()
```

LISTING 20.2 continued

```
21:  {
22:      const int MaxCats = 5;
23:      Cat *CatHouse[MaxCats];
24:      int i;
25:      for (i = 0; i<MaxCats; i++)
26:      {
27:          CatHouse[i] = new Cat(i);
28:          TelepathicFunction();
29:      }
30:
31:      for ( i = 0; i<MaxCats; i++)
32:      {
33:          delete CatHouse[i];
34:          TelepathicFunction();
35:      }
36:      return 0;
37:  }
38:
39:  void TelepathicFunction()
40:  {
41:      std::cout << "There are " << Cat::GetHowMany()
42:          << " cats alive!\n";
43:  }
```

OUTPUT

```
There are 1 cats alive
There are 2 cats alive
There are 3 cats alive
There are 4 cats alive
There are 5 cats alive
There are 4 cats alive
There are 3 cats alive
There are 2 cats alive
There are 1 cats alive
There are 0 cats alive
```

ANALYSIS The static member variable HowManyCats is declared to have private access on line 13 of the Cat declaration. The public accessor function, GetHowMany(), is declared to be both public and static on line 10.

Because GetHowMany() is public, it can be accessed by any function, and because it is static there is no need to have an object of type Cat on which to call it. Therefore, on line 41, the function TelepathicFunction() is able to access the public static accessor even though it has no access to a Cat object. Of course, you could have called GetHowMany() on the Cat objects available in main(), just as with any other accessor functions.

20

Static member functions do not have a this pointer; therefore, they cannot be declared const. Also, because member data variables are accessed in member functions using the this pointer, static member functions cannot access any non-static member variables!

Containment

As you have seen in previous examples, it is possible for the member data of a class to include objects of another class. C++ programmers say that the outer class contains the inner class. Therefore, an Employee class might contain string objects (for the name of the employee) as well as integers (for the employee's salary), and so forth.

Listing 20.3 is a stripped-down but useful String class.

LISTING 20.3   The String Class

```
0:  #include <iostream>
1:  #include <string.h>
2:
3:  class String
4:  {
5:  public:
6:      // constructors
7:      String();
8:      String(const char *const);
9:      String(const String &);
10:     ~String();
11:
12:     // overloaded operators
13:     char & operator[](int offset);
14:     char operator[](int offset) const;
15:     String operator+(const String&);
16:     void operator+=(const String&);
17:     String & operator= (const String &);
18:
19:     // General accessors
20:     int GetLen()const { return itsLen; }
21:     const char * GetString() const { return itsString; }
22:     // static int ConstructorCount;
23:
24:  private:
25:     String(int);          // private constructor
26:     char * itsString;
27:     int itsLen;
28:  };
```

LISTING 20.3   continued

```
29:
30:    // default constructor creates string of 0 bytes
31:    String::String()
32:    {
33:        itsString = new char[1];
34:        itsString[0] = '\0';
35:        itsLen=0;
36:        // std::cout << "\tDefault string constructor\n";
37:        // ConstructorCount++;
38:    }
39:
40:    // private (helper) constructor, used only by
41:    // class methods for creating a new string of
42:    // required size.  Null filled.
43:    String::String(int len)
44:    {
45:        itsString = new char[len+1];
46:        int i;
47:        for (i = 0; i<=len; i++)
48:            itsString[i] = '\0';
49:        itsLen=len;
50:        // std::cout << "\tString(int) constructor\n";
51:        // ConstructorCount++;
52:    }
53:
54:    String::String(const char * const cString)
55:    {
56:        itsLen = strlen(cString);
57:        itsString = new char[itsLen+1];
58:        int i;
59:        for (i = 0; i<itsLen; i++)
60:            itsString[i] = cString[i];
61:        itsString[itsLen]='\0';
62:        // std::cout << "\tString(char*) constructor\n";
63:        // ConstructorCount++;
64:    }
65:
66:    String::String (const String & rhs)
67:    {
68:        itsLen=rhs.GetLen();
69:        itsString = new char[itsLen+1];
70:        int i;
71:        for ( i = 0; i<itsLen;i++)
72:            itsString[i] = rhs[i];
73:        itsString[itsLen] = '\0';
74:        // std::cout << "\tString(String&) constructor\n";
75:        // ConstructorCount++;
76:    }
77:
```

20

LISTING 20.3   continued

```
 78:  String::~String ()
 79:  {
 80:      delete [] itsString;
 81:      itsLen = 0;
 82:      // std::cout << "\tString destructor\n";
 83:  }
 84:
 85:  // operator equals, frees existing memory
 86:  // then copies string and size
 87:  String& String::operator=(const String & rhs)
 88:  {
 89:      if (this == &rhs)
 90:          return *this;
 91:      delete [] itsString;
 92:      itsLen=rhs.GetLen();
 93:      itsString = new char[itsLen+1];
 94:      int i;
 95:      for (i = 0; i<itsLen;i++)
 96:          itsString[i] = rhs[i];
 97:      itsString[itsLen] = '\0';
 98:      return *this;
 99:      // std::cout << "\tString operator=\n";
100:  }
101:
102:  //non constant offset operator, returns
103:  // reference to character so it can be
104:  // changed!
105:  char & String::operator[](int offset)
106:  {
107:      if (offset > itsLen)
108:          return itsString[itsLen-1];
109:      else
110:          return itsString[offset];
111:  }
112:
113:  // constant offset operator for use
114:  // on const objects (see copy constructor!)
115:  char String::operator[](int offset) const
116:  {
117:      if (offset > itsLen)
118:          return itsString[itsLen-1];
119:      else
120:          return itsString[offset];
121:  }
122:
123:  // creates a new string by adding current
124:  // string to rhs
125:  String String::operator+(const String& rhs)
126:  {
```

LISTING 20.3   continued

```
127:        int  totalLen = itsLen + rhs.GetLen();
128:        int i,j;
129:        String temp(totalLen);
130:        for (i = 0; i<itsLen; i++)
131:            temp[i] = itsString[i];
132:        for (j = 0; j<rhs.GetLen(); j++, i++)
133:            temp[i] = rhs[j];
134:        temp[totalLen]='\0';
135:        return temp;
136:    }
137:
138:    // changes current string, returns nothing
139:    void String::operator+=(const String& rhs)
140:    {
141:        int rhsLen = rhs.GetLen();
142:        int totalLen = itsLen + rhsLen;
143:        int i,j;
144:        String  temp(totalLen);
145:        for (i = 0; i<itsLen; i++)
146:            temp[i] = itsString[i];
147:        for (j = 0; j<rhs.GetLen(); j++, i++)
148:            temp[i] = rhs[i-itsLen];
149:        temp[totalLen]='\0';
150:        *this = temp;
151:    }
152:
153:    // int String::ConstructorCount = 0;
```

OUTPUT   This program has no output.

ANALYSIS   On line 22 the static member variable `ConstructorCount` is declared, and on line 153 it is initialized. This variable is incremented in each string constructor.

Listing 20.4 describes an `Employee` class that contains three string objects. Note that a number of statements are commented out; they will be used in later listings.

20

> Put the code from Listing 20.3 into a file called STRING.HPP. Then any time you need the `String` class you can include Listing 20.3 by using #include. For example, at the top of Listing 20.4 #include "String.hpp" appears. This adds the `String` class to your program.

LISTING 20.4   The `Employee` Class and Main Program

```
0:  #include "String.hpp"
1:  // iostream already included
```

LISTING 20.4   continued

```
 2:  using std::cout; // this file uses std::cout
 3:
 4:
 5:  class Employee
 6:  {
 7:  public:
 8:      Employee();
 9:      Employee(char *, char *, char *, long);
10:      ~Employee();
11:      Employee(const Employee&);
12:      Employee & operator= (const Employee &);
13:
14:      const String & GetFirstName() const { return itsFirstName; }
15:      const String & GetLastName() const { return itsLastName; }
16:      const String & GetAddress() const { return itsAddress; }
17:      long GetSalary() const { return itsSalary; }
18:
19:      void SetFirstName(const String & fName)
20:          { itsFirstName = fName; }
21:      void SetLastName(const String & lName)
22:          { itsLastName = lName; }
23:      void SetAddress(const String & address)
24:          { itsAddress = address; }
25:      void SetSalary(long salary) { itsSalary = salary; }
26:  private:
27:      String    itsFirstName;
28:      String    itsLastName;
29:      String    itsAddress;
30:      long      itsSalary;
31:  };
32:
33:  Employee::Employee():
34:      itsFirstName(""),
35:      itsLastName(""),
36:      itsAddress(""),
37:      itsSalary(0)
38:  {}
39:
40:  Employee::Employee(char * firstName, char * lastName,
41:      char * address, long salary):
42:      itsFirstName(firstName),
43:      itsLastName(lastName),
44:      itsAddress(address),
45:      itsSalary(salary)
46:  {}
47:
48:  Employee::Employee(const Employee & rhs):
49:      itsFirstName(rhs.GetFirstName()),
50:      itsLastName(rhs.GetLastName()),
```

LISTING 20.4   continued

```
51:        itsAddress(rhs.GetAddress()),
52:        itsSalary(rhs.GetSalary())
53:    {}
54:
55:    Employee::~Employee() {}
56:
57:    Employee & Employee::operator= (const Employee & rhs)
58:    {
59:        if (this == &rhs)
60:            return *this;
61:
62:        itsFirstName = rhs.GetFirstName();
63:        itsLastName = rhs.GetLastName();
64:        itsAddress = rhs.GetAddress();
65:        itsSalary = rhs.GetSalary();
66:
67:        return *this;
68:    }
69:
70:    int main()
71:    {
72:        Employee Edie("Jane","Doe","1461 Shore Parkway", 20000);
73:        Edie.SetSalary(50000);
74:        String LastName("Levine");
75:        Edie.SetLastName(LastName);
76:        Edie.SetFirstName("Edythe");
77:
78:        cout << "Name: ";
79:        cout << Edie.GetFirstName().GetString();
80:        cout << " " << Edie.GetLastName().GetString();
81:        cout << ".\nAddress: ";
82:        cout << Edie.GetAddress().GetString();
83:        cout << ".\nSalary: " ;
84:        cout << Edie.GetSalary();
85:        return 0;
86:    }
```

20

OUTPUT
```
Name; Edythe Levine
Address: 1461 Shore Parkway
Salary: 50000
```

ANALYSIS   Listing 20.4 shows the Employee class, which contains three string objects: itsFirstName, itsLastName, and itsAddress.

On line 72 an Employee object is created, and four values are passed in to initialize it. On line 73, the Employee access function SetSalary() is called, with the constant value 50000. Note that in a real program this would either be a dynamic value (set at runtime) or a constant.

On line 74, a string is created and initialized using a C++ string constant. This string object is then used as an argument to SetLastName() on line 75.

On line 76, the Employee function SetFirstName() is called with yet another string constant. However, if you are paying close attention you will notice that Employee does not have a function SetFirstName() that takes a character string as its argument; SetFirstName() requires a constant string reference.

The compiler resolves this because it knows how to make a string from a constant character string. It knows this because you told it how to do so on line 8 of Listing 20.3.

Accessing Members of the Contained Class

Employee objects do not have special access to the member variables of String. If the employee object Edie tried to access the member variable itsLen of its own itsFirstName member variable, it would get a compile-time error. This is not much of a burden, however. The accessor functions provide an interface for the String class, and the Employee class need not worry about the implementation details any more than it worries about how the integer variable, itsSalary, stores its information.

Filtering Access to Contained Members

Note that the String class provides the operator+. The designer of the Employee class has blocked access to the operator+ being called on Employee objects by declaring that all the string accessors, such as GetFirstName(), return a constant reference. Because operator+ is not (and can't be) a const function (because it changes the object it is called on), attempting to write the following will cause a compile-time error:

```
String buffer = Edie.GetFirstName() + Edie.GetLastName();
```

GetFirstName() returns a constant String, and you can't call operator+ on a constant object.

To fix this, overload GetFirstName() to be non-const:

```
const String & GetFirstName() const { return itsFirstName; }
String & GetFirstName()  { return itsFirstName; }
```

Note that the return value is no longer const and that the member function itself is no longer const. Changing the return value is not sufficient to overload the function name; you must change the constancy of the function itself. By providing both a const and a non-const version, the compiler will invoke the const version wherever possible (for example, when a client calls GetFirstName) and the non-const version as needed (for example, when invoked with the operator+.

The Cost of Containment

It is important to note that the user of an `Employee` class pays the price of each of those string objects every time one is constructed or a copy of the `Employee` is made.

Uncommenting the `cout` statements in Listing 20.3 (lines 38, 52, 64, 76, 84, and 101) reveals how often these are called.

Copying by Value Versus by Reference

When you pass `Employee` objects by value, all their contained strings are copied as well, and therefore copy constructors are called. This is very expensive; it takes up memory and it takes time.

When you pass `Employee` objects by reference (using pointers or references), all this is saved. This is why C++ programmers work hard never to pass anything larger than 4 bytes by value.

Friend Classes

Sometimes you will create classes together, as a set. These paired classes may need access to one another's private members, but you may not want to make that information public.

NEW TERM   If you want to expose your private member data or functions to another class, you must declare that class to be a *friend*. This extends the interface of your class to include the friend class.

It is important to note that friendship cannot be transferred. Just because you are my friend and Joe is your friend doesn't mean Joe is my friend. Friendship is not inherited, either. Again, just because you are my friend and I'm willing to share my secrets with you doesn't mean I'm willing to share my secrets with your children.

Finally, friendship is not commutative. Assigning `Class One` to be a friend of `Class Two` does not make `Class Two` a friend of `Class One`. Just because you are willing to tell me your secrets doesn't mean I am willing to tell you mine.

Declarations of friend classes should be used with extreme caution. If two classes are inextricably entwined, and one must frequently access data in the other, there may be good reason to use this declaration. But use it sparingly; it is often just as easy to use the public accessor methods. Doing so allows you to change one class without having to recompile the other.

20

You will often hear novice C++ programmers complain that friend declarations "undermine" the encapsulation so important to object-oriented programming. This is, frankly, errant nonsense. The friend declaration makes the declared friend part of the class interface and is no more an undermining of encapsulation than is public derivation.

Friend Functions

At times, you will want to grant the friend level of access, not to an entire class, but to only one or two functions of that class. You can do this by declaring the member functions of the other class to be friends, rather than declaring the entire class to be a friend. In fact, you can declare any function, whether or not it is a member function of another class, to be a friend function.

Pointers to Functions

Just as an array name is a constant pointer to the first element of the array, a function name is a constant pointer to the function. It is possible to declare a pointer variable that points to a function, and to invoke the function by using that pointer. This can be very useful; it allows you to create programs that decide which functions to invoke based on user input.

The only tricky part about function pointers is understanding the type of the object being pointed to. A pointer to `int` points to an integer variable, and a pointer to a function must point to a function of the appropriate return type and signature.

In the declaration

```
long (* funcPtr) (int);
```

`funcPtr` is declared to be a pointer (note the `*` in front of the name) that points to a function that takes an integer parameter and returns a `long`. The parentheses around `* funcPtr` are necessary because the parentheses around `int` bind more tightly—that is, they have higher precedence than the indirection operator (`*`). Without the first parenthesis, this would declare a function that takes an integer and returns a pointer to a `long`. (Remember that spaces are meaningless here.)

Examine these two declarations:

```
long * Function (int);
long (* funcPtr) (int);
```

The first, Function (), is a *function* taking an integer and returning a pointer to a variable of type long. The second, funcPtr, is a *pointer* to a function taking an integer and returning a variable of type long.

The declaration of a function pointer will always include the return type and the parentheses indicating the type of the parameters, if any. Listing 20.5 illustrates the declaration and use of function pointers.

LISTING 20.5   Pointers to Functions

```
0:   // Listing 20.5 Using function pointers
1:   #include <iostream>
2:
3:   void Square (int&,int&);
4:   void Cube (int&, int&);
5:   void Swap (int&, int &);
6:   void GetVals(int&, int&);
7:   void PrintVals(int, int);
8:
9:   int main()
10:  {
11:      void (* pFunc) (int &, int &);
12:      bool fQuit = false;
13:
14:      int valOne=1, valTwo=2;
15:      int choice;
16:      while (fQuit == false)
17:      {
18:          std::cout << "(0)Quit (1)Change Values "
19:              << "(2)Square (3)Cube (4)Swap: ";
20:          std::cin >> choice;
21:          switch (choice)
22:          {
23:          case 1:
24:              pFunc = GetVals;
25:              break;
26:          case 2:
27:              pFunc = Square;
28:              break;
29:          case 3:
30:              pFunc = Cube;
31:              break;
32:          case 4:
33:              pFunc = Swap;
34:              break;
35:          default :
36:              fQuit = true;
37:              break;
38:          }
```

20

LISTING 20.5   continued

```
39:
40:             if (fQuit)
41:                 break;
42:
43:             PrintVals(valOne, valTwo);
44:             pFunc(valOne, valTwo);
45:             PrintVals(valOne, valTwo);
46:         }
47:         return 0;
48:  }
49:
50:  void PrintVals(int x, int y)
51:  {
52:      std::cout << "x: " << x << " y: " << y << std::endl;
53:  }
54:
55:  void Square (int & rX, int & rY)
56:  {
57:      rX *= rX;
58:      rY *= rY;
59:  }
60:
61:  void Cube (int & rX, int & rY)
62:  {
63:      int tmp;
64:
65:      tmp = rX;
66:      rX *= rX;
67:      rX = rX * tmp;
68:
69:      tmp = rY;
70:      rY *= rY;
71:      rY = rY * tmp;
72:  }
73:
74:  void Swap(int & rX, int & rY)
75:  {
76:      int temp;
77:      temp = rX;
78:      rX = rY;
79:      rY = temp;
80:  }
81:
82:  void GetVals (int & rValOne, int & rValTwo)
83:  {
84:      std::cout << "New value for ValOne: ";
85:      std::cin >> rValOne;
86:      std::cout << "New value for ValTwo: ";
87:      std::cin >> rValTwo;
88:  }
```

OUTPUT

```
  (0)Quit (1)Change Values (2)Square (3)Cube (4)Swap: 1
x: 1 y:2
New value for ValOne: 2
New value for ValTwo: 3
x: 2 y:3
  (0)Quit (1)Change Values (2)Square (3)Cube (4)Swap: 3
x: 2 y:3
x: 8 y: 27
  (0)Quit (1)Change Values (2)Square (3)Cube (4)Swap: 2
x: 8 y: 27
x:64 y:729
  (0)Quit (1)Change Values (2)Square (3)Cube (4)Swap: 4
x:64 y:729
x:729 y:64
  (0)Quit (1)Change Values (2)Square (3)Cube (4)Swap: 0
```

ANALYSIS On lines 3–6 four functions are declared, each with the same return type and signature, returning void and taking two references to integers.

On line 11, pFunc is declared to be a pointer to a function that returns void and takes two integer reference parameters. Any of the previous functions can be pointed to by pFunc. The user is repeatedly offered the choice of which functions to invoke, and pFunc is assigned accordingly. On lines 43–45, the current value of the two integers is printed, the currently assigned function is invoked, and then the values are printed again.

Shorthand Invocation

The pointer to a function does not need to be dereferenced, although you are free to do so. Therefore, if pFunc is a pointer to a function taking an integer and returning a variable of type long, and you assign pFunc to a matching function, you can invoke that function with either

```
pFunc(x);
```

or

```
(*pFunc)(x);
```

The two forms are identical. The former is just a shorthand version of the latter.

Arrays of Pointers to Functions

Just as you can declare an array of pointers to integers, you can declare an array of pointers to functions returning a specific value type and with a specific signature. (See Listing 20.6.)

20

LISTING 20.6   Using an Array of Pointers to Functions

```
0:    // Listing 20.6 arrays of pointers to functions
1:    #include <iostream>
2:
3:    void Square (int&,int&);
4:    void Cube (int&, int&);
5:    void Swap (int&, int &);
6:    void GetVals(int&, int&);
7:    void PrintVals(int, int);
8:
9:    int main()
10:   {
11:       int valOne=1, valTwo=2;
12:       int choice,i;
13:       const int MaxArray = 5;
14:       void (*pFuncArray[MaxArray])(int&, int&);
15:
16:       for (i=0;i<MaxArray;i++)
17:       {
18:           std::cout << "(1)Change Values "
19:               << "(2)Square (3)Cube (4)Swap: ";
20:           std::cin >> choice;
21:           switch (choice)
22:           {
23:           case 1:
24:               pFuncArray[i] = GetVals;
25:               break;
26:           case 2:
27:               pFuncArray[i] = Square;
28:               break;
29:           case 3:
30:               pFuncArray[i] = Cube;
31:               break;
32:           case 4:
33:               pFuncArray[i] = Swap;
34:               break;
35:           default:
36:               pFuncArray[i] = 0;
37:           }
38:       }
39:
40:       for (i=0;i<MaxArray; i++)
41:       {
42:           pFuncArray[i](valOne,valTwo);
43:           PrintVals(valOne,valTwo);
44:       }
45:       return 0;
46:   }
47:
```

LISTING 20.6   continued

```
48:   void PrintVals(int x, int y)
49:   {
50:       std::cout << "x: " << x << " y: " << y << std::endl;
51:   }
52:
53:   void Square (int & rX, int & rY)
54:   {
55:       rX *= rX;
56:       rY *= rY;
57:   }
58:
59:   void Cube (int & rX, int & rY)
60:   {
61:       int tmp;
62:
63:       tmp = rX;
64:       rX *= rX;
65:       rX = rX * tmp;
66:
67:       tmp = rY;
68:       rY *= rY;
69:       rY = rY * tmp;
70:   }
71:
72:   void Swap(int & rX, int & rY)
73:   {
74:       int temp;
75:       temp = rX;
76:       rX = rY;
77:       rY = temp;
78:   }
79:
80:   void GetVals (int & rValOne, int & rValTwo)
81:   {
82:       std::cout << "New value for ValOne: ";
83:       std::cin >> rValOne;
84:       std::cout << "New value for ValTwo: ";
85:       std::cin >> rValTwo;
86:   }
```

20

OUTPUT

```
(1)Change Values (2)Square (3)Cube (4)Swap: 1
(1)Change Values (2)Square (3)Cube (4)Swap: 2
(1)Change Values (2)Square (3)Cube (4)Swap: 3
(1)Change Values (2)Square (3)Cube (4)Swap: 4
(1)Change Values (2)Square (3)Cube (4)Swap: 2
New Value for ValOne: 2
New Value for ValTwo: 3
x: 2 y: 3
```

```
x: 4 y: 9
x: 64 y: 729
x: 729 y: 64
x: 531441 y:4096
```

ANALYSIS On lines 16–37, the user is asked to pick the functions to invoke, and each member of the array is assigned the address of the appropriate function. On lines 40–44, each function is invoked in turn. The result is printed after each invocation.

Passing Pointers to Functions to Other Functions

The pointers to functions (and arrays of pointers to functions, for that matter) can be passed to other functions that may take action and then call the right function using the pointer.

For example, you might improve Listing 20.6 by passing the chosen function pointer to another function (outside of `main()`) that will print the values, invoke the function, and then print the values again. Listing 20.7 illustrates this variation.

LISTING 20.7   Passing Pointers to Functions as Function Arguments

```
 0:  // Listing 20.7 Without function pointers
 1:  #include <iostream>
 2:  using namespace std; // this file uses std:: objects
 3:
 4:  void Square (int&,int&);
 5:  void Cube (int&, int&);
 6:  void Swap (int&, int &);
 7:  void GetVals(int&, int&);
 8:  void PrintVals(void (*)(int&, int&),int&, int&);
 9:
10:  int main()
11:  {
12:      int valOne=1, valTwo=2;
13:      int choice;
14:      bool fQuit = false;
15:
16:      void (*pFunc)(int&, int&);
17:
18:      while (fQuit == false)
19:      {
20:          cout << "(0)Quit (1)Change Values "
21:              << "(2)Square (3)Cube (4)Swap: ";
22:          cin >> choice;
23:          switch (choice)
24:          {
25:          case 1:
26:              pFunc = GetVals;
```

LISTING 20.7   continued

```
27:                break;
28:            case 2:
29:                pFunc = Square;
30:                break;
31:            case 3:
32:                pFunc = Cube;
33:                break;
34:            case 4:
35:                pFunc = Swap;
36:                break;
37:            default:
38:                fQuit = true;
39:                break;
40:            }
41:            if (fQuit == true)
42:                break;
43:            PrintVals ( pFunc, valOne, valTwo);
44:        }
45:
46:        return 0;
47:    }
48:
49:    void PrintVals( void (*pFunc)(int&, int&),int& x, int& y)
50:    {
51:        cout << "x: " << x << " y: " << y << endl;
52:        pFunc(x,y);
53:        cout << "x: " << x << " y: " << y << endl;
54:    }
55:
56:    void Square (int & rX, int & rY)
57:    {
58:        rX *= rX;
59:        rY *= rY;
60:    }
61:
62:    void Cube (int & rX, int & rY)
63:    {
64:        int tmp;
65:
66:        tmp = rX;
67:        rX *= rX;
68:        rX = rX * tmp;
69:
70:        tmp = rY;
71:        rY *= rY;
72:        rY = rY * tmp;
73:    }
74:
75:    void Swap(int & rX, int & rY)
```

20

LISTING 20.7   continued

```
76:  {
77:      int temp;
78:      temp = rX;
79:      rX = rY;
80:      rY = temp;
81:  }
82:
83:  void GetVals (int & rValOne, int & rValTwo)
84:  {
85:      cout << "New value for ValOne: ";
86:      cin >> rValOne;
87:      cout << "New value for ValTwo: ";
88:      cin >> rValTwo;
89:  }
```

OUTPUT

```
 (0)Quit (1)Change Values (2)Square (3)Cube (4)Swap: 1
x: 1 y:2
New value for ValOne: 2
New value for ValTwo: 3
x: 2 y:3
 (0)Quit (1)Change Values (2)Square (3)Cube (4)Swap: 3
x: 2 y:3
x: 8 y: 27
 (0)Quit (1)Change Values (2)Square (3)Cube (4)Swap: 2
x: 8 y: 27
x:64 y:729
 (0)Quit (1)Change Values (2)Square (3)Cube (4)Swap: 4
x:64 y:729
x:729 y:64
 (0)Quit (1)Change Values (2)Square (3)Cube (4)Swap: 0
```

ANALYSIS   On line 16, pFunc is declared to be a pointer to a function returning void and taking two parameters, both of which are integer references. On line 8, PrintVals is declared to be a function taking three parameters. The first is a pointer to a function that returns void but takes two integer reference parameters, and the second and third arguments to PrintVals are integer references. The user is again prompted which functions to call, and then on line 43 PrintVals is called.

Go find a C++ programmer and ask him what this declaration means:

```
void PrintVals(void (*)(int&, int&),int&, int&);
```

This is the kind of declaration that you will use infrequently and will probably look up in the book each time you need it, but it will save your program on those rare occasions when it is exactly the required construct.

Using `typedef` with Pointers to Functions

The construct void (*)(int&, int&) is cumbersome, at best. You can use typedef to simplify this, by declaring a type VPF as a pointer to a function returning void and taking two integer references. Listing 20.8 rewrites the beginning of Listing 20.7 using this typedef statement.

LISTING 20.8   Using `typedef` to Make Pointers to Functions More Readable

```
0:  // Listing 20.8. using typedef
1:  #include <iostream>
2:  using namespace std; // this file uses std:: objects
3:
4:  void Square (int&,int&);
5:  void Cube (int&, int&);
6:  void Swap (int&, int &);
7:  void GetVals(int&, int&);
8:  typedef  void (*VPF) (int&, int&) ;
9:  void PrintVals(VPF,int&, int&);
10:
11: int main()
12: {
13:     int valOne=1, valTwo=2;
14:     int choice;
15:     bool fQuit = false;
16:
17:     VPF pFunc;
18:
19:     while (fQuit == false)
20:     {
21:         cout << "(0)Quit (1)Change Values"
22:             << "(2)Square (3)Cube (4)Swap: ";
23:         cin >> choice;
24:         switch (choice)
25:         {
26:         case 1:
27:             pFunc = GetVals;
28:             break;
29:         case 2:
30:             pFunc = Square;
31:             break;
32:         case 3:
33:             pFunc = Cube;
34:             break;
35:         case 4:
36:             pFunc = Swap;
37:             break;
38:         default:
```

20

LISTING 20.8   continued

```
39:                 fQuit = true;
40:                 break;
41:             }
42:             if (fQuit == true)
43:                 break;
44:             PrintVals ( pFunc, valOne, valTwo);
45:         }
46:     return 0;
47: }
48:
49: void PrintVals( VPF pFunc,int& x, int& y)
50: {
51:     cout << "x: " << x << " y: " << y << endl;
52:     pFunc(x,y);
53:     cout << "x: " << x << " y: " << y << endl;
54: }
55:
56: void Square (int & rX, int & rY)
57: {
58:     rX *= rX;
59:     rY *= rY;
60: }
61:
62: void Cube (int & rX, int & rY)
63: {
64:     int tmp;
65:
66:     tmp = rX;
67:     rX *= rX;
68:     rX = rX * tmp;
69:
70:     tmp = rY;
71:     rY *= rY;
72:     rY = rY * tmp;
73: }
74:
75: void Swap(int & rX, int & rY)
76: {
77:     int temp;
78:     temp = rX;
79:     rX = rY;
80:     rY = temp;
81: }
82:
83: void GetVals (int & rValOne, int & rValTwo)
84: {
85:     cout << "New value for ValOne: ";
86:     cin >> rValOne;
87:     cout << "New value for ValTwo: ";
```

LISTING 20.8   continued

```
88:      cin >> rValTwo;
89:  }
```

OUTPUT

```
 (0)Quit (1)Change Values (2)Square (3)Cube (4)Swap: 1
x: 1 y:2
New value for ValOne: 2
New value for ValTwo: 3
x: 2 y:3
 (0)Quit (1)Change Values (2)Square (3)Cube (4)Swap: 3
x: 2 y:3
x: 8 y: 27
 (0)Quit (1)Change Values (2)Square (3)Cube (4)Swap: 2
x: 8 y: 27
x:64 y:729
 (0)Quit (1)Change Values (2)Square (3)Cube (4)Swap: 4
x:64 y:729
x:729 y:64
 (0)Quit (1)Change Values (2)Square (3)Cube (4)Swap: 0
```

ANALYSIS   On line 8, `typedef` is used to declare `VPF` to be of the type function that returns `void` and takes two parameters, both integer references.

On line 9, the function `PrintVals()` is declared to take three parameters, a `VPF` and two integer references. On line 17, `pFunc` is now declared to be of type `VPF`.

Once the type `VPF` is defined, all subsequent uses, to declare `pFunc` and `PrintVals()`, are much cleaner.

Pointers to Member Functions

Up until this point, all the function pointers you've created have been for general, non-class functions. It is also possible to create pointers to functions that are members of classes.

To create a pointer to member function, use the same syntax as with a pointer to a function, but include the class name and the scoping operator (`::`). Thus, if `pFunc` points to a member function of the class `Shape`, which takes two integers and returns `void`, the declaration for `pFunc` is the following:

```
void (Shape::*pFunc) (int, int);
```

Pointers to member functions are used in exactly the same way as pointers to functions, except that they require an object of the correct class on which to invoke them. Listing 20.9 illustrates the use of pointers to member functions.

20

Some compilers do not support the use of a function name as a synonym for
its address. If your compiler gives you a warning or error with this listing, try
changing lines 71–76 to

```
71:    case 1:
72:        pFunc = & Mammal::Speak;
73:        break;
74:    default:
75:        pFunc = & Mammal::Move;
76:        break;
```

and then make the same change on all subsequent listings. (Note addition
of ampersand (&) on each line.)

LISTING 20.9   Pointers to Member Functions

```
0:   //Listing 20.9 Pointers to member functions
1:   #include <iostream>
2:
3:   enum BOOL {FALSE, TRUE};
4:
5:   class Mammal
6:   {
7:   public:
8:       Mammal():itsAge(1) {   }
9:       virtual ~Mammal() { }
10:      virtual void Speak() const = 0;
11:      virtual void Move() const = 0;
12:  protected:
13:      int itsAge;
14:  };
15:
16:  class Dog : public Mammal
17:  {
18:  public:
19:      void Speak()const { std::cout << "Woof!\n"; }
20:      void Move() const { std::cout << "Walking to heel...\n"; }
21:  };
22:
23:  class Cat : public Mammal
24:  {
25:  public:
26:      void Speak()const { std::cout << "Meow!\n"; }
27:      void Move() const { std::cout << "slinking...\n"; }
28:  };
29:
30:  class Horse : public Mammal
31:  {
```

LISTING 20.9   continued

```
32:  public:
33:      void Speak()const { std::cout << "Winnie!\n"; }
34:      void Move() const { std::cout << "Galloping...\n"; }
35:  };
36:
37:  int main()
38:  {
39:      void (Mammal::*pFunc)() const =0;
40:      Mammal* ptr =0;
41:      int Animal;
42:      int Method;
43:      bool fQuit = false;
44:
45:      while (fQuit == false)
46:      {
47:          std::cout << "(0)Quit (1)dog (2)cat (3)horse: ";
48:          std::cin >> Animal;
49:          switch (Animal)
50:          {
51:          case 1:
52:              ptr = new Dog;
53:              break;
54:          case 2:
55:              ptr = new Cat;
56:              break;
57:          case 3:
58:              ptr = new Horse;
59:              break;
60:          default:
61:              fQuit = true;
62:              break;
63:          }
64:          if (fQuit)
65:              break;
66:
67:          std::cout << "(1)Speak  (2)Move: ";
68:          std::cin >> Method;
69:          switch (Method)
70:          {
71:          case 1:
72:              pFunc = Mammal::Speak;
73:              break;
74:          default:
75:              pFunc = Mammal::Move;
76:              break;
77:          }
78:
79:          (ptr->*pFunc)();
80:          delete ptr;
```

20

LISTING 20.9   continued

```
81:        }
82:        return 0;
83:   }
```

OUTPUT   (0)Quit (1)Dog (2)Cat (3)Horse: 1
(1)Speak (2)Move: 1
Woof!
(0)Quit (1)Dog (2)Cat (3)Horse: 2
(1)Speak (2)Move: 1
Meow!
(0)Quit (1)Dog (2)Cat (3)Horse: 3
(1)Speak (2)Move: 2
Galloping
(0)Quit (1)Dog (2)Cat (3)Horse: 0

ANALYSIS   On lines 5–14, the abstract data type Mammal is declared with two pure virtual methods, Speak() and Move(). Mammal is subclassed into Dog, Cat, and Horse, each of which overrides Speak() and Move().

The main() function asks the user to choose which type of animal to create, and then a new subclass of Animal is created on the free store and assigned to ptr on lines 49–63.

The user is then prompted for which method to invoke, and that method is assigned to the pointer pFunc. On line 79, the method chosen is invoked by the object created, by using the pointer ptr to access the object and pFunc to access the function.

Finally, on line 80, delete is called on the pointer ptr to return the memory set aside for the object to the heap. Note that there is no reason to call delete on pFunc because this is a pointer to code, not to an object on the heap. In fact, attempting to do so will generate a compile-time error.

Arrays of Pointers to Member Functions

As with pointers to functions, pointers to member functions can be stored in an array. The array can be initialized with the addresses of various member functions, and those can be invoked by offsets into the array. Listing 20.10 illustrates this technique.

LISTING 20.10   Array of Pointers to Member Functions

```
0:   //Listing 20.10 Array of pointers to member functions
1:   #include <iostream>
2:
3:   class Dog
4:   {
```

LISTING 20.10   continued

```
 5:  public:
 6:      void Speak()const { std::cout << "Woof!\n"; }
 7:      void Move() const { std::cout << "Walking to heel...\n"; }
 8:      void Eat() const { std::cout << "Gobbling food...\n"; }
 9:      void Growl() const { std::cout << "Grrrrr\n"; }
10:      void Whimper() const { std::cout << "Whining noises...\n"; }
11:      void RollOver() const { std::cout << "Rolling over...\n"; }
12:      void PlayDead() const
13:          { std::cout << "Is this the end of Little Caeser?\n"; }
14:  };
15:
16:  typedef void (Dog::*PDF)()const ;
17:  int main()
18:  {
19:      const int MaxFuncs = 7;
20:      PDF DogFunctions[MaxFuncs] =
21:          {   Dog::Speak,
22:              Dog::Move,
23:              Dog::Eat,
24:              Dog::Growl,
25:              Dog::Whimper,
26:              Dog::RollOver,
27:              Dog::PlayDead
28:          };
29:
30:      Dog* pDog =0;
31:      int Method;
32:      bool fQuit = false;
33:
34:      while (!fQuit)
35:      {
36:          std::cout << "(0)Quit (1)Speak (2)Move (3)Eat (4)Growl";
37:          std::cout << " (5)Whimper (6)Roll Over (7)Play Dead: ";
38:          std::cin >> Method;
39:          if (Method == 0)
40:          {
41:              fQuit = true;
42:              break;
43:          }
44:          else
45:          {
46:              pDog = new Dog;
47:              (pDog->*DogFunctions[Method-1])();
48:              delete pDog;
49:          }
50:      }
51:      return 0;
52:  }
```

20

` (0)Quit (1)Speak (2)Move (3)Eat (4)Growl (5)Whimper (6)Roll Over`
` (7)Play Dead: 1`
` Woof!`
`  (0)Quit (1)Speak (2)Move (3)Eat (4)Growl (5)Whimper (6)Roll Over`
` (7)Play Dead: 4`
` Grrrrrr`
`  (0)Quit (1)Speak (2)Move (3)Eat (4)Growl (5)Whimper (6)Roll Over`
` (7)Play Dead: 7`
` Is this the end of Little Caesar?`
`  (0)Quit (1)Speak (2)Move (3)Eat (4)Growl (5)Whimper (6)Roll Over`
` (7)Play Dead: 0`

On lines 3–14, the class Dog is created with seven member functions all sharing the same return type and signature. On line 16, a typedef declares PDF to be a pointer to a member function of Dog that takes no parameters and returns no values, and that is const: the signature of the seven member functions of Dog.

On lines 20–29, the array DogFunctions is declared to hold seven such member functions, and it is initialized with the addresses of these functions.

On lines 36 and 37, the user is prompted to pick a method. Unless he picks Quit, a new Dog is created on the heap, and then the correct method is invoked on the array on line 47. Here's another good line to show to any hotshot C++ programmers you know; ask them what this does:

```
(pDog->*DogFunctions[Method-1])();
```

Once again, this is a bit esoteric, but when you need a table built from member functions, it can make your program far easier to read and understand.

Summary

In this hour, you learned how to create static member variables in your class. Each class, rather than each object, has one instance of the static member variable. It is possible to access this member variable without an object of the class type by fully qualifying the name, assuming you've declared the static member to have public access.

Static member variables can be used as counters across instances of the class. Because they are not part of the object, the declaration of static member variables does not allocate memory, and static member variables must be defined and initialized outside the declaration of the class.

Static member functions are part of the class in the same way that static member variables are. They can be accessed without a particular object of the class and can be used to access static member data. Static member functions cannot be used to access non-static member data because they do not have a this pointer.

Because static member functions do not have a `this` pointer, they also cannot be made `const`. `const` in a member function indicates that the `this` pointer is `const`.

In this hour, you also saw how to delegate functionality to a contained object. Containment is restricted in that the new class does not have access to the protected members of the contained class, and it cannot override the member functions of the contained object.

You saw how to declare both friend functions and friend classes. Friend classes should be used with caution, but they can help you find a middle ground between providing access only to the member methods of a class and making methods and data public.

Finally, you saw how to create pointers to functions and pointers to member functions, and how to use those pointers to invoke methods dynamically.

Q&A

Q Why use static data when you can use global data?

A Static data is scoped to the class. It therefore is available only through an object of the class—through an explicit and full call using the class name if the data are public, or by using a static member function. Static data is typed to the class type, however, and the restricted access and strong typing makes static data safer than global data.

Q Why use static member functions when you can use global functions?

A Static member functions are scoped to the class, and can be called only by using an object of the class or an explicit full specification (such as `ClassName::FunctionName()`).

Q Why not make all classes friends of all the classes they use?

A Making one class a friend of another exposes the implementation details and reduces encapsulation. The ideal is to keep as many of the details of each class as possible hidden from all other classes.

20

HOUR 21

The Preprocessor

Most of your source code files are written in C++. Your source code files are translated by the compiler into machine code which is ready to be executed by the computer. Before the compiler runs, however, the preprocessor runs, and this provides an opportunity for conditional compilation. In this hour, you will learn

- What conditional compilation is and how to manage it
- How to write macros using the preprocessor
- How to use the preprocessor in finding bugs

The Preprocessor and the Compiler

Every time you run your compiler, your preprocessor runs first. The preprocessor looks for preprocessor instructions, each of which begins with a pound symbol (#). The effect of each of these instructions is a change to the text of the source code. The result is a new source code file: a temporary file that you normally don't see, but that you can instruct the compiler to save for later examination.

The compiler does not use your original source code file; it reads the output of the pre-processor and compiles that file. `#include` instructs the preprocessor to find the file whose name follows the `#include` directive and to write it into the intermediate file at that location. It is as if you had typed that entire file right into your source code, and by the time the compiler sees the source code, the included file is there.

Seeing the Intermediate Form

Just about every compiler has a "switch" that instructs the compiler to save the intermediate file. You can set this switch either in the integrated development environment (IDE) or at the command line. Check your compiler manual for the right switches to set for your compiler if you'd like to examine the intermediate file.

Using #define

NEW TERM   The `#define` command defines a string substitution. If you write

```
#define BIG 512
```

you have instructed the precompiler to substitute the string `512` wherever it sees the string `BIG`. But this is not a string in the C++ sense. The characters `512` are substituted in your source code wherever the token `BIG` is seen. A *token* is a string of characters that can be used wherever a string or constant or other set of letters might be used. Therefore, if you write

```
#define BIG 512
int myArray[BIG];
```

the intermediate file produced by the precompiler will look like this:

```
int myArray[512];
```

Note that the `#define` statement is gone. Precompiler statements are all removed from the intermediate file; they do not appear in the final source code at all.

Using #define for Constants

One way to use `#define` is as a substitute for constants. This is almost never a good idea, however, because `#define` merely makes a string substitution and does no type checking. There are tremendous advantages to using the `const` keyword rather than `#define`.

Using #define for Tests

A second way to use #define is simply to declare that a particular character string is defined. Therefore, you could write

```
#define BIG
```

Later, you can test whether BIG has been defined and take action accordingly. The precompiler commands to test whether a string has been defined are #ifdef (to see whether the string has been defined) and #ifndef (to test whether it has *not* been defined). Both of these must be followed by the command #endif before the block ends (before the next closing brace).

#ifdef evaluates to true if the string it tests has been defined already. Therefore, you can write this:

```
#ifdef DEBUG
cout << "Debug defined";
#endif
```

When the precompiler reads the #ifdef, it checks a table it has built to see if you've defined DEBUG. If so, the #ifdef evaluates to true, and everything to the next #else or #endif is written into the intermediate file for compiling. If it evaluates to false, nothing between #ifdef DEBUG and the next #else or #endif will be written into the intermediate file; it will be as if it was never in the source code in the first place.

Note that #ifndef is the logical reverse of #ifdef. #ifndef evaluates to true if the string has not been defined up to that point in the file.

The #else Precompiler Command

As you might imagine, the term #else can be inserted between either #ifdef or #ifndef and the closing #endif. Listing 21.1 illustrates how all these terms are used.

LISTING 21.1 Using #define

```
 0:  #define DemoVersion
 1:  #define DOS_VERSION 5
 2:  #include <iostream>
 3:
 4:  int main()
 5:  {
 6:      std::cout << "Checking on the definitions of DemoVersion,"
 7:          << "DOS_VERSION and WINDOWS_VERSION...\n";
 8:
 9:  #ifdef DemoVersion
10:      std::cout << "DemoVersion defined.\n";
```

21

LISTING 21.1   continued

```
11:  #else // DemoVersion
12:      std::cout << "DemoVersion not defined.\n";
13:  #endif // DemoVersion
14:
15:  #ifndef DOS_VERSION
16:      std::cout << "DOS_VERSION not defined!\n";
17:  #else // DOS_VERSION
18:      std::cout << "DOS_VERSION defined as: "
19:          << DOS_VERSION << std::endl;
20:  #endif // DOS_VERSION
21:
22:  #ifdef WINDOWS_VERSION
23:      std::cout << "WINDOWS_VERSION defined!\n";
24:  #else // WINDOWS_VERSION
25:      std::cout << "WINDOWS_VERSION was not defined.\n";
26:  #endif // WINDOWS_VERSION
27:
28:      std::cout << "Done.\n";
29:      return 0;
30:  }
```

OUTPUT
```
Checking on the definitions of DemoVersion,
➥DOS_VERSION and WINDOWS_VERSION...
DemoVersion defined
DOS_VERSION defined as: 5
WINDOWS_VERSION was not defined.
Done.
```

ANALYSIS   On lines 0 and 1, DemoVersion and DOS_VERSION are defined, with DOS_VERSION defined with the string 5. On line 9, the existence of DemoVersion is tested by the precompiler, and because DemoVersion is defined, albeit with no value, the test is true and the string on line 10 is printed.

Line 15 tests DOS_VERSION to see if it is not defined.

Because DOS_VERSION is defined, this test fails and line 18 is compiled, rather than line 16. Here the string 5 is substituted for the word DOS_VERSION, and this is seen by the compiler as

```
cout << "DOS_VERSION defined as: " << 5 << endl;
```

Note that the first word, DOS_VERSION, is not substituted because it is in a quoted string. The second DOS_VERSION is substituted. This causes the compiler to see 5, as if you had typed 5 there.

Finally, on line 22, the precompiler tests for WINDOWS_VERSION. Because you did not define WINDOWS_VERSION, the test fails and line 25 is compiled rather than line 23.

Inclusion and Inclusion Guards

You will create projects with many different files. You will probably organize your directories so that each class has its own header file (.HPP) with the class declaration, and its own implementation file (.CPP) with the source code for the class methods.

Your main() function will be in its own .CPP file, and all the .CPP files will be compiled into .OBJ files, which will then be linked together into a single program by the linker.

Because your programs will use methods from many classes, many header files will be included in each file. Also, header files often need to include one another. For example, the header file for a derived class's declaration must include the header file for its base class.

Imagine that the Animal class is declared in the file ANIMAL.HPP. The Dog class, which derives from Animal, must include the file ANIMAL.HPP in DOG.HPP, or Dog will not be able to derive from Animal. The Cat header also includes ANIMAL.HPP for the same reason. If you create a method that uses both a Cat and a Dog, you will be in danger of including ANIMAL.HPP twice.

This will generate a compile-time error, because it is not legal to declare a class (Animal) twice, even though the declarations are identical. You can solve this problem with *inclusion guards*. At the top of your ANIMAL header file, you will write these lines:

```
#ifndef ANIMAL_HPP
#define ANIMAL_HPP
...                        // the whole file goes here
#endif
```

This says, "If you haven't defined the term ANIMAL_HPP, go ahead and define it now." Between the #define statement and the closing #endif are the entire contents of the file.

The first time your program includes this file, it reads the first line, and the test evaluates to true; that is, you have not yet defined ANIMAL_HPP. Thus, this file goes ahead and defines ANIMAL_HPP and then includes the entire file.

The second time your program includes the ANIMAL.HPP file, it reads the first line, and the test evaluates false; ANIMAL_HPP has been defined. It therefore skips to the next #else (there isn't one) or the next #endif (at the end of the file). Thus, it skips the entire contents of the file, and the class is not declared twice.

The actual name of the defined symbol (ANIMAL_HPP) is not important, although it is customary to use the filename in all uppercase with the dot (.) changed to an underscore. This is purely convention, however.

21

It never hurts to use inclusion guards. Often they will save you hours of debugging time.

Defining on the Command Line

Almost all C++ compilers will let you `#define` values either from the command line or from the integrated development environment (and usually both). Therefore, you can leave out lines 1 and 2 from Listing 21.1 and define `DemoVersion` and `BetaTestVersion` from the command line for some compilations and not for others.

It is common to put in special debugging code surrounded by `#ifdef DEBUG` and `#endif`. This allows all the debugging code to be easily removed from the source code when you compile the final version: Just don't define the term `DEBUG`.

Undefining

If you have a name defined and you'd like to turn it off from within your code, you can use `#undef`. This works as the antidote to `#define`.

Conditional Compilation

By combining `#define` or command-line definitions with `#ifdef`, `#else`, and `#ifndef`, you can write one program that compiles different code depending on what is already `#defined`. This can be used to create one set of source code to compile on two different platforms, such as DOS and Windows.

Another common use of this technique is to conditionally compile in some code based on whether `DEBUG` has been defined, as you'll see in a few moments.

Macro Functions

The `#define` directive can also be used to create macro functions. A *macro function* is created using `#define`. Macros take arguments much like functions do. The preprocessor will substitute the substitution string for whatever argument it is given. For example, you can define the macro `TWICE` as

```
#define TWICE(x) ( (x) * 2 )
```

and then write in your code

```
TWICE(4)
```

The entire string `TWICE(4)` will be removed, and the value 8 will be substituted! When the precompiler sees the 4, it will substitute ((4) * 2), which will then evaluate to 4 * 2 or 8.

A macro can have more than one parameter, and each parameter can be used repeatedly in the replacement text. Two common macros are `MAX` and `MIN`:

```
#define MAX(x,y) ( (x) > (y) ? (x) : (y) )
#define MIN(x,y) ( (x) < (y) ? (x) : (y) )
```

Note that in a macro function definition, the opening parenthesis for the parameter list must immediately follow the macro name, with no spaces. The preprocessor is not as forgiving of white space as is the compiler.

If you were to write

```
#define MAX (x,y) ( (x) > (y) ? (x) : (y) )
```

and then to try to use `MAX` like this,

```
int x = 5, y = 7, z;
z = MAX(x,y);
```

the intermediate code would be

```
int x = 5, y = 7, z;
z = (x,y) ( (x) > (y) ? (x) : (y) ) (x,y)
```

A simple text substitution would be done, rather than invoking the macro function. So the token `MAX` would have substituted for it (x,y) ((x) > (y) ? (x) : (y)), and then that would be followed by the (x,y) that followed `MAX`.

When the space between `MAX` and (x,y) is removed, however, the intermediate code becomes

```
int x = 5, y = 7, z;
z = 7;
```

Why All the Parentheses?

You may be wondering why there are so many parentheses in many of the macros presented so far. The preprocessor does not demand that parentheses be placed around the arguments in the substitution string. However, the parentheses help you to avoid unwanted side effects when you pass complicated values to a macro. For example, if you define `MAX` as

```
#define MAX(x,y) x > y ? x : y
```

and pass in the values 5 and 7, the macro works as intended. But if you pass in a more complicated expression, you'll get unintended results, as shown in Listing 21.2.

LISTING 21.2   Using Parentheses in Macros

```
 0:   // Listing 21.2 Macro Expansion
 1:   #include <iostream>
 2:
 3:   #define CUBE(a) ( (a) * (a) * (a) )
 4:   #define THREE(a) a * a * a
 5:
 6:   int main()
 7:   {
 8:       long x = 5;
 9:       long y = CUBE(x);
10:       long z = THREE(x);
11:
12:       std::cout << "y: " << y << std::endl;
13:       std::cout << "z: " << z << std::endl;
14:
15:       long a = 5, b = 7;
16:       y = CUBE(a+b);
17:       z = THREE(a+b);
18:
19:       std::cout << "y: " << y << std::endl;
20:       std::cout << "z: " << z << std::endl;
21:       return 0;
22:   }
```

OUTPUT
```
y: 125
z: 125
y: 1728
z: 82
```

ANALYSIS   On line 3 the macro CUBE is defined, with the argument a put into parentheses each time it is used. On line 4 the macro THREE is defined without the parentheses.

In the first use of these macros, the value 5 is given as the parameter, and both macros work fine. CUBE(5) expands to ((5) * (5) * (5)), which evaluates to 125, and THREE(5) expands to 5 * 5 * 5, which also evaluates to 125.

In the second use, on lines 15–17, the parameter is 5 + 7. In this case, CUBE(5+7) evaluates to

```
( (5+7) * (5+7) * (5+7) )
```

which evaluates to

```
( (12) * (12) * (12) )
```

which in turn evaluates to 1,728. THREE(5+7), however, evaluates to

```
5 + 7 * 5 + 7 * 5 + 7
```

Because multiplication has a higher precedence than addition, this becomes

```
5 + (7 * 5) + (7 * 5) + 7
```

which evaluates to

```
5 + (35) + (35) + 7
```

which finally evaluates to 82.

Macros Versus Functions and Templates

Macros suffer from four problems in C++. The first is that they can be confusing if they get large, because all macros must be defined on one line. You can extend that line by using the backslash character (\), but large macros quickly become difficult to manage.

The second problem is that macros are expanded in line each time they are used. This means that if a macro is used a dozen times, the substitution will appear 12 times in your program, rather than once as a function call will. On the other hand, they are usually quicker than a function call because the overhead of a function call is avoided.

The fact that they are expanded inline leads to the third problem, which is that the macro does not appear in the intermediate source code used by the compiler, and thus is unavailable in most debuggers. This makes debugging macros tricky.

The final problem, however, is the biggest: Macros are not type-safe. While it is convenient that absolutely any argument can be used with a macro, this completely undermines the strong typing of C++ and so is anathema to C++ programmers. Templates overcome this problem, as you'll see in two hours.

String Manipulation

The preprocessor provides two special operators for manipulating strings in macros. The stringizing operator (#) substitutes a quoted string for whatever follows the stringizing operator. The concatenation operator (##) bonds two strings together into one.

Stringizing

The stringizing operator(#) puts quotes around any characters following the operator, up to the next white space. So, if you write:

```
#define WRITESTRING(x) cout << #x
```

and then call

```
WRITESTRING(This is a string);
```

21

the precompiler will turn it into this:

```
cout << "This is a string";
```

Note that the string This is a string is put into quotes, as required by cout.

Concatenation

The concatenation operator (##) enables you to bond together more than one term into a new word. The new word is actually a token that can be used as a class name, a variable name, an offset into an array, or anywhere else a series of letters might appear.

Assume for a moment that you have five functions, named fOnePrint, fTwoPrint, fThreePrint, fFourPrint, and fFivePrint. You can then declare

```
#define fPRINT(x) f ## x ## Print
```

and then use it with fPRINT(Two) to generate fTwoPrint, and with fPRINT(Three) to generate fThreePrint.

At the conclusion of Hour 19, "Linked Lists," a PartsList class was developed. This list could only handle objects of type List. Let's say that this list works well, and you'd like to be able to make lists of animals, cars, computers, and so on.

One approach would be to create AnimalList, CarList, ComputerList, and so forth, cutting and pasting the code in place. This would quickly become a nightmare, because every change to one list would have to be written to all the others.

An alternative is to use macros and the concatenation operator. For example, you could define

```
#define Listof(Type)  class Type##List \
{ \
public: \
Type##List(){} \
private:          \
int itsLength; \
};
```

This example is overly sparse, but the idea would be to put in all the necessary methods and data. When you were ready to create an AnimalList, you would write

```
Listof(Animal)
```

and this would be turned into the declaration of the AnimalList class. There are some problems with this approach, all of which are discussed in detail in Hour 23, "Templates," when templates are discussed.

Predefined Macros

Many compilers predefine a number of useful macros, including __DATE__, __TIME__, __LINE__, and __FILE__. Each of these names is surrounded by two underscore characters to reduce the likelihood that the names will conflict with names you've used in your program.

When the precompiler sees one of these macros, it makes the appropriate substitutes. For __DATE__, the current date is substituted. For __TIME__, the current time is substituted. __LINE__ and __FILE__ are replaced with the source code line number and filename, respectively. You should note that this substitution is made when the source is precompiled, not when the program is run. If you asked the program to print __DATE__, you would not get the current date; you would get the date the program was compiled. These defined macros are very useful in debugging.

assert()

Many compilers offer an assert() macro. The assert() macro returns true if its parameter evaluates true, and takes some kind of action if it evaluates false. Many compilers will abort the program on an assert() that fails, others will throw an exception. (See Hour 20, "Special Classes, Functions, and Pointers.")

One powerful feature of the assert() macro is that the preprocessor collapses it into no code at all if DEBUG is not defined. It is a great help during development, and when the final product ships there is neither a performance penalty nor an increase in the size of the executable version of the program.

Rather than depending on the compiler-provided assert(), you are free to write your own assert() macro. Listing 21.3 provides a simple assert() macro and shows its use.

LISTING 21.3 A Simple assert() Macro

```
0:  // Listing 21.3 ASSERTS
1:  #define DEBUG
2:  #include <iostream>
3:
4:  #ifndef DEBUG
5:      #define ASSERT(x)
6:  #else
7:      #define ASSERT(x) \
8:          if (! (x)) \
9:          { \
10:             std::cout << "ERROR!! Assert " << #x << " failed\n"; \
11:             std::cout << " on line " << __LINE__ << "\n"; \
12:             std::cout << " in file " << __FILE__ << "\n";  \
```

21

Listing 21.3 continued

```
13:              }
14:    #endif
15:
16:    int main()
17:    {
18:        int x = 5;
19:        std::cout << "First assert: \n";
20:        ASSERT(x==5);
21:        std::cout << "\nSecond assert: \n";
22:        ASSERT(x != 5);
23:        std::cout << "\nDone.\n";
24:        return 0;
25:    }
```

Output

```
First assert:

Second assert:
ERROR!! Assert x!=5 failed
 on line 24
 in file test2103.cpp
```

Analysis On line 1, the term DEBUG is defined. Typically, this would be done from the command line (or the IDE) at compile time, so that you could turn it on and off at will. On lines 7–13, the assert() macro is defined. Typically, this would be done in a header file, and that header (ASSERT.HPP) would be included in all your implementation files.

On line 4, the term DEBUG is tested. If it is not defined, assert() is defined to create no code at all. If DEBUG is defined, the functionality defined on lines 7–13 is applied.

The assert() itself is one long statement, split across seven source code lines, as far as the precompiler is concerned. On line 8, the value passed in as a parameter is tested; if it evaluates false, the statements on lines 10–12 are invoked, printing an error message. If the value passed in evaluates true, no action is taken.

Debugging with assert()

When writing your program, you will often know deep down in your soul that something is true: A function has a certain value, a pointer is valid, and so forth. It is the nature of bugs that what you know to be true might not be true under some conditions. For example, you know that a pointer is valid, yet the program crashes. assert() can help you find this type of bug, but only if you make it a regular practice to use assert() statements liberally in your code. Every time you assign or are passed a pointer as a parameter or function return value, be sure to assert that the pointer is valid. Any time your code depends on a particular value being in a variable, assert() that it is true.

There is no penalty for frequent use of assert() statements; they are removed from the code when you undefine debugging. They also provide good internal documentation, reminding the reader of what you believe is true at any given moment in the flow of the code.

Side Effects

It is not uncommon to find that a bug appears only after the assert() statements are removed. This is almost always due to the program unintentionally depending on side effects of things done in assert()s and other debug-only code. For example, if you write

```
ASSERT (x = 5)
```

when you mean to test whether x == 5, you will create a particularly nasty bug.

Let's say that just prior to this assert(), you called a function that set x equal to 0. With this assert() you think you are testing whether x is equal to 5; in fact, you are setting x equal to 5. The test returns true, because x = 5 not only sets x to 5, but returns the value 5; and because 5 is non-zero, the test evaluates to true.

After you pass the assert() statement, x really is equal to 5 (you just set it!). Your program runs just fine, and you're ready to ship it, so you turn debugging off. Now the assert() disappears and you are no longer setting x to 5. Because x was set to 0 just before this, it remains at 0 and your program breaks.

In frustration, you turn debugging back on, but hey! Presto! The bug is gone. Once again, this is rather funny to watch, but not to live through, so be very careful about side effects in debugging code. If you see a bug that only appears when debugging is turned off, take a look at your debugging code with an eye out for nasty side effects.

Class Invariants

Most classes have some conditions that should always be true whenever you are finished with a class member function. These are called class invariants, and they are the *sine qua non* of your class. For example, it may be true that your CIRCLE object should never have a radius of 0, or that your ANIMAL should always have an age greater than 0 and less than 100.

It can be very helpful to declare an Invariants() method that returns true only if each of these conditions is still true. You can then insert Assert(Invariants()) at the start and completion of every class method. The exception would be that your Invariants() would not be expected to return true before your constructor runs or after your destructor ends. Listing 21.4 demonstrates the use of the Invariants() method in a trivial class.

21

LISTING 21.4   Using Invariants()

```
0:   // Listing 21.4 Invariants
1:   #define DEBUG
2:   #define SHOW_INVARIANTS
3:   #include <iostream>
4:   #include <string.h>
5:
6:   #ifndef DEBUG
7:   #define ASSERT(x)
8:   #else
9:   #define ASSERT(x) \
10:      if (! (x)) \
11:      { \
12:          std::cout << "ERROR!! Assert " << #x << " failed\n"; \
13:          std::cout << " on line " << __LINE__  << "\n"; \
14:          std::cout << " in file " << __FILE__ << "\n";  \
15:      }
16:  #endif
17:
18:  class String
19:  {
20:  public:
21:      // constructors
22:      String();
23:      String(const char *const);
24:      String(const String &);
25:      ~String();
26:
27:      char & operator[](int offset);
28:      char operator[](int offset) const;
29:
30:      String & operator= (const String &);
31:      int GetLen()const { return itsLen; }
32:      const char * GetString() const { return itsString; }
33:      bool Invariants() const;
34:
35:  private:
36:      String (int);          // private constructor
37:      char * itsString;
38:      unsigned short itsLen;
39:  };
40:
41:  // default constructor creates string of 0 bytes
42:  String::String()
43:  {
44:      itsString = new char[1];
45:      itsString[0] = '\0';
46:      itsLen=0;
47:      ASSERT(Invariants());
```

LISTING 21.4 continued

```
48:   }
49:
50:   // private (helper) constructor, used only by
51:   // class methods for creating a new string of
52:   // required size.  Null filled.
53:   String::String(int len)
54:   {
55:       itsString = new char[len+1];
56:       for (int i = 0; i<=len; i++)
57:           itsString[i] = '\0';
58:       itsLen=len;
59:       ASSERT(Invariants());
60:   }
61:
62:   // Converts a character array to a String
63:   String::String(const char * const cString)
64:   {
65:       itsLen = strlen(cString);
66:       itsString = new char[itsLen+1];
67:       for (int i = 0; i<itsLen; i++)
68:           itsString[i] = cString[i];
69:       itsString[itsLen]='\0';
70:       ASSERT(Invariants());
71:   }
72:
73:   // copy constructor
74:   String::String (const String & rhs)
75:   {
76:       itsLen=rhs.GetLen();
77:       itsString = new char[itsLen+1];
78:       for (int i = 0; i<itsLen;i++)
79:           itsString[i] = rhs[i];
80:       itsString[itsLen] = '\0';
81:       ASSERT(Invariants());
82:   }
83:
84:   // destructor, frees allocated memory
85:   String::~String ()
86:   {
87:       ASSERT(Invariants());
88:       delete [] itsString;
89:       itsLen = 0;
90:   }
91:
92:   // operator equals, frees existing memory
93:   // then copies string and size
94:   String& String::operator=(const String & rhs)
95:   {
96:       ASSERT(Invariants());
```

21

LISTING 21.4   continued

```
 97:        if (this == &rhs)
 98:            return *this;
 99:        delete [] itsString;
100:        itsLen=rhs.GetLen();
101:        itsString = new char[itsLen+1];
102:        for (int i = 0; i<itsLen;i++)
103:            itsString[i] = rhs[i];
104:        itsString[itsLen] = '\0';
105:        ASSERT(Invariants());
106:        return *this;
107:    }
108:
109:    //non constant offset operator, returns
110:    // reference to character so it can be
111:    // changed!
112:    char & String::operator[](int offset)
113:    {
114:        ASSERT(Invariants());
115:        if (offset > itsLen)
116:            return itsString[itsLen-1];
117:        else
118:            return itsString[offset];
119:        ASSERT(Invariants());
120:    }
121:
122:    // constant offset operator for use
123:    // on const objects (see copy constructor!)
124:    char String::operator[](int offset) const
125:    {
126:        ASSERT(Invariants());
127:        if (offset > itsLen)
128:            return itsString[itsLen-1];
129:        else
130:            return itsString[offset];
131:        ASSERT(Invariants());
132:    }
133:
134:    // ensure that the string has some length or
135:    // the pointer is null and the length is zero
136:    bool String::Invariants() const
137:    {
138:    #ifdef SHOW_INVARIANTS
139:        std::cout << " String OK ";
140:    #endif
141:        return ( (itsLen && itsString) || (!itsLen && !itsString) );
142:    }
143:
144:    class Animal
145:    {
```

LISTING 21.4 continued

```
146:  public:
147:      Animal():itsAge(1),itsName("John Q. Animal")
148:          {ASSERT(Invariants());}
149:      Animal(int, const String&);
150:      ~Animal(){}
151:      int GetAge() { ASSERT(Invariants()); return itsAge;}
152:      void SetAge(int Age)
153:          {
154:              ASSERT(Invariants());
155:              itsAge = Age;
156:              ASSERT(Invariants());
157:          }
158:      String& GetName() { ASSERT(Invariants()); return itsName;  }
159:      void SetName(const String& name)
160:          {
161:              ASSERT(Invariants());
162:              itsName = name;
163:              ASSERT(Invariants());
164:          }
165:      bool Invariants();
166:  private:
167:      int itsAge;
168:      String itsName;
169:  };
170:
171:  Animal::Animal(int age, const String& name):
172:  itsAge(age),
173:  itsName(name)
174:  {
175:      ASSERT(Invariants());
176:  }
177:
178:  bool Animal::Invariants()
179:  {
180:  #ifdef SHOW_INVARIANTS
181:      std::cout << " Animal OK ";
182:  #endif
183:      return (itsAge > 0 && itsName.GetLen());
184:  }
185:
186:  int main()
187:  {
188:      Animal sparky(5,"Sparky");
189:      std::cout << "\n" << sparky.GetName().GetString() << " is ";
190:      std::cout << sparky.GetAge() << " years old.";
191:      sparky.SetAge(8);
192:      std::cout << "\n" << sparky.GetName().GetString() << " is ";
193:      std::cout << sparky.GetAge() << " years old.";
194:      return 0;
195:  }
```

21

OUTPUT

```
String OK  String OK  String OK  String OK  String OK  String OK
➥String OK  String OK  Animal OK  String OK  Animal OK
Sparky is  Animal OK 5 years old. Animal OK  Animal OK  Animal OK
Sparky is  Animal OK 8 years old. String OK
```

ANALYSIS

On lines 6–16, the `assert()` macro is defined. If `DEBUG` is defined, this macro will write out an error message when the `assert()` macro evaluates `false`.

On line 33, the `String` class member function `Invariants()` is declared; it is defined on lines 135–141. The constructor is declared on lines 22–24, and on line 47, after the object is fully constructed, `Invariants()` is called to confirm proper construction.

This pattern is repeated for the other constructors, and the destructor calls `Invariants()` only before it sets out to destroy the object. The remaining class functions call `Invariants()` both before taking any action and then again before returning. This both affirms and validates a fundamental principal of C++: Member functions other than constructors and destructors should work on valid objects and should leave them in a valid state.

On line 164, class `Animal` declares its own `Invariants()` method, implemented on lines 177–183. Note on lines 147, 150, 153, 155, 160, and 162 that inline functions can call the `Invariants()` method.

Printing Interim Values

In addition to asserting that something is true using the `assert()` macro, you may want to print the current values of pointers, variables, and strings. This can be very helpful in checking your assumptions about the progress of your program and in locating off-by-one bugs in loops. Listing 21.5 illustrates this idea.

LISTING 21.5   Printing Values in `DEBUG` Mode

```
0:  // Listing 21.5 - Printing values in DEBUG mode
1:  #include <iostream>
2:  #define DEBUG
3:
4:  #ifndef DEBUG
5:  #define PRINT(x)
6:  #else
7:  #define PRINT(x) \
8:      std::cout << #x << ":\t" << x << std::endl;
9:  #endif
10:
11: int main()
12: {
13:     int x = 5;
14:     long y = 738981;
```

LISTING 21.5   continued

```
15:        PRINT(x);
16:        for (int i = 0; i < x; i++)
17:        {
18:            PRINT(i);
19:        }
20:
21:        PRINT (y);
22:        PRINT("Hi.");
23:        int *px = &x;
24:        PRINT(px);
25:        PRINT (*px);
26:        return 0;
27:    }
```

OUTPUT

```
x:            5
i:            0
i:            1
i:            2
i:            3
i:            4
y:            73898
"Hi.":        Hi.
px:           0x2100 (You may recieve a value other than 0x2100)
*px:          5
```

ANALYSIS   The macro on lines 4–9 provides printing of the current value of the supplied parameter. Note that the first thing fed to cout is the stringized version of the parameter; that is, if you pass in x, cout receives "x".

Next cout receives the quoted string ":\t", which prints a colon and then a tab. Third, cout receives the value of the parameter (x) and then finally endl, which writes a new line and flushes the buffer.

Debugging Levels

In large, complex projects, you may want more control than simply turning DEBUG on and off. You can define debug levels, and test for these levels when deciding which macros to use and which to strip out.

To define a level, simply follow the #define DEBUG statement with a number. While you can have any number of levels, a common system is to have four levels: HIGH, MEDIUM, LOW, and NONE. Listing 21.6 illustrates how this might be done, using the String and Animal classes from Listing 21.4. The definitions of the class methods other than Invariants() have been left out to save space, because they are unchanged from Listing 21.4.

21

LISTING 21.6 Levels of Debugging

```
0:  // Listing 21.6 Debugging Levels
1:  #include <iostream>
2:  #include <string.h>
3:
4:  enum LEVEL { NONE, LOW, MEDIUM, HIGH };
5:
6:  #define DEBUGLEVEL HIGH
7:
8:  #if DEBUGLEVEL < LOW  // must be low, medium or high
9:  #define ASSERT(x)
10: #else
11: #define ASSERT(x) \
12:     if (! (x)) \
13:     { \
14:         std::cout << "ERROR!! Assert " << #x << " failed\n"; \
15:         std::cout << " on line " << __LINE__  << "\n"; \
16:         std::cout << " in file " << __FILE__ << "\n";  \
17:     }
18:   #endif
19:
20: #if DEBUGLEVEL < MEDIUM
21: #define EVAL(x)
22: #else
23: #define EVAL(x) \
24:     std::cout << #x << ":\t" << x << endl;
25: #endif
26:
27: #if DEBUGLEVEL < HIGH
28: #define PRINT(x)
29: #else
30: #define PRINT(x) \
31:     std::cout << x << std::endl;
32: #endif
33:
34: class String
35: {
36: public:
37:     // constructors
38:     String();
39:     String(const char *const);
40:     String(const String &);
41:     ~String();
42:
43:     char & operator[](int offset);
44:     char operator[](int offset) const;
45:
46:     String & operator= (const String &);
47:     int GetLen()const { return itsLen; }
```

LISTING 21.6 continued

```
48:        const char * GetString() const
49:            { return itsString; }
50:        bool Invariants() const;
51:
52:   private:
53:        String (int);          // private constructor
54:        char * itsString;
55:        unsigned short itsLen;
56:   };
57:
58:   bool String::Invariants() const
59:   {
60:        PRINT("(String Invariants Checked)");
61:        return ( (bool) (itsLen && itsString) ||
62:            (!itsLen && !itsString) );
63:   }
64:
65:   class Animal
66:   {
67:   public:
68:        Animal():itsAge(1),itsName("John Q. Animal")
69:        {ASSERT(Invariants());}
70:
71:        Animal(int, const String&);
72:        ~Animal(){}
73:
74:        int GetAge()
75:        {
76:            ASSERT(Invariants());
77:            return itsAge;
78:        }
79:
80:        void SetAge(int Age)
81:        {
82:            ASSERT(Invariants());
83:            itsAge = Age;
84:            ASSERT(Invariants());
85:        }
86:        String& GetName()
87:        {
88:            ASSERT(Invariants());
89:            return itsName;
90:        }
91:
92:        void SetName(const String& name)
93:        {
94:            ASSERT(Invariants());
95:            itsName = name;
```

21

LISTING 21.6   continued

```
 96:             ASSERT(Invariants());
 97:         }
 98:
 99:         bool Invariants();
100:    private:
101:         int itsAge;
102:         String itsName;
103:    };
104:
105:    // default constructor creates string of 0 bytes
106:    String::String()
107:    {
108:         itsString = new char[1];
109:         itsString[0] = '\0';
110:         itsLen=0;
111:         ASSERT(Invariants());
112:    }
113:
114:    // private (helper) constructor, used only by
115:    // class methods for creating a new string of
116:    // required size.  Null filled.
117:    String::String(int len)
118:    {
119:         itsString = new char[len+1];
120:         for (int i = 0; i<=len; i++)
121:             itsString[i] = '\0';
122:         itsLen=len;
123:         ASSERT(Invariants());
124:    }
125:
126:    // Converts a character array to a String
127:    String::String(const char * const cString)
128:    {
129:         itsLen = strlen(cString);
130:         itsString = new char[itsLen+1];
131:         for (int i = 0; i<itsLen; i++)
132:             itsString[i] = cString[i];
133:         itsString[itsLen]='\0';
134:         ASSERT(Invariants());
135:    }
136:
137:    // copy constructor
138:    String::String (const String & rhs)
139:    {
140:         itsLen=rhs.GetLen();
141:         itsString = new char[itsLen+1];
142:         for (int i = 0; i<itsLen;i++)
143:             itsString[i] = rhs[i];
144:         itsString[itsLen] = '\0';
```

LISTING 21.6 continued

```
145:        ASSERT(Invariants());
146:   }
147:
148:   // destructor, frees allocated memory
149:   String::~String ()
150:   {
151:        ASSERT(Invariants());
152:        delete [] itsString;
153:        itsLen = 0;
154:   }
155:
156:   // operator equals, frees existing memory
157:   // then copies string and size
158:   String& String::operator=(const String & rhs)
159:   {
160:        ASSERT(Invariants());
161:        if (this == &rhs)
162:            return *this;
163:        delete [] itsString;
164:        itsLen=rhs.GetLen();
165:        itsString = new char[itsLen+1];
166:        for (int i = 0; i<itsLen;i++)
167:            itsString[i] = rhs[i];
168:        itsString[itsLen] = '\0';
169:        ASSERT(Invariants());
170:        return *this;
171:   }
172:
173:   //non constant offset operator, returns
174:   // reference to character so it can be
175:   // changed!
176:   char & String::operator[](int offset)
177:   {
178:        ASSERT(Invariants());
179:        if (offset > itsLen)
180:            return itsString[itsLen-1];
181:        else
182:            return itsString[offset];
183:        ASSERT(Invariants());
184:   }
185:
186:   // constant offset operator for use
187:   // on const objects (see copy constructor!)
188:   char String::operator[](int offset) const
189:   {
190:        ASSERT(Invariants());
191:        if (offset > itsLen)
192:            return itsString[itsLen-1];
193:        else
```

21

LISTING 21.6   continued

```
194:            return itsString[offset];
195:        ASSERT(Invariants());
196: }
197:
198: Animal::Animal(int age, const String& name):
199: itsAge(age),
200: itsName(name)
201: {
202:     ASSERT(Invariants());
203: }
204:
205: bool Animal::Invariants()
206: {
207:     PRINT("(Animal Invariants Checked)");
208:     return (itsAge > 0 && itsName.GetLen());
209: }
210:
211: int main()
212: {
213:     const int AGE = 5;
214:     EVAL(AGE);
215:     Animal sparky(AGE,"Sparky");
216:     std::cout << "\n" << sparky.GetName().GetString();
217:     std::cout << " is ";
218:     std::cout << sparky.GetAge() << " years old.";
219:     sparky.SetAge(8);
220:     std::cout << "\n" << sparky.GetName().GetString();
221:     std::cout << " is ";
222:     std::cout << sparky.GetAge() << " years old.";
223:     return 0;
224: }
```

OUTPUT

```
AGE:     5
 (String Invariants Checked)
 (String Invariants Checked)
 (String Invariants Checked)
 (String Invariants Checked)
 (String Invariants Checked)
 (String Invariants Checked)
 (String Invariants Checked)
 (String Invariants Checked)
 (String Invariants Checked)
 (String Invariants Checked)

Sparky is (Animal Invariants Checked)
5 Years old. (Animal Invariants Checked)
 (Animal Invariants Checked)
 (Animal Invariants Checked)
```

```
Sparky is (Animal Invariants Checked)
8 years old. (String Invariants Checked)
 (String Invariants Checked)

// run again with DEBUG = MEDIUM

AGE:    5
Sparky is 5 years old.
Sparky is 8 years old.
```

ANALYSIS On lines 8–18, the assert() macro is defined to be stripped if DEBUGLEVEL is less than LOW (that is DEBUGLEVEL is NONE). If any debugging is enabled, the assert() macro will work. On lines 20–25, EVAL is declared to be stripped if DEBUGLEVEL is less than MEDIUM; if DEBUGLEVEL is NONE or LOW then EVAL is stripped.

Finally, on lines 27–32, the PRINT macro is declared to be stripped if DEBUGLEVEL is less than HIGH. PRINT is used only when DEBUGLEVEL is high, and you can eliminate this macro by setting DEBUGLEVEL to MEDIUM, and still maintain your use of EVAL and of assert().

PRINT is used within the Invariants() methods to print an informative message. EVAL is used on line 214 to evaluate the current value of the constant integer AGE.

DO use uppercase for your macro names. This is a pervasive convention, and other programmers will be confused if you don't.

DON'T allow your macros to have side effects. Don't increment variables or assign values from within a macro.

DO surround all arguments with parentheses in macro functions.

Summary

In this hour you learned more details about working with the preprocessor. Each time you run the compiler, the preprocessor runs first and translates your preprocessor directives such as #define and #ifdef.

The preprocessor does text substitution, although, with the use of macros, these can be somewhat complex. By using #ifdef, #else, and #ifndef, you can accomplish conditional compilation, compiling in some statements under one set of conditions and in another set of statements under other conditions. This can assist in writing programs for more than one platform, and is often used to conditionally include debugging information.

21

Macro functions provide complex text substitution based on arguments passed at compile time to the macro. It is important to put parentheses around every argument in the macro to ensure that the correct substitution takes place.

Macro functions, and the preprocessor in general, are less important in C++ than they were in C. C++ provides a number of language features, such as `const` variables and templates, that offer superior alternatives to using the preprocessor.

Q&A

Q If C++ offers better alternatives than the preprocessor, why is this option still available?

A First, C++ is backward compatible with C, and all significant parts of C must be supported in C++. Second, there are some uses of the preprocessor that are still employed frequently in C++, such as inclusion guards.

Q Why use macro functions when you can use a regular function?

A Macro functions are expanded inline and are used as a substitute for repeatedly typing the same commands with minor variations. However, templates offer a better alternative.

Q What is the alternative to using the preprocessor to print interim values during debugging?

A The best alternative is to use `watch` statements within a debugger. For information on `watch` statements, consult your compiler or debugger documentation.

HOUR **22**

Object-Oriented Analysis and Design

It is easy to become focused on the syntax of C++ and to lose sight of how and why you use these techniques to build programs. In this hour, we will pause and consider the following:

- How to analyze problems from an object-oriented perspective
- How to design your program from an object-oriented perspective
- How to design for reusability and extensibility

The Development Cycle

Many volumes have been written about the development cycle. Some propose a *waterfall* method, in which designers determine what the program should do; architects determine how the program will be built, what classes will be used, and so forth; and then programmers implement the design and architecture. By the time the design and architecture are given to the programmer, they are complete; all the programmer need do is implement the required functionality.

Even if the waterfall method worked, it would probably be a poor method for writing good programs. As the programmer proceeds, there is a necessary and natural feedback between what has been written so far and what remains to be done. While it is true that good C++ programs are designed in great detail before a line of code is written, it is not true that that design remains unchanged throughout the cycle.

The amount of design that must be finished up front, before programming begins, is a function of the size of the program. A highly complex effort, involving dozens of programmers working for many months, will require a more fully articulated architecture than a quick-and-dirty utility written in one day by a single programmer.

This chapter focuses on the design of large, complex programs that will be expanded and enhanced over many years. Many programmers enjoy working at the bleeding edge of technology; they tend to write programs whose complexity pushes at the limits of their tools and understanding. In many ways, C++ was designed to extend the complexity that a programmer or team of programmers can manage.

This chapter examines a number of design problems from an object-oriented perspective. The goal is to review the analysis process, and then to understand how you apply the syntax of C++ to implement these design objectives.

Simulating an Alarm System

NEW TERM A *simulation* is a computer model of a part of a real-world system. There are many reasons to build a simulation, but a good design must start with an understanding of what questions you hope the simulation will answer.

As a starting point, examine this problem: You have been asked to simulate the alarm system for a house. The house is a center-hall colonial with four bedrooms, a finished basement, and an under-the-house garage.

The downstairs has the following windows: three in the kitchen, four in the dining room, one in the half-bathroom, two each in the living room and the family room, and two small windows next to the front door. All four bedrooms are upstairs; each bedroom has two windows except for the master bedroom, which has four. There are two baths, each with one window. Finally, there are four half-windows in the basement and one window in the garage.

Normal access to the house is through the front door. Additionally, the kitchen has a sliding glass door, and the garage has two doors for the cars and one door for easy access to the basement. There is also a cellar door in the backyard.

All the windows and doors are alarmed, and there is a panic button on each phone and one next to the bed in the master bedroom. The grounds are alarmed as well, although these alarms are carefully calibrated so that they are not set off by small animals or birds.

There is a central alarm system in the basement that sounds a warning chirp when the alarm has been tripped. If the alarm is not disabled within a set amount of time, the police are called. If a panic button is pushed, the police are called immediately.

The alarm is also wired into the fire and smoke detectors and the sprinkler system. The alarm system itself is fault tolerant, has its own internal backup power supply, and is encased in a fireproof box.

Conceptualization

NEW TERM   In the *conceptualization* phase, you try to understand what the customer hopes to gain from the program: What is this program for? What questions might this simulation answer? For example, you might be able to use the simulation to answer the questions, "How long might a sensor be broken before anyone notices?" or "Is there a way to defeat the window alarms without the police being notified?"

The conceptualization phase is a good time to think about what is inside the program and what is outside. Are the police represented in the simulation? Is control of the actual house alarm in the system itself?

Analysis and Requirements

The conceptualization phase gives way to the analysis phase. During analysis, your job as object-oriented analyst is to help the customer understand what he requires from the program. Exactly what behavior will the program exhibit? What kinds of interactions can the customer expect?

NEW TERM   These requirements are typically captured in a series of documents. These documents might include *use cases*. A *use case* is a description of how the system will be used. It describes interactions and use patterns, helping the programmer capture the design goals of the system.

High-Level and Low-Level Design

After the product is fully understood and the requirements have been captured in the appropriate documentation, it is time to move on to the high-level design. During this phase of the design the programmer doesn't worry about the platform, operating system, or programming language issues. He concentrates, instead, on how the system will work: What are the major components? How do they interact with one another?

One way to approach this problem is to set aside issues relating to the user interface and to focus only on the components of the problem space.

 The *problem space* is the set of problems and issues your program is trying to solve. The *solution space* is the set of possible solutions to the problems.

As your high-level design evolves you'll want to begin thinking about the responsibilities of the objects you identify—what they do and what information they hold. You also want to think about their collaborations—what objects they interact with.

For example, clearly you have sensors of various types, a central alarm system, buttons, wires, and telephones. Further thought convinces you that you must also simulate rooms, perhaps floors, and possibly groups of people such as owners and police.

The sensors can be divided into motion detectors, trip wires, sound detectors, smoke detectors, and so forth. All these are types of sensors, although there is no such thing as a sensor *per se*. This is a good indication that sensor is an abstract data type (ADT).

As an ADT, the class Sensor would provide the complete interface for all types of sensors, and each derived type would provide the implementation. Clients of the various sensors would use them without regard to which type of sensor they are, and they would each "do the right thing" based on their real type.

To create a good ADT, you need to have a complete understanding of what sensors do (rather than how they work). For example, are sensors passive devices or are they active? Do they wait for some element to heat up, a wire to break, or a piece of caulk to melt, or do they probe their environment? Perhaps some sensors have only a binary state (alarm state or OK), but others have a more analog state (what is the current temperature?). The interface to the abstract data type should be sufficiently complete to handle all the anticipated needs of the myriad derived classes.

Other Objects

The design continues in this way, teasing out the various other classes that will be required to meet the specification. For example, if a log is to be kept, probably a timer will be needed; should the timer poll each sensor, or should each sensor file its own report periodically?

The user is going to need to be able to set up, disarm, and program the system, so a terminal of some sort will be required. You might want a separate object in your simulation for the alarm program itself.

What Are the Classes?

As you solve these problems, you will begin to design your classes. For example, you already have an indication that HeatSensor will derive from Sensor. If the sensor is to make periodic reports, it might also derive via multiple inheritance from Timer, or it might have a timer as a member variable.

The HeatSensor will probably have member functions, such as CurrentTemp() and SetTempLimit(), and will probably inherit functions such as SoundAlarm() from its base class, Sensor.

A frequent issue in object-oriented design is that of encapsulation. You can imagine a design in which the alarm system has a setting for MaxTemp. The alarm system asks the heat sensor what the current temperature is, compares it to the maximum temperature, and sounds the alarm if it is too hot. One could argue that this violates the principle of encapsulation. Perhaps it would be better if the alarm system didn't know or care about the details of temperature analysis—arguably that should be in the HeatSensor.

Whether or not you agree with that argument, it is the kind of decision you want to focus on during the analysis of the problem. To continue this analysis, one could argue that only the sensor and the Log object should know any details of how sensor activity is logged; the Alarm object shouldn't know or care.

Good encapsulation is marked by each class having a coherent and complete set of responsibilities, and no other class having the same responsibilities. If the Sensor is responsible for noting the current temperature, no other class should have that responsibility.

On the other hand, other classes might help deliver the necessary functionality. For example, while it might be the responsibility of the Sensor class to note and log the current temperature, it might implement that responsibility by delegating to a Log object the job of actually recording the data.

Maintaining a firm division of responsibilities makes your program easier to extend and maintain. When you decide to change the alarm system for an enhanced module, its interface to the log and to the sensors will be narrow and well defined. Changes to the alarm system should not affect the Sensor classes, and vice versa.

Should the HeatSensor have a ReportAlarm() function? All sensors will need the capability to report an alarm. This is a good indication that ReportAlarm() should be a virtual method of Sensor, and that Sensor might be an abstract base class. It is possible that

`HeatSensor` will chain up to `Sensor`'s more general `ReportAlarm()` method; the overridden function will just fill in the details it is uniquely qualified to supply.

How Are Alarms Reported?

When your sensors report an alarm condition, they will want to provide a lot of information to the object that phones the police and to the log. It may well be that you'll want to create a `Condition` Class, whose constructor takes a number of measurements. Depending on the complexity of the measurements, these too might be objects, or they might be simple scalar values such as integers.

It is possible that `Condition` objects are passed to the central alarm object; or that `Condition` objects are subclassed into `Alarm` objects, which themselves know how to take emergency action. Perhaps there is no central object; instead, there might be sensors that know how to create `Condition` objects. Some `Condition` objects would know how to log themselves; others might know how to contact the police.

A well-designed, event-driven system need not have a central coordinator. One can imagine the sensors all independently receiving and sending message objects to one another, setting parameters, taking readings, monitoring the house. When a fault is detected, an `Alarm` object is created that logs the problem (by sending a message to the `Log` object?) and takes the appropriate action.

Event Loops

To simulate such an event-driven system, your program needs to create an event loop. An event loop is typically an infinite loop such as `while(1)` that gets messages from the operating system (mouse clicks, keyboard presses, and so on) and dispatches them one by one, returning to the loop until an exit condition is satisfied. Listing 22.1 shows a rudimentary event loop.

LISTING 22.1   A Simple Event Loop

```
0:  // Listing 22.1
1:  #include <iostream>
2:
3:  class Condition
4:  {
5:  public:
6:      Condition() { }
7:      virtual ~Condition() {}
8:      virtual void Log() = 0;
9:  };
10:
```

LISTING 22.1 continued

```
11:    class Normal : public Condition
12:    {
13:    public:
14:        Normal() { Log(); }
15:        virtual ~Normal() {}
16:        virtual void Log()
17:            { std::cout << "Logging normal conditions...\n"; }
18:    };
19:
20:    class Error : public Condition
21:    {
22:    public:
23:        Error() {Log();}
24:        virtual ~Error() {}
25:        virtual void Log() { std::cout << "Logging error!\n"; }
26:    };
27:
28:    class Alarm : public Condition
29:    {
30:    public:
31:        Alarm ();
32:        virtual   ~Alarm() {}
33:        virtual void Warn() { std::cout << "Warning!\n"; }
34:        virtual void Log() { std::cout << "General Alarm log\n"; }
35:        virtual void Call() = 0;
36:    };
37:
38:    Alarm::Alarm()
39:    {
40:        Log();
41:      Warn();
42:    }
43:
44:    class FireAlarm : public Alarm
45:    {
46:    public:
47:        FireAlarm(){Log();};
48:        virtual ~FireAlarm() {}
49:        virtual void Call() { std::cout<< "Calling Fire Dept.!\n"; }
50:        virtual void Log() { std::cout << "Logging fire call.\n"; }
51:    };
52:
53:    int main()
54:    {
55:        int input;
56:        int okay = 1;
57:        Condition * pCondition;
58:        while (okay)
59:        {
```

LISTING 22.1   continued

```
60:             std::cout << "(0)Quit (1)Normal (2)Fire: ";
61:             std::cin >> input;
62:             okay = input;
63:             switch (input)
64:             {
65:             case 0:
66:                 break;
67:             case 1:
68:                 pCondition = new Normal;
69:                 delete pCondition;
70:                 break;
71:             case 2:
72:                 pCondition = new FireAlarm;
73:                 delete pCondition;
74:                 break;
75:             default:
76:                 pCondition = new Error;
77:                 delete pCondition;
78:                 okay = 0;
79:                 break;
80:             }
81:         }
82:     return 0;
83: }
```

OUTPUT
```
(0)Quit (1)Normal (2)Fire: 1
Logging normal conditions...
(0)Quit (1)Normal (2)Fire: 2
General Alarm log
Warning!
Logging fire call.
(0)Quit (1)Normal (2)Fire: 0
```

ANALYSIS The simple loop created on lines 58–81 enables the user to enter input simulating a normal report from a sensor and a report of a fire. Note that the effect of this report is to spawn a Condition object whose constructor calls various member functions.

Calling virtual member functions from a constructor can cause confusing results if you are not mindful of the order of construction of objects. For example, when the FireAlarm object is created on line 72, the order of construction is Condition, Alarm, FireAlarm. The Alarm constructor calls Log, but it is Alarm's Log() that is invoked, not FireAlarm's, despite Log() being declared virtual. This is because at the time Alarm's constructor runs, there is no FireAlarm object. Later, when FireAlarm itself is constructed, its constructor calls Log() again, and this time FireAlarm::Log() is called.

PostMaster: A Case Study

Here's another problem on which to practice your object-oriented analysis: You have been hired by Acme Software, Inc., to start a new software project and to hire a team of C++ programmers to implement your program. Jim Grandiose, vice-president of New Product Development, is your new boss. He wants you to design and build PostMaster, a utility to read electronic mail from various unrelated e-mail providers. The potential customer is a business person who uses more than one e-mail product, for example, CompuServe, America Online, Internet Mail, Lotus Notes, and so forth.

The customer will be able to teach PostMaster how to connect to each of the e-mail providers. PostMaster will get the mail and then present it in a uniform manner, enabling the customer to organize the mail, reply, forward letters among services, and so forth.

PostMaster Professional, to be developed as version two of PostMaster, is already anticipated. It will add an administrative assistant mode that will enable the user to designate another person to read some or all of the mail, to handle routine correspondence, and so forth. There is also speculation in the marketing department that an artificial-intelligence component might add the capability for PostMaster to pre-sort and prioritize the mail based on subject and content keywords and associations.

Other enhancements have been talked about, including the capability to handle not only mail but discussion groups, such as Internet newsgroups and mail lists. It is obvious that Acme has great hopes for PostMaster, and you are under severe time constraints to bring it to market, although you seem to have a nearly unlimited budget.

Measure Twice, Cut Once

You set up your office and order your equipment; your first order of business is then to get a good specification for the product. After examining the market, you decide to recommend that development be focused on a single platform, and you set out to decide among UNIX, Macintosh, and Windows.

You have many painful meetings with Jim Grandiose. It becomes clear that there is no right choice, so you decide to separate the front end—that is, the user interface (or UI)—from the back end—the communications and database part. To get things going quickly, you decide to write for Windows, followed later by UNIX and perhaps the Mac.

This simple decision has enormous ramifications for your project. It quickly becomes obvious that you will need a class library or a series of libraries to handle memory management, the various user interfaces, and perhaps also the communications and database components.

Mr. Grandiose believes strongly that projects live or die by having one person with a clear vision, so he asks that you do the initial architectural analysis and design before hiring any programmers. You set out to analyze the problem.

Divide and Conquer

It quickly becomes obvious that you really have more than one problem to solve. You divide the project into these significant subprojects:

- Communications: The capability for the software to dial into the e-mail provider via modem, or to connect over a network.

- Database: The capability to store data and to retrieve it from disk.

- E-mail: The capability to read various e-mail formats and to write new messages to each system.

- Editing: Providing state-of-the-art editors for the creation and manipulation of messages.

- Platform issues: The various UI issues presented by each platform.

- Extensibility: Planning for growth and enhancements.

- Organization and scheduling: Managing the various developers and their code interdependencies. Each group must devise and publish schedules, and then be able to plan accordingly. Senior management and marketing need to know when the product will be ready.

You decide to hire a manager to handle one of these items, organization and scheduling. You then hire senior developers to help you analyze and design, and then to manage the implementation of the remaining areas. These senior developers will create the following teams:

- Communications: Responsible for both dial-up and network communications. They deal with packets, streams, and bits rather than with e-mail messages *per se*.

- Message Format: Responsible for converting messages from each e-mail provider to a canonical form (PostMaster standard), and back. It is also this team's job to write these messages to disk and to get them back off the disk as needed.

- Message editors: This group is responsible for the entire UI of the product, on each platform. It is their job to ensure that the interface between the back end and the front end of the product is sufficiently narrow so that extending the product to other platforms does not require duplication of code.

Message Format

You decide to focus on the message format first, setting aside the issues relating to communications and user interface. These will follow after you understand more fully what it is you are dealing with. There is little sense in worrying about how to present the information to the user until you understand what kind of information it is.

An examination of the various e-mail formats reveals that they have many things in common, despite their various differences. Each e-mail message has a point of origination, a destination, and a creation date. Nearly all such messages have a title or subject line, and a body that might consist of simple text, rich text (text with formatting), graphics, and perhaps even sound or other fancy additions. Most such e-mail services also support attachments so that users can send programs and other files.

You confirm your early decision that you will read each mail message out of its original format and into PostMaster format. This way you will only have to store one record format, and writing to and reading from the disk will be simplified. You also decide to separate the header information (sender, recipient, date, title, and so on) from the body of the message. Often the user will want to scan the headers without necessarily reading the contents of all the messages. You anticipate that a time might come when users will want to download only the headers from the message provider, without getting the text at all, but for now you intend that version one of PostMaster will always get the full message, although it might not display it to the user.

Initial Class Design

This analysis of the messages leads you to design the Message class. In anticipation of extending the program to non-e-mail messages, you derive EmailMessage from the abstract base Message. From EmailMessage you derive PostMasterMessage, InterchangeMessage, CISMessage, ProdigyMessage, and so forth.

Messages are a natural choice for objects in a program handling mail messages, but finding all the right objects in a complex system is the single greatest challenge of object-oriented programming. In some cases, such as with messages, the primary objects seem to fall out of your understanding of the problem. More often, however, you have to think long and hard about what you are trying to accomplish to find the right objects.

Don't despair. Most designs are not perfect the first time. A good starting point is to describe the problem out loud. Make a list of all the nouns and verbs you use when describing the project. The nouns are good candidates for objects. The verbs might be the methods of those objects (or they might be objects in their own right). This is not a foolproof method, but it is a good technique to use when getting started on your design.

That was the easy part. Now the question arises, "Should the message header be a separate class from the body?" If so, do you need parallel hierarchies—NewsGroupBody and NewsGroupHeader as well as EmailBody and EmailHeader?

Parallel hierarchies are often a warning sign of a bad design. It is a common error in object-oriented design to have a set of objects in one hierarchy and a matching set of manager objects in another. The burden of keeping these hierarchies up-to-date and in synch with each other soon becomes overwhelming: a classic maintenance nightmare.

There are no hard and fast rules, of course, and at times such parallel hierarchies are the most efficient way to solve a particular problem. Nonetheless, if you see your design moving in this direction, you should rethink the problem; there might be a more elegant solution available.

When the messages arrive from the e-mail provider they will not necessarily be separated into header and body; many will be one large stream of data that your program will have to disentangle. Perhaps your hierarchy should reflect that idea directly.

Further reflection on the tasks at hand leads you to try to list the properties of these messages, with an eye toward introducing capabilities and data storage at the right level of abstraction. Listing properties of your objects is a good way to find the data members, as well as to shake out other objects you might need.

Mail messages will need to be stored, as will the user's preferences, phone numbers, and so forth. Storage clearly needs to be high up in the hierarchy. Should the mail messages necessarily share a base class with the preferences?

Rooted Hierarchies Versus Non-Rooted

There are two overall approaches to inheritance hierarchies: You can have all, or nearly all, of your classes descend from a common root class; or you can have more than one inheritance hierarchy. An advantage of a common root class is that you often can avoid multiple inheritance; a disadvantage is that many times implementation will percolate up into the base class.

A set of classes is rooted if all share a common ancestor.

Non-rooted hierarchies do not all share a common base class.

Because you know that your product will be developed on many platforms, and because multiple inheritance is complex and not necessarily well supported by all compilers on all platforms, your first decision is to use a rooted hierarchy and single inheritance. You decide to identify those places where multiple inheritance might be used in the future. You can then design so that breaking apart the hierarchy and adding multiple inheritance at a later time need not be traumatic to your entire design.

You decide to prefix the name of all your internal classes with the letter p, so that you can easily and quickly tell which classes are yours and which are from other libraries.

Your root class will be pObject. Virtually every class you create will descend from this object. pObject itself will be kept fairly simple; only the data that absolutely every item shares will appear in this class.

If you want a rooted hierarchy, you'll want to give the root class a fairly generic name (like pObject) and few capabilities. The point of a root object is to be able to create collections of all its descendants and refer to them as instances of pObject. The trade-off is that rooted hierarchies often percolate interface up into the root class.

The next likely candidates for top-of-the-hierarchy status are pStored and pWired. pStored objects are saved to disk at various times (for example, when the program is not in use), and pWired objects are sent over the modem or network. Because nearly all your objects will need to be stored to disk, it makes sense to push this functionality up high in the hierarchy. Because all the objects that are sent over the modem must be stored, but not all stored objects must be sent over the wire, it makes sense to derive pWired from pStored.

Each derived class acquires all the knowledge (data) and functionality (methods) of its base class, and each should have one discrete additional capability. Thus pWired might add various methods, but all these methods are designed to facilitate transfer of data over a modem.

It is possible that all wired objects are stored, or that all stored objects are wired, or that neither of those statements is true. If only some wired objects are stored, and only some stored objects are wired, you will be forced either to use multiple inheritance or to hack around the problem. A potential hack for such a situation would be to inherit, for example, Wired from Stored, and then to make the stored methods do nothing or return an error for those objects that are sent via modem but are never stored.

In fact, you realize that some stored objects clearly are not wired; for example, user preferences. All wired objects, however, are stored, so your inheritance hierarchy so far is as reflected in Figure 22.1.

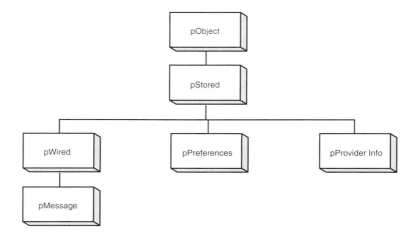

FIGURE **22.1**
*Initial inheritance
hierarchy.*

Designing the Interfaces

It is important, at this stage of designing your product, to avoid being concerned with implementation. You want to focus all your energies on designing a clean interface among the classes, and then delineating what data and methods each class will need.

It is often a good idea to have a solid understanding of the base classes before trying to design the more derived classes, so you decide to focus on pObject, pStored and pWired.

The root class, pObject, will only have those data and methods that are common to everything on your system. Perhaps every object should have a unique identification number. You could create pID (PostMaster ID) and make that a member of pObject; but first you must ask yourself, "Does any object that is not stored and not wired need such a number?" That begs the question, "Are there any objects that are not stored, but that are part of this hierarchy?"

If there are no such objects, you might want to consider collapsing pObject and pStored into one class; after all, if all objects are stored, what is the point of the differentiation? Thinking this through, you realize that there might be some objects, such as address objects, that it would be beneficial to derive from pObject but that will never be stored on their own; if they are stored it will be as part of some other object.

This tells you that, for now, having a separate pObject class would be useful. You can imagine that there will be an address book that will be a collection of pAddress objects, and while no pAddress will ever be stored on its own, there would be utility in having each one have its own unique identification number. You tentatively assign pID to pObject; that means that pObject, at a minimum, will look like this:

```
class pOjbect
{
public:
   pObject();
   ~pObject();
   pID GetID()const;
   void SetID();
private:
   pID  itsID;
}
```

There are a number of things to note about this class declaration. First, this class is not declared to derive from any other; this is your root class. Second, there is no attempt to show implementation, even for methods such as GetID() that are likely to have inline implementation when you are done.

Third, const methods are already identified; this is part of the interface, not the implementation. Finally, a new data type is implied: pID. Defining pID as a type rather than using, for example, unsigned long puts greater flexibility into your design.

If it turns out that you don't need an unsigned long, or that an unsigned long is not sufficiently large, you can modify pID. That modification will affect every place pID is used, and you won't have to track down and edit every file with a pID in it.

For now, you use typedef to declare pID to be ULONG which, in turn, you declare to be unsigned long. This raises the question: Where do these declarations go?

When programming a large project, an overall design of the files is needed. A standard approach, one that you will follow for this project, is that each class appears in its own header file, and the implementation for the class methods appears in an associated .CPP file. Thus, you will have a file called OBJECT.HPP and another called OBJECT.CPP. You anticipate having other files such as MSG.HPP and MSG.CPP with the declaration of pMessage and the implementation of its methods, respectively.

The Buy/Build Decision

Buy it or write it? One question you will confront throughout the design phase of your program is which routines you might buy and which you must write yourself. It is entirely possible that you can take advantage of existing commercial libraries to solve some or all your communications issues. Licensing fees and other non-technical concerns must also be resolved.

It is often advantageous to purchase such a library, and to focus your energies on your specific program rather than to reinvent the wheel about secondary technical issues. You might even want to consider purchasing libraries that were not necessarily intended for use with C++, if they can provide fundamental functionality you'd otherwise have to engineer yourself. This can be instrumental in helping you hit your deadlines.

Building a Prototype

For a project as large as PostMaster, it is unlikely that your initial design will be complete and perfect. It would be easy to become overwhelmed by the sheer scale of the problem, and trying to create all the classes and to complete their interface before writing a line of working code is a recipe for disaster.

There are a number of good reasons to try out your design on a prototype—a quick-and-dirty working example of your core ideas. There are a number of different types of prototypes, however, each meeting different needs.

An interface design prototype provides the chance to test the look and feel of your product with potential users.

A functionality prototype does not have the final user interface, but enables users to try out various features, such as forwarding messages or attaching files.

Finally, an architecture prototype might be designed to give you a chance to develop a smaller version of the program and to assess how easily your design decisions will scale up as the program is fleshed out.

It is imperative to keep your prototyping goals clear. Are you examining the user interface, experimenting with functionality, or building a scale model of your final product? A good architecture prototype makes a poor user-interface prototype, and vice versa.

It is also important to keep an eye on over-engineering of the prototype, or becoming so concerned with the investment you've made in the prototype that you are reluctant to tear down the code and redesign as you progress.

The 80/80 Rule

A good design rule of thumb at this stage is to design for those things that 80% of the people want to do 80% of the time, and to set aside your concerns about the remaining 20%. The boundary conditions will need to be addressed sooner or later, but the core of your design should focus on the 80/80.

Accordingly, you might decide to start by designing the principal classes, setting aside the need for the secondary classes. Further, when you identify multiple classes that will have similar designs with only minor refinements, you might choose to pick one representative class and focus on that, leaving until later the design and implementation of its close cousins.

> There is another rule, the 80/20 rule, that states: "The first 20% of your program will take 80% of your time to code; the remaining 80% of your program will take the other 80% of your time!"

Designing the `PostMasterMessage` Class

In keeping with these considerations, you decide to focus on the `PostMasterMessage`. This is the class that is most directly under your control.

As part of its interface, `PostMasterMessage` will need to talk with other types of messages, of course. You hope to be able to work closely with the other message providers, and to get their message format specifications, but for now you can make some smart guesses just by observing what is sent to your computer as you use their services.

In any case, you know that every `PostMasterMessage` will have a sender, a recipient, a date, and a subject, as well as the body of the message and perhaps attached files. This tells you that you'll need accessor methods for each of these attributes, as well as methods to report on the size of the attached files, the size of the messages, and so forth.

Some of the services to which you will connect will use rich text—that is, text with formatting instructions to set the font, character size, and attributes such as bold and italic. Other services do not support these attributes, and those that do might or might not use their own proprietary scheme for managing rich text. Your class will need conversion methods for turning rich text into plain ASCII, and perhaps for turning other formats into PostMaster formats.

The Application Programming Interface

An Application Programming Interface (API) is a set of documentation and routines for using a service. Many of the mail providers will give you an API so that PostMaster mail will be able to take advantage of their more advanced features, such as rich text and embedding files. You will also want to publish an API for PostMaster so that other providers can plan for working with PostMaster in the future.

Your PostMasterMessage class needs to have a well-designed public interface, and the conversion functions will be a principal component of PostMaster's API. Listing 22.2 illustrates what PostMasterMessage's interface looks like so far.

This listing does not define the base class (MailMessage), and it will not compile.

LISTING 22.2   PostMasterMessage's Interface

```
0:  // Listing 22.2 the PostMasterMessage class
1:
2:  class PostMasterMessage : public MailMessage
3:  {
4:  public:
5:      PostMasterMessage();
6:      PostMasterMessage(
7:          pAddress Sender,
8:          pAddress Recipient,
9:          pString Subject,
10:         pDate creationDate);
11:
12:     // other constructors here
13:     // remember to include copy constructor
14:     // as well as constructor from storage
15:     // and constructor from wire format
16:     // Also include constructors from other formats
17:     ~PostMasterMessage();
18:     pAddress& GetSender() const;
19:     void SetSender(pAddress&);
20:     // other member accessors
21:
22:     // operator methods here, including operator equals
23:     // and conversion routines to turn PostMaster messages
24:     // into messages of other formats.
25:
26:  private:
27:     pAddress itsSender;
28:     pAddress itsRecipient;
29:     pString  itsSubject;
30:     pDate itsCreationDate;
31:     pDate itsLastModDate;
32:     pDate itsReceiptDate;
33:     pDate itsFirstReadDate;
34:     pDate itsLastReadDate;
35:  };
```

OUTPUT This listing has no output.

ANALYSIS Class `PostMasterMessage` is declared to derive from `MailMessage`. A number of constructors will be provided, facilitating the creation of `PostMasterMessages` from other types of mail messages.

A number of accessor methods are anticipated for reading and setting the various member data, as well as operators for turning all or part of a message into other message formats. You anticipate storing these messages to disk and reading them from the wire, so accessor methods are noted for those purposes as well.

Programming in Large Groups

Even this preliminary architecture is enough to indicate how the various development groups ought to proceed. The Communications group can go ahead and start work on the communications back end, negotiating a narrow interface with the Message Format group.

The Message Format group will probably lay out the general interface to the `Message` classes, as was begun earlier, and then will turn its attention to the question of how to write data to the disk and read it back. After this disk interface is well understood, the team will be in a good position to negotiate the interface to the communications layer.

The message editors will be tempted to create editors with an intimate knowledge of the internals of the message class, but this would be a bad design mistake. They too must negotiate a very narrow interface to the message class; message editor objects should know very little about the internal structure of messages.

Ongoing Design Considerations

As the project continues, you will repeatedly confront this basic design issue: In which class should you put a given set of functionality (or information)? Should the message class have this function, or should the address class? Should the editor store this information, or should the message store it itself?

Your classes should operate on a need-to-know basis, much like secret agents. They shouldn't share any more knowledge than is absolutely necessary.

Design Decisions

As you progress with your program, you will face hundreds of design issues. They will range from the more global questions, "What do we want this to do?" to the more specific, "How do we make this work?"

Although the details of your implementation won't be finalized until you ship the code, and some of the interfaces will continue to shift and change as you work, you must ensure that your design is well understood early in the process. It is imperative that you know what you are trying to build before you write the code. The single most frequent cause of software dying on the vine must be that there is not sufficient agreement, early enough in the process, about what is being built.

Decisions, Decisions

To get a feel for what the design process is like, examine this question, "What will be on the menu?" For PostMaster, the first choice is probably New Mail Message, and this immediately raises another design issue: When the user selects New Mail Message, what happens? Does an editor get created, which in turn creates a mail message, or does a new mail message get created, which then creates the editor?

The command you are working with is New Mail Message, so creating a new mail message seems like the obvious thing to do. But what happens if the user clicks Cancel after starting to write the message? Perhaps it would be cleaner to first create the editor and have it create (and own) the new message.

The problem with this approach is that the editor will need to act differently if it is creating a message than if it were editing the message; whereas if the message is created first, and then handed to the editor, only one set of code needs to exist because everything is an edit of an existing message.

If a message is created first, who creates it? Is it created by the menu command code? If so, does the menu also tell the message to edit itself, or is this part of the constructor method of the message?

It makes sense for the constructor to do this at first glance; after all, every time you create a message you'll probably want to edit it. Nonetheless, this is not a good design idea. First, it is very possible that the premise is wrong; you might create "canned" messages (that is, error messages mailed to the system operator) that are not put into an editor. Second, and more important, a constructor's job is to create an object; it should do no more and no less than that. After a mail message is created, the constructor's job is done. Adding a call to the edit method just confuses the role of the constructor and makes the mail message vulnerable to failures in the editor.

Worse yet, the edit method will call another class—the editor— causing its constructor to be called. But the editor is not a base class of the message, nor is it contained within the message; it would be unfortunate if the construction of the message depended on successful construction of the editor.

Finally, you won't want to call the editor at all if the message can't be successfully created; yet successful creation would, in this scenario, depend on calling the editor! Clearly you want to fully return from message's constructor before calling `Message::Edit()`.

Working with Driver Programs

NEW TERM One approach to surfacing design issues is to create a *driver program* early in the process. A *driver program* is a function that exists only to demonstrate or test other functions. For example, the driver program for PostMaster might offer a very simple menu that will create `PostMasterMessage` objects, manipulate them, and otherwise exercise some of the design.

Listing 22.3 illustrates a somewhat more robust definition of the `PostMasterMessage` class and a simple driver program.

LISTING 22.3   A Driver Program for `PostMasterMessage`

```
0:  // Listing 22.3
1:  #include <iostream>
2:  #include <string.h>
3:
4:  typedef unsigned long pDate;
5:  enum SERVICE { PostMaster, Interchange,
6:      CompuServe, Prodigy, AOL, Internet };
7:
8:  class String
9:  {
10:  public:
11:      // constructors
12:      String();
13:      String(const char *const);
14:      String(const String &);
15:      ~String();
16:
17:      // overloaded operators
18:      char & operator[](int offset);
19:      char operator[](int offset) const;
20:      String operator+(const String&);
21:      void operator+=(const String&);
22:      String & operator= (const String &);
23:      friend std::ostream & operator<<
24:              (std::ostream& theStream, String& theString);
25:      // General accessors
26:      int GetLen()const { return itsLen; }
27:      const char * GetString() const { return itsString; }
28:      // static int ConstructorCount;
29:
```

LISTING 22.3   continued

```
30:  private:
31:      String (int);          // private constructor
32:      char * itsString;
33:      int itsLen;
34:  };
35:
36:  // default constructor creates string of 0 bytes
37:  String::String()
38:  {
39:      itsString = new char[1];
40:      itsString[0] = '\0';
41:      itsLen=0;
42:      // std::cout << "\tDefault string constructor\n";
43:      // ConstructorCount++;
44:  }
45:
46:  // private (helper) constructor, used only by
47:  // class methods for creating a new string of
48:  // required size.  Null filled.
49:  String::String(int len)
50:  {
51:      itsString = new char[len+1];
52:      int i;
53:      for ( i = 0; i<=len; i++)
54:          itsString[1] = '\0';
55:      itsLen=len;
56:      // std::cout << "\tString(int) constructor\n";
57:      // ConstructorCount++;
58:  }
59:
60:  // Converts a character array to a String
61:  String::String(const char * const cString)
62:  {
63:      itsLen = strlen(cString);
64:      itsString = new char[itsLen+1];
65:      int i;
66:      for ( i = 0; i<itsLen; i++)
67:          itsString[i] = cString[i];
68:      itsString[itsLen]='\0';
69:      // std::cout << "\tString(char*) constructor\n";
70:      // ConstructorCount++;
71:  }
72:
73:  // copy constructor
74:  String::String (const String & rhs)
75:  {
76:      itsLen=rhs.GetLen();
77:      itsString = new char[itsLen+1];
78:      int i;
```

LISTING 22.3   continued

```
79:        for (i = 0; i<itsLen;i++)
80:            itsString[i] = rhs[i];
81:        itsString[itsLen] = '\0';
82:        // std::cout << "\tString(String&) constructor\n";
83:        // ConstructorCount++;
84:    }
85:
86:    // destructor, frees allocated memory
87:    String::~String ()
88:    {
89:        delete [] itsString;
90:        itsLen = 0;
91:        // std::cout << "\tString destructor\n";
92:    }
93:
94:    String& String::operator=(const String & rhs)
95:    {
96:        if (this == &rhs)
97:            return *this;
98:        delete [] itsString;
99:        itsLen=rhs.GetLen();
100:        itsString = new char[itsLen+1];
101:        int i;
102:        for (i = 0; i<itsLen;i++)
103:            itsString[i] = rhs[i];
104:        itsString[itsLen] = '\0';
105:        return *this;
106:        // std::cout << "\tString operator=\n";
107:    }
108:
109:    //non constant offset operator, returns
110:    // reference to character so it can be changed
111:    char & String::operator[](int offset)
112:    {
113:        if (offset > itsLen)
114:            return itsString[itsLen-1];
115:        else
116:            return itsString[offset];
117:    }
118:
119:    // constant offset operator for use
120:    // on const objects (see copy constructor!)
121:    char String::operator[](int offset) const
122:    {
123:        if (offset > itsLen)
124:            return itsString[itsLen-1];
125:        else
126:            return itsString[offset];
127:    }
```

LISTING 22.3 continued

```
128:
129:  // creates a new string by adding current
130:  // string to rhs
131:  String String::operator+(const String& rhs)
132:  {
133:      int  totalLen = itsLen + rhs.GetLen();
134:      String temp(totalLen);
135:      int i,j;
136:      for (i = 0; i<itsLen; i++)
137:          temp[i] = itsString[i];
138:      for (j = 0; j<rhs.GetLen(); j++, i++)
139:          temp[i] = rhs[j];
140:      temp[totalLen]='\0';
141:      return temp;
142:  }
143:
144:  // changes current string, returns nothing
145:  void String::operator+=(const String& rhs)
146:  {
147:      int rhsLen = rhs.GetLen();
148:      int totalLen = itsLen + rhsLen;
149:      String  temp(totalLen);
150:      int i,j;
151:      for ( i = 0; i<itsLen; i++)
152:          temp[i] = itsString[i];
153:      for ( j = 0; j<rhs.GetLen(); j++, i++)
154:          temp[i] = rhs[i-itsLen];
155:      temp[totalLen]='\0';
156:      *this = temp;
157:  }
158:
159:  // int String::ConstructorCount = 0;
160:
161:  std::ostream& operator<<(
162:                                              std::ostream& theStream,
163:                                      String& theString)
164:  {
165:      theStream << theString.GetString();
166:      return theStream;
167:  }
168:
169:  class pAddress
170:  {
171:  public:
172:      pAddress(SERVICE theService,
173:              const String& theAddress,
174:              const String& theDisplay):
175:          itsService(theService),
176:          itsAddressString(theAddress),
```

LISTING 22.3   continued

```
177:            itsDisplayString(theDisplay)
178:        {}
179:        // pAddress(String, String);
180:        // pAddress();
181:        // pAddress (const pAddress&);
182:        ~pAddress(){}
183:        friend std::ostream& operator<<(
184:           std::ostream& theStream, pAddress& theAddress);
185:        String& GetDisplayString()
186:          { return itsDisplayString; }
187: private:
188:        SERVICE itsService;
189:        String itsAddressString;
190:        String itsDisplayString;
191: };
192:
193: std::ostream& operator<<
194:    ( std::ostream& theStream, pAddress& theAddress)
195: {
196:        theStream << theAddress.GetDisplayString();
197:        return theStream;
198: }
199:
200: class PostMasterMessage
201: {
202: public:
203: //   PostMasterMessage();
204:
205:        PostMasterMessage(const pAddress& Sender,
206:                          const pAddress& Recipient,
207:                          const String& Subject,
208:                          const pDate& creationDate);
209:
210:        ~PostMasterMessage(){}
211:
212:        void Edit(); // invokes editor on this message
213:
214:        pAddress& GetSender()  { return itsSender; }
215:        pAddress& GetRecipient()  { return itsRecipient; }
216:        String& GetSubject()  { return itsSubject; }
217:        //   void SetSender(pAddress& );
218:        // other member accessors
219:
220:        // operator methods here, including operator equals
221:        // and conversion routines to turn PostMaster messages
222:        // into messages of other formats.
223:
224: private:
225:        pAddress itsSender;
```

LISTING 22.3   continued

```
226:        pAddress itsRecipient;
227:        String  itsSubject;
228:        pDate itsCreationDate;
229:        pDate itsLastModDate;
230:        pDate itsReceiptDate;
231:        pDate itsFirstReadDate;
232:        pDate itsLastReadDate;
233:    };
234:
235:    PostMasterMessage::PostMasterMessage(
236:        const pAddress& Sender,
237:        const pAddress& Recipient,
238:        const String& Subject,
239:        const pDate& creationDate):
240:        itsSender(Sender),
241:        itsRecipient(Recipient),
242:        itsSubject(Subject),
243:        itsCreationDate(creationDate),
244:        itsLastModDate(creationDate),
245:        itsFirstReadDate(0),
246:        itsLastReadDate(0)
247:    {
248:        std::cout << "Post Master Message created. \n";
249:    }
250:
251:    void PostMasterMessage::Edit()
252:    {
253:        std::cout << "PostMasterMessage edit function called\n";
254:    }
255:
256:
257:    int main()
258:    {
259:        pAddress Sender(
260:            PostMaster, "jliberty@PostMaster", "Jesse Liberty");
261:        pAddress Recipient(
262:            PostMaster, "sliberty@PostMaster","Stacey Liberty");
263:        PostMasterMessage PostMasterMessage(
264:            Sender, Recipient, "Saying Hello", 0);
265:        std::cout << "Message review... \n";
266:        std::cout << "From:\t\t"
267:            << PostMasterMessage.GetSender() << std::endl;
268:        std::cout << "To:\t\t"
269:            << PostMasterMessage.GetRecipient() << std::endl;
270:        std::cout << "Subject:\t"
271:            << PostMasterMessage.GetSubject() << std::endl;
272:        return 0;
273:    }
```

OUTPUT

```
Post Master Message created.
Message review...
From:      Jesse Liberty
To:        Stacey Liberty
Subject:   Saying Hello
```

ANALYSIS On line 4, pDate is type-defined to be an unsigned long. It is not uncommon for dates to be stored as a long integer, typically as the number of seconds since an arbitrary starting date such as January 1, 1900. In this program, this is a placeholder; you would expect to eventually turn pDate into a real class.

On line 5, an enumerated constant, SERVICE, is defined to enable the address objects to keep track of what type of address they are, including PostMaster, CompuServe, and so forth.

Lines 8–167 represent the interface to and implementation of String, along much the same lines as you have seen in previous chapters. The String class is used for a number of member variables in all the message classes and in various other classes used by messages, and as such, it is pivotal in your program. A full and robust String class will be essential to making your message classes complete.

On lines 169–191, the pAddress class is declared. This represents only the fundamental functionality of this class, and you would expect to flesh this out after your program is better understood. These objects represent essential components in every message: both the sender's address and that of the recipient. A fully functional pAddress object will be able to handle forwarding messages, replies, and so forth.

It is the pAddress object's job to keep track of both the display string and the internal routing string for its service. One open question for your design is whether there should be one pAddress object, or whether it should be subclassed for each service type. For now the service is tracked as an enumerated constant that is a member variable of each pAddress object.

Lines 200–233 show the interface to the PostMasterMessage class. In this particular listing, this class stands on its own, but very soon you'll want to make this part of its inheritance hierarchy. When you do redesign this to inherit from Message, some of the member variables might move into the base classes, and some of the member functions might become overrides of base class methods.

A variety of other constructors, accessor functions, and other member functions will be required to make this class fully functional. Note that what this listing illustrates is that your class does not have to be 100% complete before you can write a simple driver program to test some of your assumptions.

22

On lines 251–254, the `Edit()` function is stubbed out in just enough detail to indicate where the editing functionality will be put after this class is fully operational.

Lines 257–273 represent the driver program. Currently this program does nothing more than exercise a few of the accessor functions and the `operator<<` overload. Nonetheless, this gives you the starting point for experimenting with `PostMasterMessages` and a framework within which you can modify these classes and examine the impact.

Summary

In this hour you saw how to bring together many of the elements of C++ syntax and apply them to object-oriented analysis, design, and programming. The development cycle is not a linear progression from clean analysis through design and culminating in programming; rather, it is, in fact, cyclical. The first phase is typically analysis of the problem, with the results of that analysis forming the basis for the preliminary design.

After a preliminary design is complete, programming can begin; but the lessons learned during the programming phase are fed back into the analysis and design. As programming progresses, testing and then debugging begin. The cycle continues, never really ending, although discrete points are reached. There comes a time, however, when it is appropriate to ship the product. Don't hesitate, ship it!

When analyzing a large problem from an object-oriented viewpoint, the interacting parts of the problem are often the objects of the preliminary design. The designer keeps an eye out for process, hoping to encapsulate discrete activities into objects whenever possible.

A class hierarchy must be designed, and fundamental relationships among the interacting parts must be established. The preliminary design is not meant to be final, and functionality will migrate among objects as the design solidifies.

It is a principal goal of object-oriented analysis to hide as much of the data and implementation as possible and to build discrete objects that have a narrow and well-defined interface. The clients of your object should not need to understand the implementation details of how they fulfill their responsibilities.

Q&A

Q **In what way is object-oriented analysis and design fundamentally different from other approaches?**

A Prior to the development of these object-oriented techniques, analysts and programmers tended to think of programs as functions that acted on data. Object-oriented programming focuses on the integrated data and functionality as discrete units that have both knowledge (data) and capabilities (functions). Procedural programs, on the other hand, focus on functions and how they act on data. It has been said that Pascal and C programs are collections of procedures, and C++ programs are collections of classes.

Q Is object-oriented programming finally the silver bullet that will solve all programming problems?

A No, it was never intended to be. For large, complex problems, however, object-oriented analysis, design, and programming can provide the programmer with tools to manage enormous complexity in ways that were previously impossible.

HOUR 23

Templates

In the past few years, C++ has added a few new features. One of the more exciting and powerful new aspects of C++ is templates. Templates enable you to build type-safe collections. In this hour you will learn

- What templates are and how to use them
- Why templates supply a better alternative to macros
- How to create class templates

What Are Templates?

In Hour 19, you learned how to make a linked list. Your linked list was nicely encapsulated: The list knew only about its head pointer; the head pointer delegated its work to internal pointers, and so forth.

The one glaring problem with the linked list was that it only knew how to handle the particular data objects it was created to work with. If you wanted to put anything else into your linked list, you couldn't do it. You couldn't for example, make a linked list of Car objects, or of Cats, or of any other object that wasn't of the same type as those in the original list.

To solve this problem, you can create a List base class and derive from it the CarList and CatsList classes. You can then cut and paste much of the LinkedList class into the new CatsList declaration. Next week, however, when you want to make a list of Car objects, you have to make a new class and cut and paste again.

Needless to say, this is not a satisfactory solution. Over time, the List class and its derived classes will have to be extended. Making sure that all the changes are propagated to all the related classes will then be a nightmare.

Templates offer a solution to this problem. In addition, unlike old-fashioned macros, templates are an integrated part of the language, type-safe and very flexible.

NEW TERM Templates provide you with the capability to create a general class and pass types as *parameters* to the template to build specific instances of the parameterized type.

Parameterized Types

Templates enable you to teach the compiler how to make a list of any type of thing, rather than creating a set of type-specific lists. A PartsList is a list of parts; a CatList is a list of cats. The only way in which they differ is the type of the thing on the list. With templates, the type of the thing on the list becomes a parameter to the definition of the class.

NEW TERM The act of creating an object (from a class)or a specific type from a template is called *instantiation*, and the individual classes are called *instances* of the template.

Template Definition

You declare a parameterized List object (a template for a list) by writing

```
1: template <class T>    // declare the template and the parameter
2: class List            // the class being parameterized
3: {
4: public:
5:    List();
6:    // full class declaration here
7: };
```

The keyword template is used at the beginning of every declaration and definition of a template class. The parameters of the template are after the keyword template; they are the items that will change with each instance. For example, in the list template shown in the previous code snippet, the type of the objects stored in the list will change. One instance might store a list of Integers, whereas another might store a list of Animals.

In this example, the keyword class is used, followed by the identifier T. The keyword class indicates that this parameter is a type. The identifier T is used throughout the rest of the template definition to refer to the parameterized type. One instance of this class will substitute int everywhere T appears, and another will substitute Cat.

To declare an int and a Cat instance of the parameterized list class, you would write

```
List<int> anIntList;
List<Cat> aCatList;
```

The object anIntList is of the type list of integers; the object aCatList is of the type ListOfCats. You can now use the type List<int> anywhere you would normally use a type—as the return value from a function, as a parameter to a function, and so forth.

Listing 23.1 parameterizes the List object. This is an excellent technique for building templates: Get your object working on a single type, as we did in Hour 19, "Linked Lists." Then by parameterizing, generalize your object to handle any type.

LISTING 23.1   Demonstrating Parameterized Lists

```
 0:  // ************************************************
 1:  //    FILE:         Listing 23.1
 2:  //
 3:  //    PURPOSE:     Demonstrate parameterized list
 4:  //    NOTES:
 5:  //
 6:  //  COPYRIGHT:   Copyright  1997 Liberty Associates, Inc.
 7:  //                   All Rights Reserved
 8:  //
 9:  // Demonstrates an object-oriented approach to parameterized
10:  // linked lists. The list delegates to the node.
11:  // The node is an abstract Object type. Three types of
12:  // nodes are used, head nodes, tail nodes and internal
13:  // nodes. Only the internal nodes hold Object.
14:  //
15:  // The Object class is created to serve as an object to
16:  // hold in the linked list.
17:  //
18:  // ************************************************
19:  #include <iostream>
20:
21:  enum { kIsSmaller, kIsLarger, kIsSame};
22:
23:  // Object class to put into the linked list
24:  // Any class in this linked list must support two methods:
```

LISTING 23.1   continued

```
25:    // Show (displays the value) and
26:    // Compare (returns relative position)
27:    class Data
28:    {
29:    public:
30:        Data(int val):myValue(val){}
31:        ~Data()
32:        {
33:            std::cout << "Deleting Data object with value: ";
34:            std::cout << myValue << "\n";
35:        }
36:        int Compare(const Data &);
37:        void Show() { std::cout << myValue << std::endl; }
38:    private:
39:        int myValue;
40:    };
41:
42:    // compare is used to decide where in the list
43:    // a particular object belongs.
44:    int Data::Compare(const Data & theOtherObject)
45:    {
46:        if (myValue < theOtherObject.myValue)
47:            return kIsSmaller;
48:        if (myValue > theOtherObject.myValue)
49:            return kIsLarger;
50:        else
51:            return kIsSame;
52:    }
53:
54:    // Another class to put into the linked list
55:    // Again, every class in this linked
56:    // list must support two methods:
57:    // Show (displays the value) and
58:    // Compare (returns relative position)
59:    class Cat
60:    {
61:    public:
62:        Cat(int age): myAge(age){}
63:        ~Cat()
64:        {
65:            std::cout << "Deleting ";
66:            std::cout << myAge << " years old Cat.\n";
67:        }
68:        int Compare(const Cat &);
69:        void Show()
70:        {
71:            std::cout << "This cat is ";
72:            std::cout << myAge << " years old\n";
73:        }
```

LISTING 23.1 continued

```
74:   private:
75:       int myAge;
76:   };
77:
78:
79:   // compare is used to decide where in the list
80:   // a particular object belongs.
81:   int Cat::Compare(const Cat & theOtherCat)
82:   {
83:       if (myAge < theOtherCat.myAge)
84:           return kIsSmaller;
85:       if (myAge > theOtherCat.myAge)
86:           return kIsLarger;
87:       else
88:           return kIsSame;
89:   }
90:
91:
92:   // ADT representing the node object in the list
93:   // Every derived class must override Insert and Show
94:   template <class T>
95:   class Node
96:   {
97:   public:
98:       Node(){}
99:       virtual ~Node(){}
100:       virtual Node * Insert(T * theObject)=0;
101:       virtual void Show() = 0;
102:   private:
103:   };
104:
105:   template <class T>
106:   class InternalNode: public Node<T>
107:   {
108:   public:
109:       InternalNode(T * theObject, Node<T> * next);
110:       ~InternalNode(){ delete myNext; delete myObject; }
111:       virtual Node<T> * Insert(T * theObject);
112:       virtual void Show()
113:       {
114:           myObject->Show();
115:           myNext->Show();
116:       } // delegate!
117:   private:
118:       T * myObject;  // the Object itself
119:       Node<T> * myNext;    // points to next node in the linked list
120:   };
121:
```

LISTING 23.1 continued

```
122:  // All the constructor does is initialize
123:  template <class T>
124:  InternalNode<T>::InternalNode(T * theObject, Node<T> * next):
125:  myObject(theObject),myNext(next)
126:  {
127:  }
128:
129:  // the meat of the list
130:  // When you put a new object into the list
131:  // it is passed to the node which figures out
132:  // where it goes and inserts it into the list
133:  template <class T>
134:  Node<T> * InternalNode<T>::Insert(T * theObject)
135:  {
136:      // is the new guy bigger or smaller than me?
137:      int result = myObject->Compare(*theObject);
138:
139:      switch(result)
140:      {
141:      // by convention if it is the same as me it comes first
142:      case kIsSame:        // fall through
143:      case kIsLarger:     // new Object comes before me
144:          {
145:              InternalNode<T> * ObjectNode =
146:              new InternalNode<T>(theObject, this);
147:              return ObjectNode;
148:          }
149:      // it is bigger than I am so pass it on to the next
150:      // node and let HIM handle it.
151:      case kIsSmaller:
152:          myNext = myNext->Insert(theObject);
153:          return this;
154:      }
155:      return this;   // appease MSC
156:  }
157:
158:  // Tail node is just a sentinel
159:  template <class T>
160:  class TailNode : public Node<T>
161:  {
162:  public:
163:      TailNode(){}
164:      virtual ~TailNode(){}
165:      virtual Node<T> * Insert(T * theObject);
166:      virtual void Show() { }
167:  private:
168:  };
169:
170:  // If Object comes to me, it must be inserted before me
```

LISTING 23.1   continued

```
171:   // as I am the tail and NOTHING comes after me
172:   template <class T>
173:   Node<T> * TailNode<T>::Insert(T * theObject)
174:   {
175:       InternalNode<T> * ObjectNode =
176:       new InternalNode<T>(theObject, this);
177:       return ObjectNode;
178:   }
179:
180:   // Head node has no Object, it just points
181:   // to the very beginning of the list
182:   template <class T>
183:   class HeadNode : public Node<T>
184:   {
185:   public:
186:       HeadNode();
187:       virtual ~HeadNode() { delete myNext; }
188:       virtual Node<T> * Insert(T * theObject);
189:       virtual void Show() { myNext->Show(); }
190:   private:
191:       Node<T> * myNext;
192:   };
193:
194:   // As soon as the head is created
195:   // it creates the tail
196:   template <class T>
197:   HeadNode<T>::HeadNode()
198:   {
199:       myNext = new TailNode<T>;
200:   }
201:
202:   // Nothing comes before the head so just
203:   // pass the Object on to the next node
204:   template <class T>
205:   Node<T> * HeadNode<T>::Insert(T * theObject)
206:   {
207:       myNext = myNext->Insert(theObject);
208:       return this;
209:   }
210:
211:   // I get all the credit and do none of the work
212:   template <class T>
213:   class LinkedList
214:   {
215:   public:
216:       LinkedList();
217:       ~LinkedList() { delete myHead; }
218:       void Insert(T * theObject);
219:       void ShowAll() { myHead->Show(); }
```

23

LISTING 23.1   continued

```
220:  private:
221:      HeadNode<T> * myHead;
222:  };
223:
224:  // At birth, i create the head node
225:  // It creates the tail node
226:  // So an empty list points to the head which
227:  // points to the tail and has nothing between
228:  template <class T>
229:  LinkedList<T>::LinkedList()
230:  {
231:      myHead = new HeadNode<T>;
232:  }
233:
234:  // Delegate, delegate, delegate
235:  template <class T>
236:  void LinkedList<T>::Insert(T * pObject)
237:  {
238:      myHead->Insert(pObject);
239:  }
240:
241:  // test driver program
242:  int main()
243:  {
244:      Cat * pCat;
245:      Data * pData;
246:      int val;
247:      LinkedList<Cat>  ListOfCats;
248:      LinkedList<Data> ListOfData;
249:
250:      // ask the user to produce some values
251:      // put them in the list
252:      for (;;)
253:      {
254:          std::cout << "What value? (0 to stop): ";
255:          std::cin >> val;
256:          if (!val)
257:              break;
258:          pCat = new Cat(val);
259:          pData= new Data(val);
260:          ListOfCats.Insert(pCat);
261:          ListOfData.Insert(pData);
262:      }
263:
264:      // now walk the list and show the Object
265:      std::cout << "\n";
266:      ListOfCats.ShowAll();
267:      std::cout << "\n";
268:      ListOfData.ShowAll();
```

LISTING 23.1 continued

```
269:        std::cout << "\n *********** \n\n";
270:        return 0;  // The lists fall out of scope and are destroyed!
271:    }
```

OUTPUT

```
What value? (0 to stop): 5
What value? (0 to stop): 13
What value? (0 to stop): 2
What value? (0 to stop): 9
What value? (0 to stop): 7
What value? (0 to stop): 0

This cat is 2 years old
This cat is 5 years old
This cat is 7 years old
This cat is 9 years old
This cat is 13 years old

2
5
7
9
13

***********

Deleting Data object with value: 13
Deleting Data object with value: 9
Deleting Data object with value: 7
Deleting Data object with value: 5
Deleting Data object with value: 2
Deleting 13 years old Cat.
Deleting 9 years old Cat.
Deleting 7 years old Cat.
Deleting 5 years old Cat.
Deleting 2 years old Cat.
```

ANALYSIS The first thing to notice is the striking similarity to the listing in Hour 19. Go ahead, find the original listing; I'll wait right here…. As you can see, little has changed.

The biggest change is that each of the class declarations and methods is now preceded by

```
template class <T>
```

This tells the compiler that you are parameterizing this list on a type that you will define later, when you instantiate the list. For example, the declaration of the Node class now becomes

```
template <class T>
class Node
```

This indicates that Node will not exist as a class in itself, but rather that you will instantiate Nodes of Cats and Nodes of Data objects. The actual type you'll pass in is represented by T.

Thus, InternalNode now becomes InternalNode<T> (read that as "InternalNode of T"). And InternalNode<T> points not to a Data object and another Node; rather, it points to a T (whatever type of object) and a Node<T>. You can see this on lines 118 and 119.

Look carefully at Insert, defined on lines 133–156. The logic is just the same, but where we used to have a specific type (Data) we now have T. Thus, on line 134 the parameter is a pointer to a T. Later, when we instantiate the specific lists, the T will be replaced by the compiler with the right type (Data or Cat).

The important thing is that the InternalNode can continue working, indifferent to the actual type. It knows to ask the objects to compare themselves. It doesn't care whether Cats compare themselves in the same way Data objects do. In fact, we can rewrite this so that Cats don't keep their age; we can have them keep their birth date and compute their relative age on the fly, and the InternalNode won't care a bit.

Using Template Items

You can treat template items as you would any other type. You can pass them as parameters, either by reference or by value, and you can return them as the return values of functions, also by value or by reference. Listing 23.2 demonstrates how to pass Template objects.

LISTING 23.2   Demonstrating Parameterized Lists

```
0:  // ************************************************
1:  //    FILE:         Listing 23.2
2:  //
3:  //    PURPOSE:      Demonstrate parameterized list
4:  //    NOTES:
5:  //
6:  //  COPYRIGHT:   Copyright (C) 1997 Liberty Associates, Inc.
7:  //                  All Rights Reserved
8:  //
9:  // Demonstrates an object-oriented approach to parameterized
10: // linked lists. The list delegates to the node.
11: // The node is an abstract Object type. Three types of
12: // nodes are used, head nodes, tail nodes and internal
13: // nodes. Only the internal nodes hold Object.
14: //
15: // The Object class is created to serve as an object to
```

LISTING 23.2   continued

```
16:  // hold in the linked list.
17:  //
18:  // ************************************************
19:
20:  #include <iostream>
21:
22:  enum { kIsSmaller, kIsLarger, kIsSame};
23:
24:  // Object class to put into the linked list
25:  // Any class in this linked list must support two methods:
26:  // Show (displays the value) and
27:  // Compare (returns relative position)
28:  class Data
29:  {
30:  public:
31:      Data(int val):myValue(val){}
32:      ~Data()
33:      {
34:          std::cout << "Deleting Data object with value: ";
35:          std::cout << myValue << "\n";
36:      }
37:      int Compare(const Data &);
38:      void Show() { std::cout << myValue << std::endl; }
39:  private:
40:      int myValue;
41:  };
42:
43:  // compare is used to decide where in the list
44:  // a particular object belongs.
45:  int Data::Compare(const Data & theOtherObject)
46:  {
47:      if (myValue < theOtherObject.myValue)
48:          return kIsSmaller;
49:      if (myValue > theOtherObject.myValue)
50:          return kIsLarger;
51:      else
52:          return kIsSame;
53:  }
54:
55:  // Another class to put into the linked list
56:  // Again, every class in this linked
57:  // list must support two methods:
58:  // Show (displays the value) and
59:  // Compare (returns relative position)
60:  class Cat
61:  {
62:  public:
63:      Cat(int age): myAge(age){}
64:      ~Cat()
```

LISTING 23.2   continued

```
65:        {
66:            std::cout << "Deleting " << myAge
67:                << " years old Cat.\n";
68:        }
69:        int Compare(const Cat &);
70:        void Show()
71:        {
72:            std::cout << "This cat is " << myAge
73:                << " years old\n";
74:        }
75: private:
76:        int myAge;
77: };
78:
79:
80: // compare is used to decide where in the list
81: // a particular object belongs.
82: int Cat::Compare(const Cat & theOtherCat)
83: {
84:        if (myAge < theOtherCat.myAge)
85:            return kIsSmaller;
86:        if (myAge > theOtherCat.myAge)
87:            return kIsLarger;
88:        else
89:            return kIsSame;
90: }
91:
92:
93: // ADT representing the node object in the list
94: // Every derived class must override Insert and Show
95: template <class T>
96: class Node
97: {
98: public:
99:        Node(){}
100:        virtual ~Node(){}
101:        virtual Node * Insert(T * theObject)=0;
102:        virtual void Show() = 0;
103: private:
104: };
105:
106: template <class T>
107: class InternalNode: public Node<T>
108: {
109: public:
110:        InternalNode(T * theObject, Node<T> * next);
111:        virtual ~InternalNode(){ delete myNext; delete myObject; }
112:        virtual Node<T> * Insert(T * theObject);
113:        virtual void Show() // delegate!
```

LISTING 23.2 continued

```
114:        {
115:            myObject->Show(); myNext->Show();
116:        }
117:   private:
118:        T * myObject;   // the Object itself
119:        Node<T> * myNext;    // points to next node in the linked list
120:   };
121:
122:   // All the constructor does is initialize
123:   template <class T>
124:   InternalNode<T>::InternalNode(T * theObject, Node<T> * next):
125:   myObject(theObject),myNext(next)
126:   {
127:   }
128:
129:   // the meat of the list
130:   // When you put a new object into the list
131:   // it is passed to the node which figures out
132:   // where it goes and inserts it into the list
133:   template <class T>
134:   Node<T> * InternalNode<T>::Insert(T * theObject)
135:   {
136:        // is the new guy bigger or smaller than me?
137:        int result = myObject->Compare(*theObject);
138:
139:        switch(result)
140:        {
141:        // by convention if it is the same as me it comes first
142:        case kIsSame:        // fall through
143:        case kIsLarger:     // new Object comes before me
144:            {
145:                InternalNode<T> * ObjectNode =
146:                new InternalNode<T>(theObject, this);
147:                return ObjectNode;
148:            }
149:        // it is bigger than I am so pass it on to the next
150:        // node and let HIM handle it.
151:        case kIsSmaller:
152:            myNext = myNext->Insert(theObject);
153:            return this;
154:        }
155:        return this;  // appease MSC
156:   }
157:
158:
159:   // Tail node is just a sentinel
160:   template <class T>
161:   class TailNode : public Node<T>
162:   {
```

LISTING 23.2 continued

```
163:    public:
164:        TailNode(){}
165:        virtual ~TailNode(){}
166:        virtual Node<T> * Insert(T * theObject);
167:        virtual void Show() { }
168:    private:
169:    };
170:
171:    // If Object comes to me, it must be inserted before me
172:    // as I am the tail and NOTHING comes after me
173:    template <class T>
174:    Node<T> * TailNode<T>::Insert(T * theObject)
175:    {
176:        InternalNode<T> * ObjectNode =
177:            new InternalNode<T>(theObject, this);
178:        return ObjectNode;
179:    }
180:
181:    // Head node has no Object, it just points
182:    // to the very beginning of the list
183:    template <class T>
184:    class HeadNode : public Node<T>
185:    {
186:    public:
187:        HeadNode();
188:        virtual ~HeadNode() { delete myNext; }
189:        virtual Node<T> * Insert(T * theObject);
190:        virtual void Show() { myNext->Show(); }
191:    private:
192:        Node<T> * myNext;
193:    };
194:
195:    // As soon as the head is created
196:    // it creates the tail
197:    template <class T>
198:    HeadNode<T>::HeadNode()
199:    {
200:        myNext = new TailNode<T>;
201:    }
202:
203:    // Nothing comes before the head so just
204:    // pass the Object on to the next node
205:    template <class T>
206:    Node<T> * HeadNode<T>::Insert(T * theObject)
207:    {
208:        myNext = myNext->Insert(theObject);
209:        return this;
210:    }
211:
```

LISTING 23.2 continued

```
212:   // I get all the credit and do none of the work
213:   template <class T>
214:   class LinkedList
215:   {
216:   public:
217:       LinkedList();
218:       ~LinkedList() { delete myHead; }
219:       void Insert(T * theObject);
220:       void ShowAll() { myHead->Show(); }
221:   private:
222:       HeadNode<T> * myHead;
223:   };
224:
225:   // At birth, i create the head node
226:   // It creates the tail node
227:   // So an empty list points to the head which
228:   // points to the tail and has nothing between
229:   template <class T>
230:   LinkedList<T>::LinkedList()
231:   {
232:       myHead = new HeadNode<T>;
233:   }
234:
235:   // Delegate, delegate, delegate
236:   template <class T>
237:   void LinkedList<T>::Insert(T * pObject)
238:   {
239:       myHead->Insert(pObject);
240:   }
241:
242:   void myFunction(LinkedList<Cat>& ListOfCats);
243:   void myOtherFunction(LinkedList<Data>& ListOfData);
244:
245:   // test driver program
246:   int main()
247:   {
248:       LinkedList<Cat>  ListOfCats;
249:       LinkedList<Data> ListOfData;
250:
251:       myFunction(ListOfCats);
252:       myOtherFunction(ListOfData);
253:
254:       // now walk the list and show the Object
255:       std::cout << "\n";
256:       ListOfCats.ShowAll();
257:       std::cout << "\n";
258:       ListOfData.ShowAll();
259:       std::cout << "\n *********** \n\n";
260:       return 0;  // The lists fall out of scope and are destroyed!
```

23

LISTING 23.2   continued

```
261:   }
262:
263:   void myFunction(LinkedList<Cat>& ListOfCats)
264:   {
265:       Cat * pCat;
266:       int val;
267:
268:       // ask the user to produce some values
269:       // put them in the list
270:       for (;;)
271:       {
272:           std::cout << "\nHow old is your cat? (0 to stop): ";
273:           std::cin >> val;
274:           if (!val)
275:               break;
276:           pCat = new Cat(val);
277:           ListOfCats.Insert(pCat);
278:       }
279:   }
280:   }
281:
282:   void myOtherFunction(LinkedList<Data>& ListOfData)
283:   {
284:       Data * pData;
285:       int val;
286:
287:       // ask the user to produce some values
288:       // put them in the list
289:       for (;;)
290:       {
291:           std::cout << "\nWhat value? (0 to stop): ";
292:           std::cin >> val;
293:           if (!val)
294:               break;
295:           pData = new Data(val);
296:           ListOfData.Insert(pData);
297:       }
298:
299:   }
```

OUTPUT

```
How old is your cat? (0 to stop): 12

How old is your cat? (0 to stop): 2

How old is your cat? (0 to stop): 14

How old is your cat? (0 to stop): 6
```

```
How old is your cat? (0 to stop): 0

What value? (0 to stop): 3

What value? (0 to stop): 9

What value? (0 to stop): 1

What value? (0 to stop): 5

What value? (0 to stop): 0

This cat is 2 years old
This cat is 6 years old
This cat is 12 years old
This cat is 14 years old

1
3
5
9

   * * * * * * * * * * * *

Deleting Data object with value: 9
Deleting Data object with value: 5
Deleting Data object with value: 3
Deleting Data object with value: 1
Deleting 14 years old Cat.
Deleting 12 years old Cat.
Deleting 6 years old Cat.
Deleting 2 years old Cat.
```

ANALYSIS This code is much like the previous example, but this time we pass the LinkedLists by reference to their respective functions for processing. This is a powerful feature. After the lists are instantiated, they can be treated as fully defined types, passed into functions, and returned as values.

The Standard Template Library

C++ defines a *Standard Template Library* (STL). All the major compiler vendors now offer the STL as part of their compiler. The STL is a library of template-based container classes, including vectors, lists, queues, and stacks. The STL also includes a number of common algorithms, including sorting and searching.

The goal of the STL is to give you an alternative to reinventing the wheel for these common requirements. The STL is tested and debugged, offers high performance, and it's free! Most important, the STL is reusable; when you understand how to use an STL container, you can use it in all your programs without reinventing it.

Summary

In this hour you learned how to create and use templates. Templates are a built-in facility of C++ used to create parameterized types—types that change their behavior based on parameters passed in at creation. They are a way to reuse code safely and effectively.

The definition of the template determines the parameterized type. Each instance of the template is an actual object that can be used like any other object—as a parameter to a function, as a return value, and so forth.

Q&A

Q Why use templates when macros will do?

A Templates are type-safe and built into the language.

Q What is the difference between the parameterized type of a template function and the parameters to a normal function?

A A regular function (non-template) takes parameters on which it may take action. A template function allows you to parameterize the type of a particular parameter to the function.

Q When do you use templates and when do you use inheritance?

A Use templates when all the behavior or virtually all the behavior is unchanged, but the type of the item on which your class acts is different. If you find yourself copying a class and changing only the type of one or more of its members, it might be time to consider using a template.

HOUR 24

Exceptions and Error Handling

The code you've seen in this book was created for illustration purposes. It has not dealt with errors, so that you will not be distracted from the central issues being presented. Real-world programs, on the other hand, must take error conditions into consideration. In fact, in real-world programs, anticipating and handling errors can be the largest part of the code!

In this final hour, you will learn

- What exceptions are
- How exceptions are used and what issues they raise
- How to create bug-free code
- Where to go from here

Bugs, Errors, Mistakes, and Code Rot

It has been said that if cities were built like software is built, the first woodpecker to come along would level civilization. The fact is that all too many commercial programs, from some of the biggest vendors in the business, have bugs. Serious bugs.

Although this is true, that does not make it okay; and writing robust, bug-free programs should be the number-one priority of anyone serious about programming. I would argue that the single biggest problem in the software industry is buggy, unstable code. Certainly the biggest expense in many major programming efforts is testing, finding, and fixing bugs.

There are a number of discrete kinds of bugs that can trouble a program. The first is poor logic: The program does just what you asked, but you haven't thought through the algorithms properly. The second is syntactic: You used the wrong idiom, function, or structure. These two are the most common, and they are the ones most programmers are on the lookout for. Far harder to find are subtle bugs that pop up only when the user does something unexpected. These little logic bombs can lurk quietly and undisturbed, like a land mine after the war is over. You think everything is okay and then suddenly— BAM!—someone steps in the wrong place and your program blows up.

Research and real-world experience have shown beyond a doubt that the later in the development process you find a problem, the more it costs to fix it. The least expensive problems or bugs to fix are the ones you manage to avoid creating. The next cheapest are those the compiler spots. The C++ standards force compilers to put a lot of energy into making more and more bugs show up at compile time.

Bugs that get compiled but are caught at the first test—those that crash every time—are less expensive to find and fix than those that are flaky and only crash once in a while.

A bigger problem than logic or syntactic bugs is unnecessary fragility: Your program works just fine if the user enters a number when you ask for one, but it crashes if the user enters letters. Other programs crash if they run out of memory, or if the floppy disk is left out of the drive, or if the modem drops the line.

To combat this kind of fragility, programmers strive to make their programs bulletproof. A *bulletproof* program is one that can handle anything that comes up at runtime, from bizarre user input to running out of memory.

It is important to distinguish among bugs. There are those that arise because the programmer made a mistake in syntax. There are also logic errors that arise because the programmer misunderstood the problem or how to solve it. Finally there are exceptions that arise because of unusual but predictable problems such as running out of resources (memory or disk space).

Handling the Unexpected

Programmers use powerful compilers and sprinkle their code with asserts to catch programming errors. They use design reviews and exhaustive testing to find logic errors.

Exceptions are different, however. You can't eliminate exceptional circumstances; you can only prepare for them. Your users will run out of memory from time to time, and the only question is what you will do. Your choices are these:

- Crash the program.
- Inform the user and exit gracefully.
- Inform the user and allow the user to try to recover and continue.
- Take corrective action and continue without disturbing the user.

Although it is not necessary or even desirable for every program you write to automatically and silently recover from all exceptional circumstances, it is clear that you must do better than crashing.

C++ exception handling provides a type-safe, integrated method for coping with the predictable but unusual conditions that arise while running a program.

Exceptions

New Term   In C++, an *exception* is an object that is passed from the area of code where a problem occurs to the part of the code that is going to handle the problem. When an exception occurs it is said to be "*raised*" or "*thrown*". When an exception is handled, it is said to be "*caught*".

The type of the exception determines which area of code will handle the problem; and the contents of the object thrown, if any, may be used to provide feedback to the user.

The basic idea behind exceptions is fairly straightforward:

- The actual allocation of resources (for example, the allocation of memory or the locking of a file) is usually done at a very low level in the program.
- The logic of what to do when an operation fails, memory cannot be allocated, or a file cannot be locked is usually high in the program, with the code for interacting with the user.
- Exceptions provide an express path from the code that allocates resources to the code that can handle the error condition. If there are intervening layers of functions, they are given an opportunity to clean up memory allocations, but are not required to include code whose only purpose is to pass along the error condition.

How Exceptions Are Used

try blocks are created to surround areas of code that might have a problem. A try block is a block, surrounded by braces, in which an exception might be thrown. For example:

```
try
{
    SomeDangerousFunction();
}
```

A catch block is the block immediately following a try block, in which exceptions are handled. For example:

```
try
{
    SomeDangerousFunction();
}
catch(OutOfMemory)
{
    // take some actions
}
catch(FileNotFound)
{
    // take other action
}
```

The basic steps in using exceptions are:

1. Identify those areas of the program in which you begin an operation that might raise an exception, and put them in try blocks.

2. Create catch blocks to catch the exceptions if they are thrown, to clean up allocated memory, and to inform the user as appropriate. Listing 24.1 illustrates the use of both try blocks and catch blocks.

When an exception is thrown (or raised), control transfers to the catch block immediately following the current try block.

LISTING 24.1   Raising an Exception

```
0:  // Listing 24.1 throwing exceptions
1:  #include <iostream>
2:
3:  const int DefaultSize = 10;
4:
5:  // define the exception class
6:  class xBoundary
7:  {
8:  public:
```

LISTING 24.1 continued

```
 9:         xBoundary() {}
10:         ~xBoundary() {}
11:    private:
12:    };
13:
14:    class Array
15:    {
16:    public:
17:         // constructors
18:         Array(int itsSize = DefaultSize);
19:         Array(const Array &rhs);
20:         ~Array() { delete [] pType;}
21:
22:         // operators
23:         Array& operator=(const Array&);
24:         int& operator[](int offSet);
25:         const int& operator[](int offSet) const;
26:
27:         // accessors
28:         int GetitsSize() const { return itsSize; }
29:
30:         // friend function
31:         friend std::ostream& operator<< (std::ostream&, const Array&);
32:
33:    private:
34:         int *pType;
35:         int  itsSize;
36:    };
37:
38:
39:    Array::Array(int size):
40:    itsSize(size)
41:    {
42:         pType = new int[size];
43:         for (int i = 0; i<size; i++)
44:             pType[i] = 0;
45:    }
46:
47:
48:    Array& Array::operator=(const Array &rhs)
49:    {
50:         if (this == &rhs)
51:             return *this;
52:         delete [] pType;
53:         itsSize = rhs.GetitsSize();
54:         pType = new int[itsSize];
55:         for (int i = 0; i<itsSize; i++)
56:             pType[i] = rhs[i];
57:         return *this;
```

LISTING 24.1   continued

```
58:    }
59:
60:    Array::Array(const Array &rhs)
61:    {
62:        itsSize = rhs.GetitsSize();
63:        pType = new int[itsSize];
64:        for (int i = 0; i<itsSize; i++)
65:            pType[i] = rhs[i];
66:    }
67:
68:
69:    int& Array::operator[](int offSet)
70:    {
71:        int size = GetitsSize();
72:        if (offSet >= 0 && offSet < GetitsSize())
73:            return pType[offSet];
74:        throw xBoundary();
75:        return pType[offSet]; // to appease MSC!
76:    }
77:
78:
79:    const int& Array::operator[](int offSet) const
80:    {
81:        int mysize = GetitsSize();
82:        if (offSet >= 0 && offSet < GetitsSize())
83:            return pType[offSet];
84:        throw xBoundary();
85:        return pType[offSet]; // to appease MSC!
86:    }
87:
88:    std::ostream& operator<< (std::ostream& output,
89:                            const Array& theArray)
90:    {
91:        for (int i = 0; i<theArray.GetitsSize(); i++)
92:            output << "[" << i << "] " << theArray[i] << std::endl;
93:        return output;
94:    }
95:
96:    int main()
97:    {
98:        Array intArray(20);
99:        try
100:        {
101:            for (int j = 0; j< 100; j++)
102:            {
103:                intArray[j] = j;
104:                std::cout << "intArray[" << j
105:                    << "] okay..." << std::endl;
106:            }
```

LISTING 24.1 continued

```
107:        }
108:        catch (xBoundary)
109:        {
110:            std::cout << "Unable to process your input!\n";
111:        }
112:        std::cout << "Done.\n";
113:        return 0;
114: }
```

OUTPUT
```
intArray[0] okay...
intArray[1] okay...
intArray[2] okay...
intArray[3] okay...
intArray[4] okay...
intArray[5] okay...
intArray[6] okay...
intArray[7] okay...
intArray[8] okay...
intArray[9] okay...
intArray[10] okay...
intArray[11] okay...
intArray[12] okay...
intArray[13] okay...
intArray[14] okay...
intArray[15] okay...
intArray[16] okay...
intArray[17] okay...
intArray[18] okay...
intArray[19] okay...
Unable to process your input!
Done.
```

ANALYSIS Listing 24.1 presents a somewhat stripped-down Array class, created just to illustrate this simple use of exceptions. On lines 6–12, a very simple exception class is declared, xBoundary. The most important thing to notice about this class is that there is absolutely nothing that makes it an exception class. In fact, any class, with any name and any number of methods and variables, will do just fine as an exception. What makes this an exception is only that it is *thrown*, as shown on line 74, and that it is caught, as shown on line 108!

The offset operators throw xBoundary when the client of the class attempts to access data outside the array (lines 74 and 84). This is far superior to the way normal arrays handle such a request; they just return whatever garbage happens to be in memory at that location, a sure-fire way to crash your program.

On line 99, the keyword try begins a try block that ends on line 107. Within that try block, 100 integers are added to the array that was declared on line 98.

On line 108, the catch block to catch xBoundary exceptions is declared.

---

try Blocks

A try block is a set of statements that begin with the word try followed by an opening brace, and end with a closing brace.

For example:

```
try
{
    Function();
}
```

---

catch Blocks

A catch block is a series of statements, each of which begins with the word catch, followed by an exception type in parentheses, followed by an opening brace, and ending with a closing brace.

For example:

```
Try
{
    Function();
}
Catch (OutOfMemory)
{
    // take action
}
```

Using try Blocks and catch Blocks

Figuring out where to put your try blocks is probably the hardest part of using exceptions; it is not always obvious which actions might raise an exception. The next question is where to catch the exception. It might be that you'll want to throw all memory exceptions where the memory is allocated, but you'll want to catch the exceptions high in the program where you deal with the user interface.

When trying to determine try block locations, look to where you allocate memory or use resources. Other things to look for are out-of-bounds errors, illegal input, and so forth.

Catching Exceptions

Here's how catching exceptions works: When an exception is thrown, the call stack is examined. The *call stack* is the list of function calls created when one part of the program invokes another function.

The call stack tracks the execution path. If `main()` calls the function `Animal::GetFavoriteFood()`, and `GetFavoriteFood()` calls `Animal::LookupPreferences()`, which in turn calls `fstream::operator>>()`, all these are on the call stack. A recursive function might be on the call stack many times.

The exception is passed up the call stack to each enclosing block. As the stack is unwound, the destructors for local objects on the stack are invoked, and the objects are destroyed.

After each `try` block are one or more `catch` statements. If the exception matches one of the `catch` statements, it is considered to be handled by having that statement execute. If it doesn't match any, the unwinding of the stack continues.

If the exception reaches all the way to the beginning of the program (`main()`) and is still not caught, the function `terminate()` is called, which in turn calls `abort()` to abort the program.

It is important to note that the exception unwinding of the stack is a one-way street. As it progresses, the stack is unwound, and objects on the stack are destroyed. There is no going back: After the exception is handled, the program continues after the `try` block of the `catch` statement that handled the exception.

Thus, in Listing 24.1, execution will continue on line 111, the first line after the `try` block of the `catch` statement that handled the `xBoundary` exception. Remember that when an exception is raised, program flow continues after the `catch` block, not after the point where the exception was thrown.

More Than One `catch` Specification

It is possible for more than one condition to cause an exception. In this case, the `catch` statements can be lined up one after another, much like the conditions in a `switch` statement. The equivalent to the `default` statement is the "catch everything" statement, indicated by `catch(...)`.

Catching by Reference and Polymorphism

You can take advantage of the fact that exceptions are just classes to use them polymorphically. By passing the exception by reference, you can use the inheritance hierarchy to take the appropriate action based on the runtime type of the exception. Listing 24.2 illustrates using exceptions polymorphically. The output reflects running the program three times, first passing in an array size of 5, then 50,000, and finally 12.

LISTING 24.2   Polymorphic Exceptions

```
0:  // Listing 24.2 catching exceptions polymorphically
1:  #include <iostream>
2:
3:  const int DefaultSize = 10;
4:
5:  // define the exception classes
6:  class xBoundary {};
7:
8:  class xSize
9:  {
10: public:
11:     xSize(int size):itsSize(size) {}
12:     ~xSize(){}
13:     virtual int GetSize() { return itsSize; }
14:     virtual void PrintError()
15:     { std::cout << "Size error. Received: "
16:         << itsSize << std::endl; }
17: protected:
18:     int itsSize;
19: };
20:
21: class xTooBig : public xSize
22: {
23: public:
24:     xTooBig(int size):xSize(size){}
25:     virtual void PrintError()
26:     {
27:         std::cout << "Too big! Received: ";
28:         std::cout << xSize::itsSize << std::endl;
29:     }
30: };
31:
32: class xTooSmall : public xSize
33: {
34: public:
35:     xTooSmall(int size):xSize(size){}
36:     virtual void PrintError()
37:     {
38:         std::cout << "Too small! Received: ";
39:         std::cout << xSize::itsSize << std::endl;
40:     }
41: };
42:
```

LISTING 24.2   continued

```
43:   class xZero  : public xTooSmall
44:   {
45:   public:
46:       xZero(int size):xTooSmall(size){}
47:       virtual void PrintError()
48:       {
49:           std::cout << "Zero!!. Received: ";
50:           std::cout << xSize::itsSize << std::endl;
51:       }
52:   };
53:
54:   class xNegative : public xSize
55:   {
56:   public:
57:       xNegative(int size):xSize(size){}
58:       virtual void PrintError()
59:       {
60:           std::cout << "Negative! Received: ";
61:           std::cout << xSize::itsSize << std::endl;
62:       }
63:   };
64:
65:   class Array
66:   {
67:   public:
68:       // constructors
69:       Array(int itsSize = DefaultSize);
70:       Array(const Array &rhs);
71:       ~Array() { delete [] pType;}
72:
73:       // operators
74:       Array& operator=(const Array&);
75:       int& operator[](int offSet);
76:       const int& operator[](int offSet) const;
77:
78:       // accessors
79:       int GetitsSize() const { return itsSize; }
80:
81:       // friend function
82:       friend std::ostream& operator<< (std::ostream&, const Array&);
83:
84:
85:   private:
86:       int *pType;
87:       int  itsSize;
88:   };
89:
90:   Array::Array(int size):
91:   itsSize(size)
```

LISTING 24.2   continued

```
 92:   {
 93:       if (size == 0)
 94:           throw xZero(size);
 95:
 96:       if (size < 0)
 97:           throw xNegative(size);
 98:
 99:       if (size < 10)
100:           throw xTooSmall(size);
101:
102:       if (size > 30000)
103:           throw xTooBig(size);
104:
105:       pType = new int[size];
106:       for (int i = 0; i<size; i++)
107:           pType[i] = 0;
108:   }
109:
110:   int& Array::operator[] (int offset)
111:   {
112:       int size = GetitsSize();
113:       if (offset >= 0 && offset < GetitsSize())
114:           return pType[offset];
115:       throw xBoundary();
116:       return pType[offset];
117:   }
118:
119:   const int& Array::operator[] (int offset) const
120:   {
121:       int size = GetitsSize();
122:       if (offset >= 0 && offset < GetitsSize())
123:           return pType[offset];
124:       throw xBoundary();
125:       return pType[offset];
126:   }
127:
128:   int main()
129:   {
130:       try
131:       {
132:           int choice;
133:           std::cout << "Enter the array size: ";
134:           std::cin >> choice;
135:           Array intArray(choice);
136:           for (int j = 0; j< 100; j++)
137:           {
138:               intArray[j] = j;
139:               std::cout << "intArray[" << j << "] okay..."
140:                   << std::endl;
```

LISTING 24.2 continued

```
141:            }
142:        }
143:        catch (xBoundary)
144:        {
145:            std::cout << "Unable to process your input!\n";
146:        }
147:        catch (xSize& theException)
148:        {
149:            theException.PrintError();
150:        }
151:        catch (...)
152:        {
153:            std::cout << "Something went wrong,"
154:                << "but I've no idea what!" << std::endl;
155:        }
156:        std::cout << "Done.\n";
157:        return 0;
158:    }
```

OUTPUT

```
Enter the array size: 5
Too small! Received: 5
Done.

Enter the array size: 50000
Too big! Received: 50000
Done.

Enter the array size: 12
intArray[0] okay...
intArray[1] okay...
intArray[2] okay...
intArray[3] okay...
intArray[4] okay...
intArray[5] okay...
intArray[6] okay...
intArray[7] okay...
intArray[8] okay...
intArray[9] okay...
intArray[10] okay...
intArray[11] okay...
Unable to process your input!
Done.
```

ANALYSIS Listing 24.2 declares a virtual method in the xSize class, PrintError(), that prints an error message and the actual size of the class. This is overridden in each of the derived classes.

On line 147, the exception object is declared to be a reference. When `PrintError()` is called with a reference to an object, polymorphism causes the correct version of `PrintError()` to be invoked. The first time through we ask for an array of size 5. This causes the `TooSmall` exception to be thrown; that is the `xSize` exception caught on line 147. The second time through we ask for an array of 50,000 and that causes the `TooBig` exception to be thrown. This is also caught on line 147, but polymorphism causes the right error string to print. When we finally ask for an array of size 12, the array is populated until the `xBoundary` exception is thrown and caught on line 143.

Next Steps

With templates and exceptions under your belt, you are well equipped with some of the more advanced aspects of C++. Before you put the book down, however, let's take a moment to discuss some points about writing professional-quality code. When you go beyond hobbyist interest and work as part of a development team, you must write code that not only works, but that can be understood by others. Your code also must be maintained and supported both by you, as the customer's demands change, and also by others after you leave the project.

Style

Although it doesn't matter which style you adopt, it is important to adopt a consistent coding style. A consistent style makes it easier to guess what you meant by a particular part of the code, and you avoid having to look up whether or not you spelled the function with an initial cap the last time you invoked it.

The following guidelines are arbitrary; they are based on the guidelines used in projects I've worked on in the past, and they've worked well. You can just as easily make up your own, but these will get you started.

As Emerson said, "Foolish consistency is the hobgoblin of small minds," but having some consistency in your code is a good thing. Make up your own, but then treat it as if it were dispensed by the programming gods.

Braces

How to align braces can be the most controversial topic between C and C++ programmers. Here are the tips I suggest:

- Matching braces should be aligned vertically.
- The outermost set of braces in a definition or declaration should be at the left mar-

gin. Statements within should be indented. All other sets of braces should be in line with their leading statement.

- No code should appear on the same line as a brace. For example

```
if (condition==true)
{
    j = k;
    SomeFunction();
}
m++;
```

Long Lines

Keep lines to the width displayable on a single screen. Code that is off to the right is easily overlooked, and scrolling horizontally is annoying. When a line is broken, indent the following lines. Try to break the line at a reasonable place, and try to leave the intervening operator at the end of the previous line (as opposed to the beginning of the following line) so it is clear that the line does not stand alone and that there is more coming.

In C++, functions tend to be far shorter than they were in C, but the old, sound advice still applies. Try to keep your functions short enough to print the entire function on one page.

Tab size should be four spaces. Make sure your editor converts each tab to four spaces.

switch Statements

Indent switches as follows to conserve horizontal space:

```
switch(variable)
{
case ValueOne:
      ActionOne();
      break;
case ValueTwo:
      ActionTwo();
      break;
default:
      assert("bad Action");
      break;
}
```

Program Text

There are several tips you can use to create code that is easy to read. Code that is easy to read is easy to maintain:

- Use white space to help readability.

- Objects and arrays are really referring to one thing. Don't use spaces within object references (., ->, [ ]).

- Unary operators are associated with their operand, so don't put a space between them. Do put a space on the side away from the operand. Unary operators include !, ~, ++, —, -, * (for pointers), & (casts), and `sizeof`.

- Binary operators should have spaces on both sides: +, =, *, /, %, >>, <<, <, >, ==, !=, &, |, &&, ||, ?:, =, +=, and so on.

- Don't use lack of spaces to indicate precedence (4+ 3*2).

- Put a space after commas and semicolons, not before.

- Parentheses should not have spaces on either side.

- Keywords, such as `if`, should be set off by a space: `if (a == b)`.

- The body of a comment should be set off from the `//` with a space.

- Place the pointer or reference indicator next to the type name, not the variable name. Do this:
  ```
  char* foo;
  int& theInt;
  ```
  rather than this:
  ```
  char *foo;
  int &theInt;
  ```

- Do not declare more than one variable on the same line.

Identifier Names

Here are some guidelines for working with identifiers.

- Identifier names should be long enough to be descriptive.

- Avoid cryptic abbreviations.

- Take the time and energy to spell things out.

- Short names (i, p, x, and so on) should only be used where their brevity makes the code more readable and where the usage is so obvious that a descriptive name is not needed.

- The length of a variable's name should be proportional to its scope.

- Make sure identifiers look and sound different from one another to minimize confusion.

- Function (or method) names are usually verbs or verb-noun phrases: `Search()`, `Reset()`, `FindParagraph()`, `ShowCursor()`. Variable names are usually abstract nouns, possibly with an additional noun: `count`, `state`, `windSpeed`, `windowHeight`. Boolean variables should be named appropriately: `windowIconized`, `fileIsOpen`.

Spelling and Capitalization of Names

Spelling and capitalization should not be overlooked when creating your own style. Some tips for these areas include the following:

- Identifiers should use mixed case—no underscores. Function names, methods, class, `typedef`, and `struct` names should begin with a capitalized letter (often called Pascal Case, as in `MyFunction`). Elements like data members or locals should begin with a lowercase letter (often called Camel Case, as in `myVariable`).

- Enumerated constants should begin with a few lowercase letters as an abbreviation for the `enum`. For example:

```
enum TextStyle
{
    tsPlain,
    tsBold,
    tsItalic,
    tsUnderscore,
};
```

Comments

Comments can make it much easier to understand a program. Often, you will not work on a program for several days or even months, while you turn your attention to higher priority projects. In this time you can forget what certain code does or why it has been included. Problems in understanding code can also occur when someone else reads your code. Comments that are applied in a consistent, well-thought-out style can be well worth the effort. There are several tips to remember concerning comments:

- Wherever possible, use C++ `//` comments rather than the `/* */` style.

- Higher-level comments are infinitely more important than process details. Add value; do not merely restate the code. For example:

```
n++; // n is incremented by one
```

This comment isn't worth the time it takes to type it in. Concentrate on the semantics of functions and blocks of code. Say what a function does. Indicate side effects, types of parameters, and return values. Describe all assumptions that are made (or not made), such as "assumes n is non-negative" or "will return –1 if x is invalid." Within complex logic, use comments to indicate the conditions that exist at that point in the code.

- Use complete English sentences with appropriate punctuation and capitalization. The extra typing is worth it. Don't be overly cryptic, and don't abbreviate. What seems exceedingly clear to you as you write code can be amazingly obtuse in a few months.
- Use blank lines freely to help the reader understand what is going on. Separate statements into logical groups.

Access

The way you access portions of your program should also be consistent. Some tips for access include these:

- Always use `public:`, `private:`, and `protected:` labels; don't rely on the defaults.
- List the public members first, then protected, then private. List the data members in a group after the methods.
- Put the constructor(s) first in the appropriate section, followed by the destructor. List overloaded methods with the same name adjacent to each other. Group accessor functions together when possible.
- Consider alphabetizing the method names within each group and alphabetizing the member variables. Be sure to alphabetize the filenames in `include` statements.
- Even though the use of the `virtual` keyword is optional when overriding, use it anyway; it helps to remind you that it is virtual, and also keeps the declaration consistent.

Class Definitions

Try to keep the definitions of methods in the same order as the declarations. It makes things easier to find.

When defining a function, place the return type and all other modifiers on a previous line so that the class name and function name begin on the left margin. This makes it much easier to find functions.

`include` Files

Try as hard as you can to keep from including files into header files. The ideal minimum is the header file for the class that the current class derives from. Other mandatory includes will be those for objects that are members of the class being declared. Classes that are merely pointed to or referenced only need forward references of the form.

Don't leave out an `include` file in a header just because you assume that whatever `.cpp` file includes this one will also have the needed `include`.

> All header files should use inclusion guards.

assert()

Use assert() freely. It helps find errors, but it also clarifies the assumptions for the reader. It also helps to focus the writer's thoughts around what is valid and what isn't.

const

Use const wherever appropriate: for parameters, variables, and methods. Often there is a need for both a const and a non-const version of a method; don't leave one out if both are needed. Be very careful when explicitly casting from const to non-const and vice versa—there are times when this is the only way to do something—but be certain that it makes sense, and include a comment.

24

Next Steps

You've worked hard, and you are now a competent C++ programmer, but you are by no means finished. There is much more to learn, and many more books to read as you move from novice C++ programmer to expert.

The following sections recommend a number of specific books, and these recommendations reflect only my personal experience and opinions. There are dozens of books on each of these topics, however, so be sure to get other opinions before purchasing.

Where to Get Help and Advice

The very first thing you will want to do as a C++ programmer will be to tap into one or more C++ conferences on an online service. These groups supply immediate contact with hundreds or thousands of C++ programmers who can answer your questions, offer advice, and provide a sounding board for your ideas.

Required Reading

An excellent next book in your C++ education is *Effective C++* (ISBN: 0201924889) by Scott Meyers, from Addison-Wesley Publishing, 1997.

You might also want to consider some of my other books, including *C++ Unleashed* (SAMS, ISBN: 0-672-31241-7, 1999) for advanced C++ techniques and *Clouds To Code* (Wrox Press, ISBN: 1861000952) to see how a real-world application is built with C++ using object-oriented analysis and design.

Finally, you might want to take a look at *The Complete Idiot's Guide to a Career In Computer Programming* (Que, ISBN: 0-7897-1995-9, 1999) for information about how to apply your skills to getting a great job.

Staying in Touch

If you have comments, suggestions, or ideas about this book or other books, I'd love to hear them. Please visit my Web site: www.LibertyAssociates.com. I look forward to hearing from you.

PART VII
Appendices

Appendix

APPENDIX A

Binary and Hexadecimal

You learned the fundamentals of arithmetic so long ago, it is hard to imagine what it would be like without that knowledge. When you look at the number 145 you instantly see "one hundred and forty-five" without much reflection.

Understanding binary and hexadecimal requires that you re-examine the number 145 and see it not as a number, but as a code for a number.

Start small: Examine the relationship between the number three and "3." The numeral 3 is a squiggle on a piece of paper; the number three is an idea. The numeral is used to represent the number.

The distinction can be made clear by realizing that three, 3, |||, III, and *** all can be used to represent the same idea of three.

In base 10 (decimal) math you use the numerals 0, 1, 2, 3, 4, 5, 6, 7, 8, and 9 to represent all numbers. How is the number 10 represented?

One can imagine that we would have evolved a strategy of using the letter A to represent ten; or we might have used IIIIIIIII to represent that idea. The Romans used X. The Arabic system, which we use, makes use of position in conjunction with numerals to represent values. The first (right-most) column is used for "ones," and the next column is used for tens. Thus, the number fifteen is represented as 15 (read "one, five"); that is, 1 ten and 5 ones.

Certain rules emerge, from which some generalizations can be made:

1. Base 10 uses the digits 0–9.

2. The columns are powers of ten: 1s, 10s, 100s, and so on.

3. If the third column is 100, the largest number you can make with two columns is 99. More generally, with n columns you can represent 0 to (10^n-1). Thus, with 3 columns you can represent 0 to $(103-1)$ or 0–999.

Other Bases

It is not a coincidence that we use base 10; we have 10 fingers. One can imagine a different base, however. Using the rules found in base 10, you can describe base 8:

1. The digits used in base 8 are 0–7.

2. The columns are powers of 8: 1s, 8s, 64s, and so on.

3. With n columns you can represent 0 to (8^n-1).

To distinguish numbers written in each base, write the base as a subscript next to the number. The number fifteen in base 10 would be written as 15_{10} and read as "one, five, base ten."

Thus, to represent the number 15_{10} in base 8 you would write 17_8. This is read "one, seven, base eight." Note that it can also be read "fifteen" as that is the number it continues to represent.

Why 17? The 1 means 1 eight, and the 7 means 7 ones. One eight plus seven ones equals fifteen. Consider fifteen asterisks:

```
*****   *****
*****
```

The natural tendency is to make two groups, a group of ten asterisks and another of five. This would be represented in decimal as 15 (1 ten and 5 ones). You can also group the asterisks as

```
****      *******
****
```

That is, eight asterisks and seven. That would be represented in base eight as 17_8. That is, one eight and seven ones.

Around the Bases

You can represent the number fifteen in base ten as 15_{10}, in base nine as 169, in base 8 as 17_8, in base 7 as 21_7. Why 21_7? In base 7 there is no numeral 8. In order to represent fifteen, you will need two sevens and one 1.

How do you generalize the process? To convert a base ten number to base 7, think about the columns: in base 7 they are ones, sevens, forty-nines, three-hundred forty-threes, and so on. Why these columns? They represent 7^0, 7^1, 7^2, 7^4, and so forth. Create a table for yourself:

4	3	2	1
7^3	7^2	7^1	7^0
343	49	7	1

The first row represents the column number. The second row represents the power of 7. The third row represents the decimal value of each number in that row.

To convert from a decimal value to base 7, here is the procedure: Examine the number and decide which column to use first. If the number is 200, for example, you know that column 4 (343) is 0, and you don't have to worry about it.

To find out how many 49s there are, divide 200 by 49. The answer is 4, so put 4 in column 3 and examine the remainder: 4. There are no 7s in 4, so put a zero in the sevens column. There are 4 ones in 4, so put a 4 in the 1s column. The answer is 404_7.

To convert the number 968 to base 6:

5	4	3	2	1
6^4	6^3	6^2	6^1	6^0
1296	216	36	6	1

There are no 1296s in 968, so column 5 has 0. Dividing 968 by 216 yields 4 with a remainder of 104. Column 4 is 4. Dividing 104 by 36 yields 2 with a remainder of 32. Column 3 is 2. Dividing 32 by 6 yields 5 with a remainder of 2. The answer therefore is 4252_6.

5	4	3	2	1
6^4	6^3	6^2	6^1	6^0
1296	216	36	6	1
0	4	2	5	2

There is a shortcut when converting from one base to another base (such as base 6 to base 10). You can multiply:

```
4 * 216 =    864
2 * 36  =     72
5 * 6   =     30
2 * 1   =      2
Total        968
```

Binary

Base 2 is the ultimate extension of this idea. There are only two digits: 0 and 1. The columns are

Col:	8	7	6	5	4	3	2	1
Power:	2^7	2^6	2^5	2^4	2^3	2^2	2^1	2^0
Value:	128	64	32	16	8	4	2	1

To convert the number 88 to base 2, you follow the same procedure: There are no 128s, so column 8 is 0. There is one 64 in 88, so column 7 is 1 and 24 is the remainder. There are no 32s in 24, so column 6 is 0. There is one 16 in 24, so column 5 is 1. The remainder is 8. There is one 8 in 8, and so column 4 is 1. There is no remainder, so the rest of the columns are 0.

```
 0     1     0     1     1     0     0     0
```

To test this answer, convert it back:

```
1 * 64 = 64
0 * 32 =  0
1 * 16 = 16
1 *  8 =  8
0 *  4 =  0
0 *  2 =  0
0 *  1 =  0
Total     88
```

Why Base 2?

The power of base 2 is that it corresponds so cleanly to what a computer needs to represent. Computers do not really know anything at all about letters, numerals, instructions, or programs. At their core they are just circuitry, and at a given juncture there either is a lot of power or there is very little.

To keep the logic clean, engineers do not treat this as a relative scale (a little power, some power, more power, lots of power, tons of power), but rather as a binary scale ("enough power" or "not enough power"). Rather than saying "enough" or "not enough," they simplify it to "yes" or "no." Yes or no, or true or false, can be represented as 1 or 0. By convention, 1 means true or yes, but that is just a convention; it could just as easily have meant false or no.

Once you make this great leap of intuition, the power of binary becomes clear: With 1s and 0s you can represent the fundamental truth of every circuit (there is power or there isn't). All a computer ever knows is, "Is you is, or is you ain't?" Is you is = 1; is you ain't = 0.

Bits, Bytes, and Nybbles

Once the decision is made to represent truth and falsehood with 1s and 0s, binary digits (or bits) become very important. Since early computers could send 8 bits at a time, it was natural to start writing code using 8-bit numbers—called bytes.

> Half a byte (4bits) is called a nybble!

With 8 binary digits you can represent up to 256 different values. Why? Examine the columns: If all 8 bits are set (1), the value is 255. If none is set (all the bits are clear or zero) the value is 0. 0–255 is 256 possible states.

What's a KB?

It turns out that 2^{10} (1,024) is roughly equal to 10^3 (1,000). This coincidence was too good to miss, so computer scientists started referring to 2^{10} bytes as 1KB or 1 kilobyte, based on the scientific prefix of kilo for thousand.

Similarly, 1024 * 1024 (1,048,576) is close enough to one million to receive the designation 1MB or 1 megabyte, and 1,024 megabytes is called 1 gigabyte (giga implies thousand-million or billion).

Binary Numbers

Computers use patterns of 1s and 0s to encode everything they do. Machine instructions are encoded as a series of 1s and 0s and interpreted by the fundamental circuitry. Arbitrary sets of 1s and 0s can be translated back into numbers by computer scientists, but it would be a mistake to think that these numbers have intrinsic meaning.

For example, the Intel 80×6 chip set interprets the bit pattern 1001 0101 as an instruction. You certainly can translate this into decimal (149), but that number per se has no meaning.Sometimes the numbers are instructions, sometimes they are values, and sometimes they are codes. One important standardized code set is ASCII. In ASCII every letter and punctuation is given a 7-digit binary representation. For example, the lowercase letter "a" is represented by 0110 0001. This is not a number, although you can translate it to the number 97 (64 + 32 + 1). It is in this sense that people say that the letter "a" is represented by 97 in ASCII; but the truth is that the binary representation of 97, 01100001, is the encoding of the letter "a," and the decimal value 97 is a human convenience.

Hexadecimal

Because binary numbers are difficult to read, a simpler way to represent the same values is sought. Translating from binary to base 10 involves a fair bit of manipulation of numbers; but it turns out that translating from base 2 to base 16 is very simple, because there is a very good shortcut.

To understand this, you must first understand base 16, which is known as hexadecimal. In base 16 there are sixteen numerals: 0, 1, 2, 3, 4, 5, 6, 7, 8, 9, A, B, C, D, E, and F. The last six are arbitrary; the letters A–F were chosen because they are easy to represent on a keyboard. The columns in hexadecimal are

4	3	2	1
16^3	16^2	16^1	16^0
4096	256	16	1

To translate from hexadecimal to decimal, you can multiply. Thus, the number F8C represents:

$$F * 256 = 15 * 256 = 3840$$
$$8 * 16 = \qquad 128$$
$$C * 1 = 12 * 1 = \qquad 12$$
Total $\qquad$ 3980

Translating the number FC to binary is best done by translating first to base 10, and then to binary:

$$F * 16 = 15 * 16 = 240$$
$$C * 1 = 12 * 1 = \quad 12$$
Total $\qquad$ 252

Converting 252_{10} to binary requires the chart:

```
Col:        9   8   7   6   5   4   3   2   1
Power:      2⁸  2⁷  2⁶  2⁵  2⁴ 2³ 2² 2¹ 2⁰
Value:     256 128  64  32  16  8   4   2   1
```

There are no 256s.
1 128 leaves 124
1 64 leaves 60
1 32 leaves 28
1 16 leaves 12
1 8 leaves 4
1 4 leaves 0
0
0
1   1   1   1   1   1   0   0

Thus, the answer in binary is 1111 1100.

Now, it turns out that if you treat this binary number as two sets of 4 digits, you can do a magical transformation.

The right set is 1100. In decimal that is 12, or in hexadecimal it is C.

The left set is 1111, which in base 10 is 15, or in hexadecimal is F.

Thus, you have:

1111 1100

F   C

Putting the two hexadecimal numbers together is FC, which is the real value of 1111 1100. This shortcut always works. You can take any binary number of any length, and reduce it to sets of 4, translate each set of four to hexadecimal, and put the hexadecimal numbers together to get the result in hexadecimal. Here's a much larger number:

1011 0001 1101 0111

The columns are 1, 2, 4, 8, 16, 32, 64, 128, 256, 512, 1024, 2048, 4096, 8192, 16384, and 32768.

```
1 * 1 =          1
1 * 2=           2
1 * 4 =          4
0 * 8 =          0
```

```
1 * 16 =              16
0 * 32 =               0
1 * 64 =              64
1 * 128 =            128

1 * 256 =            256
0 * 512 =              0
0 * 1024 =             0
0 * 2048 =             0

1 * 4096 =          4,096
1 * 8192 =          8,192
0 * 16384 =            0
1 * 32768 =        32,768
Total              45,527
```

Converting this to hexadecimal requires a chart with the hexadecimal values.

65535   4096   256   16   1

There are no 65,536s in 45,527 so the first column is 4,096. There are 11 4096s (45,056), with a remainder of 471. There is one 256 in 471 with a remainder of 215. There are 13 16s (208) in 215 with a remainder of 7. Thus, the hexadecimal number is B1D7.

Checking the math:

```
B (11) * 4096 =     45,056
1 * 256 =              256
D (13) * 16 =          208
7 * 1 =                  7
Total               45,527
```

The shortcut version would be to take the original binary number, 1011000111010111, and break it into groups of 4: 1011 0001 1101 0111. Each of the four then is evaluated as a hexadecimal number:

```
1011 =
1 * 1 =       1
1 * 2 =       2
0 * 4 =       0
1 * 8 =       8
Total        11
```

Hex: B

0001 =
1 * 1 =   1
0 * 2 =   0
0 * 4 =   0
0 * 8 =   0
Total   1
Hex: 1

1101 =
1 * 1 =   1
0 * 2 =   0
1 * 4 =   4
1 * 8 =   8
Total   13
Hex: D

0111 =
1 * 1 =   1
1 * 2 =   2
1 * 4 =   4
0 * 8 =   0
Total   7
Hex: 7

Total Hex: B1D7

A

APPENDIX B

Glossary

Hour 1

Library   A collection of linkable files that were supplied with your compiler, you purchased separately, or created yourself.

Function   A block of code that performs a service, such as adding two numbers or printing to the screen.

Class   The definition of a new type. A class is implemented as data and related functions.

Compiler   Software that can translate a program from human-readable form to machine code, producing an object file that will later be linked (see linker) and run.

Linker   A program that builds an executable (runnable) file from the object code files produced by the compiler.

Hour 2

Compiling   The first step in transforming code from a compiler into what is called object code in an object file (.obj).

Linking   The second step in creating an executable file; links together the object files produced by a compiler into an executable program.

Executable Program   A program that runs on your operating system.

Interpreter   An interpreter translates a program from human-readable form to machine code while the program is running.

Procedural Programming   A series of actions performed on a set of data.

Structured Programming   A systematic approach to breaking programs down into procedures.

Encapsulation   Creating self-contained objects.

Data Hiding   Hiding the state of a class in private member variables.

Inheritance   Creating a new type that can extend the characteristics of an existing type.

Polymorphism   The ability to treat many sub-types as if they were of the same base type.

Preprocessor   A program that runs before your compiler and handles lines that begin with a pound (#) symbol.

Comment   Text which does not affect the operation of your program, but which is added to instruct or inform the programmer.

Signature   The name of a function and its arguments.

Hour 3

Variable   A named memory location in which you can store a value.

RAM   Random Access Memory.

Type   The size and characteristics of an object.

Signed   A variable type that can hold negative and positive values.

Unsigned   A variable type that can hold only positive values.

ASCII (American Standard Code for Information Interchange)   A system for encoding the characters, numerals, and punctuation used by many computers.

Case-Sensitive   When uppercase and lowercase letters are considered to be different (myVal is not the same as Myval).

Typedef   A type definition.

Constant   Data storage locations whose value will not change while the program is running.

Literal Constant   A value typed directly into the program, such as 35.

Symbolic Constant   A typed and named value marked as constant such as BoilingPoint.

Enumerated Constants   A named set of constants.

Hour 4

Statement   A way to control the sequence of execution, evaluate an expression, or do nothing (the null statement).

Whitespace   Spaces, tabs, and new lines.

Compound Statement   Replaces a single statement with a series of statements between an opening brace and a closing brace.

Expression   Any statement that returns a value.

Operator   A symbol that causes the compiler to take an action.

Operand   A mathematical term referring to the part of an expression operated upon by an operator.

Assignment Operator (=) Causes the operand on the left side of the assignment operator to have its value changed to the value on the right side of the assignment operator.

L-Value   An l-value is an operand that can be on the left side of an operator.

R-Value   An r-value is an operand that can be on the right side of an operator.

Relational Operators   Determine whether two numbers are equal or if one is greater or less than the other.

Incrementing   Increasing a value by 1.

Decrementing   Decreasing a value by 1.

Prefix Operator   The prefix operator (++myAge) increments before evaluation.

Postfix Operator   The postfix operator (myAge++) increments after evaluation.

Precedence Value   The precedence value tells the compiler the order in which to evaluate operators.

Hour 5

Stack   A special area of memory allocated for your program to hold the data required by each of the functions in your program.

B

Function Declaration   Tells the compiler the name, return type, and parameters of the function.

Prototype   Declaration of a function.

Function Definition   Tells the compiler how the function works; it is the body of the function.

Function Parameter List   The list of all the parameters and their types, separated by commas.

Local Variables   Variables that exist only within a function.

Scope   Where a variable is visible and can be accessed.

Global Variables   Variables accessible from anywhere within the program.

Hour 6

Iteration   Doing the same thing again and again.

Hour 7

Clients   Other classes or functions that make use of your class.

Member Variables (also known as **Data Members**)   The variables in your class.

Data Members   See **Member Variables**.

Member Functions (also called **Member Methods**)   The functions of your class.

Member Methods   See **Member Functions**.

Object   An instance of a class.

Public Access   Access available to methods of all classes.

Private Access   Access available only to the methods of the class itself or to methods of classes derived from the class.

Accessor Methods   Methods used to access private member variables.

Method Definition   A definition that begins with the name of the class followed by two colons, the name of the function, and its parameters.

Default Constructor   A constructor with no parameters.

Hour 8

Constant member function A constant member function promises that it won't change the value of any of the members of the class.

Hour 9

Pointer A variable that holds a memory address.

Indirection Accessing the value at an address held by a pointer.

Hour 11

Reference An alias to an object.

Hour 13

Shallow Copy Copies the exact values of one object's member variables to another object. Also called a member-wise copy.

Deep Copy Copies the values of member variables, and creates copies of objects pointed to by member pointers.

Hour 14

Unary Operator An operator which takes only one term, such as a++, as opposed to a binary operator which takes two terms, such as a+b.

Binary operator An operator which takes two terms, such as a+b.

Ternary operator An operator which takes three terms. In C++ there is only one ternary operator, the ?: operator, used as

```
a < b ? true : false;
```

which will return true if a is less than b, and otherwise will return false.

Arity How many terms an operator takes. The possible values for a C++ operator's arity are unary, binary, and ternary.

Hour 15

Array A collection of objects all of the same type.

Subscript Offsets into an array. The fourth element of myArray would be accessed as myArray[3];

String An array of characters ending with a null character.

Hour 16

Stubbing Out   Writing only enough of a function to compile, leaving the details for later.

Overriding   When a derived class creates a member function that changes the implementation of a function in the base class. The overridden method must have the same return type and signature as the base method.

Hour 19

Linked List   A data structure that consists of nodes linked to one another.

Singly Linked List   A linked list in which nodes point to the next node in the list, but not back to the previous.

Doubly Linked List   A linked list in which nodes point both to the next node in the list and also the previous node in the list.

Tree   A complex data structure built from nodes, each of which points to two or more other nodes.

Hour 20

Friend   Keyword to provide another class with access to the current class's private member variables and methods.

Hour 21

`#define`   A command that defines a string substitution.

Token   A string of characters.

Hour 22

Waterfall   A method in which each stage is completed before the product is passed on to the next stage. Each stage is discrete and self-contained.

Simulation   A computer model of part of a real-world system.

Conceptualization   The core idea of the software project.

Use case   A description of how the system will be used.

Problem space   The set of problems and issues your program will try to solve.

Solution space   The set of possible solutions to the problem.

Driver program   A test program.

Hour 23

Template   Provides the ability to create a general class or method and pass types as parameters.

Instantiation   Creating an object from a class, or a type from a template.

Hour 24

Exception   An object that is passed from the area of code where a problem occurs to the part of the code that is going to handle the problem.

B

INDEX

Other Related Titles

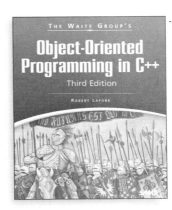

Object-Oriented Programming in C++
Robert Lafore
1-57169-160-x
$34.99 US/$50.95 CAN

STY C++ in 21 Days, 4E
Jesse Liberty
067332072x
$39.99 US/$59.95 CAN

STY UML in 24 Hours, 2E
Joseph Schmuller
0-672-32238-2
$29.99 US/$37.95 CAN

C++ Primer Plus, 3E
Stephen Prata
1-57169-162-6
$35.00 US/$49.99 CAN

**STY C++ for Linux
in 21 Days**
*Jesse Liberty and
David Horvath*
0-672-31895-4
$39.99 US/$59.95 CAN

**STY C++ in 21 Days,
CCE, 4E**
Jesse Liberty
0-672-32207-2
$49.99 US/$74.95 CAN

STY C in 24 Hours, 2E
Tony Zhang
0-672-31861-x
$24.99 US/$37.95 CAN

C++ Unleashed
Jesse Liberty
0-672-31239-5
$39.99 US/$59.95 CAN

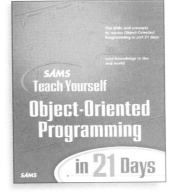

**STY Object-Oriented
Programming in 21 Days**
Tony Sintes
0-672-32109-2
$39.99 US/$59.95 CAN

www.samspublishing.com

All prices are subject to change.